Press, Politics and the Public Sphere in Europe and North America, 1760–1820

Newspapers are a vital component of print and political cultures, and as such they informed as well as documented the social and political upheavals of the eighteenth and nineteenth centuries. However, despite the huge influence attributed to them by both contemporary observers and historians, our knowledge of the nature and function of the newspaper press itself remains scant. *Press, Politics and the Public Sphere in Europe and North America, 1760–1820* aims to fill this gap by examining aspects of the press in several European countries and America, both individually and comparatively, during this particularly turbulent and important period. Contributors explore the relationship between newspapers and social change, specifically in the context of the part played by the press in the political upheavals of the time. The collection examines the relationship between newspapers and public opinion, and attempts to define their place in the emergence of a 'public sphere'.

HANNAH BARKER is Senior Lecturer in History at the University of Manchester. She is the author of *Newspapers, Politics, and Public Opinion in Late Eighteenth-Century England* (1998), *Newspapers, Politics and English Society, 1695–1855* (2000) and editor, with David Vincent, of *Language, Print and Electoral Politics 1790–1832* (2001).

SIMON BURROWS is Lecturer in Modern History at the University of Leeds. He is the author of *French Exile Journalism and European Politics, 1792–1814* (2000), and has published articles in a variety of journals, including the *International History Review*, *French History*, the *Journal of European Studies* and *Eighteenth-Century Life*.

Press, Politics and the Public Sphere in Europe and North America, 1760–1820

Edited by

Hannah Barker
University of Manchester

and

Simon Burrows
University of Leeds

CAMBRIDGE UNIVERSITY PRESS
Cambridge, New York, Melbourne, Madrid, Cape Town, Singapore, São Paulo

Cambridge University Press
The Edinburgh Building, Cambridge CB2 8RU, UK

Published in the United States of America by Cambridge University Press, New York

www.cambridge.org
Information on this title: www.cambridge.org/9780521662079

© Cambridge University Press 2002

This publication is in copyright. Subject to statutory exception
and to the provisions of relevant collective licensing agreements,
no reproduction of any part may take place without the written
permission of Cambridge University Press.

First published 2002
This digitally printed version 2007

A catalogue record for this publication is available from the British Library

ISBN 978-0-521-66207-9 hardback
ISBN 978-0-521-03714-3 paperback

Contents

Notes on contributors		*page* vii
Acknowledgements		ix
	Introduction	1
	HANNAH BARKER AND SIMON BURROWS	
1	The cosmopolitan press, 1760–1815	23
	SIMON BURROWS	
2	The Netherlands, 1750–1813	48
	NICOLAAS VAN SAS	
3	Germany, 1760–1815	69
	ECKHART HELLMUTH AND WOLFGANG PIERETH	
4	England, 1760–1815	93
	HANNAH BARKER	
5	Ireland, 1760–1820	113
	DOUGLAS SIMES	
6	America, 1750–1820	140
	DAVID COPELAND	
7	France, 1750–89	159
	JACK CENSER	
8	The French revolutionary press	182
	HUGH GOUGH	
9	Italy, 1760–1815	201
	MAURIZIO ISABELLA	
10	Russia, 1790–1830	224
	MIRANDA BEAVEN REMNEK	
Index		248

Notes on the contributors

HANNAH BARKER is Senior Lecturer in History at the University of Manchester. She is author of *Newspapers, Politics and Public Opinion in Late Eighteenth-Century England* (1998) and *Newspapers, Politics and English Society, 1695–1855* (2000). She is also co-editor of *Gender in Eighteenth-Century England* (1997), with Elaine Chalus, and *Language, Print and Electoral Politics, 1790–1832* (2001), with David Vincent.

SIMON BURROWS is Lecturer in Modern History at the University of Leeds. He has published several articles on the London-based French press between 1769 and 1814, as well as *French Exile Journalism and European Politics, 1792–1814* (2000).

JACK CENSER is Professor of History at George Mason University. He is author of *Liberty, Equality, Fraternity: Exploring the French Revolution* (with Lynn Hunt), *The French Press in the Age of Enlightenment* (1994) and *Prelude to Power: The Parisian Radical Press, 1789–91* (1976), and has written numerous articles on the historiography of the French Revolution. He has also edited three books: *Press and Politics in Pre-Revolutionary France* (1987), *French Revolution and Intellectual History* (1989) and *Visions and Revisions in Eighteenth-Century France* (1997).

DAVID COPELAND is the A. J. Fletcher Professor of Communications at Elon University. He is the author of *Colonial American Newspapers: Character and Content* (1997) and *Debating the Issues in Colonial Newspapers* (2000), as well as several articles on the press in eighteenth-century colonial America.

HUGH GOUGH is professor of history at University College, Dublin. He has published many works on both French and Irish history, including *The Newspaper Press in the French Revolution* (1988), *Ireland and the French Revolution* (1990) and *The Terror in the French Revolution* (1998).

ECKHART HELLMUTH is Professor of History at the University of Munich. He works on both German and English history, and amongst his publications are *Natural Law and Bureaucratic Perspectives: Studies in Prussian Intellectual and Social History in the Eighteenth Century* (1985), and *Liberty and Licentiousness: The Discourse on the Liberty of the Press in Seventeenth- and Eighteenth-Century Britain* (2000). He has also edited *The Transformation of Political Culture: England and Germany in the Late Eighteenth Century* (1990) and *Rethinking Leviathan: The Eighteenth-Century State in Britain and Germany* (1998), with John Brewer.

MAURIZIO ISABELLA works in Brussels, where he conducts independent research. His publications include '"Una scienza dell'amor patrio": public economy, freedom and civilisation in Giuseppe Pecchio's works (1827–1830)', *Journal for Modern Italian Studies* (1999) and 'Italian exiles and British politics before and after 1848', in Rudolf Muhs and Sabine Freitag, (eds.), *Flotsam of Revolution. European Exiles in Mid-Victorian England* (Oxford, 2002). He is currently working on a biography of the Lombard exiled economist and journalist, Giuseppe Pecchio.

WOLFGANG PIERETH is Lecturer in Modern History at the University of Munich. He has published *Bayerns Presspolitik und die Neuordnung Deutschlands nach den Befreiungskriegen* (1999), as well as a number of articles on press, propaganda and censorship in nineteenth-century Germany. He is also editor of *Das 19. Jahrhundert. Ein Lesebuch zur deutschen Geschichte 1815–1918* (1997).

MIRANDA BEAVEN REMNEK is Professor of Russian and Central European Studies at the University of Minnesota, where she also coordinates the library's Russian and central European collections. She has written a number of articles on print culture in pre-revolutionary Russia, especially the early nineteenth century, and is editor of *Books in Russia and the Soviet Union: Past and Present* (1991).

DOUGLAS SIMES is Senior Lecturer at the University of Waikato, New Zealand. He is currently writing a book on the Ultra-Tories and has produced several articles on the influential *Dublin University Magazine* and on the Brunswick Clubs.

NICOLAAS VAN SAS is Professor of Modern History at the University of Amsterdam. He is the author of *Onze Natuurlijkste Bondgenoot. Nederland, Engeland en Europa, 1813–1831* (1985) and *Talen van het vaderland. Over patriottisme en nationalisme* (1996). He has edited a number of books, including one on the concept of Fatherland in the Netherlands from early modern times till World War II and one on Dutch *lieux-de-mémoire*.

Acknowledgements

We are grateful to the following, for their generous help in compiling this volume: Rodney Barker, Joe Bergin, Jeremy Black, Oliver Bleskie, Carlo Capra, Elaine Chalus, Malcolm Crook, Simon Dixon, Paul Hoftijzer, Ann Hughes, Michael John, Colin Jones, Otto Lanckhorst, Gary Marker, Monica McLean, Louise McReynolds, James Raven, Raymond Richards, Cynthia Whittaker, and our anonymous readers.

Introduction

Hannah Barker and Simon Burrows

As a vital component of print culture, newspapers feature prominently in most recent accounts of social and political change in the late eighteenth and early nineteenth centuries. This is as true for historians exploring the new 'cultural interpretation' of the French Revolution as it is for those studying Europe's emergent middle classes or the commercialisation of Western culture. Yet despite the priority both historians and contemporaries have attributed to the influence of the newspaper press, its role is poorly integrated into most narrative accounts, and not enough is known about the press itself, especially in terms of national comparison.[1] This is particularly problematic given the central role that many historians attribute to newspapers in the formation of 'public opinion' and a pan-European 'public sphere' independent of government but critical of the actions of authority.[2]

This book seeks to address this need by offering a number of nationally based case studies, assessing their common features and divergences and exploring the role of the newspaper in political and social change. The choice of 'national boundaries' as organising categories serves an essential purpose here, because the political and legal frameworks which defined the parameters and possibilities of the press, as well as the broad contours of societies and economies, were to a high degree co-extensive with national borders, even in ancien regime Europe. Furthermore, the extent and processes by which nationhood was defined from the 1760s to the 1820s rank among the most problematic and pressing issues confronting historians of the period, and accounts of the processes of nation-building and defining national identity often privilege the press.[3] Within our predominantly 'national' framework, chapters covering communities lacking statehood (Ireland and pre-revolutionary America), geographic units incorporating many states (Germany and Italy) and a chapter on the cosmopolitan press offer varied perspectives on links between the press and shifting senses of community and national identity.

Many recent press studies have stressed the extent to which newspapers and the political and print cultures in which they arise help to define one another. Thus, the study of the press cannot be isolated from the broader contexts in which it operates. Different contexts can lead to considerable divergences, even at a single historical moment.[4] In considering a representative range of national press cultures, contributors to this volume take a variety of approaches. They examine the structure of the press; the methods used to control it by political authorities and their effectiveness; the journalistic texts themselves; and the political role of newspapers within the public sphere, however defined. They investigate who owned the papers, who wrote for them, how they were distributed and who read them, and attempt to assess how far audience composition and the social backgrounds of journalists, editors and proprietors determined the nature of the messages the press contained. They also investigate how far newspaper circulations, regularity of publication, audience size, price, marketing methods and availability determined the social and geographic penetration of newspapers, their level of independence from patronage and their political roles. Moreover, they describe the journalistic texts, their presentation and format, the topics they covered, the way issues were presented and the messages, overt and implicit, that they contained. Such a comprehensive approach to the comparative role of national newspaper presses reveals important differences. Divergent press traditions helped to shape radically different national political cultures, calling many generalisations about the role of the press into question. Our approach also recognises that different national presses developed according to national political chronologies, and thus allowed our contributors a certain flexibility about end-dates. In particular, we felt that abrupt changes in political circumstances during the revolutionary period so altered press regimes in several countries that it made no sense to offer a unitary coverage of the whole period 1760–1820. Thus, there are separate chapters on pre-revolutionary and revolutionary France, and discussion of those states where the vestiges of press liberty were extinguished by Napoleonic expansion – the Netherlands and Italy – ends around 1800. However, the subsequent experience of these states from 1800 until the restoration fits within the broader narrative outlined in the chapter on the cosmopolitan press. Despite these divergences of experience, as European and American national presses grew from common origins, and common analytical frameworks have influenced the academic study of their development, it is possible to raise common themes here.

When newspapers began to emerge in the early seventeenth century, they were the product of a relatively mature print culture, which according to Marshall McLuhan, was already shaping the entire experience of Western civilisation.[5] Drawing upon a variety of disciplines, McLuhan suggested that the impact of the invention of movable type printing (as developed by Gutenberg in the mid-fifteenth century) was not limited to its technological advantages: by restructuring modes of communication it also restructured social and cultural practices, intellectual habits and cognition itself. Building on McLuhan's approach, Elizabeth Eisenstein attempts to identify, define and explore the precise nature of the shift from oral and manuscript culture to print.[6] Eisenstein argues that as print increased dissemination exponentially, it amplified messages and made standardisation possible. It led to the reorganisation of texts and reference guides, promoting rationalisation, codification and cataloguing of information and new processes of data collection. Whereas continual copying of manuscripts in scribal culture led to the cumulative corruption of texts, print culture allowed for processes of feedback, correction and improved editions. Printing also greatly improved the preservation of data, fixing the knowledge base, and reinforcing messages and stereotypes through amplification and repetition. Access to this knowledge base was through the ever-improving world of the printed text. There, solitary practices of reading and research replaced the shared oral knowledge of the past, promoting the retreat into increasingly 'private worlds' that historians have detected in the early modern period. The development of habits of critical thought through comparison and criticism of multiple texts promoted intellectual and religious fragmentation as critical analysis of texts considered authoritative in the Middle Ages called their authority into question. When combined with the propaganda potential of the printing press to disseminate such findings, printing became a major force behind the success of the Reformation and the secularisation of European society. Printing also appeared to be a prerequisite of the evolution of new forms of political and social organisation, especially nation states predicated on the twin pillars of bureaucratic administration and political consent founded upon a national community of identity expressed primarily through the medium of print.[7]

Although Eisenstein's approach has been criticised, not least by Adrian Johns, as being too deterministic and overplaying print's fixity and claims to authority, the implications of the influence of multiple texts remain vital, especially with regard to the spread of news.[8] Yet, sadly, as Mitchell Stephens has pointed out, Eisenstein almost ignores the journalistic uses of print.[9] However, following lines suggested by Eisenstein's analysis, other historians have explored the historical implications of serial production. As some of the first disposable, mass-produced products, news publications have been implicated in the development of new modes of production. They were also the most important forum for the development of modern advertising. Serial publications offered a regular point of contact between producers and their potential clients and made possible the evolution and practice of mass marketing, branding and promoting new products.[10] They also helped to restructure a reader's sense of time and space, creating an impression of engagement with a wider continuous drama of 'public' events, within which their lives and communities took on new meanings and political participation became thinkable. By the early nineteenth century, if not sooner, these processes were beginning to provide the basis for an emerging modern, democratic, consumer society, albeit one initially restricted socially and geographically. Thus, most cultural historians would agree that the shift to a culture based on print is heavily implicated in almost every significant change connected with the advent of political and social modernity.

The place of the newspaper press within this culture of print underwent fundamental shifts during the eighteenth century. In many places, though at different moments, the newspaper began to supersede the pamphlet as the dominant printed form for political discourse and the dissemination of news. At the same time, it began to occupy a more prominent position alongside other institutions and social networks which both informed and articulated public debate. However, defining what does – or does not – constitute a 'newspaper' is problematic. Exact definitions of appearance, periodicity, content and format usually raise more difficulties than they resolve.[11] Contributors to this work take a varied approach to this problem, though all assume that newspapers are printed publications that appear frequently, at regular intervals, in dated (or numbered) instalments, containing a miscellaneous variety of stories per issue in a consistent and recognisable format. They should be available to the general public, usually for sale individually or by subscription, and attempt to provide readers with a regular diet of the most up-to-date news available. Nevertheless, for practical purposes, what constitutes a newspaper varies according to context. By the mid-eighteenth century, daily newspapers were available in some European countries, but elsewhere bi-weekly, weekly, fortnightly or even monthly political periodicals still functioned as the primary news media. Thus, in a British context Hannah Barker is concerned primarily with broad-sheet publications appearing with daily to weekly frequency, and can ignore monthly periodicals and 'reviews' which were, in general, not as central to news transmission and political opinion formation. In contrast, Miranda Beaven Remnek's chapter on Russia, where the daily press was small and lacking in political importance, is concerned largely with the monthly 'thick press', which often contained the freshest news available.[12] In some other national contexts, including Ireland and pre-revolutionary France, both sorts of journals seem to have been important, fulfilling different functions. Yet these differences in format in themselves are indicative, as our contributors show, of significant variations in the contours of the 'public sphere', the tempo of news transmission and the pulse of political and economic life, as well as in the relationships between editors and readers, rulers and subjects.

Although newspapers only began to take their full modern form in the early eighteenth century, they were the outcome of a long evolutionary process. Indeed, according to Claude Lévi-Strauss the desire for news ('communication of messages') is a basic human trait, part of the communication process that binds cultures together.[13] The earliest European news organs were hand-written official news bulletins in ancient Rome.[14] Although after the fall of the Roman Empire, European communications, trade and news networks collapsed, there was a revival of international demand for news in the later Middle Ages and Renaissance. In part, this was driven by the development of a world-wide trade in European hands and ever more sophisticated speculative means to finance it. Consequently, reliable news information became an increasingly valuable commodity, as merchants and financiers tried to ensure they received the best possible prices and attempted to make accurate assessments of risk. Hence, great commercial centres, where news was both most available and of greatest value, became the largest and most innovative journalistic centres, led by Venice in the sixteenth century, Amsterdam in the seventeenth century and London in the eighteenth century.[15]

The first 'newspapers' evolved from hand-written Venetian *Gazzette*. These *Gazzette* originally appeared in the mid-sixteenth century, and pioneered the publication of a diverse set of reports, each under the dateline of its place of origin, in a single issue. The format of the *Gazzette* was extremely influential, and remained commonplace for over two centuries. By 1609, however, printed newsbooks were appearing in Germany, and around 1620, Dutch printers began to produce weekly printed papers, known as *corantos*, in Dutch, English and French.[16]

Nevertheless, the market for news to which this nascent press catered was small and developed slowly. The first printed 'newspapers' would probably have had circulations in the low hundreds and tended to appear only weekly.[17] Even in the eighteenth century, French provincial newspapers could break even at 200–50 copies and give their publishers a moderate but respectable living on 400–50.[18] In America, the *Boston News-Letter*, although successful, had an initial print-run of just 250 in 1704.[19] Despite the commercial possibilities of a relatively low circulation, daily newspaper publication still spread slowly, hindered by licensing and censorship regimes and the challenge of acquiring sufficient material. The first daily paper, the *Einkommende Zeitung*, was published in Leipzig in 1650. A London daily did not appear until 1702, France did not have a successful daily until 1777, and America's first daily only appeared in 1783.[20] A weekly provincial press developed in England from 1701 and in France from the 1750s, but both drew much of their political news from the metropolitan press.[21]

Early newspapers were also limited because of the available technology. Essentially the presses used in the eighteenth century were the same as those used by Gutenburg three centuries earlier, with only minor adaptations. These presses could seldom produce more than 250 impressions per hour.[22] Speed of output could only be increased by adding another press, which required hiring an additional printer and compositor. Thus, prior to the technological advances of the late eighteenth and nineteenth centuries, printers gained no significant economies of scale by increasing existing capacity. Even late eighteenth-century innovations such as the Stanhope press and the Columbian press only marginally increased the speed of production. With the introduction of the König steam press, first used to print *The Times* of 29 November 1814, it become possible to greatly increase output. König's machine impressed 1,100 pages per hour, but by 1830 steam-driven machines could produce 4,000 imprints per hour.[23] Nevertheless, it was some years before demand levels were sufficient for successful newspapers elsewhere to switch to steam presses.

The steam press accelerated the transformation of newspaper production into a large-scale capital intensive industry, especially after the construction of steam railways from the 1830s onwards made it possible for metropolitan daily papers to serve truly national audiences. But this transformation of newspapers into larger enterprises was already under way, in Britain at least, by 1800. For much of the eighteenth century it required very little capital to establish a successful newspaper. Many early newspapers were published and edited by their printers, but over time the roles of editor, printer and sometimes proprietor became separate. By the later eighteenth century most London newspapers were large-scale capital enterprises with several shareholders, a salaried editor and a small staff of journalists.[24] Elsewhere, newspapers were often smaller ventures. In the early nineteenth century, American townships with populations as low as 300 had their own newspapers run by a single printer-editor and many French revolutionary publications were established by editor-proprietors who were the sole-journalists.[25] Before steam transport, most newspapers tended to serve predominantly local audiences; for example, the majority of Parisian newspapers and periodicals produced in the Revolution were sold in the metropolis.[26]

Yet if newspapers tended to serve geographically defined communities, the information sources they used to compile their texts were international. In the late eighteenth century modern reporting practices were still in their infancy and staff correspondents virtually unknown. Nor were there any specialist agencies collecting and circulating news. Nevertheless, there was a wide variety of sources of information available to the press, forming what Jeremy Black has called 'a far from enclosed system of information'.[27] Early newspapers relied above all on foreign newspapers and hand-written news letters, which they recycled shamelessly. Journalists also sought up-to-date information from private and mercantile correspondence, books and printed ephemera, travellers' and merchants' reports, coffee-house gossip and other oral sources. The unreliable nature of some of this material was indicated by the use of ubiquitous phrases such as 'we hear' or its French equivalent *'on dit'* in much newspaper reporting.[28] However, by the mid-eighteenth century, journalists could also draw on official publications including government gazettes, and often published the full text of important documents, leaving readers to interpret them. But increasingly, journalists began to find an editorial voice and to print their own material and analysis. *The Times* was a leader in this field, sending staff to cover the French Revolution from Paris.[29] International newspapers like the *Gazette de Leyde* and *Courier de l'Europe* appear to have used paid correspondents in foreign cities even earlier.[30] Nevertheless, they, like many European newspapers, continued to present news in a series of dry, diplomatic-style dispatches under their (putative) cities of origin and a dateline well into the nineteenth century. In some cases papers did not even give news of their own city, probably both because it was liable to censorship and because local news still circulated through local networks by oral means.[31]

Governments and political elites had many ways to restrict the circulation and content of news. Licensing regulations, prior censorship and restrictive privileges were widespread practices. In the Netherlands, papers required a privilege to publish and discussion of Dutch internal affairs was restricted until the Patriot Revolution of 1783–7.[32] In ancien regime France, French political news could not be printed at all unless it was reproduced from the sterile *Gazette de France* (and at a fee for breach of privilege); under Napoleon after 1807 uncensored papers could only take political news from the official *Moniteur*.[33] Patronage rewards, political subsidy, bribery and fees to publish or suppress items were common even where instruments of prior censorship or licensing systems did not exist. Moreover, libel and sedition laws were often draconian. In Britain the authors, editors, publishers and hawkers of newspapers could all be imprisoned and pilloried in cases of criminal libel, and until Fox's 'Libel Act' of 1792, the decision of guilt rested with the judge, not a jury. In other states journalists could be imprisoned at the sovereign's pleasure. Such was the fate of over 800 publishers and writers in ancien regime France, including the journalists Jacques-Pierre Brissot and Simon-Nicolas-Henri Linguet.[34] Moreover, although there were increasing debates in many European countries about the liberty to publish and the benefits of a free press which challenged absolutist practices of secret government, support for the idea of a totally unfettered media was novel. Prior to the ratification of the First Amendment in the United States in 1791, no country in the Western world granted their citizens freedom of printed expression as a basic right.[35] Even when it was granted it proved a precarious liberty. In France the freedom of expression enshrined in the Declaration of the Rights of Man and Citizen lasted only from August 1789 to August 1792; in the United States the Alien and Sedition Acts of 1798 were used to persecute Republican editors for several years.[36]

However, despite the fact that governments often feared the subversive potential of the press, and might try to control it, newspapers often enjoyed a greater freedom than other legally printed products, partly because old regime governments tended to lack the machinery to monitor the newspaper press effectively. But governments also needed the press, especially international newspapers, to persuade or influence policy-makers and the political nation in other states. To do this effectively, they had to use news channels that enjoyed that public's confidence, which in turn required that they use the most reputable news organs: those which maintained the appearance of independence by publishing documents from both parties to a dispute. In attempting to persuade, moreover, governments tacitly accepted the legitimacy of the judgements of a 'public', however limited. As the eighteenth century wore on, governments thus began to develop news management techniques rather than attempting to suppress information.[37] Many countries also sought to restrict access to newspapers, sometimes by insisting on sale by subscription, sometimes, as in Britain, by 'taxes on knowledge'. But newspapers, by their very nature, were a poor and unlikely medium for truly subversive materials, since they needed to maintain a fixed office and regular impression, and could be suppressed easily or intercepted in the post, the main means of newspaper distribution beyond metropolitan areas.

Despite lingering worries about the effects of the press and other forms of print on the lower orders, governments were beginning to encourage increased educational provision, and literacy was rising across most of Europe. Although determining the potential literate audience is fraught with difficulties, and even the most basic measures of literacy remain problematic,[38] it is still possible to make some broad generalisations. Literacy was highest in north-western Europe, where by 1800 over half of adult males in most areas could sign their names – the standard measure of basic literacy used by historians – and more still had simple reading ability. England and Scotland, north-eastern France, Germany and Scandinavia could even boast low-level mass literacy skills, unlike the Iberian peninsula, Mediterranean basin, Russia and eastern and central Europe. In France literacy rates were high but uneven. In one north-eastern town male signature literacy was already 83 per cent in 1700. By the eve of the Revolution, 60 per cent of women in north-eastern France were also literate. In contrast, in the south and west, where resistance to the Revolution was strongest, literacy rates were considerably lower, perhaps preventing the penetration of new, revolutionary ideas. Literacy levels were also low in much of Ireland, where 90 per cent female illiteracy was the norm. However, literacy almost everywhere was on an upward trend, in marked contrast to earlier periods, though progress was often slow. German records suggest that 10 per cent of those over six years old could read with ease by 1750 and around 25 per cent by 1800. Within populations, it is possible also to make generalisations about the structure of literacy rates. Usually the most literate were concentrated at the top of the social scale, men were more literate than women and the young more literate than the old. Urban populations tended to be more literate than rural ones, since they had more access to educational opportunities and greater everyday contact with printed matter. In London by the 1750s, 92 per cent of bridegrooms and 74 per cent of brides could sign their names. In Amsterdam, 85 per cent of bridegrooms could sign their names by 1780.[39] In addition, by the late 1700s, some continental states, following an example set by Prussia in 1717, were beginning to decree systems of universal primary education, although in practice the results were limited.[40] Thus, by the late eighteenth century, there was already a potential mass reading 'public' for newspapers, drawn from a wide cross-section of society in many European states.

But the literate were not the only consumers of print culture. Sharing newspapers and reading them aloud in coffee houses or other public places were common practices in the eighteenth century. Contemporary accounts – as most of our contributors note – suggest that on average each copy of a newspaper was consumed by several readers, perhaps as many as a dozen or more. Thus, reconstructing the size of the audience, its geographic and social location, and how and how frequently they consumed newspapers would be a problem for historians even if adequate financial records and subscription lists had survived. If the precise size and character of the audience for print was and remains unclear, many contemporaries were still convinced of its importance. In the eighteenth and early nineteenth centuries, editors and journalists often referred to their audience as the 'public' and invoked the concept of 'public opinion' when discussing the legitimacy of acts of authority. But both they and subsequent historians have often been vague about the nature of 'public opinion', how it operated, and to whom it belonged. Evidently it did not include the whole population, and indeed the 'public' was often juxtaposed against its other, the 'mob'. But was this 'public' a mere concept, or was there some sort of reality behind it – did consumers of print and the press that 'represented' them genuinely participate in policy formation? If so, was membership of this 'participatory public' in practice defined primarily through involvement with the press, and was it co-extensive with newspaper readership? Or was it restricted to a narrower group of readers who contributed articles or letters to newspapers, wrote tracts, or perhaps had access to officials and policy-makers? Then again, it might be a broader group, comprising not only regular readers of newspapers, but those who met and discussed political issues in coffee shops, Masonic lodges, taverns, salons and the other focal points of eighteenth-century urban culture.

If 'public opinion' did influence political life, how was it structured? Was it an essentially unitary consensual force, as many contemporary writers including Jean-Jacques Rousseau argued, and most French revolutionaries seem tragically to have believed? Or was it divided and fragmentary? If so, how could a fragmentary 'public opinion' operate in monarchical states which were by nature unitary? Was 'public opinion' the outcome of enlightened, disinterested debate and hence the embodiment of reason, as both Immanuel Kant and Rousseau seemed to believe, or was it ultimately contestable and malleable as the propagandists described by Keith Michael Baker and their patrons seemed to have intuited?[41] The profoundest meditations on these topics are those of the German philosopher Jürgen Habermas on the development of a 'bourgeois public sphere' (*bürgerliche Öffentlichkeit*).[42] This has provided many historians with a theoretical basis from which to explore the political culture of the ancien regime.

For Habermas, the political public sphere was part of a specific stage in early capitalist commercial relations. It was directly linked to the growth of a self-conscious bourgeoisie and the emergence of a 'reasoning public' which could be critical of administration and sought to influence political power. The space within which this new public operated – 'the tension-charged field of state-society relations'– was the public sphere.[43] The public sphere was dependent upon new networks of communications on two levels. First, because factors like a press and a reading public allowed the exchange of information and ideas. Second, these developments themselves created a new institutional context for political action. Habermas argues that the political public sphere issued directly from the

Introduction

public literary sphere based in the institutions of Enlightenment sociability, such as salons, coffee houses, clubs, debating societies and above all (particularly in terms of this book) periodical literature.

For Habermas, then, the political public sphere was open to anyone with access to print. This degree of participation contrasts forcibly with older modes of political action which centred on the royal court or oligarchical elites and were conducted in secret. Habermas's public sphere was essentially egalitarian. The judgements of the rational-critical public differentiated between individuals and their arguments only in the quality of their critical reasoning, thus ignoring the hierarchical distinctions of ancien regime society. No sphere of human activity was exempt from the scrutiny of this new rational-critical public. This being the case, the opinion of the public increasingly assumed the role of a legitimising tribunal which judged the acts of political authority and invoked the universal and constant force of reason against the supposedly chaotic commands of arbitrary will and traditional institutions. However, despite Habermas's assertion that the public sphere had to be accessible to all, it was never truly democratic. He acknowledged that his analysis of the 'liberal model' of the public sphere failed to incorporate the 'plebeian public sphere', composed of the *Volk* or *peuple*. Instead, he defined the public sphere as essentially 'bourgeois', sociologically separate both from the public power of ruling elites and from the 'people', who lacked the skills and opportunity to make public use of their reason. The basis of public opinion, Habermas argues, was 'class interest', but the ideological fiction of universal access was maintained, and was indeed vital, to the continued existence of the public sphere. Habermas seeks to make up for the absence of 'the people' in his model by arguing that they were nevertheless represented by the public sphere, since the public's opinion was 'objectively congruent' with the general interest.[44]

Although Habermas addresses the specific cases of England, France and Germany, his model is, in principle, applicable more widely, since it focuses on historical categories and their functions rather than on historical events. Habermas dates the formation of the bourgeois or public sphere in France to the mid-eighteenth century, and somewhat later in Germany, but emphasises their limited nature in comparison with the 'ideal type' represented by England, where the strength of liberal capitalism and a lack of censorship allowed for a freer formulation of the public sphere than was possible under the heavy censorship of ancien regime societies. France and Germany are relegated by Habermas to the status of 'continental variants'. It was only in England, prior to 1789, he argues, that the individual bourgeois could articulate a political critique of government based on the interests of private property, rather than take part in the 'pre-political' literary public spheres of France and Germany, which were principally aimed at self-enlightenment. The events of the Revolution, however, created in France 'overnight, if in a less durable form, what in England took more than a century to develop: the institutions of a politically reasoning public'. In the years which followed, both German and French law were altered to suit a capitalist model of free-market relations, thereby guaranteeing property rights and protecting the interests of bourgeois society in line with English law, demonstrating that the bourgeois public sphere had reached its most developed state as it was able to compel state authority to respond to its needs.[45]

Habermas's model of societal change has important implications for press historians, stressing as it does the role of print in facilitating the emergence of the public sphere. Indeed, it is a popular contention amongst cultural historians – many of whom draw heavily on the work of Habermas – that developments in the production, dissemination and use of printed texts are deeply implicated in the cultural origins and outcomes of many important events in the eighteenth and nineteenth centuries, not least the French Revolution. Numerous studies of France have explored the emergence and construction of a critical public which was increasingly hostile to established authority in the generations prior to the Revolution.[46] This public was largely formed through the medium of print, in which newspapers were important, although arguably other forms of publication – such as the illegal pamphlets and 'philosophic books' studied by Robert Darnton or the legally circulated trial briefs examined by Sarah Maza – played a more decisive role.[47] However, the importance of newspapers in the public sphere is demonstrated by Jean Sgard's work on the French-language press in eighteenth-century France, Holland and Switzerland, which argues for a 'common rhetoric', indicating a shared readership and explicitly appealing to a unified 'public sphere'.[48] Jeremy Popkin argues for a continuity in the pre-revolutionary and revolutionary newspaper press in France. He has highlighted the growth of the pre-revolutionary press, which offered its readers a detailed picture of politics, publicised opposition to royal policies and was 'in no sense clandestine or subversive', but was rather an established part of the French political system before 1789.[49] Just how broad a vision of politics this press offered is explored in Jack Censer's chapter in this volume.

Historians of Germany have tended to focus on the early nineteenth century as the period when bourgeois association, in the form of clubs and philanthropic societies, resulted in the type of middle-class emancipation and self-affirmation fundamental to the formation of bourgeois civil society.[50] But it is also evident that the process by which an educated German elite constituted itself as a public was well under way in the eighteenth century.[51] Indeed, the growth of associations, leagues of friendship, clubs, lodges and reading societies has led to one German historian identifying the eighteenth century as 'the sociable century'.[52] As Eckhart Hellmuth points out, German associations were more fragile and elitist than English ones; nevertheless, the public sphere in Germany developed significantly in the eighteenth century.[53] Hans Bödeker has shown that the periodical press not only grew quickly in this period, but also widened its field of reporting to pay increasing attention to political, social and economic subjects.[54] In such a climate, in the last decades of the eighteenth century, claims Bödeker, 'the new reading, reasoning public of educated people was born'.[55]

Historians of America have also made use of Habermas's conception of the public sphere. In *Civil Tongues and Polite Letters in British America*, David Shields explores the culture of eighteenth-century literary societies which, he argues, forged the grounds for a widening participation in a polite culture of rational discourse. David Waldstreicher's work on popular nationalism, *In the Midst of Perpetual Fetes*, asserts that local rituals and print culture allowed people to participate in, and define, the political culture of the new nation, producing 'the true political public sphere of the early Republic'. Mary Ryan's *Civic Wars* explores the experience of democracy in nineteenth-century America and uses the idea of 'the public' to analyse America's diverse peoples, presenting public life as a 'trial of contestation'.[56] In addition, press historians have stressed the decisive role of newspapers in the creation of a separate American national consciousness, in both the later colonial period and after independence, and in promoting communal loyalty to the institutions and ideals of the new Republic.[57]

Although historians have raised problems with Habermas's model, in particular his emphasis on rational-critical debate[58] and use of a Marxist model of historical change, which appears to exclude non-bourgeois participation,[59] his account of the emergence of the public sphere remains extremely useful for historians, not least because it describes very wide-ranging social and cultural developments. Yet, as the contributors to this volume make clear, any emphasis on a specifically *bourgeois* public sphere, which appears to associate newspapers narrowly with the middle class, is not particularly helpful. Although the newspaper trade developed first along important trade routes and newspaper proprietors everywhere tended to be profit-seeking entrepreneurs, it would be misleading to associate eighteenth- and nineteenth-century newspaper readership too closely with the commercial middle classes. In states with the most developed presses – America, Britain, the Netherlands, Germany – newspaper reading extended well beyond this social group. By the 1830s, one in two American households subscribed to a newspaper and broadly similar levels may have been achieved in Britain and the Netherlands. In all three cases the social penetration of newspapers went far deeper than the middle classes by the 1780s if not earlier. The same might be said of revolutionary France. In contrast, our contributors have also highlighted the prevalence of nobles among the reading public in Russia, ancien regime Italy and pre-revolutionary France. Moreover, Hugh Gough's chapter notes that noble readers continued to be important to some newspapers well into the revolutionary decade – although he also emphasises the importance of papers aimed a 'popular' opinion. Elsewhere, for example in revolutionary Italy, radical papers also existed, but as Maurizio Isabella points out, they were unable to carve out a popular constituency. In Italy the revolution had little appeal beyond the urban elites who formed the bureaucratic cadres of the French sister-republics. Tackling the question from another angle Simon Burrows's chapter suggests that until the end of the Napoleonic period a separate international press existed to serve the political needs of a narrow cosmopolitan francophone elite, and that this audience was neither bourgeois nor interested in political debate above information. Finally, Miranda Beaven Remnek argues that in early nineteenth-century Russia the press did not have a primarily bourgeois constituency because the merchant class was small, largely illiterate and occupied an economically precarious position. Nevertheless, her evidence suggests that they formed perhaps 10 per cent of the readership of Russian papers, and their insignificance can be overstated. In Russia the widest interest in political news was among the nobility, although an emergent intelligentsia were the heaviest users of some other sorts of periodical, especially journals.

Despite the fact that the public sphere was often quite broadly based, we should not assume that it was necessarily robust or that the triumph of a liberal, democratic and free press was inevitable. Rather than enjoying independence from state power, the press enjoyed a contingent autonomy, and proved weak in the face of a hegemonic or tyrannical government intent on exerting the full force of state power. Armed force extinguished the public sphere in the Netherlands in both 1787 and 1798, in Italy, in revolutionary France and, to a slightly lesser extent, in Napoleonic Germany. In the Napoleonic period, the French succeeded in silencing critical discussion across Europe and established a virtual monopoly over agenda-setting information, shutting out whole categories of news information. Yet even Napoleonic France was limited by a lack of resources with which to monitor all titles through prior censorship, instead allowing news only from approved sources. If this suggests a certain weakness in the apparatus of even the strongest state, it is equally necessary to note that mechanisms for political control existed everywhere. Even in America, Britain, Ireland and the Dutch Republic legal prosecutions and criminal libel trials were used for much of our period as a means of silencing, or intimidating, opposition journalists, though with mixed results. Popular violence or political coups also constrained journalists in the Netherlands, revolutionary France and revolutionary America. Dedication to publishing in such circumstances often required considerable prudence, occasional courage and ideological commitment.

Moreover, it seems misleading to overemphasise the separation of the public sphere from the state. National governments traditionally played a crucial role in the growth of the public sphere, since in most cases its early development – at least in terms of the newspaper press – took place under state aegis and tutelage. This is displayed most clearly in Eckhart Hellmuth's and Wolfgang Peireth's contribution on Germany, where state employees and politicians were heavily involved in the formation of the press. The state and its legal framework set the boundaries for public discussion, and in continental Europe under the ancien regime that usually precluded the discussion of domestic news. Indeed, gazettes, especially as initially envisaged by Richelieu and shaped by Renaudot, were tools of ancien regime state power. Whether produced by governments or entrepreneurs, they served to represent the needs of political interest groups and above all the rulers of the continental states where they were based until the end of the eighteenth century and beyond. In general this involved maintaining a discreet silence over domestic political affairs. This was true even in the Netherlands, where the press otherwise enjoyed a broad *de facto* freedom, and yet until the 1780s, as the chapter by Nicolaas van Sas shows, much domestic political discussion took place by proxy in the Spectators.

Except in Britain, America and the Netherlands, where ordinary citizens appear to have contributed to public debate through their published letters, readers had little role in debating policies in newspapers. In much of Continental Europe, newspapers only offered a forum for debate during revolutionary disturbance. For most of our period, letters from readers were few, and those that did appear tended to be from influential figures. Participation in newspaper debate was thus largely restricted to editors and political actors, suggesting that the distinction between newspapers and other print products (especially pamphlets) has often been overdrawn. When public discussion of policy occurred in print in ancien regime states, most of it was away from the primary news media – in periodicals and pamphlets – and at a pace which precluded intense on-going debate over day-to-day policies. Certainly the press played a vital role in providing information and materials for informed debate, but it left readers to discuss them in the other forums of civil society. Indeed, it is probable in ancien regime states – as Miranda Beaven Remnek suggests was the case in nineteenth-century Russia – that political discussion took place in the other spheres of enlightened sociability precisely because the press was so controlled.

We can see from the contexts in which a free press did start to emerge that its existence was not inevitable, and was certainly not the result of any gradual liberalisation of society and move towards modernity. It seems fair to suggest that it usually took a revolutionary intervention – a cataclysmic collapse or reorganisation of state power – rather than gradual evolution, to allow the emergence of what Habermas would characterise as a mature political press, that is to say one that operated under the guarantee of legal protections and achieved greater public participation. This was true, to some extent, even in England, where it was the outcome of the lapsing of the Licensing Act in the aftermath of the Glorious Revolution. In America a 'mature' political press was the product of the struggles for independence from Britain and to forge a new nation, and in the Netherlands, the outcome of the Patriot Revolution of the 1780s. In France a mature political press existed in its purest form for but a brief moment between 1789 and 1792, and after 1799 Napoleon largely succeeded in excluding the public from the public sphere.

Yet these reservations about the emergence and extent of press freedom in our period should not lead us to conclude that newspapers were always or necessarily subservient to state interests. Nor should we assume that state moves to suppress freedom of expression diminished popular support for such an ideal – indeed, quite the opposite appears to have been the case in several national contexts. The degree of press autonomy from government and a widely held view that an independent press was an essential ingredient of enlightened society resulted in different interest groups, above all the international powers, competing for the sanction of public opinion in the gazettes and similar newspapers, by parading their cases before their readers. In states without ancien regime press structures – Britain, America and Ireland, the Dutch Republic, revolutionary France, and to some degree revolutionary Italy and revolutionary and Napoleonic Germany – a less regulated but more politically charged publishing environment existed. Here the most popular newspapers tended to be the most politically engaged, and in many cases papers were established or directly influenced by ambitious politicians, governments or political pressure groups. Thus, in the fledgling United States, David Copeland has noted that most papers were affiliated to political parties; in England, Hannah Barker has described the vigorous nature of partisan press politics; while in revolutionary France, Hugh Gough's piece suggests most readers identified passionately with the political agenda of their chosen paper. In the most polarised of these societies there was little scope for neutrality: as Douglas Simes's essay shows, this was as true for Ireland after 1798 as for France in the aftermath of 1789. An objective tone was often a route to ruin, whereas intolerant, sometimes even murderous, partisanship, had wide appeals in some sections of the community.

Newspapers could thus be distinctly subversive. Given the prevailing technological conditions before the widespread use of steam printing, where only a small amount of capital and a few hundred readers were required to launch a successful venture, the press had an explosive potential wherever controls on printing broke down or liberal press laws were introduced. In revolutionary contexts – including Ireland – newspapers were instrumental in the politicisation of populations and in displaying and interpreting the new politics of popular assemblies to the public. They expressed, shaped and directed revolutionary fervour and were instrumental in fomenting unrest, inciting violence and scripting political action. But even under absolutist press regimes, as demonstrated especially by Jack Censer's chapter, newspapers had the ability to challenge authority implicitly, by showing political power as something that was contested by competing authorities, displaying alternative, foreign governmental arrangements to the public, and spreading political information. In the process, they implicitly challenged the ideological foundation of absolutism, by forcing rulers to justify their positions, and thus tacitly admit that they could be wrong and that policy options should be subject to broader debate. Despite their limitations, newspapers were universally acknowledged as a power to be reckoned with, or at least contained, and during our period they offered both implicit and explicit challenges to government. If tangible evidence of their influence is hard to come by, there can be little doubt that by the end of the period under discussion, even more than the beginning, the influence of the press was widely recognised. By the middle decades of the nineteenth century, it was setting agendas, forging political identities and commenting on everyday political issues in a way which would have been unthinkable in most ancien regime states, and which prepared the way for mass politics in many states by the end of the century.

NOTES

1 The main international comparative studies of the press in English are Anthony Smith, *The Newspaper: An International History* (London, 1979); Mitchell Stephens, *A History of News From the Drum to the Satellite* (New York, 1988). See also Bob Harris, *Politics and the Rise of the Press: Britain and France 1620–1800* (London, 1996); Leonore O'Boyle, 'The image of the journalist in France, Germany and England, 1815–1848', *Comparative Studies in History and Society*, 10 (1967–8), 290–317.

2 This concept originates in the seminal work of Jürgen Habermas, *The Structural Transformation of the Public Sphere: An Inquiry into a Category of Bourgeois Society*, trans. Thomas Burger (Cambridge, MA, 1989).
3 The work of Benedict Anderson on 'imagined' national communities is especially useful here: Benedict Anderson, *Imagined Communities: Reflections on the Origin and Spread of Nationalism* (London, 1983).
4 Adrian Johns, *The Nature of the Book: Print and Knowledge in the Making* (Chicago and London, 1998), esp. pp. 636–7, argues strongly for the importance of different cultural settings in making distinctive print cultures.
5 Marshall McLuhan, *The Gutenberg Galaxy: the Making of Typographic Man* (Toronto, 1962).
6 Eisenstein's ideas on this subject originally appeared as 'Some conjectures about the impact of printing on Western Society', *Journal of Modern History*, 40 (1968), 1–56. They are repeated and applied in Elizabeth L. Eisenstein, *The Printing Press as an Agent of Change: Communication and Cultural Transformation in Early Modern Europe*, 2 vols. (Cambridge, 1979), and its abridgement, *The Printing Revolution in Early Modern Europe* (Cambridge, 1983).
7 Eisenstein, *Printing Press* and Eisenstein, *Printing Revolution*.
8 For his critique of Eisenstein see Johns, *The Nature of the Book*, esp. pp. 2–28.
9 Stephens, *History of News*, p. 4.
10 On newspapers and the commercialisation of culture see: Neil McKendrick, John Brewer and J. H. Plumb, *The Birth of a Consumer Society: The Commercialisation of Eighteenth-Century England* (London, 1982); J. H. Plumb, *The Commercialisation of Leisure in Eighteenth Century England* (Reading, 1973); C. J. Ferdinand, 'Selling it to the Provinces: News and Commerce Round Eighteenth-Century Salisbury', in John Brewer and Roy Porter (eds.), *Consumption and the World of Goods* (London, 1993), 393–411; T. R. Nevett, *Advertising in Britain: A History* (London, 1982), pp. 15–17; Colin Jones, 'The Great Chain of Buying: medical advertisement, the bourgeois public sphere, and the origins of the French Revolution', *American Historical Review*, vol. 101, 1(1996), 13–40. But note also the critique of existing explanations of the 'consumer revolution' in Colin Campbell, *The Romantic Ethic and the Spirit of Consumerism* (Oxford, 1987), chs. 2–3. Most recent histories of advertising in America, such as Michael Schudson, *Advertising, the Uneasy Persuasion: Its Dubious Impact on American Society* (New York, 1984), ch. 5, ignore the period prior to 1850.
11 For example, a random sampling of accounts of the evolution of the English newspaper variously identify the first English language newspapers as a Dutch *coranto* produced in 1620, newsbooks published in 1641 (tentatively), and the *Oxford Gazette*, published in 1665. Stephens, *History of News*, p. 157; Joad Raymond, *The Invention of the Newspaper: English Newsbooks 1641–1649* (Oxford, 1996); Charles E. Clark, *The Public Prints: the Newspaper in Anglo-American Culture, 1665–1740* (Oxford, 1994). Smith, *The Newspaper*, pp. 9–13 and 24–5, traces four stages of development internationally before 'the eighteenth century went on to create the newspaper in its complete form'. Nevertheless, he says the first known 'daily newspaper' appeared in Germany in 1650.
12 See below and Louise MacReynolds, *The News under Russia's Old Regime* (Princeton, NJ, 1991), pp. 18–21.

13 Claude Lévi-Strauss, *Structural Anthropology*, vol. I, trans. Claire Jackson and Brooke Grundfest Schoepf (London, 1968), p. 296.
14 Stephens, *History of News*, pp. 64–5, 68–71.
15 James Burke, *The Day the Universe Changed* (Boston, 1985), pp. 91–112; Clark, *The Public Prints*; Tessa Watt, *Cheap Print and Popular Piety, 1550–1640* (Cambridge, 1991); R. W. Scribner, *For the Sake of Simple Folk: Popular Propaganda in the German Reformation* (Oxford, 1994); Stephens, *History of News*.
16 Smith, *The Newspaper*, pp. 157–8.
17 For example, as late as 1740, no American newspaper had a regular print-run of over 600: Clark, *The Public Prints*, p. 259. However, Joad Raymond, *The Invention of the Newspaper*, pp. 233–8, argues plausibly that in the 1640s, newsbook print-runs were probably considerably higher than traditional estimates of 250–850.
18 Jeremy D. Popkin, *The Right-Wing Press in France, 1792–1800* (Chapel Hill, NC, 1980), pp. 177–9; Gilles Feyel, 'Les Frais d'impression et de diffusion de la presse parisienne entre 1789 et 1792', in Pierre Rétat (ed.), *La Révolution du journal 1788–94* (Paris, 1989), 77–99, p. 96.
19 Clark, *The Public Prints* pp. 15, 77–8.
20 Smith, *The Newspaper*, pp. 24–5; Jeremy Black, *The English Press in the Eighteenth Century* (Beckenham, 1987), p. 12; Hugh Gough, *The Newspaper Press in the French Revolution* (London, 1988); Jack Censer, *The French Press in the Age of Enlightenment* (London and New York, 1994), p. 10; Edwin Emery, *The Press in America: An Interpretative History of the Mass Media*, 3rd edn (Englewood Cliffs, NJ, 1972), p. 134.
21 G. A. Cranfield, *The Development of the Provincial Newspaper, 1700–1760* (Oxford, 1962), p. 13; Censer, *French Press*, pp. 8–10 and 54–5.
22 S. H. Steinberg, *500 Years of Printing*, 3rd edn (Harmondsworth, 1974), p. 280. G. A. Cranfield, *The Press and Society from Caxton to Northcliffe* (London and New York, 1978), p. 152. Raymond, *The Invention of the Newspaper*, p. 234, considers this rate 'high but by no means implausible' for the seventeenth century. Stephens, *A History of News*, refers to a production rate of 125 'papers' per hour, but appears to mean printing on two sides of paper.
23 'First Newspaper Printed by Steam', *The Times*, 29 November 1814, cited in James Grant, *The Newspaper Press: Its Origin – Progress – and Present Position*, 2 vols. (London, 1871), vol. I, pp. 453–4; Steinberg, *500 Years of Printing*, p. 280.
24 Stephens, *History of News*, p. 162; Raymond, *Invention of the Newspaper*, p. 8; Hannah Barker, *Newspapers, Politics and Public Opinion in Late Eighteenth-Century England* (Oxford, 1997), ch. 2.
25 Smith, *The Newspaper*, p. 91; William J. Murray, *The Right-Wing Press in the French Revolution* (Woodbridge, 1986), p. 30.
26 Gough, *Newspaper Press*, p. 212.
27 Black, *English Press*, p. 87.
28 The use of this phrase is examined by Jean Sgard, 'On dit', in Harvey Chisick (ed.), *The Press in the French Revolution: Studies on Voltaire and the Eighteenth Century*, vol. 287 (Oxford, 1991), 25–32.
29 Neal Ascherson (ed.), *The Times Reports on the French Revolution* (London, 1975), p. xvi; Stanley Morison *et al.*, *The History of The Times*, vol. I, *The Thunderer in the Making* (London, 1935), pp. 41–3.

30 Jeremy D. Popkin, *News and Politics in the Age of Revolution: Jean Luzac's Gazette de Leyde* (Ithaca, NY, and London, 1989), pp. 71–5; Gunnar and Mavis von Proschwitz, *Beaumarchais et le Courier de l'Europe: documents inédits ou peu connus*, 2 vols.: *Studies on Voltaire and the Eighteenth Century*, vols. 273–4 (Oxford, 1990), vol. I, p. 30.
31 Stephens, *History of News*, pp. 164–8.
32 Smith, *The Newspaper*, p. 79; chapter by van Sas below.
33 Censer, *French Press*, pp. 141–2; Gough, *Newspaper Press*, p. 3; Jeremy D. Popkin, *Revolutionary News: The Press in France 1789–1799* (Durham, NC, and London, 1990), p. 177; Robert B. Holtman, *Napoleonic Propaganda* (New York, 1969 reprint), pp. 46, 53.
34 Hannah Barker, *Newspapers, Politics and English Society, 1695–1855* (Harlow, 2000), ch. 4; David Pottinger, *The French Book Trade in the Ancien Regime, 1500–1791* (Cambridge, MA, 1958), p. 79.
35 Smith, *The Newspaper*, p. 79.
36 See chapters by David Copeland and Hugh Gough below.
37 On these points see Popkin, *News and Politics*; chapter by Burrows below.
38 The most common measure of literacy used by historians – the ability of individuals to sign their name on marriage certificates – although having the advantage of near universality can only reveal a limited amount. It only indicates a basic ability in one of several skills associated with literacy, the ability to hold a pen to write a few possibly well-practised words. It does not reveal much about reading ability in a society where reading and writing were taught separately and many women who could read were apparently never taught to write. Moreover, signature literacy reveals only a little about the level of writing skills and nothing about an individual's ability to understand and assimilate texts. For discussions of this topic see David Cressy, 'Literacy in context: meaning and measurement in early modern England' in Brewer and Porter (eds.), *Consumption and Goods*, pp. 305–19; R. A. Houston, *Literacy in Early Modern Europe: Culture and Education 1500–1800* (London and New York, 1988), ch. 6.
39 Houston, *Literacy in Early Modern Europe*, esp. pp. 150–4.
40 Ibid., p. 46.
41 See Keith Michael Baker, *Inventing the French Revolution: Essays on French Political Culture in the Eighteenth Century* (Cambridge, 1990).
42 Habermas, *Structural Transformation*.
43 Ibid., p. 29.
44 Ibid., p. 87. Benjamin Nathans has pointed out that the term used by Habermas, *bürgerliche Öffentlichkeit* can be translated as either 'civil public sphere' or 'bourgeois public sphere' and that this ambiguity in translation reflects a fundamental ambiguity in the concept itself in terms of its links to class: Benjamin Nathans, 'Habermas's "public sphere" in the era of the French Revolution', *French Historical Studies*, 16, 3 (1990), 620–44, p. 622n.
45 Habermas, *Structural Transformation*, part 3.
46 See Roger Chartier, *The Cultural Origins of the French Revolution*, trans. Lydia G. Cochrane (Durham, NC, 1991); Keith Michael Baker, *Inventing the French Revolution*; François Furet, *Interpreting the French Revolution*, trans. Elborg Forster (Cambridge, 1981); Mona Ozouf, *Festivals and the French Revolution*,

trans. Alan Sheridan (Cambridge, MA, 1988); Lynn Hunt, *Politics, Culture, and Class in the French Revolution* (Berkeley, CA, 1984).
47 Darnton argues that 'philosophic books' depicting sexual, political and pecuniary corruption at Louis XV's court played a central role in the desacralisation of the monarchy and the political education of the French public; Sara Maza that the concept of a rational-critical 'public opinion' as an alternative legitimising tribunal was both facilitated and reflected by the practice of opposing litigants in high-profile court cases publishing their uncensored trial briefs. See Robert Darnton, 'The high enlightenment and the low-life of literature in pre-revolutionary France', *Past and Present*, 60 (1971), 81–115, and Darnton, *The Forbidden Best-Sellers of Pre-Revolutionary France* (London, 1996); Sarah Maza, *Private Lives and Public Affairs: The Causes Célèbres of Pre-Revolutionary France* (Berkeley, CA, 1993). Darnton's work has been highly controversial: for a summary view of the current state of the debate, see H. T. Mason (ed.), *The Darnton Debate: Books and Revolution in the Eighteenth Century* (Oxford, 1998).
48 Jean Sgard, 'Journale und Journalisten im Zeitalter der Aufklärung', in H. U. Gumbrecht, R. Reichardt and T. Schleich (eds.), *Sozialgeschichte der Aufklärung in Frankreich* (Munich, 1981); see also Jean Sgard (ed.), *Dictionnaire de journaux*, 2 vols. (Paris, 1991).
49 Jeremy D. Popkin,'The prerevolutionary origins of political journalism', in Keith Michael Baker (ed.), *The French Revolution and the Creation of Modern Political Culture*, vol. I, *The Political Culture of the Old Regime* (Oxford, 1987), p. 209 and passim.
50 See *Lesegesellschaften und bürgerliche Emanzipation: Ein europäischer Vergleich*, ed. Otto Dann (Munich, 1982); David Blackbourn and Geoff Eley, *The Peculiarities of German History: Bourgeois Society and Politics in Nineteenth-Century Germany* (Oxford, 1984); R. Van Dülmen, *Die Gesellschaft der Aufklärer: Zur bürgerlichen Emanzipation und aufklärischen Kultur in Deutschland* (Frankfurton-Main, 1986); David Blackbourn, *Populists and Patricians: Essays in Modern German History* (London, 1987).
51 Hans Erich Bödeker, 'Prozesse und Strukturen politischer Bewusstseinsbildung der deutschen Aufklärung', in Hans Eric Bödeker and Ulrich Herman (eds.), *Aufklärung als Politisierung – Politisierung als Aufklärung* (Hamburg, 1987), 10–31; 'Journals and public opinion: the politicization of the German Enlightenment in the second half of the eighteenth century', in Eckhart Hellmuth (ed.), *The Transformation of Political Culture: England and Germany in the Late Eighteenth Century* (Oxford, 1990), 423–46.
52 U. Im Hof, *Das gesellige Jahrhundert: Gesellschaft und Gesellschaften im Zeitalter der Aufklärung* (Munich, 1982). See also T. Nipperdey, 'Verein als soziale Struktur in Deutschland im späten 18. und frühen 19. Jahrhundert', in Nipperdey, (ed.), *Gesellschaft, Kultur, Theorie* (Göttingen, 1976), 174–205.
53 Eckhart Hellmuth, 'Towards a comparative study of political culture: the cases of late eighteenth-century England and Germany', in Hellmuth (ed.), *Transformation of Political Culture*, 1–38, p. 25.
54 Bödeker, 'Journals and public opinion'.
55 Ibid., p. 425.

56 David S. Shields, *Civil Tongues and Polite Letters in British America* (Chapel Hill, NC, 1997); David Waldstreicher, *In the Midst of Perpetual Fetes: The Making of American Nationalism* (Chapel Hill, NC, 1997), quote from p. 293; Mary P. Ryan, *Civic Wars: Democracy and Public Life in the American City During the Nineteenth Century* (Berkeley, CA, 1997).

57 See for example Charles E. Clark, *The Public Prints: The Newspaper in Anglo-American Culture, 1655–1740* (Oxford, 1994).

58 Nathans, 'Habermas's "Public Sphere" in the era of the French Revolution', pp. 628–9. For example, whilst Keith Michael Baker, Jack Censer and Jeremy Popkin believe that the pre-revolutionary public sphere centred on competing ideologies, Darnton concluded that the type of radical libellous literature that he described did not contain any political programme, and implied a politics that revolved around personalities rather than issues or ideas: Robert Darnton, *The Literary Underground of the Old Regime* (Cambridge, MA, 1982), pp. 34ff. Historians of America have also drawn attention to the fact that the sociability of the public sphere was often defined by wit, humour and theatricality, rather than reason. Popular interventions into public discussions were largely moral, affective and even passionate, and are, John Brooke contends, 'particularly problematical for Habermas's insistence that the public sphere be one of rational discourse': John L. Brooke, 'Reason and passion in the public sphere: Habermas and the cultural historians', *Journal of Interdisciplinary History*, 24, 1 (summer, 1998), 43–67, p. 54.

59 See, for example, Geoff Eley, 'Nations, publics, and political cultures: placing Habermas in the nineteenth century', in Craig Calhoun (ed.), *Habermas and the Public Sphere* (Cambridge MA, 1989), 289–339, p. 304; Joan Landes, *Women and the Public Sphere in the Age of the French Revolution* (Ithaca, NY, 1988); Brooke, 'Reason and passion in the public sphere', p. 55; Mary P. Ryan, 'Gender and public access: women's politics in nineteenth-century America', in Calhoun (ed.), *Habermas and the Public Sphere*, pp. 259–88. However, see also Habermas, 'Further reflections on the public sphere', in Calhoun (ed.), *Habermas and the Public Sphere*, pp. 421–61.

1 The cosmopolitan press, 1759–1815

Simon Burrows

The celebrated cosmopolitanism of Enlightenment Europe was bound together by a common elite culture, a common elite language (French) and a common news media. In consequence, it is surely not unreasonable to envisage a European public, and even a pan-European public sphere, albeit a narrow and largely aristocratic one, which transcended national publics. For from the Huguenot diaspora to the Napoleonic period, there existed beyond French borders a French-language press that aimed to provide a steady flow of news information and, increasingly, opinion, to an international elite. This press – comprising political newspapers produced beyond France's direct sphere of influence for a European audience – is the subject of this chapter. Although these papers were written in French, and at times circulated widely inside France, the chapter's focus will be on Europe generally, both because the role of international papers inside ancien regime France is discussed below in Jack Censer's chapter, and because they had difficulty circulating there after 1792. Journals aimed primarily at local francophones in Belgium, Switzerland, Germany, Poland and other countries are not considered here, nor are the specialised journals that proliferated in eighteenth-century Europe. While most international papers were what Jerzy Lojek has termed 'international gazettes',[1] a few periodicals – such as the *Journal encyclopédique* or Jean-Gabriel Peltier's émigré publications – which contained substantial news sections are also worthy of mention. However, they could not compete with the gazettes for freshness, and risked accusations of providing 'news which is not news'.[2] This survey is also limited by the secondary literature, for despite extensive recent work on the international French press in the Enlightenment,[3] our knowledge and bibliographic sources are still patchy,[4] and the situation with regard to émigré papers is worse.[5]

Despite the international focus of the cosmopolitan press, there is no escaping the fact that the French Revolution was the most decisive event in its history. Before 1789, French readers found their freshest, most independent news of France in gazettes produced outside the Bourbon realm.

Table 1 *Leading extra-territorial gazettes during the late ancien regime*

Common title	Place of Publication	Dates	Rank[7]
Courier de l'Escaut	Malines (?) (Austrian Netherlands)	1784–1819?	3 / 12
Courrier d'Avignon	Avignon (Papal territory)	1733–1793	3 / *
Courier de l'Europe	London, with Boulogne reprint	1776–1826	2 / 4
Courier du Bas-Rhin	Cleves, Wesel (Prussia)	1767–1807?	1 / 2
Gazette d'Altona	Altona (Denmark)	1758?–1775+[8]	3 / 11
Gazette d'Amsterdam	Amsterdam (United Provinces)	1663?–1795?	2 / 5
Gazette d'Utrecht	Utrecht (United Provinces)	1689?–1787	2 / 3
Gazette de Berne	Berne (Switzerland)	1689–1798	3 / *
Gazette de Cologne	Cologne (Archbishopric of)	1734–1794	3 / 7
Gazette de La Haye	The Hague (United Provinces)	1744–1790?	3 / 6
Gazette de Leyde	Leiden (United Provinces)	1677–1811	1 / 1
Gazette des Deux-Ponts	Mannheim (duchy of Deux-Ponts)	1770–1798	3 / 8
Gazette de Bruxelles	Brussels (Austrian Netherlands)	1649–1791	3 / 10

After the collapse of royal control over the printed word in July 1789, foreign gazettes no longer offered either advantage. In Paris new journals whose coverage focused heavily, often exclusively, on events inside France, now Europe's hottest news story, proliferated as France's boldest political publicists returned from exile, while foreign gazettes lagged days behind. But although the market for foreign gazettes inside France rapidly dried up, a lively French-language press survived outside the country until the end of the Napoleonic era, staffed largely by émigrés.

Before the revolution, the international francophone press was large and increasingly influential, but it remained significant thereafter. Between 1760 and 1789 about sixty French-language political papers were produced outside France for an international audience, although many were short-lived.[6] The most significant are listed in table 1. All these papers were classic *international gazettes*, most of which appeared twice-weekly, and provided readers with news bulletins and official texts (such as relations, laws, ordinances, peace treaties and remonstrances), usually without comment, in a set order, under the putative place and dateline of the report's origin. Often several reports would cover the same story, giving different versions. Readers themselves were expected to make sense of these discordant reports. This gazette form prospered for over 130 years, largely due to its commercial orientation: gazettes existed primarily to sell news information, not to peddle ideology, in marked contrast to the papers of the revolutionary era. Editorial comment was therefore very limited – far less significant in terms of space and emphasis than news bulletins and official texts.[9]

Table 2 *Leading émigré political papers in Europe, 1789–1815*[15]

Title	Emigré editors	Place	Dates
Abeille du nord	Barons d'Angely	Altona	1799–1810
L'Ambigu	Peltier	London	1802–1818
Annales politiques du XIXe siècle	Paoli de Chagny	Hamburg Ratisbon	1805–1806
Censeur	Bertin d'Antilly and Mesmont	Hamburg	1799–1800
Correspondance politique	Peltier	London	1793–1794
Courier d'Angleterre	Regnier	London	1805–1815
Courier de Londres = Courier de l'Europe	Verduisant, abbé Calonne, Montlosier, Regnier, Gérard	London	1776–1826
Mercure britannique	Mallet Du Pan	London	1798–1800
Mercure de France	Anonymous committee of six	London	1800–1801
Mercure universel	Paoli de Chagny	Ratisbon	1797?–1803
Paris pendant l'année	Peltier	London	1795–1802
Le Pour et le contre	Paoli de Chagny and Sabatier de Castres	Hamburg	1805
Reveil	Mesmont	Hamburg	1798–1799
Spectateur du Nord	Baudus and Villers	Hamburg	1797–1802

Nevertheless, within these parameters, different gazettes developed differences in tone and approach, especially as the Revolution approached, and from the late 1760s three leading papers, the *Courier du Bas-Rhin*, *Gazette de Leyde* and *Courier de l'Europe* (founded 1776), began increasing editorial comment.[10] When French subscriptions to international gazettes dropped sharply after 1789, reputation, political engagement – and in the case of the *Courier de l'Europe* ideological prostitution – helped these three papers to survive. For by 1791–2, faced with the demands of partisan politics, it was becoming difficult for international gazettes to retain their detachment and appeal.[11] Hence, most disappeared in the 1790s and several others came under the influence of the émigrés, including the *Gazette de Cologne*, *Courier du Bas-Rhin* and *Courier de l'Europe*.[12] However, the 1790s also witnessed the establishment of numerous papers by the émigrés themselves. London alone had eleven émigré papers between 1793 to 1818, including the *Courier de l'Europe*, which under the title *Courier de Londres* survived until 1826, adapting its politics to political contingency.[13] A brief survey of titles produced elsewhere identified thirty-three more papers edited by émigrés on mainland Europe and in the United States.[14] The most important European émigré papers are listed in table 2.

From 1759 to the Revolution, France was the most important market for the cosmopolitan press. Although ancien regime French readers had been introduced to an illegal literature of ideas by a flourishing clandestine pamphlet trade, they found fresh, miscellaneous political news – especially of France – hard to come by until the 1760s. The handful of foreign gazettes that were permitted to circulate in the post – notably the *Courrier d'Avignon*, *Gazette d'Amsterdam* and *Gazette d'Utrecht* – were prohibitively expensive, and the only domestic newspaper, the *Gazette de France*, was insipid, heavily censored, court-centred and offered little French political news.[16] However, after the so-called 'postal revolution' of 1759, the government tolerated the importation under licence of various foreign gazettes and granted a monopoly over their distribution at a moderate fixed price via the postal service. The postal revolution cut prices by around 70 per cent and thereafter sales of international gazettes rose rapidly: 3,100 subscribers in 1747 had become 14,000 by 1781. This compares with a circulation of almost 30,000 for domestically produced newspapers.[17] After the postal revolution France became the most important market for international gazettes. As a result they proliferated and the French government gained increased powers of suasion over them.

Total sales of international gazettes and individual titles were closely connected to political events. They boomed in the Seven Years War, fell back after the peace, peaked again during the American Revolution, and then began to climb again in the pre-revolutionary crisis.[18] After the French Revolution subscriptions inside France to all categories of foreign news periodical fell to negligible levels. However, there was also a significant market beyond France. In November 1778, the *Courier de l'Europe*'s London print-run was 700,[19] a level that was probably relatively constant until further boosted by the pre-Revolution and coming of the émigrés.[20] Until the Revolution a much larger edition for the continent was printed at Boulogne. The *Gazette de Leyde*'s circulation peaked during the American Revolution at 4,200 subscribers, of whom only 2,500 lived in France or Brabant, plus perhaps 2,000 more for counterfeit editions.[21] The *Courier du Bas-Rhin*, although banned in revolutionary France, had a circulation of 1340 in 1793 and 530 in 1801.[22] Among émigré journals, Peltier's *Correspondance politique* boasted at least 225 subscribers in Britain and 450 in continental Europe and Mallet Du Pan's twice-monthly *Mercure britannique* probably had 2,000 to 2,500 subscribers plus perhaps 1,500 more for its various counterfeit editions. Regnier's *Courier d'Angleterre* distributed an average of 490 copies per issue in 1808.[23] Surviving evidence allows us to speculate that before the Revolution international gazettes had a total of perhaps 10–15,000 subscribers outside France, roughly matching their circulation inside. This total excludes the phenomenally successful *Annales politiques, civiles et littéraires du dix-huitième siècle* of

Simon-Nicolas-Henri Linguet, more a commentary on political events than a newspaper, which sold over 20,000 copies Europe-wide. After the Revolution, despite enormous upheavals in the market and the collapse of many international gazettes, French extra-territorial papers continued to have several thousand subscribers outside France. These numbers, though small, were not insignificant, especially given multiple readers and the social status of the readership.

Although detailed subscription lists do not survive, there is no doubt that the extra-territorial French press served an elite audience. Jeremy Popkin's analysis of the content of the *Gazette de Leyde* convincingly demonstrates that it performed the main function of an 'elite press', delivering the highest possible quality political news to a wealthy cosmopolitan audience. Like the other French international gazettes and émigré papers, it was almost wholly reliant on subscription revenue.[24] However, what little advertising it carried targeted the wealthiest strata of ancien regime society, the potential purchasers of large estates and luxury goods across Europe and beyond. For according to the abbé Bianchi 'the Dutch gazettes are read at Constantinople, Smyrna, Cairo, in the Levant, in both Indies, just as at the Hague and in the cafés of Amsterdam'.[25] German papers were also widely available. The *Gazette des Deux-Ponts*'s distribution spanned London, Versailles, the Rhineland, Berlin, Rome and Vienna while in 1768 the newly founded *Courier du Bas-Rhin* was circulating widely in France, Germany, Austria, Bohemia, the Low Countries, Switzerland and Italy.[26] As Popkin notes, the international gazettes were required reading for diplomats and politicians,[27] but they were also available to readers from other social strata. Paul Benhamou found French readers could pay to read international gazettes in the premises of Parisian *gazetiers*, and in numerous *cabinets de lecture* (public reading rooms), *sociétés d'amateurs* (associations of literature enthusiasts who subscribed for journals collectively) and *chambres de lecture* (clubs of individuals who gathered to read and discuss papers purchased in common) across France. There were also a large number of sociable sites where gazettes, though not the primary attraction, were usually available *gratis*, including cafés, clubs, gambling dens and smoking rooms.[28] International gazettes might be encountered in the remotest corners of Europe and the Mediterranean. By the late 1780s, a French soldier in the Russian army in Moldavia could buy fresh editions of the *Gazette de Leyde* from Jewish merchants, and the comte de La Motte could read the paper in a Glasgow café.[29] A decade later, while campaigning in Egypt, Napoleon updated himself on French affairs from copies of the *Courier de Londres* acquired from the British navy,[30] while French police reports reveal that in 1811 Peltier's *L'Ambigu* was circulating at Tunis 'in the cafés, *auberges* and other public places'.[31]

These examples suggest that international gazettes were reaching social groups well beyond politicians, diplomats and courtly and aristocratic elites and that a variety of titles were available to the public at a modest price in moderate-sized towns across Europe and even beyond.

After the Revolution, émigré papers continued to serve an elite audience. Mallet Du Pan's *Mercure britannique*'s readers included British princes and ministers, various European diplomats, Tsar Paul I, the Duke of Brunswick, the Prince of Brazil and 'many other persons of rank and of parliamentary and literary distinction'.[32] The *Courier d'Angleterre* circulated among some of the Tsar's leading Francophobe advisors, Swedish aristocrats and the leading counter-revolutionary publicists.[33] But émigré journals also served other audiences, notably French exiles and French-speaking merchants.

The most successful international gazettes were based along major trade routes, mostly in smaller states with considerable autonomy and liberal censorship regimes. The oldest were established in the United Provinces by Huguenot refugees in the late seventeenth century. Others were published in the German Rhineland, the German free city of Hamburg, the neighbouring Danish free city of Altona and a handful of small states along the French frontier. These included the principality of Bouillon; the Prussian enclave of Cleves (home to the *Courier du Bas-Rhin*); the Duchy of Deux-Ponts and the papal enclave of Avignon. London emerged as a publishing centre belatedly, and only for political reasons. Cut off from the sources of Continental news, it only became a viable base in the 1770s and early 1780s, when Britain's struggle to retain its American colonies became Europe's leading story. The *Courier de l'Europe* was launched to take advantage of these circumstances, but its proprietors soon felt the need for a Continental edition at Boulogne. After the peace, subscriptions fell sharply. Moreover, until the French Revolution, London's French journalists were widely acknowledged to be the lowest class of muck-rakers. The *Courier de l'Europe*'s founding editor, Alphonse-Joseph de Serres de La Tour, was a romantic refugee from royal justice, who had absconded to London with the aristocratic wife of his well-connected employer. His successors Charles Théveneau de Morande and Joseph Perkins MacMahon were blackmailers and *libellistes*. Morande was also a French spy. London only became the premier French extra-territorial news centre once more in the mid-1790s, as revolutionary armies advanced, quashing Dutch and German press liberty. Increasingly, only London seemed to offer both a reasonably free press beyond the reach of French influence and a significant French community. By 1798 Mallet Du Pan could write to a friend: 'As for the public ... one must leave the continent in order to speak to it; for there is no longer anywhere where anyone can print a line against the Directory and its manoeuvres ... Only in England can one write, think, speak or act.'[34]

Before the Revolution, France had few career journalists. According to William Murray, Mallet Du Pan and Linguet were probably the first.[35] However, both began their journalistic careers beyond French borders, and there the situation is not so clear. In London several pre-revolutionary exiles worked on more than one paper, including Serres de La Tour, Perkins MacMahon and Morande. Jean Manzon, the Piedmontese editor of the *Courier du Bas-Rhin*, and his arch-rival Jean Luzac, who edited the *Gazette de Leyde* from 1772 to 1798, should also be considered career journalists. So perhaps should Jacques-Pierre Brissot, who was the indexer of Linguet's *Annales* and an administrator and later journalist with the *Courier de l'Europe* before establishing a succession of papers. The revolutionary journalistic partners Pascal Boyer and Antoine-Marie Cerisier also began their careers with the extra-territorial press before 1789.

Among numerous motives that drew these men to journalism, money was certainly important. The profits for a successful journalist-proprietor were considerable. According to Brissot, Serres de La Tour often boasted that he earned more money in a year from his one-third share in the *Courier de l'Europe*'s profits than Jean-Jacques Rousseau had made in a lifetime as a *philosophe*.[36] Likewise, Jean Luzac's revenues from the *Gazette de Leyde* exceeded those of the entire University of Leiden, where he was also a professor.[37] Even émigré journalists earned considerable sums. Mallet Du Pan's income as editor-proprietor of the *Mercure britannique* exceeded the lavish salary of 18,000 livres he had earned in the 1780s as political editor of Panckoucke's *Mercure de France*, despite a much smaller circulation. His rival Peltier lived extravagantly, and journalism helped him to recover from a series of bankruptcies.

Journalism also offered exiles an opportunity to remain politically involved. For many it was a conscious choice for this reason and even before 1789 the most successful journalists were characterised by their ideological commitment. Both Jean Luzac and Manzon promoted moderate variants of Enlightenment: Luzac championing representative bodies, Manzon supporting enlightened absolutism, penal reform and d'Holbachian materialism.[38] Linguet used his journal primarily as a 'tribune' to advance his views rather than record news,[39] and his example was followed from 1787 by Morande, who, finding an independent journalistic voice, espoused the cause of patriotic reform in his editorials and *Lettres d'un voyageur*. Morande's articles were highly engaged, topical and prescriptive. They broke new ground in French newspaper journalism and attempted to lead public debate. Nothing like them appeared in other French-language newspapers during the pre-Revolution.[40] Their style was imitated by journalists in revolutionary Paris, where it created a 'new type of demagogue', the tribune of the people, who transformed Linguet's activism into calls for direct action.[41] Commitment to a cause became a hallmark of émigré journalism too, as Mallet Du Pan made explicit when he declared the *Mercure britannique*'s aim 'of reviving in every quarter the courage of governments and nations overwhelmed or menaced by the French Republic; of showing them the necessity of resistance, and inspiring the hope of success, if supported by united endeavours and the rectitude of intention'.[42]

Given their audience and the sensitive information and heterodox ideas they sometimes carried, it is hardly surprising that ancien regime governments sought to contain or control the content of international papers. Their most obvious expedient was to ban gazettes from circulating on their own territories. Joseph II punished the *Gazette de Leyde* by giving a third party exclusive rights to reprint and disseminate the journal in the Habsburg realms, allowing news to circulate but hitting the newspaper's owners in the pocket.[43] Until 1759 the French also permitted cheap reprints, but found that this left editors no financial incentive to adopt a moderate tone: perhaps this is why they eventually decided to admit cheap foreign gazettes.[44] They also found that temporary interdictions were more flexible. They briefly banned the *Courier du Bas Rhin* in 1767 for publishing extracts of an anti-religious tract; the *Gazette d'Utrecht* in 1771 in order to intimidate other papers; and the *Courier de l'Europe* in 1776 for publishing a letter mistreating Marie-Antoinette and Maurepas.[45]

However, bans could not prevent the circulation of unfavourable news information on foreign soil and among the policy-makers and diplomatic corps of rival powers. Ancien regime governments therefore often resorted to diplomatic complaints to silence recalcitrant journalists, with varying success.[46] From the late seventeenth century onwards there was a steady stream of diplomatic complaints against Dutch international gazettes.[47] The authorities in the Netherlands often took positive action in response to complaints. One from the Prussian government in 1790 led to a temporary interdiction on the *Gazette de La Haye*, which resulted in its permanent closure.[48] But such brutal effectiveness was rare and the influence that the Prussians enjoyed in Holland after their intervention in the patriot revolution in 1787 was exceptional. Usually diplomatic complaints had lesser effects. Jean Veycrusse has traced thirty complaints against Dutch gazettes in French archives dating from the period 1760–1785, most originating from the highest levels of French society rather than government. Of these thirty cases, the French government took action over twenty-eight, pressurising the journalists to back down and print retractions or corrections in at least twenty-four.[49] Complaints elsewhere forced similar retractions: in 1768 the *Gazette de Berne* was forced to print a humiliating retraction of a 'false and calumnious' notice which had wrongly attributed a scandalous banned work to Voltaire, after the *philosophe* complained to the Bernese authorities.[50] Sometimes complaints resulted in sanctions. In 1776, Etienne Luzac was reprimanded for offending the Grand Master of the Order of Malta and ordered not to print commentaries in future.[51]

Despite the high success rate of such complaints, warnings, bans and admonitions seldom had much lasting effect. In the Netherlands, at least, this was in part due to the devolved power structure, and the same was possibly true, to a certain extent, in the Holy Roman Empire. Moreover, if pushed too hard, editors might imitate Gueudeville who, finding his *Esprit des cours de l'Europe* suppressed in 1701, merely changed its title.[52] Or they might move their operation, like Pierre Rousseau, whose peripatetic *Journal encyclopédique* moved from Liège to Brussels before finally finding a safe home in Bouillon.[53] Moreover, bans and complaints could prove counter-productive. Jean-Baptiste de la Varenne, editor of the *Glaneur historique*, welcomed them, believing that they promoted sales, while in 1776 the *Mémoires secrètes* predicted that the *Courier de l'Europe*'s notoriety would win it many subscribers once the French government lifted its interdiction.[54] Dutch editors could sometimes afford to be defiant. In response to French complaints in 1772 Etienne Luzac replied that if he limited himself to French news published in the *Gazette de France*, 'it would alert the French public that we were holding back and produce the opposite of the desired effect'.[55] In the same year he refused to bow to Danish complaints that he had refused to endorse charges brought against the reforming minister Struensee, who was executed after a palace coup. However, Luzac's bold declaration that he would 'never depart from the truth either out of enmity or from a desire to please men in high places' was largely bluster. Already in 1771, following French complaints, he had ceased publishing material on the Maupeou crisis in France.[56] The *Gazette d'Amsterdam*, *Gazette de La Haye* and *Gazette d'Utrecht* bowed before similar pressure.[57]

Nevertheless, Etienne Luzac's comments showed that governments were caught in a cleft stick. If they wanted to persuade a broad European public of their version of events, they had to use news channels that enjoyed that public's confidence and maintained their appearance of independence by publishing documents from all parties. In turn, this meant that governments were forced to attempt to persuade. In the process they admitted tacitly that they recognised the legitimacy of the judgements of a 'public', however limited, and existence of alternative sources of authority and hence, that monarchs were not the only political actors within their states.[58]

Realising that they could not always suppress hostile news coverage, governments sought more effective means to moderate and guide coverage of affairs in the international press. One way to achieve this was to attempt to bribe editors and proprietors. Thus, Manzon – who readily sold his pen on issues which affected neither Prussian interests nor his own personal crusades – was paid to push a pro-Polish line by the Polish King, Stanislaus-Augustus Poniatowski, until 1772–3, when Russian pressure forced the journalist to change tack.[59] In the 1740s, it was rumoured that the French had bribed the only Dutch gazettes permitted to enter France. It was said that Du Breuil, the editor of the *Gazette d'Amsterdam*, was paid 2,000 livres for allowing the French ambassador to vet his paper, while Madame de Limiers was said to have received 12–15,000 livres for pro-French coverage in the *Gazette d'Utrecht*.[60] The French postal revolution of 1759 was also a form of bribe, for by opening the frontiers to other selected gazettes and slashing the cost of postage, the French were opening up the largest market in Europe. No editor could afford to ignore this incentive, although one complained that the circumspection required to gain admission had made his gazette too 'dull' for readers outside France.[61] Moreover, according to manuscript newsletters the French government 'bought' the *Courier de l'Europe* during the American Revolution with a mass-subscription, allegedly for 4,000 copies, an improbably high amount.[62] But if it was to remain a credible organ they had to allow it considerable leeway for, as its proprietor remarked, it would lose all interest if it was sensed to be written from Paris.[63] This paradox dogged the French in their attempts to moderate the foreign gazettes. It would also prove problematic to British attempts to use the émigré press after 1803.

Governments also began to develop techniques of news management. Several German powers established international gazettes as a means to exercise direct control over a paper while promoting their interests with an international public. The *Gazette de Cologne*, founded in 1734, fought assiduously for causes supported by its prince-bishop electors. It opposed the *philosophes* and religious laxity and became a mouthpiece for the Jesuits after their expulsion from France.[64] The liberal Duke Christian IV of Deux-Ponts, who had close ties with the *philosophes*, established a literary journal to be their organ and contemporaries saw a similar influence behind the *Gazette des Deux-Ponts*, which was edited under bureaucratic supervision.[65] So was the *Courier du Bas-Rhin*, which served notoriously as a Prussian 'propaganda bridgehead' into Western Europe.[66] However, although his paper regularly published Prussian-inspired disinformation and commentaries on international affairs and was no freer in its domestic coverage than the *Gazette de France*, Manzon's relationship with the Prussian authorities was complex and far from servile. His paper, like many other international gazettes, was not permitted to report freely or comment on events in its homeland.[67] However, he was allowed to follow instructions on international affairs with considerable interpretative latitude, and expected to comment freely on the internal politics of other countries and philosophic matters.[68] The French attempted to control news flows internally by releasing a flood of supportive information and suppressing contrary stories and externally by feeding information to their vassal papers in Avignon and London.[69] Furthermore, in the 1770s, they launched a number of substitute papers, including Panckoucke's 'clandestine' foreign papers the *Journal de Genève* and *Journal de Bruxelles*, and the propagandist *Affaires de l'Angleterre et de l'Amérique*.[70] American diplomatic agents supplied propaganda essays to the handful of international gazettes that accepted such pieces, but such efforts were dependent on individual initiative. Moreover, the Americans had little control over editors. When John Adams decided to stop sending materials to the *Gazette de Leyde* and start patronising the *Gazette d'Amsterdam* after Jean Luzac argued for peace based on a territorial compromise, it did nothing to popularise the American cause.[71]

A more sophisticated method of control was to direct reporting at source. Stanislaus-Augustus tried to ensure a pro-Polish coverage by supplying bulletins to Dutch and German journalists;[72] and in the early 1780s, if not earlier, the French established close supervision over the Parisian correspondents of the foreign gazettes. Certainly, a system of direction existed from January 1781, when they arrested several Parisian newsmongers, including Pascal Boyer, formerly a correspondent for the *Courier de l'Europe* and Charles Fouilhoux, who corresponded with the *Gazette d'Utrecht*. Both were rapidly released on a good behaviour bond and given official sanction and materials to continue their trade. Moreover, the government apparently arranged for Boyer to run a news bureau supplying the *Courier du Bas-Rhin*, *Gazette de Leyde* and possibly Europe's best-selling paper, the German-language Hamburg *Correspondenten*.[73] Systematic supervision may have existed already in the 1770s, for in March 1780 the British press entrepreneur Samuel Swinton alerted the editor of his new gazette, the *Gazette anglo-françoise-américaine*, that his Paris correspondent also supplied the *Gazette de Cologne*, *Gazette d'Utrecht*, *Gazette d'Amsterdam* and *Gazette de Leyde*.[74]

Whether newspaper editors were fully aware of their correspondents' links to the French administration is not entirely clear, but this relationship was indicative of the gazetteers' symbiotic reliance on government. Journalists needed governments to supply fresh and reliable information, whilst governments wished to suppress certain stories, at the same time as publicising others. By the early 1780s, these developments had created an integrated system of political reporting covering all Europe, especially with regard to bulletins from France. Thus, in late July 1789, exactly the same initial report of the fall of the Bastille appears in the *Gazette de Leyde*, *Gazette de Berne* and *Courier du Bas-Rhin*, with only slight editorial variations.[75] This inter-textuality has important implications for our understanding of European public opinion and responses to key issues, especially the generally warm reception given to the early stages of the French Revolution. The response was similar across Europe, at least in part, because across the Continent elites were reading similar reports based on the same printed and manuscript sources in international gazettes. And in many cases these reports also served as sources for domestic papers.

Given the degree of integration of the international gazettes, it is worth making a few generalisations about editorial content, especially as editorial interventions became increasingly common after 1750. From the late 1760s and early 1770s, after the founding of the *Courier du Bas Rhin* and *Courier de l'Europe*, and Jean Luzac's accession to the editorship of the *Gazette de Leyde*, ideological discourses also begin to appear more frequently in these papers.[76] The most reticent among them was the *Gazette de Leyde*. Although in this period it was Europe's paper of record and aimed at comprehensive and impartial reporting, Jean Luzac's commitment to representative, though not democratic, forms of government was evident in editorial comments and his willingness to accept American propaganda materials. His stance was even clearer in the 1780s when he emerged as a leader of the moderate faction of the patriots during the Dutch Patriot Revolution.[77] Luzac's arch-rival, Jean Manzon, who edited the *Courier du Bas-Rhin*, was more outspoken, especially in favour of enlightened absolutism. In his 'Cleves' column and long notes and explications, Manzon offered both opinion and interpretation, often while launching tirades against other newspapers.[78] More innovative still was the London-based *Courier de l'Europe*, whose early numbers resembled British newspapers and offered regular coverage of the sessions of parliament, large numbers of readers' letters, essays, occasional poems and literary contributions. This formula proved too radical for readers, and the paper rapidly adopted the traditional quarto form of the international gazettes and reduced cultural content and correspondence. However, it continued to offer more commercial news and cultural and literary content than its Continental counterparts and from 1787, as we have seen, contained Morande's essay articles, which advocated political reform as the means to 'regenerate' France.

All three leading gazettes promoted Enlightenment, albeit in diluted and divergent forms, and the same is generally true, though to a lesser extent, of most of their competitors. All international gazettes tended to favour freedom to circulate information, but few, if any, supported unbridled freedom of expression. To varying degrees they supported more humane punishments and legal codification. They also tended – with rare exceptions such as the *Gazette de Cologne* – to be secular, anti-Jesuit and, in Manzon's case, materialist. Most favoured political emancipation and representative government, usually supporting representative bodies in their struggles against ministerial and monarchic power. Even Manzon believed liberty should be the ultimate aim and crowning achievement of a strong regime, but he saw absolutism as the only guarantee against social disintegration. In fact, Manzon's fear of demagoguery and democratic forces was shared by the other international journalists, but in a more muted manner. The political preferences of the international gazettes thus covered the spectrum of enlightened elite opinion. However, after 1770 the unity of that elite was strained in the face of political developments. The American Revolution and Dutch Patriot Revolution of the 1780s in particular were decisive in formulating European opinion prior to 1789. As these political developments were reported and interpreted by the press, it is legitimate to ask whether the international gazettes contributed to the spread and development of reformist and democratic ideas.

It has been suggested that the ideals of the American Revolution, with their emphasis on liberty and the principle of no taxation without representation, constituted a direct challenge to the powers of ancien regime Europe, and that the publication of American proclamations and constitutions in the gazettes was deeply subversive.[79] However, as Jack Censer's contribution to this volume suggests, we should exercise caution with such claims, even in a French context. Moreover, 1789 appears to have changed the way in which European readers understood these documents.[80] The response of the *Gazette des Deux-Ponts*, whose editors viewed the insurgents' struggle as a just battle against ministerial despotism, is probably typical.[81] Jean Luzac seems to have taken the Americans' part largely for similar reasons.[82]

The coverage of representative politics, especially the British parliament, has also been seen as subversive, especially in France.[83] In 1793, Peltier even accused the *Courier de l'Europe* of precipitating the Revolution by creating a vogue for opposition.[84] Again, it is necessary to urge caution. However, it seems fair to argue that through the *Courier de l'Europe* in particular, educated Europeans became familiar with the political vocabulary of British representative politics, leading old French terms such as *opposition, majorité, minorité* and *responsabilité* to be invested with modern political meanings.[85] But conversely British political life was often depicted as tumultuous, divisive and faction-ridden, and this may have reinforced prejudices against representative politics, at least in their British incarnation. The *Courier du Bas-Rhin* admired Britain, but saw her 'liberties' as a distraction to mask ministerial despotism at a deeper level: it argued that Voltaire received more protection in France than John Wilkes in Britain.[86] Morande likened the British constitution to a beautiful woman showing the blemishes of age.[87] These ambiguous depictions may help to explain the rejection of the British political model by the French Constituent Assembly in September 1789, despite decades of Anglophilia in enlightened circles.

Events in the Netherlands in the 1780s – where traditional tensions between the Stadholderate and representative provincial estates backed by urban interests erupted into open conflict – also seem to have had a decisive influence on the political views of many international journalists. Dutch papers like the *Gazette de Leyde* and *Gazette d'Amsterdam* gave the so-called *patriots* vigorous support in their struggle against the Stadholder – until silenced by Prussian intervention in 1787 – as did the French-sponsored *Courier de l'Europe*, keen to support France's traditional allies. The *Courier du Bas-Rhin*, not surprisingly took the Stadholder's part, castigating the *patriots*, whom it labelled '*le parti démagogique*' and accused of bribing correspondents to papers like the *Gazette de Cologne* in order to mislead European opinion.[88] The *Gazette d'Amsterdam* in contrast stigmatised the Stadholder's supporters as 'the party opposed to liberty' and accused them of wishing to sow disunity among the patriots.[89] The rebellion in the neighbouring Austrian Netherlands (modern Belgium) was treated in a somewhat different manner. Manzon naturally was antipathetic: a typical report in December 1786 denounced staff at the University of Louvain for fomenting resistance to reforms that all Europe applauded.[90] But this time the Dutch patriot Luzac and French agent Morande concurred with him. While both applauded outbursts of popular resistance to despotism elsewhere in Europe, they had little sympathy for the conservative, priest-led rebellion against the enlightened rationalising policies of Joseph II.[91]

The international gazettes' response to the French Revolution is perhaps best illustrated by considering their reports of a pivotal event, the fall of the Bastille. As we have seen, the *Courier du Bas-Rhin*, *Gazette de Leyde* and *Gazette de Berne* all carried the same report, save for minor editorial differences. The report glorifies the success of the '*Peuple*' on a day which 'will forever be celebrated in our annals'. It told of the storming of the Bastille and murder and decapitation of its governor, de Launay, but spoke of his treason in ordering his troops to fire on the crowd and gloated, 'How the instruments of despotism quake in horror once the people throw off their yoke and takes their vengeance.' However, the report also shows characteristic elite anxieties about popular violence, though it excuses it on this occasion, asserting, 'Posterity may excuse the people of Paris to some extent; today they fought only for their liberty and only immolated those who provoked and betrayed them.' Crucially, however, the *Gazette de Leyde* deleted this phrase, hinting at a lesser sympathy; and another summary report in the same issue talks disdainfully about the 'vile populace' and their hopes of pillage amidst the disorder.

A survey of reports in four other gazettes shows the prevalence of similar viewpoints. All speak of the *'Peuple'* rather than a mob. The *Gazette d'Amsterdam*'s correspondent was horrified by de Launay's decapitation, but described the people as 'justly incensed' (*'irrités'*) by his actions and rejoiced that the fall of the Bastille had saved France.[92] The *Gazette des Deux-Ponts* lamented the dismissal of Necker that had provoked the disturbances; celebrated the heroism and impetuosity of the attackers; and described de Launay as a 'traitor' and 'the people' as a 'model of wisdom' – a phrase bearing chilling similarities to the Rousseauist rhetoric of St-Just and Robespierre.[93] Later, the paper gave sensationalist reports of the demolition of *'cette horrible prison'* and discoveries in its ruins and archives.[94] The *Courier de l'Europe*'s main account saw Necker – 'the only man who could save France' – as a victim of an aristocratic party and briefly glossed over the events of this *'tumulte horrible'*. However, the editorial column explained that the rebellion was against the abuses of centuries rather than Louis XVI; stressed that the murders were not premeditated or cruel, because 'they weren't committed in cold blood'; and asserted the King had showed his love for his people by submission to their will.[95] The *Courrier d'Avignon*, perhaps the most lukewarm paper, explained the motives for the murder of de Launay and Flesselles but described the events as 'deplorable'; nevertheless, it felt that the King's response was the best way to appease the situation.[96]

This elitist, ambiguous response to the Revolution – praising reforms, looking forward to regeneration but deploring and fearing mob action and demagoguery – continued to characterise the leading international gazettes for the next couple of years. From 1789 to 1791 Morande saw the Revolution as part of a pan-European movement for liberty and upheld the principles of 1789 while castigating extremists of both left and right. Although he claimed to be a *patriote royaliste*, he insisted that the new constitution took precedence over the King.[97] My sampling of the *Gazette d'Amsterdam* in early 1790 suggests it was anti-*aristocrat*, supportive of Lafayette and Necker, and alarmed by both the activities of royalist intriguers such as Favras and extreme press liberty. The *Gazette des Deux-Ponts* welcomed the Revolution wholeheartedly until the National Assembly abolished feudal dues in August 1789, thereby threatening the Duke's property rights and income, but did not totally abandon the Revolution until the rise of the Jacobins.[98] The *Gazette de Leyde*, despite huge misgivings about the revolutionaries, was optimistic the constitution would re-establish order and applauded the abolition of Church land and the Le Chapelier law, which severely curtailed workers' rights. However, like the *Gazette des Deux-Ponts*, it refused to collude in the National Assembly's official lie that Louis XVI had been kidnapped when he fled to Varennes and by late 1791 the paper was 'vehemently anti-revolutionary'.[99] Thus, by early 1792, the international francophone press was thoroughly politicised and ideologically committed to counter-revolution: the ancien regime international press system had come to an end.

The ancien regime system worked largely because of a balance of power preventing any state from being able to assert itself without provoking counter-measures. This guaranteed the survival of smaller states and allowed princelings of tiny enclaves like Bouillon to gamble on sheltering controversial publications in return for economic benefits. In effect, if international gazettes remained moderate in their comment, they would survive. But this impunity was precariously posited on the survival of the existing states' system and, with the coming of the French Revolution, proved unsustainable. International newspapers were banned from France under the Jacobin Republic and again in 1797. As the French Republic expanded, her government began a more systematic campaign against hostile newspapers across Europe, especially after Napoleon Bonaparte seized power in November 1799, until by 1803, the Whig lawyer Sir James Mackintosh could claim credibly that Britain had 'the only free press remaining in Europe'.[100]

The Napoleonic assault on the independence of the European public sphere began in January 1800 with a decree reducing the Parisian press from seventy-three to thirteen titles. By 1811, further decrees, forced mergers, bankruptcies and suppressions had reduced them to just four and the government controlled the appointment of editors. In 1807, the provincial political press was limited to one paper per *département*, to be edited by the prefect.[101] Foreign news was only permitted if it had already appeared in the official *Moniteur*. Hostile papers were forbidden from circulating in France, as were German-language papers save the pro-French *Minerva*. However, the European newspaper-reading public was too extensive to be served only by French subsidised newspapers, so similar measures were extended to conquered territories and satellite states. For example, a press censor was established in Amsterdam and after the

Act of Mediation in Switzerland (1802) the press there also came under French control.[102] The German press was finally subjugated after the campaign of 1806–7, when several international gazettes including the *Courier du Bas-Rhin*, the *Gazette de Frankfort*, the *Gazette de Bayreuth* and several Hamburg papers were suppressed.[103] The *Correspondenten* was reduced to abject servitude, forced to publish as a bilingual news-sheet and rapidly lost subscribers.[104] Indeed, the only significant German paper not to fall under direct government control in this period was the *Allgemeine Zeitung*, and even it was effectively bent to Napoleon's will and forced to depend on the *Moniteur* for material.[105] Besides, after 1804, when he had the Nuremburg publisher J. P. Palm seized and shot, few publishers dared to defy Bonaparte.

Napoleon also sought to silence or convert 'enemy writers' beyond his immediate sphere of influence, using a mixture of intimidation, payment, argument and diplomatic complaints. As a result, in July 1800, the Hamburg Senate suppressed the *Censeur* and arrested its authors, although Russian pressure prevented their extradition.[106] Likewise, by 1801, two leading émigré editors, Louis Baudus of the *Spectateur du nord* and Montlosier of the *Courier de Londres*, were won over to the new regime.[107] However, during the Peace of Amiens (1802–3), Bonaparte failed to silence criticism in the London press and above all Peltier's journals and the *Courier de Londres*, now edited by Jacques Regnier, a *pur* royalist. Although keen to placate Bonaparte, the British ministry insisted that they could not legally expel Peltier, agreeing instead to bring him to court, where he was found guilty on a charge of criminal libel. Nevertheless, the French were dissatisfied with the British government, feeling that their denial of legal authority to punish Peltier was provocative hypocrisy, especially as the Aliens Act was used to expel pro-French editors in both 1793 and 1803. The dispute rapidly soured relations between Britain and France, accentuating mutual perceptions that the other acted through malevolence and hastening the descent into war. Contemporary observers including the French Foreign Minister Talleyrand, the British Ambassador Whitworth and Napoleon's secretary Bourienne agreed that the press issue was a decisive factor in the outbreak of a war which, at that stage, both sides would have preferred to avoid.[108]

The objective of French press policy was to prevent certain types of news becoming known, especially those damaging to the army, France's allies, social harmony or popular sovereignty. Many subjects, including religious affairs, the Bourbons, military movements and Napoleon's actions or speeches, could only be discussed if reports had already appeared in the *Moniteur*. Other topics, including events in Spain and Rome in 1808, were placed under temporary interdict; the word 'Poland' was banned.[109]

These bans were not intended merely to portray Napoleon as the only public actor in Europe and to keep French citizens and subject peoples in ignorance. Their other purpose was to establish a French monopoly over the distribution of 'agenda-setting' information, keeping enemies and wavering allies alike in the dark as to French intentions, dispositions and weaknesses. Nor should it be forgotten that alternative sources of information for governments were breaking down in the Napoleonic period. Postal services between combatants were interrupted. Merchant activity and correspondence were inhibited, especially after the instigation of the British blockade and Napoleon's Continental system. Diplomatic reports, themselves often partly reliant on press sources, were constrained by censorship, blockade and war. Even foreign travellers, traditionally a useful information source, found their movements inhibited by the new 'rules' of revolutionary warfare, especially after Napoleon arrested all Britons unfortunate enough to be in Paris at the opening of hostilities in 1803.

In consequence, after 1803, Napoleon's enemies were forced to rely increasingly on self-serving reports from spy-masters like Fauche-Borel and the comte d'Antraigues for information and – as the British Foreign Minister Castlereagh explained – on French-language journals for 'Conveying instruction to the Continent when no other means could be found.'[110] Thus, the British government hired émigré newspapers to fight its propaganda war, including Peltier's *l'Ambigu*, the *Courier de Londres* and Regnier's *Courier d'Angleterre*, a succession of journals produced in Germany by Paoli de Chagny, the Altona-based *Abeille du Nord* and possibly Hyde Neuville's *Journal des dames* in New York. In response the French obtained the suppression of Paoli de Chagny's *Mercure universel* at Regensburg and bans on the *Courier de Londres* in the Batavian Republic, Hamburg and Saxony in 1804–5.[111] Moreover, in April 1805, Regnier was sacked from the editorship of the *Courier de Londres*, apparently at the instigation of the British government, possibly to remove an obstacle to peace negotiations.[112]

After the battle for Germany was lost, the British propaganda campaign switched to Russia and Sweden, where Regnier's new paper, the *Courier d'Angleterre*, as well as the *Courier de Londres* and *l'Ambigu* were distributed at British expense with the connivance of the local authorities. After the peace of Tilsit between France and Russia and the coup d'état of 13 March 1809 in Sweden, this connivance was withdrawn, but highly placed anti-French elements in both countries continued to distribute the papers by clandestine means until the Francophobes regained the ascendant in 1811.[113] From 1808, following Napoleon's invasion of the Iberian peninsula, émigré propaganda papers were also distributed there, and sometimes translated into Spanish and Portuguese.[114]

Despite the importance of their objectives, the British Foreign Office failed to exercise a close supervision over what its hirelings wrote, due to lack of resources and limited means of coercion, especially as government subscriptions to émigré journals were not necessarily essential to their financial survival. Although the *Courier d'Angleterre* folded rapidly following the peace, the *Courier de Londres* and *l'Ambigu* both published for several years after the remaining émigrés went home in 1814 and the government withdrew support in 1815. Thus, although funding to these three papers exceeded the entire sum the government expended 'corrupting' the British press in the 1780s and 1790s, the émigré journals' support for the British government was contingent rather than absolute. But the émigré press also enjoyed considerable freedom because the government wished its links with the papers to remain a secret. This allowed them sufficient latitude to expound disagreeable doctrines, including polemical articles that justified and incited Napoleon's assassination.[115]

Such murderous partisanship would have been unthinkable to the late eighteenth-century international gazettes and represented a considerable mutation. They had belonged to a world of controlled knowledge and aspired, at most, to freedom of information, not freedom of opinion. For the wider public they provided materials, rather than a forum, for policy discussion. Only the established political authorities who produced these materials and a handful of more outspoken newspaper editors actually participated in debate in their pages. Nevertheless, by exposing political actors to scrutiny, by forcing them to justify their positions in public documents, in freeing information flows and in cautiously supporting political reforms, the international gazettes were agents for the diffusion of Enlightenment, cosmopolitanism and confident reformism among Europe's francophone elites. But after the Revolution polarised Europe, the international gazettes and émigré organs that survived beyond French reach became organs of party and committed advocates of counter-revolution, shedding their characteristic detachment in the process. After 1802, when most émigrés returned to France and the pan-European public sphere was systematically transformed into a French-controlled space, exile journals were reduced to serving the interests of allied propaganda and forlorn, outspoken vitriolic attacks on Bonaparte. Finally, in the era of romanticism, nationalism and the steam press after 1815, the cosmopolitan press had outlived its purposes and rapidly disappeared. The old Europe of francophone elites bound together by common language, culture, values and media had gone forever, the emigration was over and, as one journalist remarked, with the coming of peace 'a French newspaper printed in London is the most useless thing in the world for the [British] government'.[116] In the revolutionary struggles, the pan-European public had disintegrated.

NOTES

1 Jerzy Lojek, 'Gazettes internationales de la langue française dans la seconde moitié du XVIIIème siècle', in P. Deyon (ed.), *Modèles et moyens de la réflexion politique au XVIIIe siècle*, 3 vols. (Lille, 1977), vol. 1, 369–82.
2 Laus de Boissy to Société Typographique de Neuchâtel, 9 March 1780, Ms. STN 1173, fos. 320–1, Bibliothèque publique de la ville de Neuchâtel, cited in Michel Schlup, 'Diffusion et lecture du *Journal helvétique*, au temps de la Société Typographique de Neuchâtel, 1769–1782', in Hans Bots (ed.), *La Diffusion et lecture des journaux de langue française sous l'ancien régime* (Amsterdam, 1988), 59–71, p. 69.
3 The standard bibliographical work is Jean Sgard (ed.), *Dictionnaire de journaux*, 2 vols. (Paris, 1991); Henri Duranton, Claude Labrosse and Pierre Rétat (eds.), *Les Gazettes européennes de langue française (XVIIe–XVIIIe siècles)* (Saint-Etienne, 1992) is devoted to the topic.
4 While researching this chapter I discovered a uniquely rich collection of international gazettes for the years c. 1774–90 in the Bibliothèque municipale de Versailles, most of which went unreported in the survey of holdings in Duranton *et al.* (eds.), *Gazettes européennes*, pp. 331–46. It comprises the *Courrier d'Avignon* (1775–89); *Courier du Bas-Rhin* (1774–90); *Courier de l'Europe* (1776–91); *Gazette d'Altona* (1774–5); *Gazette d'Amsterdam* (1748–91); *Gazette de Cologne* (1774–85); *Gazette de La Haye* (1752–87); *Gazette de Leyde* (1774–91); *Gazette d'Utrecht* (1750–84); and *Gazette des Deux-Ponts* (1774–84; 1789–91).
5 On the émigré press see Simon Burrows, *French Exile Journalism and European Politics, 1792–1814* (London, 2000); Hélène Maspero-Clerc, *Un Journaliste contre-révolutionnaire: Jean-Gabriel Peltier, 1760–1825* (Paris, 1973) and her articles 'Journaux d'émigrés à Londres', *Bulletin d'histoire économique et sociale de la révolution française* (hereinafter *BHESRF*) années 1972–3 (1974), 67–79; 'Montlosier, journaliste de l'émigration', *BHESRF* année 1975 (1977), 81–103; Samuel J. Marino, 'The French refugee newspapers in the United States, 1789–1825', Ph.D. thesis, University of Michigan (1962); Paul Hazard, 'Le *Spectateur du Nord*', *Revue d'histoire littéraire de France* (1906), 26–50.
6 Sgard (ed.), *Dictionnaire de journaux*. Title counts are my own and necessarily approximate. 601 French language serials appeared between 1760 and 1789; 37 per cent of French serials published before 1789 appeared outside France.
7 The first ranking figures follow the three tentative groupings given by Lojek, 'Gazettes internationales', pp. 376–80. 1 = systematically penetrated countries across Europe; 2 = widely read in France, Germany and Austria and often other countries; 3 = less widespread but widely read in more than one country. The second ranking corresponds to Lojek's rankings of individual papers,

in descending order of importance. Asterisks for the second ranking indicate that Lojek did not mention the paper, and I have tentatively assigned its first ranking.
8 Pierre Rétat's article on the *Gazette d'Altona* in Sgard (ed.), *Dictionnaire de journaux*, vol. I, pp. 493–4, says it was produced from at least 1758 to 1765. However, there are volumes for 1774–5 in the Bibliothèque municipale at Versailles and in 1795–6, Louis Baudus is known to have edited a paper with the same title.
9 Claude Labrosse and Pierre Rétat, 'Le Texte de la gazette', in Duranton et al. (eds.), *Gazette européennes*, 135–44, pp. 135–7.
10 On divergences in reporting a single story see Robert Favre and Chantal Thomas, 'Le Mariage du Dauphin et de Marie-Antoinette d'Autriche: estampe et feu d'artifice', in Duranton et al. (eds.), *Gazettes européennes*, 213–27, pp. 223–4.
11 Jeremy D. Popkin, 'The elite press in the Revolution: the *Gazette de Leyde* and the *Gazette universelle*', in Harvey Chisick (ed.), *The Press in the French Revolution: Studies on Voltaire and the Eighteenth Century*, vol. 287 (Oxford, 1991), 85–98.
12 Burrows, *French Exile Journalism*, p. 95.
13 Although Burrows, *French Exile Journalism*, lists thirteen émigré 'journals', two (Jean-Gabriel Peltier's *Dernier Tableau de Paris*, F.-D. Kirwan's *Antidote*) do not fit the definition of 'newspapers' used here. Peltier's *Tableau de l'Europe* (1794–5) and *Histoire de la restauration de la monarchie française* (1793) are marginal for inclusion.
14 Simon Burrows, 'The emigré press and the emigré community', unpublished paper delivered to '*Emigrés*-2' conference (London, July 1999). My list, drawn from secondary sources and titles encountered during research, does not pretend to be comprehensive.
15 Only papers known to have survived over six months are included, plus Paoli de Chagny's journals, which attracted French police attention but whose duration is uncertain.
16 Jack Censer, *The French Press in the Age of Enlightenment* (London and New York, 1994), p. 9.
17 Gilles Feyel, 'La Diffusion des gazettes étrangères en France et la révolution postale des années 1750', in Duranton et al. (eds.), *Gazettes européennes*, 81–99; Censer, *French Press*, pp. 10–11. These figures only apply to foreign gazettes.
18 For circulation figures see Censer, *French Press*, appendix 1, pp. 215–16, and supplementary information in Sgard (ed.), *Dictionnaire de journaux*, vol. I, pp. 272–4; Jeremy D. Popkin, *News and Politics in the Age of Revolution: Jean Luzac's Gazette de Leyde* (Ithaca, NY, and London, 1989), pp. 120–22 and Gunnar and Mavis von Proschwitz, *Beaumarchais et le Courier de l'Europe: documents inédits ou peus connus*, 2 vols.: *Studies on Voltaire and the Eighteenth Century*, vols. 273–4 (Oxford, 1990), vol. II, p. 1,004. Gazettes in terminal decline, such as the *Gazette d'Utrecht*, are rare exceptions to the pattern.
19 Hélène Maspero-Clerc, 'Une *Gazette anglo-française* pendant la guerre d'Amérique: Le *Courier de l'Europe* (1776–1788)', *Annales historiques de la révolution française* (hereinafter *AHRF*), 226 (1976), 572–94, p. 590.

20 See Burrows, *French Exile Journalism*, pp. 80–82.
21 Popkin, *News and Politics*, pp. 121–2.
22 Sgard (ed.), *Dictionnaire de journaux*, vol. I, p. 301.
23 Burrows, *French Exile Journalism*, pp. 77–84.
24 Ibid., and Popkin, *News and Politics*, p. 177. Note, however, that my survey of pre-revolutionary gazettes found that the *Gazette de Leyde*'s advertising volume was comparatively low despite its high circulation.
25 Bianchi to the Prince de Beaumont-Vintimille (no place or date or repository given), cited in Hatin, *Les Gazettes de Hollande et la presse clandestine aux XVIIe et XVIIIe Siècles* (Paris, 1865), p. 50 after *Novelle literarie* (no precise reference given).
26 Jacques Godechot, 'L'Expansion de la Déclaration des Droits de l'Homme de 1789 dans le monde', *AHRF*, 231 (1978), 201–12, p. 206; François Moureau, 'Lumières et libertés vues de Cleves par le *Courier du Bas-Rhin* de 1768', in Raymond Oberlé (ed.), *Le Concept de liberté dans l'espace rhénan supérieur* (Gap, 1976), 77–88, p. 78.
27 Popkin, *News and Politics*, pp. 128–9.
28 Paul Benhamou, 'Essai d'inventaire des instruments de lecture publique des gazettes', in Duranton et al. (eds.), *Gazettes européennes*, pp. 121–9.
29 Lojek, 'Gazettes internationales', p. 375; Jeanne de Saint-Rémy, *Memoirs of the Countess de Valois de la Motte* (Dublin, 1790), p. 167.
30 J. M. Thompson, *Napoleon* (Oxford, 1958), p. 132.
31 Nicole Gotteri (ed.), *La Police secrète du Premier Empire: bulletins quotidiens adressés par Savary à l'Empereur*, 4 vols. (Paris, 1997–2000), vol. III, p. 108.
32 John Lewis Mallet, *An Autobiographical Retrospective of the First Twenty-Five Years of his Life* (Windsor, 1890), p. 210.
33 Burrows, *French Exile Journalism*, pp. 134–9.
34 Mallet Du Pan to abbé de Pradt, undated, cited in A. Sayous, *Mémoires et correspondance de Mallet du Pan pour servir à l'histoire de la révolution française*, 2 vols. (Paris, 1851), vol. II, p. 358.
35 William Murray, 'Journalism as a Career Choice in 1789', in Chisick (ed.), *The Press in the French Revolution*, 161–88, p. 163.
36 'Mémoire pour J.-P. Brissot', 446 AP/3 (Brissot papers), fo. 28, Archives nationales, Paris.
37 Jeremy Popkin, remark made in 'Discussion', in Duranton et al. (eds.), *Gazettes européennes*, p. 77.
38 Popkin, 'News and politics'; J. J. V. M. de Vet, 'Le *Courier du Bas-Rhin* de Jean Manzon et les Provinces-Unies (1787–1795): un traitement idéologique de l'information', in Duranton et al. (eds.), *Gazettes européennes*, 107–20; Moureau, 'Lumières et libertés'.
39 Myriam Yardeni, 'Paradoxes politiques et persuasion dans les *Annales* de Linguet', in Chisick (ed.), *The Press in the French Revolution*, 211–19, p. 211.
40 On Morande's journalism and political engagement see von Proschwitz and von Proschwitz, *Beaumarchais et le Courier de l'Europe*; Simon Burrows, 'A literary low-life reassessed: Charles Théveneau de Morande in London, 1769–91', *Eighteenth-Century Life*, 22 (1998), 76–94.
41 Elizabeth Eisenstein, 'The Tribune of the People: a new species of demagogue', in Chisick (ed.), *The Press in the French Revolution*, 145–59.

42 *British Mercury*, 24 (English edition, 15 August 1799), p. 463.
43 Louis Trénard, 'La Presse d'origine étrangère', in Claude Bellanger, Jacques Godechot, Pierre Guiral and Fernand Terrou (eds.), *Histoire générale de la presse française*, 4 vols. (Paris, 1969), vol. I, 285–97, p. 288.
44 Françoise Weil, 'Un épisode de la guerre entre la *Gazette de France* et des gazettes hollandaises: l'échec du projet de transformation de la *Gazette de France* en 1762', in Duranton *et al.* (eds.), *Gazettes européennes*, 99–105; Feyel, 'Diffusion des gazettes', p. 91.
45 Moureau, 'Lumières et libertés', p. 78; Jack Censer, 'Maupeou et la presse politique', in Duranton *et al.* (eds.), *Gazettes européennes*, 290–8, p. 294; von Proschwitz and von Proschwitz, *Beaumarchais et le Courier de l'Europe*, vol. I, pp. 16–17.
46 On the problematic nature of these attempts see Pierre Rétat, 'Les Gazetiers de Hollande et les puissances politiques: une difficile collaboration', *Dix-huitième siècle*, 25 (1993), 319–35.
47 See Hatin, *Gazettes de Hollande*, pp. 90–101.
48 Otto Lankhorst, 'La *Gazette de La Haye* (1744–1790), cadette des premières gazettes néerlandaises', in Duranton *et al.* (eds.), *Gazettes européennes*, 51–64, p. 58.
49 Jean Vercruysse, 'La Reception politique des gazettes de Hollande, une lecture diplomatique', in Bots (ed.), *Diffusion et lecture*, 39–47.
50 *Gazette de Berne*, 10, 20 and 23 February 1768.
51 Hatin, *Les Gazettes de Hollande*, p. 100.
52 Louis Trénard, 'Les Gazettes étrangères', in Bellanger *et al.* (eds.), *Histoire générale*, vol. I, 143–57, p. 150.
53 J. Lenardon, 'The paradox of revolution within an étatiste mentalité', in Chisick (ed.), *The Press in the French Revolution*, 99–117, pp. 99–100.
54 Eisenstein, *Grub Street Abroad: Aspects of the French Cosmopolitan Press from the Age of Louis XIV to the Enlightenment* (Oxford, 1992), p. 19; Louis Petit de Bachaumont (attrib.), *Mémoires secrets pour servir à l'histoire de la république des lettres en France, depuis 1762 jusqu'à nos jours, ou journal d'un observateur*, 36 vols. (London, 1777–89), entry dated 24 September 1776.
55 Trénard, 'La Presse d'origine étrangère', p. 289; Jeremy D. Popkin, 'The *Gazette de Leyde* and French Politics under Louis XVI', in Jack Censer and Jeremy D. Popkin (eds.), *Press and Politics in Pre-Revolutionary France* (Berkeley, CA, 1987), 75–132, p. 85.
56 Popkin, *News and Politics*, p. 140.
57 Censer, 'Maupeou et la presse'.
58 These arguments draw on Popkin, *News and Politics*.
59 François Moureau, 'La Presse allemande de langue française (1686–1790): Etude statistique et thématique', *Aufklärungen: Frankreich und Deutschland im 18. Jahrhundert*, 1 (1985), 243–50, p. 248; Moureau, 'Lumières et libertés', p. 87; Lojek, 'Gazettes internationales', p. 376.
60 Robert Darnton, 'An Early Information Society: News and the Media in Eighteenth-Century Paris', *American Historical Review*, 105 (2000), 1–35, p. 6.
61 'Mémoire pour Louis Claude Cesar de Launay' (October 1780), MS. 6798 (Bastille papers), fos. 17–19, Bibliothèque de l'Arsenal, Paris.

62 Hatin, *Les Gazettes de Hollande*, p. 42 citing the *Correspondance secrète*; Popkin, *News and Politics*, p. 54, citing another letter, asserts 4,800. However, extensive research in French archives and memoir sources by Maspero-Clerc, Gunnar von Proschwitz and myself has produced no evidence to support this claim.
63 Swinton to Beaumarchais, 10 April 1778, published in Brian N. Morton (ed.), *Correspondance de Beaumarchais* (Paris, 1969–1978), vol. IV, pp. 102–3, and von Proschwitz and von Proschwitz, *Beaumarchais et le Courier de l'Europe*, vol. I, pp. 473–4.
64 Moureau, 'Presse allemande', p. 247.
65 Jochen Schlobach, 'Conditions politiques et matérielles de l'imprimerie et des gazettes à Deux-Ponts', in Duranton et al. (eds.), *Gazettes européennes*, 269–80.
66 Moureau, 'Presse allemande', p. 78.
67 For example, my sampling of the content of the *Gazette de Berne* for 1768 uncovered no reports of the civil strife in Geneva.
68 Moureau, 'Lumières et libertés', pp. 78–80.
69 Jack Censer, 'English politics in the *Courrier d'Avignon*', in Censer and Popkin (eds.), *Press and Politics*, 170–203, p. 173.
70 See Censer, 'Maupeou et la presse', and Censer's chapter in this book.
71 Peter Ascoli, 'American propaganda in the French language press during the American Revolution', in *La Révolution Américaine et l'Europe* (Paris, 1979), 291–305, p. 302.
72 Moreau, 'Presse allemande', p. 248; Lojek, 'Gazettes internationales', pp. 371–2.
73 Popkin, *News and Politics*, pp. 72–3; Popkin, 'The *Gazette de Leyde*', pp. 82–3.
74 Samuel Swinton to Louis Claude Cesar de Launay, Londres, 10 mars 1780, MS. 12451 (Bastille papers), fos. 212–13, Bibliothèque de l'Arsenal.
75 See *Courier du Bas-Rhin*, 25 July 1789; *Gazette de Berne*, 22 July 1789; *Gazette de Leyde*, 24 July 1789.
76 See Labrosse and Rétat 'Le Texte de la gazette'.
77 See especially Popkin, *News and Politics*, chs. 7–8 and passim.
78 De Vet, 'Le *Courier du Bas-Rhin*', p. 110; for a typical tirade see the Cleves column in *Courier du Bas-Rhin*, 20 December 1787.
79 See for example Ascoli, 'American propaganda', p. 295.
80 Indeed, Gonthier-Louis Fink, 'La Révolution américaine et la revolution française: analogies et différences selon la presse allemande 1789–98', in *Littérature et révolution française* (Paris, 1987), 88–117, shows how the German press reinterpreted the American Revolution after 1789; Fink found little discussion of issues arising from the Declaration of Independence and State Constitutions before 1789.
81 Hans Jürgen Lusebrink and Rolf Reichardt, 'Médiation culturelle et perception de l'événement. Le cas de la *Gazette des Deux-Ponts*', in Duranton et al. (eds.), *Gazettes européennes*, 229–49.
82 Popkin, *News and Politics*, p. 144.
83 Censer, 'English politics', p. 200.
84 *Correspondance politique*, 2 November 1793.
85 Von Proschwitz and von Proschwitz, *Beaumarchais et le Courier de l'Europe*, vol. I, pp. 5, 22.

86 Moureau, 'Lumières et libertés', p. 82.
87 *Courier de l'Europe*, 24 July 1789.
88 *Courier du Bas-Rhin*, 17 and 27 January 1787.
89 *Gazette d'Amsterdam*, 5 January 1787.
90 *Courier du Bas-Rhin*, 30 December 1786.
91 See for example *Courier de Londres*, 3 February, 18 April and 7 May 1790; Popkin, *News and Politics*, p. 192.
92 *Gazette d'Amsterdam*, 24 July 1789.
93 *Gazette des Deux-Ponts*, 17 and 20 July 1789.
94 Lusebrink and Reichardt, 'Médiation culturelle'.
95 *Courier de Londres*, 22 July 1789.
96 *Courrier d'Avignon*, 22 July 1789.
97 Burrows, 'Literary low-life', p. 86.
98 See 'Observations très importantes pour la maison palatine de Deux-Ponts', *Gazette des Deux-Ponts*, 28 and 30 September and 2 October 1789; Lusebrink and Reichardt, 'Médiation culturelle', p. 240.
99 *Gazette des Deux-Ponts*, 27 June 1791; Popkin, *News and politics*, pp. 211–14.
100 Jean-Gabriel Peltier, *The Trial of John Peltier* (London, 1803), p. 83.
101 Robert B. Holtman, *Napoleonic Propaganda* (Baton Rouge, LA, 1950), pp. 44–5, 54–5.
102 Ibid., pp. 50–52.
103 Ibid., pp. 46–7, 57.
104 F^{18} 12 no. 43 and 'minute of police bulletin, 8 April 1812', AF^{IV} 1521, Archives nationales, Paris.
105 Daniel Moran, 'Cotta and Napoleon: the French pursuit of the *Allgemeine Zeitung*', *Central European History*, 14 (1981), 91–109.
106 Comtesse de la Chapelle to Grenville, 9 August 1800, FO27/56, Public Record Office; MS 723 fo. 61(1), Bibliothèque historique de la ville de Paris.
107 Hazard, 'Le *Spectateur du nord*', pp. 45–50; Maspero-Clerc, 'Montlosier', pp. 95–7; Burrows, *French Exile Journalism*, pp. 50, 106.
108 See Simon Burrows, 'Culture and misperception: the outbreak of war in 1803', *International History Review*, 18 (1996), 793–818.
109 Holtman, *Napoleonic Propaganda*, pp. 52–3.
110 Hansard, *Journals of the House of Commons*, vol. 34, p. 101 (debate of 30 April 1816).
111 Simon Burrows, 'The struggle for European opinion in the Napoleonic Wars: British Francophone propaganda, 1803–14', *French History*, 11 (1997), 29–53.
112 Ibid., 41.
113 Simon Burrows, 'British Propaganda for Russia in the Napoleonic Wars: the *Courier d'Angleterre*', *New Zealand Slavonic Journal* (1993), 85–100.
114 Burrows, 'Struggle for opinion', pp. 48–9.
115 Burrows, *French Exile Journalism*, pp. 90–94.
116 Jacques Regnier to Foreign Office, 24 December 1814, FO27/109, Public Record Office.

2 The Netherlands, 1750–1813

Nicolaas van Sas

On 8 October 1804 Willem Anthonie Ockerse opened the winter series of lectures in the Amsterdam society *Doctrina et Amicitia* with a talk entitled 'What's the news?' in which he offered a light-hearted theory of human curiosity. According to Ockerse, curiosity and above all the asking of the question 'What's the news?' was a prime characteristic of the *condition humaine*. Man – and certainly also woman – could only be fulfilled in contact with other human beings. Sociability and the continuous exchange of views were part of human nature, and naturally gave rise to the urge to hear and impart news. Self-interest was obviously an important and daily inspiration for human curiosity. One person might have an interest in inheritances, another in lotteries, a third in stocks, a fourth in shipping news, a fifth in peace or war, a sixth in political events. 'What's the news?' was the first question one asked on entering polite society or coffee house, towing-barge or coach, council chamber or theatre, even – Ockerse added mischievously – sometimes church. In an ever-changing world there was always a great appetite for news. But certainly the sad and terrible events of recent years had added greatly to the demand for news. 'Good heavens! How many things formerly unthought-of have happened in the past years with an ever quickening sequence, the story of which has made humankind cry, sigh and shiver!' Ockerse profoundly hoped that one day the reply to that perennial question 'What's the news?' would be: 'Good news! – order, quiet, peace, freedom, prosperity will return to the peoples of the world, and to the Netherlands.'[1]

Ockerse was not some obscure speaker. He was a well-known figure in contemporary Dutch society, a theologian by training and long-time practising minister, but first and foremost he was an intellectual, a typical product of Dutch enlightened sociability. As such he was also a journalist – co-editor of *De Democraten*, the best political journal of the Batavian Revolution – a member of parliament in 1797 and 1798 and one of the framers of the first Dutch constitution.[2] But perhaps his most enduring claim to fame is his important study of Dutch national character, published in 1797, which propounds a theory of Dutch society and national identity, aimed at furthering the cause of a Dutch state that would be – like its French sister republic – *'une et indivisible'*.[3] In this study, Ockerse stated that the Dutch people were traditionally very interested in politics and possessed what he called 'a general and popular knowledge of political affairs and interests'. Their curiosity was continuously kept alive by news from coffee houses, newspapers and the stock exchange.[4] In this sense politics in the Dutch Republic was – as in England – 'a rather common and favourite pastime'. Indeed, in his view everybody from the loftiest regent to the lowest porter used to 'politicise' in the Dutch Republic.[5] This was certainly true for his own time – the years immediately following the Batavian Revolution of 1795 – but it was not a new phenomenon. Traditionally, according to Ockerse, there had been an extensive supply of news in the Dutch Republic. However, since the beginning of the American Revolutionary War this had expanded rapidly, reaching a new high-point during the so-called Patriot Period of 1780–87, when sales of political weeklies like *De Post van den Neder-Rhijn* and *De Politieke Kruyer* (*The Political Barrow-man*) had reached unprecedented levels.[6]

Ockerse was certainly right to stress the ready availability of news in the Netherlands. From the early seventeenth century onwards, the young Dutch Republic had established itself as the most important clearinghouse of international news. In the late sixteenth century, while still fighting off their Spanish sovereign, the Dutch rapidly developed into the foremost trading nation in the world. In the wake of this they also became a great power politically. Interests of war and trade and its central position in seventeenth-century geopolitics worked together to make the Dutch Republic, and particularly the city of Amsterdam, the global nerve-centre for the gathering and dissemination of news.[7] From 1618 onwards, we know of the existence of 'coranto': printed news-sheets which mainly provided factual information from abroad, obtained from a network of foreign correspondents. From about mid-century, in a process of piecemeal innovation, these developed into regular newspapers, first of all in Amsterdam, later also in several other towns in the core province of Holland like Haarlem (1656), The Hague (1656) and Leyden (1686). All of these were commercial enterprises initiated by local printers. Amsterdam had four officially recognised newspapers, appearing on different days of the week. However, by the end of the seventeenth century, they had merged into one, which in the eighteenth century was acquired by the city government.[8] Very gradually during the eighteenth century, other towns, at first mainly in the province of Holland, established their own newspapers, normally by granting an exclusive privilege to a local printer. By the middle of the eighteenth century, papers were being established in the capitals of the outlying provinces, including Groningen

(1742), Leeuwarden (1752) and Middelburg (1758). The most important of these news-sheets would appear three times a week, the smaller ones once or twice. Whereas in the seventeenth century no more than 600 copies would have been printed, by the 1750s this number had risen to between 4,000 and 6,000 for the four largest papers, the *Oprechte Haerlemse Courant*, the *Amsterdamsche Courant*, the *Leydse Courant* and the *'s Gravenhaegse Courant*. In 1778 the *Amsterdamsche Courant* reputedly sold 6,500 copies within the city and another 1,000 outside.[9]

Though exact information is lacking, the readership was not evenly distributed over the Republic. A rule of thumb may be that reading newspapers was mainly an urban phenomenon and that the more densely populated areas – above all the Holland heartland – would be overrepresented. The four 'national' newspapers mentioned above in the mid-eighteenth century had a combined circulation of about 20,000. If the common estimate that each issue was read by some ten people is correct, their total readership must have been about 200,000, that is 10 per cent of the overall population of the country.[10] But looking at the towns of the province of Holland in particular, it has been calculated that in this period up to a third of their adult population – male and female – must have been regular newspaper readers.[11] Indeed, when Ockerse said that in the Dutch Republic everybody was interested in the news, he was merely echoing a well-worn cliché. Already in the 1680s, the French ambassador d'Avaux said of the Dutch newspapers: *'tout le peuple les lit'*.[12] In Amsterdam, the delivery people of the *Amsterdamsche Courant* were expected to collect the papers very early in the morning, in summer at 3.30 a.m., because the workmen used to read them in the tavern before going to work.[13] Newspapers could not only be bought, they were also rented out and they could be read in taverns and coffee houses, in the stage-coach and, more comfortably, in the towing-barge.

The main newspapers were distributed nationwide and, judging from the scant evidence available, apparently also abroad, in the southern Netherlands, in Germany and in London.[14] Nonetheless, their geographical distribution patterns varied considerably. Whereas less than 15 per cent of the *Amsterdamsche Courant* was exported outside the city – which, admittedly, housed 10 per cent of the population of the Republic – a majority of subscribers to the *Oprechte Haerlemse Courant* dwelt *extra muros*.[15] The city of Amsterdam would expect to make between 20,000 and 30,000 guilders profit a year from its ownership of the *Amsterdamsche Courant*,[16] but other towns charged a so-called 'recognition fee' for the exclusive privilege to publish an urban newspaper. These papers would also be expected to print official publications free of charge. Even when exact figures are lacking, increases in the recognition-fees – especially in the 1770s – are a clear indication of the growing circulation of the urban newspapers.[17] These stiff costs would be partly met from the income of advertisements, typically placed crossways in the margins of the paper. Advertisements could contain anything from inquiries about missing persons or pets, medicine, lotteries, trees and shrubs, the sale of houses and – last but not least – new books.

Though these newspapers were local ventures, local news was not their mainstay. Rather, the editors had to be careful not to overstep the boundaries set by city regents, who were not at all willing to have their local *arcana* out on the streets. The news – including commercial and shipping information – was presented in an objective, concise manner, painstakingly avoiding any colouring or editorial comment. The writers of the *Amsterdamsche Courant* in 1767 were given very explicit instructions on what *not* to publish. They were not supposed to print anything concerning the military power of the Republic and were only allowed to publish information on domestic political affairs after having obtained permission beforehand. The style of the paper had to be simple, unostentatious, unambiguous and impartial. It should avoid offending any person, either high or low, political, military or religious, friend or enemy.[18] Despite these limitations set by local authorities, the particularist political structure of the Dutch Republic ensured a considerable freedom of the press, precisely because there was no central authority to enforce effective constraints. This was not so much freedom in principle as a practice of freedom, which in hindsight, however – like the similar matter of religious and political tolerance – came to be regarded as a matter of principle in which the Dutch Republic had stood out in contemporary Europe.

News-sheets were important because they made the Dutch Republic a very news-oriented society, but judging from their contents they were relatively unspectacular. Apart from them, the Dutch press scene of the ancien regime had two prime characteristics. One was a blossoming pamphlet culture which made up in newsworthiness, juiciness and political outspokenness (though not in objectivity and reliability) for what the rather staid newspapers lacked. All political crises in the Dutch Republic, but also all sorts of local conflicts, scandals and religious disputes, were accompanied and fuelled by a surge of pamphlets. Far more than the regular newspaper press these 'flying leaflets' profited from the so-called 'tempered freedom' of the press[19] and the fragmentation of jurisdiction which lasted till the Batavian Revolution of 1795–8. The other feature of the Dutch journalistic scene was the existence of an important French-language press, especially since the Dutch Republic had become a refuge for French Huguenot exiles. This French-language press – of which the *Gazette d'Amsterdam* was an early example, and the *Gazette de Leyde* eventually the most celebrated[20] – contributed far more than the indigenous Dutch journals to the fame of the Dutch Republic, making it a byword for freedom and tolerance in the international Republic of Letters.

Around 1750, some important changes took place in Dutch society, as historical research of the past twenty years has demonstrated time and again.[21] Outside the recognised sphere of politics and the political structure, which was still that fossilised medieval jumble fought over by the Dutch Revolt, a new civil society emerged, bringing with it a reorganisation and redefinition of the public sphere. This rearrangement of public space made full use of the existing flexibility of Dutch society, through the practical freedom already mentioned and the absence of a central authority in internal affairs, which were organised on a local or, at most, provincial basis. This cultural shift marked the breakthrough of a distinctly Dutch Enlightenment. This 'Dutchification' of the Enlightenment had far-reaching consequences for Dutch culture, society and also politics. Establishing what was national, especially in terms of culture, language and literature, came to be one of its defining characteristics.[22] The rearrangement of public space in the Dutch Enlightenment created an 'imagined community' in the sense of Benedict Anderson:[23] a community of people who did not – and indeed could not – know one another but who at the same time felt a clear sense of belonging together. Particularly in the 1760s and 1770s, Dutch society was newly defined in cultural and moral terms, as a society of patriots, trying to use the forces of Enlightenment to stem the decline of the Dutch Republic and to restore it to its former glory.

The civil society of the Dutch Enlightenment was a conglomerate of societies and associations of all sorts and shapes, stretching from the smallest poetical societies and reading clubs on a scale hardly overstepping the format of a living room, to impressive learned societies and reformist associations with a nationwide appeal.[24] But the other pillar of the Dutch Enlightenment was a plethora of new periodical publications – quite different from the newspapers mentioned above – which grew steadily in number between 1750 and 1800. A new 'communication society' was formed, transcending – indeed ignoring – the formal political boundaries of the seven sovereign provinces.

Overstepping these boundaries and rearranging the public sphere was an important phase in the cultural process of nation-building. Thus nation-building in an all-Dutch sense preceded by several decades the construction of the unitary Dutch state in 1798. Unlike the formative years of the Dutch Republic, when war and politics took pride of place, it was now cultural developments which were taking the lead. To turn the well-known concept of Ernest Gellner on its head: it was not a matter of the state producing a nation, but the other way around.[25] In this process the periodical press played a crucial role. Almost imperceptibly, a rift opened up between an increasingly fossilised state not able to meet the challenges of the times and a civil society which appeared novel and exciting and developed a dynamic of its own, in a context of universal enlightened thinking and enlightened practices. Paradoxically, these dynamics were strongly motivated by the 'decline' (or at least the perception of decline) of the Dutch Republic which was seemingly in a free fall in terms of international power and economic strength since the days of its 'Golden' seventeenth century. The causes for this decline were ultimately sought in the sphere of morals and manners. The Dutch people had supposedly lost their pristine burgher virtues and the regent class in particular was accused of disavowing its burgher origins through an increasingly luxurious lifestyle and an abdication of public responsibility.

This debate on the fundamentals of Dutch society and its pressing problems of decline and fall was inextricably bound up with new developments in Dutch press culture. It was conducted in a series of new periodical publications, mainly along the lines of Addison and Steele's *Spectator*. Already in the 1730s Justus van Effen had published his famous *Hollandsche Spectator*, in which the ills of Dutch culture and society were analysed in plain Dutch by an author who until then had always written in French. Especially in the second half of the century his example had numerous followers. These moral weeklies were organised according to a well-rehearsed formula, in which a wise and benevolent Spectator-figure gave judgment on all sorts of questions and problems. The manners and morals of polite society, matters of religion, education or the relations between the sexes were subtly connected to the problems that beset Dutch society at large. In the end the decline of the Dutch Republic was almost routinely explained in terms of the declining morals of Dutch society.

These Spectator-like publications really took off from mid-century onwards. Some lasted only a few issues; others, however, continued publication on a periodical basis for many years. According to the inventory made by P. J. Buijnsters, twelve Spectators appeared between 1718 and 1747, whereas fifty-eight new ones were published between 1747 and 1800.[26] The trend-setting *Hollandsche Spectator* itself appeared from 1731 to 1735, to be collected in twelve volumes. *De Nederlandsche Spectator*, author or authors unknown, appeared in Leyden between 1749 and 1760. *De Philantrope* was published in Amsterdam from 1756 to 1762 and some of its authors continued with *De Denker (The Thinker)* until 1774. A short-lived *Vrouwelyke Spectator (Female Spectator)* was published in 1760–61 in twenty-four issues. *De Philosooph*, written by Cornelis van Engelen, appeared between 1766 and 1769. *De Koopman (The Merchant)* – an acknowledged mine of economic information – was published in Amsterdam between 1766 and 1776, whilst *De Borger* was produced in Utrecht between 1778 and 1780. And these are only some of the best-known and long-lived Spectators in the decades before the political upheaval of the Patriot Period, which changed the political landscape and the practices of periodical publication with it.

To take just one example, between 1749 and 1751 *De Nederlandsche Criticus (The Dutch Critic)* appeared in eighty-six weekly issues. It was published in Leeuwarden, the capital of Friesland, and it was distributed widely in the rest of the country. Its editor was the Lutheran minister Statius Muller, whose name has also been connected with four other Spectators. Dissenting theologians generally played a prominent role in the dissemination of the Dutch Enlightenment and in its press culture. Introducing itself, *De Nederlandsche Criticus* described the publication of Spectators as a craze in which everyone wanted to take part: 'the Republic of Letters is in uproar and its citizens are up in arms, the printing presses are occupied and the Spectators are coming to and fro'. This particular Spectator was advertised as a collective enterprise taking the pulse of contemporary society by frequenting all social layers:

> We mean to enter all public societies of gentlemen and ladies, at court and in the coffee house, and to avoid becoming hypochondriacs we will also walk often in the market-place. We see, we hear, we speak and we keep silent as it seems fit. Everything is to our liking, we read everything as much as possible ... and subsequently we will give a free and uninhibited judgement upon it.

The explicit reason given to undertake this enterprise was 'affection ... for our dear Fatherland' because present-day society was possessed by all sorts of follies. Everyone was liable to be taken to task by *De Nederlandsche Criticus*, which hoped to reach an audience of 'learned and unlearned people, of people of high standing in society and common burghers, of the male and female sex'.[27] In its eighty-six issues all sorts of topics were tackled, with a strong bias towards religious themes. It was concerned with general morality, with matters of taste and public behaviour, with education, arts and sciences. Typical problems of the times were commented on in an authoritative manner. Though politics in a narrow sense were avoided, *De Nederlandsche Criticus* would speak out on the qualities to be expected from regents and holders of public offices.[28] Topicality and enlightened judgement were cleverly mixed to make this Spectator, like others, relevant to contemporary issues, while at the same time appearing to rise above them.

Taken together, the whole corpus of these Spectators may be regarded as the transactions of the Dutch Enlightenment (of which they were both the mouthpiece and the carrier), which is still to be explored from a wide range of possible angles and perspectives. In a recent study Dorothée Sturkenboom has imaginatively analysed, not to say reconstructed, the 'emotional culture' of the Dutch Enlightenment from the formal basis of the assembled Spectators.[29] This research could, in principle, be replicated from a whole range of viewpoints: morals and manners, religion, education, social and economic questions, and – last but not least – the crypto-political nature of much of its social comment and criticism.

The continuous discussion in weekly instalments of the morals of Dutch society played a major part in creating a new moral community of burghers.[30] Traditionally, 'burgher' was a legal category denoting the first-class citizens of the many towns which constituted the Dutch Republic. But burgher had other connotations as well. It was also a moral category, drawing strength from a seventeenth-century ideal of burgherhood that was now newly imbued with enlightened values and already pointing towards the political citizenship of the Age of the Democratic Revolutions. Almost imperceptibly the burgher, though still firmly rooted in the town where he enjoyed his civic rights, was becoming a member of a Dutch civil society and a citizen of an overall Dutch nation.

This moral and as yet only quasi-political citizenship had little to do with the economic aspirations of an emerging 'bourgeoisie' (even if this was not defined in narrow Marxist terms). Though economics did play an important part in the debate of the Dutch Enlightenment, it would be highly deceptive to reduce the impetus of this enlightened civil society merely to economic motives. The enlightened burgher of the second half of the eighteenth century was not defined in predominantly economic terms, nor in terms of social class. He could even – and often did – belong to the established upper reaches of society,[31] the 'periwig aristocracy' which was often at the receiving end of the enlightened moral critique voiced in the Spectators. At the same time, this moral community of burghers was also open to those not belonging to the Dutch Reformed Church.[32] Membership of this Church – an established church in all but name – was obligatory for all who participated in formal politics and often for those seeking to obtain public offices, including many lowly jobs in the pay of local government.

The development of nations as imagined communities, according to the views of Benedict Anderson, has been closely related to the evolution of national print cultures in the early modern period, and subsequently to the growth of the newspaper press which made the sense of belonging an everyday experience. For reading a newspaper is a ritual that can be seen – as Hegel memorably suggested – as a substitute for morning prayers: the picking-up of the same text by thousands of readers at roughly the same time creating a spirit of communion.[33] In the Dutch Republic after 1750 the process of nation-building was conducted on a weekly basis in its many moralising Spectators, redefining the public sphere and preparing the ground – as we can see with hindsight – for the fierce political battles of the 1780s.

Dutch historiography of the final decades of the eighteenth century has traditionally concentrated on its two revolutions: the so-called Patriot Revolution of 1780–87, one of the frontrunners in R. R. Palmer's series of 'democratic revolutions', and the Batavian Revolution of 1795, the Dutch version of the French Revolution, which can also be seen as the continuation of the revolutionary fervour of the 1780s.[34] Curiously enough, there have been few attempts to place these revolutions in a more cultural context. Rather the contrary: the idea of a Dutch Enlightenment was considered slightly ridiculous until perhaps thirty years ago. In recent years, however, a change of focus and a change of definition have altered the picture quite dramatically.[35] As soon as the Enlightenment was no longer defined as an essentially French-inspired and francophone phenomenon, but came to be seen as a multiple experience with a whole range of national variations, a Dutch Enlightenment was quickly discovered. Part of this discovery has been the projection of Rolf Engelsing's well-known concept of a *Leserevolution*, developed for eighteenth-century Germany, on the situation of the Dutch Republic.[36] Summarised very briefly, this implied that the Dutch Enlightenment was analysed in terms of a 'reading revolution': a substantial enlargement of the reading public on the one hand, together with a change in the manner and in the matter of reading. Instead of a continuous, *intensive* rereading of an iron repertory of selected texts (the Bible, sermons, almanacs and the like), there emerged *extensive* (that is, more casual and desultory) reading of a much greater variety of material: general information (to quench the enlightened thirst for knowledge), ephemeral literature (such as novels), periodicals and newspapers. There has been fierce debate over the last few years on the tenability of the concept of this *Leserevolution* when applied to the Dutch scene.[37] This debate has generated a great deal of information, which has particularly increased our knowledge of the eighteenth-century book trade. Unfortunately, however, the great sophistication of this research in terms of new sources tapped and new methods used – such as modern marketing theory[38] – has not been rewarded with clear and unequivocal answers, since each new specialist monograph tends to rephrase the questions and, in a sense, adds to the confusion.

Research has concentrated so far on the economics of book production and book distribution. The hard quantitative evidence now available in this field makes it difficult to uphold the idea of a reading revolution as it had been originally put forward by Engelsing's Dutch followers. In part this may be a matter of definition and of sources used, and perhaps also of focusing too much on the novel which has been considered 'practically the emblem of the reading revolution'.[39] On the other hand, recent research has done little to deny the increasing importance (from the 1770s onwards) of ephemeral literature, especially newspapers and periodicals – already noted as a matter of course by contemporary observers – not to mention the explosive growth of political literature in the 1780s. The problem is that such items can hardly be expected to appear in the inventory lists of deceased people or in the account books of booksellers, which have dominated much recent research. If the idea of a reading revolution of sorts is still tenable, it is most likely to be found in the area of periodicals, newspapers and the innumerable political tracts of the 1780s.[40] The appearance of new newspapers from the mid-1770s, the frequent publication of double numbers and the mounting circulation of the four main 'national' newspapers, all seem to support this suggestion.[41]

Though the concept of an enlightened Fatherland was carefully kept outside the realm of politics proper – it remained, after all, an 'imagined community' – it did have a growing impact on Dutch politics. Below the surface a great deal of unease had built up – especially in the Spectators – as to the way Dutch society was developing and the Dutch state was run. But it was the growing international tension, especially when France joined the American rebels against England in 1778, which really made the political climate in the Dutch Republic change. The number of political pamphlets – always a sure barometer – started to rise quickly. Also in 1778 *De Staatsman* (*The Statesman*), the first example of a new type of political journalism, began publication. It appeared fortnightly and was edited by the *philosophe* Nassau La Lecq, a distant cousin of Stadholder William V. A typical feature was the recycling of older texts of political theory, especially from the sphere of English classical republicanism.[42] *De Staatsman* commented on the international situation as well as on Dutch internal politics in a rather contemplative, long-winded manner. Its political colouring was pro-French and anti-British, calling Britain a 'friend in appearance only' and criticising the Dutch for investing in the British public debt.[43] Still, the growing political unrest from 1778 onwards was mild compared to what happened in the final days of 1780, when Britain quite suddenly and unexpectedly declared war on the Dutch. It was the shock of war and its immediate consequences in terms of shipping lost and trade routes blocked which produced a political crisis in the Dutch Republic that would last until the late summer of 1787, when a Prussian army overran the country. The outbreak of war immediately and visibly highlighted the 'decline' of the Republic, which had been debated exhaustively by the Spectators of the past decades. It also immediately produced a great surge in political literature, both pamphlets and periodicals. During the Patriot Period of 1780–7, Dutch society was politicised as it had never been before. Of course, the Dutch Republic in both the seventeenth and eighteenth centuries had witnessed several moments of high political crisis in which two 'parties', the Regents and the Orangists, had confronted one another. But this time the crisis was drawn out over several years, allowing politics to become a process in which the periodical press – surpassing the pamphlet, the typical workhorse of crisis politics – played a crucial role, precisely because it could react to developments and shape them on a continuing basis.

The public sphere demarcated by the Dutch Enlightenment was now filled with politics. This had some important consequences. The earlier civil society could not carry the pressures of the mounting political antagonism and after a while more or less collapsed, at least for the time being. Being ostensibly non-political, this civil society had accommodated people of various political leanings, united in their cultural pursuits and in their quest for a revival of the Fatherland. Now this spirit of unity, evoked so well in the moralising Spectators, was shattered by the highly polarised politics of the 1780s. In Dutch society new fault lines appeared. The traditional Regent–Orangist antithesis was replaced by the opposition between Patriots and Orangists. The Patriots took their line from the Dutch Enlightenment of the past decades, trying to translate its moral message into a political programme. With the publication of *De Post van den Neder-Rhijn*, the Patriots started a regular political press with a nationwide appeal within weeks of the outbreak of the war. They did this most effectively by simply copying the format and the formula of the popular Spectators, hoping no doubt to attract their reading public as well.[44] There was, however, one big difference. The earlier Spectators had staged a comedy of manners that, however true to life it may have seemed, was still largely a matter of fiction and imagination. The new political Spectators, of which the *Post van den Neder-Rhijn* was the first and the most successful (lasting 614 issues between January 1781 and October 1787, with a print-run of perhaps 3,000 copies),[45] employed these rituals of fiction – including the use of suggestive pseudonyms – to play the game of real politics. Polite conversation now became political conversation. Carefully constructed set-piece problems of morals and manners gave way to the great political questions of the day.

In its first year *De Post* was almost wholly devoted to international politics and the course of the war. In 1782, however, attention gradually shifted from the war itself to those held responsible for conducting it. This opened up the whole sphere of internal politics in the Dutch Republic including its structure of authority. Politics now developed a dynamic of its own, becoming more radical around 1785 and escalating into fullscale civil war in 1786-7. The catchphrase of the Patriot movement was constitutional restoration, which meant purging the ancient constitution of the Republic of all sorts of abuses that had crept in over the years. The vast patronage of the Stadholder was attacked, as was the position of city Regents, who were increasingly exposed as a self-appointed and self-serving aristocracy, unchecked by burgher influence. The editor of *De Post* was Pieter 't Hoen, a committed Patriot who was willing to put his life on the line when the Utrecht Patriots had to fight off an attack by regular Orangist troops in May 1787.[46] Much of the paper consisted of letters to the editor in the best Spectatorial mode. Thus in a sense the readers of *De Post* were also its writers, though 't Hoen allowed himself the editorial freedom to trim pieces and to combine them. *De Post* was particularly strong on the main thrust of the Patriot programme as an ideology of international power, citizen participation and moral rearmament. It also provided much practical information on what happened in the main centres of action (such as Utrecht), for instance on the foundation of urban militias, which came to be one of the chief features of organised Patriotism, or on the setting-up of political societies. When such a Fatherland Society was established in the Gelderland capital of Arnhem, *De Post* provided all the relevant details.[47] On the society's premises good Patriots could refresh themselves with a pint of beer or wine. The best newspapers were available, as was a selection of books, in order to further the 'necessary civic knowledge', but playing games was strictly forbidden. A particular point of interest to *De Post* was the protection of the freedom of the press, attacking abuse and defending, if necessary, other papers. When the Orangist prosecutor Athlone tried to have *De Post* banned in 1782, its publisher Van Paddenburg reacted by threatening to move his flourishing business, which employed eighteen people, out of Utrecht. All through the 1780s *De Post*, which had been the first in the field, succeeded in remaining the most influential of all Patriot papers. In the dying days of the Patriot movement, when the Prussian army was already in the country, a letter-writer praised *De Post* for being 'so to speak the *handbook* of the right-thinking part of the people'.[48]

The second most important Patriot paper was *De Politieke Kruyer*, edited by Johan Christiaan Hespe, which started publication in Amsterdam in September 1782. Though its politics were much the same as those of *De Post*, its tone was quite different. *De Kruyer* operated on the principle that people in authority were there to be checked, and, if need be, exposed. Whereas *De Post* was serious to the point of being laborious, the style of *De Kruyer* was more direct and sometimes even racy. Like *De Post*,

De Kruyer gave detailed information on the organisation of urban militias and political societies as well as on the attempts at constitutional reform in many cities, trying to give back to the burghers the legitimate political influence that had supposedly been theirs in medieval times.

The Patriot programme was put forward in many books and pamphlets, but it was elaborated and developed on an almost day-to-day, week-to-week basis, in a manner not shown before, in the newly founded political journals. The example of *De Post van den Neder-Rhijn* and *De Politieke Kruyer* was followed by dozens of other periodicals, though generally these were less successful and shorter-lived. Several French newspapermen such as Antoine-Marie Cérisier[49] and François Bernard were also involved in the Patriot journalistic effort. Cérisier, for instance, was the author of *Le Politique hollandais*, which started to appear in February 1781 and which provided a mix of international affairs and Dutch domestic politics.

De Post and *De Kruyer* were distributed all over the country and had a nationwide impact. They gave a sense of purpose and a sense of unity to a Patriot movement that – given the constitutional fragmentation of the country – was by nature divided, having to fight a different battle in every town, with a different agenda and a different timetable. The original constitution of the Dutch Republic was still regarded as sacrosanct, to be restored but certainly not overturned. In this context the press was the single most important unifying force of Patriotism. The politics of the Patriots were evolutionary rather than revolutionary. They generally tried to reach their goal of constitutional restoration in a legal, even legalistic manner. This was reflected in the general tone of the press, though in 1786 and 1787 this tone hardened when constitutional restoration developed into full-scale civil war. In places such as the main Patriot bulwark of Utrecht, where direct mass-action was effectively used to put pressure on the process of reform, this was due to the skills of local activists rather than to a special effort on the part of the press. There were many attempts to bring the Patriot message to the lower orders of society in specially targeted publications. What made them special, however, was not an insurrectionary tone, but an attempt to translate the Patriot programme into language that was easy to understand.

A new dimension was added to the practice of contemporary politics when the Orangist party – which was always several steps behind the Patriots – tried to create a counter-network of political papers to answer the Patriots and defend the Stadholder and his system and the traditional alliance with Britain. Rijklof Michaël van Goens, one of the most enlightened Dutchmen of his age, edited *De Ouderwetse Nederlandsche Patriot* (*The Old-fashioned Dutch Patriot*), which appeared in a print run of 700 copies, many of which were distributed free to coffee houses and political clubs.[50] Elie Luzac, the Orangist cousin of Jean Luzac, the editor of the *Gazette de Leyde*, was the author of *Reinier Vryaarts openhartige brieven* (*Reinier Vryaart's Candid Letters*), an erudite series of letters in which the follies of the Patriots were systematically exposed, and a conservative political theory was developed in the process.[51] Instead of blaming the Stadholder for everything, as the Patriots did, Luzac pointed at the city of Amsterdam as the evil influence in Dutch history and politics. An Orangist Spectator written in a more popular vein was *Vaderlandsche Byzonderheden* (*Particulars of the Fatherland*), which started to appear in Amsterdam in 1785, and routinely blamed the new-fangled Patriots and their 'Moderne Couranten' for undermining the dignity of the Stadholder through their 'vapid reasonings, filled with the most malicious traits of their corrupted ingenuity'.[52]

In terms of impact and circulation, this Orangist counter-attack was far less successful than the Patriot offensive. Whatever many ordinary people may have thought, it can safely be assumed that 'enlightened opinion' at least was inclined far more to Patriot politics than to the Orangist alternative. However, the creation of a well-defined Orangist policy was a vital stage in the development of a political culture based on contestation. It enabled a vision of politics as a choice between alternative value systems, each with distinct ideological overtones. The contribution of the periodical press to this invention of modern politics in the Dutch setting can hardly be overestimated. In the 1780s, several of the established urban newspapers shed their habitual neutrality and became more politically explicit, the *Leydse Courant* supporting the Patriots and the *'s Gravenhaegse Courant* the Orangists. The *Amsterdamsche Courant*, however, stuck to its neutral tone, losing many readers as a consequence.[53] Many contemporary observers agreed that the outbreak of the war in 1780 had both made people politically conscious and made them read.[54] Political opponents of the Patriots gave full credit to the essential role of the Patriot press in bringing about the political escalation of the 1780s. Adriaan Kluit, a Leyden law professor who doubled as an Orangist polemicist, regarded the new periodical press as the chief agent of the Patriot Revolution.[55]

At the Orangist Restoration of 1787, many Patriot activists fled the country, in the early days perhaps as many as 40,000, of which maybe 5,000 remained abroad till the Batavian Revolution of 1795. Both 't Hoen and Hespe, the editors of *De Post van den Neder-Rhijn* and *De Politieke Kruyer*, were among those who stayed abroad for the whole of the Restoration. Hespe, along with a number of other directors and writers of Patriot journals published in Holland, was explicitly excluded from the general amnesty the province of Holland granted on 15 February 1788.[56]

All Patriot periodicals were forbidden on the Orangists' return to power, and during the backlash that followed it was advisable for Patriots to lie low. But whereas all Patriot journals had to stop publication, interestingly enough, Spectators of the earlier non-political type now started to appear once again, some of them edited by former Patriots. Bernardus Bosch, a violent Patriot, had lost his job as a Protestant minister in 1787. To earn a living he started the Spectator *De Menschenvriend (The Friend of Man)* (1788–95), which attracted a readership of mainly former Patriots.[57] Together with IJsbrand van Hamelsveld, Bosch also edited *De Godsdienstvriend (The Friend of Religion)* (1788–95). Van Hamelsveld, a professor of theology in Utrecht, had been one of the ringleaders of the local Patriot movement, earning great notoriety by preaching Patriotism during his Sunday sermons in the Utrecht cathedral church. When he was ousted from his professorship in 1787, he became a man of letters, writing Spectators and undertaking translation work. After 1795, Van Hamelsveld was to turn to politics once more, becoming a member of the National Assembly in 1796. But his experiences of the 1780s had obviously taught him a lesson: during the Batavian Revolution he was constantly preaching conciliation between Dutchmen of all political backgrounds.

After the outbreak of the French Revolution in 1789, traditional newspapers reported extensively on the revolutionary events in France, taking the opportunity to regain some of the ground lost to the purely political press of the Patriot years. They provided both the Patriots and the Orangists with an increasingly frightening sequel to the events in their own country. Obviously France had now become the 'High School of Revolution', as the Patriot writer and journalist-in-exile Gerrit Paape called it.[58] The Batavian Revolution of January 1795, when the French revolutionary army overran the Republic and the Stadholder ignominiously fled to England, was a 'velvet revolution'. Its result was a foregone conclusion. The former Patriots simply took over the city and provincial councils. There was no resistance and no bloodshed. In retrospect, the long-drawn-out process of the Patriot Revolution had already broken the back of the Dutch ancien regime.

After the Revolution the political press which had been suppressed in 1787 immediately reappeared, sometimes using the same titles. *De Post van den Neder-Rhijn* became *De Nieuwe Post van den Neder-Rhijn*, whereas the satirical magazine *Janus* called itself *Janus Verrezen (Janus Resurrected)*. It was now the turn of the Orangist press to be banned. This implied there was no longer the open competition between alternative ideological systems that had been so characteristic of the 1780s. Instead, political journals came to serve as platforms for the various strands within Batavian revolutionary politics. A radical paper from the beginning of the Revolution was the *Advocaat der Nationale Vrijheid*, edited by Johan Valckenaer who had been an eye-witness of the Revolution in France and was now in favour of some intimidating revolutionary measures, including exemplary executions. The most important of the many new papers that were founded aimed at forming public opinion in the great debate developing on the constitution, which was to be framed by the newly established National Assembly of 1796.[59] In *De Republikein*, edited by Jan Konijnenburg, and especially *De Democraten*, edited by Isaac Gogel and Willem Anthonie Ockerse, a democratic political programme was worked out. *Heraclyt en Democryt* called for a revamped federalist Republic. It was no coincidence that its editor was a native of Friesland, fearing the loss of its sovereignty in a centralised state inevitably dominated by Holland. *De Democraten* was by far the most impressive political journal of the period, advocating representative democracy, a state that was '*une et indivisible*' and also an imaginative programme of popular enlightenment and national education. For it considered the Batavian Revolution to be doomed if the revolutionary process of state-building was not accompanied by a parallel process of nation-building.[60]

However important the role of the political press may have been in the three years of revolution (1795–8), providing food for debate for the many political clubs and societies which had sprung up all over the country, it was less central to the political process than in the 1780s, for the simple reason that during the Patriot Period the political press constituted the only truly national political forum. During the Batavian Revolution this role was assumed as of right by the new National Assembly. The proceedings of the National Assembly were taken down verbatim by writers in the gallery, while the *Representanten* – as the members of parliament were called – also often handed in their speeches. These reports were published daily in the *Dagverhaal* (*Journal*) of the National Assembly, a commercial publishing venture of Swart en Comp. Like other newspapers it was read in clubs and coffee houses and provided a framework for political discussion. Despite the fact that its proceedings were often laborious and its debates always long-winded – though generally of high quality – it was the National Assembly itself, rather than the political press surrounding it, which managed to set the agenda for political discussion in 1796 and 1797.

The radical coup d'état of 22 January 1798 – one of very few in Dutch history – provided the breakthrough in a constitutional debate, which had become a constitutional impasse. A unitary state organised on democratic-centralist principles was forced upon the Dutch people by the radical minority in parliament. The constitution of 1798 formally established the freedom of the press, which until then had been a matter of fact rather than of principle.[61] Paradoxically, however, the curbing of the press started almost at the same moment. The now formally instituted top-down style of government greatly facilitated the control of unwelcome political activities, such as political clubs and publications.[62] The radical centralism of 1798 paved the way for subsequent strictures on the press by the still Dutch-controlled Staatsbewind after 1801 and the satellite government of Napoleon's brother Louis (1806–10). Finally, the incorporation of his Kingdom of Holland into the French Empire in 1810 brought with it the full machinery of Napoleon's police state.[63]

A prosecution in 1802 was perhaps symbolic of these changes. It was directed against Johan Christiaan Hespe, in Patriot times the editor of *De Politieke Kruyer*, and now connected with *De Politieke Blixem*. In 1785, Hespe, as editor of *De Kruyer*, had been taken into custody for a few days and fined 3,000 guilders. This action, however, backfired heavily on the Amsterdam authorities when Hespe was celebrated all over the country as a martyr of the Patriot cause and subscriptions were organised to pay his fine.[64] In 1802, the outcome was quite different, though Hespe had remained true to himself. In one suggestive political 'day-dream', published in *De Politieke Blixem*, he predicted that Napoleon might intervene in the Batavian Republic, in another he attacked the lacklustre Staatsbewind. Hespe was imprisoned on dubious legal grounds for several months.[65] In contrast to 1785, this political prosecution did not result in added prestige for the press. On the contrary, it proved that the age of radical journalism and political scandal-mongering, Hespe's stock-in-trade, was over.

The diminishing importance of the political press from 1798 onwards was not merely a matter of curbs and controls. It was also related to the growing weariness of the general public about all matters political. By 1800, some Dutch citizens even regarded politics as a fashion that had lost its attractiveness.[66] The shifting role of the French – the liberators of 1795 had become the Napoleonic occupying force – coincided with the development of a strong and general aversion to politics among the Dutch public. This also had important consequences for the conception of the public sphere. On the one hand the Dutch withdrew into the private world of the family, on the other hand there was a revaluation of the non-political civil society and the cultural sociability of the 1760s and 1770s.

In retrospect, the political press in the Dutch Republic had its heyday during the Patriot Revolution when it played an indispensable and also largely 'unedited' role, providing much of the political dynamics of those years. Its role during the Batavian Revolution was less crucial and less spectacular. Despite the gradual erosion of freedom of the press after 1798, however, the basic function of traditional newspapers – providing the news, especially from abroad – remained intact, catering for a natural need of man, as we have seen from Ockerse's lecture of 1804. But perhaps his lecture must also be read as a guarded warning against Napoleon's continuous attempts to control this stream of information and to break with a highly valued Dutch tradition of supplying the news that was much older than the recent flurry of political journalism. When the Dutch regained their independence in 1813, the freedom of the press was immediately restored. However, this freedom was not used to revive the political journalism of Patriot and Batavian times. Quite the contrary: these journalistic battles were now seen as part and parcel of the revolutionary politics which most Dutchmen of 1813 were trying hard to forget in a spirit of national harmony and reconciliation.

NOTES

1 Willem Anthonie Ockerse, 'Wat nieuws is er? Verhandeling, gehouden in Doctrina et Amicitia. Den 8sten October 1804', in *Redevoeringen, nagelaten door W. A. Ockerse* (Amsterdam, 1826), pp. 243–66.
2 Johanna Stouten, *Willem Anthonie Ockerse (1760–1826). Leven en werk* (Amsterdam, 1982).
3 Willem Anthonie Ockerse, *Ontwerp tot eene algemeene characterkunde. Derde stukjen, behelzende het nationaal character der Nederlanderen* (Amsterdam, 1797).
4 Ibid., p. 144.
5 Ibid., pp. 145–6.
6 Ibid., pp. 146–7.
7 Maarten Schneider and Joan Hemels, *De Nederlandse krant 1618–1978. Van 'nieuwstydinghe' tot dagblad* (Baarn, 1979); G. de Bruin, *Geheimhouding en verraad. De geheimhouding van staatszaken ten tijde van de Republiek (1600–1750)* ('s-Gravenhage, 1991). See also C. G. Gibbs, 'The role of the Dutch Republic as the intellectual entrepôt of Europe in the seventeenth and eighteenth centuries', *Bijdragen en mededelingen betreffende de geschiedenis der Nederlanden*, 86 (1971), 323–49.
8 I. H. van Eeghen, 'De *Amsterdamse Courant* in de achttiende eeuw', *Jaarboek van het Genootschap Amstelodamum*, 44 (1950), 31–58.
9 Hannie van Goinga, *Alom te bekomen. Veranderingen in de boekdistributie in de Republiek 1720–1800* (Amsterdam, 1999), pp. 35–40, 288. Van Goinga's computations are based on a weighing of all published evidence available and on her own research into the *Leydse Courant*. See also Van Eeghen, 'De *Amsterdamse Courant*'; D. H. Couvée, 'The administration of the *Oprechte Haarlemse Courant*, 1738–1742', *Gazette*, 4 (1958), 91–110.
10 Van Goinga, *Alom te bekomen*, p. 288.
11 De Bruin, *Geheimhouding en verraad*, p. 409.
12 Ibid.
13 Van Eeghen, 'De *Amsterdamse Courant*', p. 45.
14 Van Goinga, *Alom te bekomen*, p. 35.
15 Van Eeghen, 'De *Amsterdamse Courant*', p. 49.
16 Ibid., p. 48.
17 Van Goinga, *Alom te bekomen*, pp. 32–4.

18 Van Eeghen, 'De *Amsterdamse Courant*', pp. 52–5.
19 H. A. Enno van Gelder, *Getemperde vrijheid. Een verhandeling over de verhouding van Kerk en Staat in de Republiek der Verenigde Nederlanden en de vrijheid van meningsuiting inzake godsdienst, drukpers en onderwijs, gedurende de 17e eeuw* (Groningen, 1972).
20 Eugène Hatin, *Les Gazettes de Hollande et la presse clandestine aux XVIIe et XVIIIe siècles* (Paris, 1865). See also W. P. Sautijn Kluit, 'Bijdrage omtrent de Fransche Amsterdamsche en Leidsche couranten', *Bijdragen voor vaderlandsche geschiedenis en oudheidkunde*, new series, 4 (1865), 28–49. On the *Gazette de Leyde*, Jeremy D. Popkin, *News and Politics in the Age of Revolution. Jean Luzac's Gazette de Leyde* (Ithaca, NY, and London, 1989). See also the chapters by Simon Burrows and Jack Censer in this volume.
21 For an English-language overview see Margaret C. Jacob and Wijnand W. Mijnhardt (eds.), *The Dutch Republic in the Eighteenth Century. Decline, Enlightenment and Revolution* (Ithaca, NY, 1992).
22 N. C. F. van Sas (ed.), *Vaderland Een geschiedenis van de vijftiende eeuw tot 1940* (Amsterdam, 1999), especially the chapters by Peter van Rooden, J. J. Kloek and N. C. F. van Sas.
23 Benedict Anderson, *Imagined Communities. Reflections on the Origin and Spread of Nationalism*, revised edn (London, 1991).
24 W. W. Mijnhardt, *Tot heil van 't menschdom. Culturele genootschappen in Nederland, 1750–1815* (Amsterdam, 1987).
25 Ernest Gellner, *Nations and Nationalism* (Oxford, 1983).
26 P. J. Buijnsters, *Spectatoriale geschriften* (Utrecht, 1991).
27 *De Nederlandsche Criticus* (Leeuwarden, 1749), 1.
28 Ibid., 24.
29 Dorothée Sturkenboom, *Spectators van hartstocht. Sekse en emotionele cultuur in de achttiende eeuw* (Hilversum, 1998).
30 Peter van Rooden, 'Godsdienst en nationalisme in de achttiende eeuw: het voorbeeld van de Republiek', in van Sas (ed.), *Vaderland*, 201–36; and J. J. Kloek, 'Reconsidering the reading revolution: the thesis of the "Reading Revolution" and a Dutch bookseller's clientele around 1800', *Poetics*, 26 (1999) 289–307, p. 304.
31 J. J. Kloek's review of Sturkenboom's *Spectators van hartstocht* in *Bijdragen en mededelingen betreffende de geschiedenis der Nederlanden*, 115 (2000), p. 125.
32 Van Rooden, 'Godsdienst en nationalisme', pp. 231–6.
33 Anderson, *Imagined Communities*, p. 35.
34 For an English-language overview of these events see Simon Schama, *Patriots and Liberators. Revolution in the Netherlands, 1780–1813* (New York, 1977).
35 For this change of focus see P. J. Buijnsters, 'Les Lumières hollandaises', *Studies on Voltaire and the Eighteenth Century*, 77 (1972), 197–215; W. W. Mijnhardt, 'De Nederlandse Verlichting. Een terreinverkenning', in *Figuren en figuraties: acht opstellen aangeboden aan J. C. Boogman* (Groningen, 1979), pp. 1–25.
36 Rolf Engelsing, 'Die Perioden der Lesergeschichte in der Neuzeit. Das statistische Ausmass und die soziokulturelle Bedeutung der Lektüre', in R. Engelsing, *Zur Sozialgeschichte deutscher Mittel- und Unterschichten* (Göttingen, 1973), 112–54.

The Netherlands 1750-1813 67

37 Particularly the still unfinished Utrecht research project of J. J. Kloek and W. W. Mijnhardt on the account books of the Middelburg bookseller Samuel van Benthem has fuelled this debate. For a recent *status quaestionis* see Kloek, 'Reconsidering the reading revolution'. Important contributions were made by Han Brouwer, *Lezen en schrijven in de provincie. De boeken van Zwolse boekverkopers, 1777–1849* (Leiden, 1995); José de Kruif, *Liefhebbers en gewoontelezers. Leescultuur in Den Haag in de achttiende eeuw* (Zutphen, 1999); van Goinga, *Alom te bekomen*; and Arianne Baggerman, *Een lot uit de loterij. Familiebelangen en uitgeverspolitiek in de Dordtse firma A. Blussé en Zoon, 1745–1823* (The Hague, 2000).
38 See de Kruif, *Liefhebbers en gewoontelezers.*
39 Kloek, 'Reconsidering the reading revolution', p. 299.
40 See Martin Welke's perceptive criticism of the Engelsing thesis in this respect, 'Gemeinsame Lektüre und frühe Formen von Gruppenbildungen im 17. und 18. Jahrhundert: Zeitungslesen in Deutschland', in Otto Dann (ed.), *Lesegesellschaften und bürgerliche Emanzipation. Ein europäischer Vergleich* (Munich, 1981), 29–53.
41 Van Goinga, *Alom te bekomen*, p. 306.
42 S. R. E. Klein, *Patriots republikanisme. Politieke cultuur in Nederland, 1766–1787* (Amsterdam, 1995), 65–76.
43 *De Staatsman*, I, part 1, pp. 163, 454.
44 P. J. Buijnsters, 'Sociologie van de spectator', in Buijnsters, *Nederlandse literatuur van de achttiende eeuw* (Utrecht, 1984), p. 72.
45 W. P. Sautijn Kluit, '*De Post van den Neder-Rhijn*', *Bijdragen voor vaderlandsche geschiedenis en oudheidkunde*, new series, 10 (1880), 293–385.
46 P. J. H. M. Theeuwen, 'Pieter 't Hoen (1744–1828). Politiek journalist en Utrechts Patriot', in *O Vrijheid! onwaardeerbaar pand! Aspecten van de Patriottenbeweging in stad en gewest Utrecht. Jaarboek Oud-Utrecht 1987*, 43–77.
47 *De Post van den Neder-Rhijn*, 315.
48 Ibid., 600–601.
49 On Cérisier see Jeremy D. Popkin, 'From Dutch Republican to French Monarchist: Antoine-Marie Cérisier and the Age of Revolution', *Tijdschrift voor Geschiedenis*, 102 (1989), 534–44.
50 J. M. Peterse, 'R. M. van Goens. Publicist voor Oranje. R. M. van Goens en *De Ouderwetse Nederlandsche Patriot* (1781–1783)', *Bijdragen en mededelingen betreffende de geschiedenis der Nederlanden*, 103 (1988), 182–208.
51 W. R. E. Velema, *Enlightenment and Conservatism in the Dutch Republic. The Political Thought of Elie Luzac (1721–1796)* (Assen, 1993).
52 *Vaderlandsche Byzonderheden*, 2 (1786), p. 97.
53 Van Eeghen, 'De *Amsterdamse Courant*', p. 47.
54 See the remarks of the Leyden publisher C. F. Koenig in his *Koninklijke verdediging* (Leiden, 1784). Commercially, however, he was far less successful in exploiting this 'lust of reading' than he boasted: Hannie van Goinga, 'Een blik op de praktijk van de Nederlandse boekhandel omstreeks 1785: Christoffel Frederik Koenig, uitgever van volksblaadjes, Leiden 1782–1786', *De achttiende eeuw*, 25 (1993), 39–72.
55 [A. Kluit], *De soevereiniteit der Staaten van Holland, verdedigd tegen de hedendaagsche leere der volks-regering* (s.l., 1785), pp. 160–61.

56 *Nederlandsche amnestien* (Dordrecht, 1789), p. 282.
57 H. F. J. M. van den Eerenbeemt, 'Bernardus Bosch: Nutsfiguur, schrijver en politicus', *De Gids*, 134 (1971), 490–91.
58 E. O. G. Haitsma Mulier, 'De receptie van de Franse revolutie in Nederland. Contemporaine reactie en geschiedschrijving', *Tijdschrift voor geschiedenis*, 102 (1989), 451–70.
59 Herman de Lange, 'De politieke pers in de Bataafse revolutie. Enkele analytische hypothesen', *Economisch en sociaal-historisch jaarboek*, 35 (1972), 6–93.
60 N. C. F. van Sas, 'Vaderlandsliefde, nationalisme en vaderlands gevoel in Nederland, 1770–1813', *Tijdschrift voor geschiedenis*, 102 (1989), 483–5.
61 A. H. Huussen Jr, 'Freedom of the Press and Censorship in the Netherlands, 1780–1810', in A. C. Duke and C. A. Tamse (eds.), *Too Mighty to be Free. Censorship and the Press in Britain and the Netherlands* (Zutphen, 1987), 107–26, and W. R. E. Velema, 'Politiek, pers en publieke opinie. Het debat over de vrijheid van drukpers in de Bataafse tijd', in *Grondwetgeving 1795–1806* (Haarlem, 1997), 65–81.
62 N. C. F. van Sas, 'La sociabilité politique des Patriotes Bataves', *Annales historiques de la révolution française*, 277 (1989), 210–24.
63 Johan Joor, *De adelaar en het lam. Onrust, opruiing en onwilligheid in Nederland ten tijde van het Koninkrijk Holland en de Inlijving bij het Franse Keizerrijk (1806–1813)* (Amsterdam, 2000).
64 W. P. Sautijn Kluit, 'De Politieke Kruyer', *Bijdragen voor vaderlandsche geschiedenis en oudheidkunde*, third series, 1 (1882), 176–263.
65 M. Elisabeth Kluit, *Cornelis Felix van Maanen, tot het herstel der onafhankelijkheid* (Groningen, 1954), pp. 118–27; Gerlof D. Homan, 'The *Staatsbewind* and freedom of the press', *Tijdschrift voor Geschiedenis*, 89 (1976), 18–24.
66 *De mode; eene satyre* (Amsterdam, 1804), p. 93.

3 Germany, 1760–1815

Eckhart Hellmuth and Wolfgang Piereth
Translated by Angela Davies

From the 1760s, the public sphere in Germany became increasingly politicised. Certain strata of German society became receptive to the idea of civil activities undertaken for the common good, displayed a new sensitivity to contemporary political and social conditions and their shortcomings, and were more prepared to voice criticism. Events such as the Seven Years War and the American War of Independence stimulated this development. The dramatic occurences of the revolutionary and Napoleonic age gave it a further boost.[1] In particular, the war with Napoleonic France had a profound impact on society, bringing with it occupation and haggling about territory, constant changes of ruler and a far-reaching reform policy which awakened and sharpened the political awareness of broad sections of the population.[2] For example, the Confederation of the Rhine was the 'subject of debate in all the journals, during which, society was quickly politicised'.[3] These upheavals cleared the deck for a debate on political basics such as national identity, legal equality and political participation.

This newly created public was to a large extent the domain of the enlightened intelligentsia, the *Gebildeten*, at least in the later eighteenth century. This group was highly diverse in terms of origin, profession, type and level of income.[4] What unified the *Gebildeten* as a group was education. As a rule, they had studied at one of the enlightened universities. Familiarity with the contemporary and classical culture ensured the homogeneity of this group. Since education, not property or social background, defined the *Gebildeten*, in principle it was an open group. At the same time, it was highly elitist, as it comprised only about 2 per cent of the total population. Although the *Gebildeten* group was middle-class at heart, it also crossed over into the nobility. It consisted essentially of three sub-groups. First, there were members of the professions who had had an academic training, such as doctors, lawyers and apothecaries. Second, there were writers, artists and journalists. And third, by far the largest constituent group of the *Gebildeten* were members of the civil service. In the widest sense this included, in addition to administrative officials and the judiciary, professors and, in the Protestant territories, the clergy and teachers. These servants of the state took part in the public discussion about state, society and the law which began from about 1750 and became much more widespread during the last quarter of the century. For civil servants with an academic training this debate naturally provided an intellectual challenge, especially as academic and literary activity offered a high degree of prestige. Thus, in addition to their professional duties, officials devoted themselves to the task of interpreting the world by writing newspaper articles, academic studies, treatises and essays.

As authors, editors and publishers the *Gebildeten* came together in informal but highly influential 'networks' which to a large extent dominated the unfolding market in information.[5] This is the context in which the profession of journalism began to develop.[6] In addition to numerous part-time 'writers',[7] there were probably about a hundred full-time journalists in late eighteenth- and early nineteenth-century Germany.[8] Their most important members included Christoph Martin Wieland and Christian Friedrich Daniel Schubart. During the wars of liberation, Joseph Görres, in particular, made a name for himself with his journal, the *Rheinische Merkur (Rhineish Mercury)* (1814–16). Increasing commercialization meant that in the second half of the eighteenth century not everyone published out of lofty political and social concerns. Journalists often sought to make money and further their careers by securing large sales for their publications, or by writing their way into a job with the state by publishing pro-government articles.[9]

The *Gebildeten* saw themselves as an authority entitled to judge, as 'the mouth of the people and the ear of the prince'.[10] At the same time, they sharply separated themselves from the masses, who, because of 'their ignorance and roughness', could have no part in shaping public opinion.[11] Yet we must not forget that there were also 'plebeian' circles of communication. Interest in printed political information among the broad and often illiterate masses rose in leaps and bounds at certain times during the eighteenth and early nineteenth centuries.[12] The clergy, teachers and pub landlords took an active part by reading political material aloud, and thus helped to politicise the public at large. In 1792, the Helmstedt professor Johann Nikolaus Bischoff noted: 'In short, everyone is eager for the most recent news of world events, from the Regent, who receives it at first hand from his envoys and messengers, down to the countryman, who hears the ... newspaper read by his political schoolmaster every Sunday in the pub.'[13] Nothing had changed in the run-up to the wars of liberation, as this announcement from Rosenheim in Bavaria, dated July 1813, shows: 'Everyone is drinking and arguing to their hearts' content; the numerous clergy there, apart from the dean, who is a most noble man, are working on the audience in their usual way.'[14]

The development of a 'modern' public sphere in Germany was closely tied to changes in reading behaviour. In the last third of the eighteenth century, a maximum of 15 per cent of the 25 million inhabitants of the German Reich could read; by the end of the century, this figure had risen to about 25 per cent.[15] While Rolf Engelsing's concept of the 'reading revolution' may be controversial,[16] there is no doubt that from the second half of the eighteenth century the reading public, especially among the middle classes, expanded considerably. People spoke of a 'reading addiction' and a 'mania for reading', which filled contemporaries with amazement and soon with real concern.[17] This change has been described as the transition from 'intensive' to 'extensive' reading.[18] In the early eighteenth century, the repetitious reading of, for example, devotional literature, had dominated; now people read more widely. The purpose of reading was no longer just to confirm and consolidate a canon of traditional beliefs and maxims; rather, the aim was to open up a new view of the world. Reading now frequently went beyond the private sphere and became an occasion for communication within society.[19] This could happen in circles of friends, but its main setting was in the context of the rapidly expanding reading societies, which were even spreading into rural areas.[20] These reading societies had two functions: first, they provided access to a stock of books which, as a rule, went far beyond the holdings of private libraries. And second, they served as a forum for debate about what had been read. This 'extensive' reading by the educated classes fundamentally undermined the monopoly of interpretation previously enjoyed by the Church and state authorities. What was read can be roughly grouped into four categories: books, journals, newspapers and pamphlets. All of them profited from the fact that changes in reading behaviour led to a boom in the literary market from the late eighteenth century.

During the second half of the eighteenth century, the book market was clearly going through an upswing. The total production of German-language books between 1700 and 1800 is estimated at about 175,000 titles. About two-thirds of these were probably published after 1760.[21] Correspondingly, the number of bookshops in Germany is thought to have 'increased by a quarter' between 1793 and 1803.[22] There is another indicator that fundamental changes had been taking place on the German book market from about 1760:[23] learned books in Latin were largely being displaced by books written for the educated general reader. They were written in German, and mostly contained practical information, or were entertaining. Whereas in 1740, 27 per cent of all new publications at the Leipzig and Frankfurt book fairs had been in Latin, by 1770 this percentage had almost halved (14.25 per cent), and by 1800 it had shrunk to a mere 3.97 per cent. Also striking is that the significance of theological works decreased constantly. In 1770, a quarter of the books on offer at the fairs had been theological or religious in content; in 1800, the figure was about 13.5 per cent. While legal and medical books kept their share of the market, other areas, such as geography, pedagogy, natural science, politics and philosophy registered a clear increase. The largest growth, however, was in the sphere of *belles-lettres*, that is, novels, poetry and drama. In 1740, these genres had had a market share of just under 6 per cent; in 1800 the figure had risen to 21.45 per cent. The novel, in particular, evoked a lasting response in readers.

The second half of the eighteenth century, however, was not only the age of the book, it was also the age of the journal. The journal is considered, with good reason, as the medium of the Enlightenment *par excellence*. Until the middle of the century, about 800 journals had been published in the German-language area, but after 1750 this market developed its own dynamic.[24] Almost 3,000 new titles appeared between 1751 and 1800, the greatest growth rates being achieved towards the end of the century. Between 1781 and 1790 alone, 1,225 new journals were published. These are remarkable figures, even if we take into account that quite a few were short-lived and did not survive after the first few issues. Consequently, only a limited number of journals could build up a steady readership. The size of print-runs varied. Normally, they would have been around 1,000; print-runs over 2,000 were a rare exception, yet a journal was financially viable if it could sell more than 500 copies.[25] When considering these – on the whole – modest figures, however, we must remember that individual copies were, as a rule, read by several people. In addition, the effectiveness of these journals was increased even further by the fact that they frequently formed a key part of the holdings of the libraries of contemporary reading societies.

The landscape of journals that emerged in this period was extraordinarily diverse. Thus there were many specialist journals on subjects such as theology, philosophy, law, medicine, education, natural sciences, economics, music, architecture and military science. Their readerships were drawn from those 'experts' in both the state apparatus and the free professions whose numbers had increased in the late eighteenth century. Publishers also discovered other specialist markets, such as women's journals[26] and fashion journals. As Bertuch's *Journal des Luxus und der Moden* (*Journal of Luxury and Fashion*) showed, these publications could be highly lucrative.[27] And finally, there were journals that concentrated on contemporary literature. Among these general reviewing organs, the *Allgemeine Deutsche Bibliothek* (*General German Library*), edited by the

Berlin publisher Friedrich Nicolai, initially stood out. In addition to specialist organs of this nature, which had a relatively clear profile, there were also journals that covered a broad spectrum of subjects. These included the moral weeklies,[28] which played a key role in broadening the reading public in the German-language area. Between 1720 and 1770, around 100 journals in this genre were published. Their content centred on developing a new understanding of 'virtue', and the spectrum of subjects addressed included, among other things, questions of upbringing and education, the home, social conduct, aesthetics, literature and language. The general magazine, however, dominated the journal landscape in the second half of the eighteenth century. The popularity of this genre was attributable not least to the fact that it treated a remarkable range of subjects. It 'regaled readers with information on discoveries, inventions, nature, history, statistics, practical matters, and occasional medical advice, all of which – interspersed where appropriate with a little poetry and moralizing – served both the readers and the common weal'.[29] The encyclopaedic character of the age was expressed here in trivialised form. The real target readership of the general magazines was the *Gebildeten*. But there were also many journals of this sort that aspired to instruct the 'common man'.

The *Intelligenzblätter* (advertisers, or information sheets) represented a unique form of journal.[30] At first they printed mainly announcements and official proclamations. But by the second half of the eighteenth century they often also had a sizeable editorial section which contained contributions in a popular enlightened vein, literary essays, or pieces on the common good, which placed them in the vicinity of the moral weeklies. While the *Intelligenzblätter* were often close to the state, or even state-owned, a substantial number were based on private initiatives. During the eighteenth century they spread throughout all the German states, and there is evidence that they were published in at least 220 cities. The average weekly print-run was between 500 and 1,000 copies, but there were some much higher figures. Around 1800 the two *Intelligenzblätter* published in Hamburg – a stronghold of the German press – had circulations of 3,000 and 5,000 respectively. In rural areas, in particular, the *Intelligenzblatt* might be the only published organ of the press. Holger Böning has therefore justifiably pointed out that *Intelligenzblätter* contributed to connecting 'the local, regionally limited publics into a national public that ignored the borders of the small states and territories'.[31]

A political press in the real sense did not emerge until after 1770. In the last three decades of the eighteenth century there were several dozen journals which dealt intensively with political topics. During the 1790s alone, twenty-four of these historical-political journals came on to the market; the following decade saw another twenty-five more titles of this sort.[32] A number of these journals had constantly rising circulation figures, which shows that they evoked a considerable response among the public. The most prominent included Schlözer's *Staatsanzeigen* (*State Advertiser*), Friedrich Karl von Moser's *Patriotisches Archiv* (*Patriotic Archive*), Schubart's *Deutsche Chronik* (*German Chronicle*) and Archenholz's *Minerva*, which was published in 1809 with a print-run of 5,000, and whose authors included the well-known journalists Friedrich (von) Gentz and Ernst Moritz Arndt. One of the most important organs of the late Enlightenment in Germany was the *Berlinische Monatsschrift* (*Berlin Monthly*) (1783–1811), edited by Joachim Erich Biester and Friedrich Gedicke.[33] Its authors included Prussia's leading intellectuals, among them Immanuel Kant and Moses Mendelssohn. The 1790s also witnessed the founding of journals which openly sympathised with the French Revolution, such as *Das Neue Graue Ungeheuer* (*The New Grey Monster*) (1795–1797) and *Die Geissel* (*The Whip*) (1797–9), which was edited by the lawyer and later judge in the French court of appeal Andreas Georg Friedrich Rebmann.[34] As a rule, the editors played a central part in these historical-political journals. They often wrote a substantial proportion of the contents themselves, and thus significantly influenced their political profile.

In order to attract readers, the historical-political journals, like the general journals, also carried travel reports, book reviews and anecdotal and biographical information.[35] But their main concern was domestic and foreign politics. They inundated their readers with a flood of information about government campaigns of various sorts, economics, commerce and military undertakings. Frequently, statistical information also formed an important part of their contents. Thus, they published figures on the budgets of individual states and territories, on the military potential of the European powers, birth and death rates, and import and export figures. By publishing data of this sort, the editors of political journals were trying to still the enormous public hunger for information. There was more, however, to this obsession with statistics. It was also a deliberate, political act which was intended to break through the secrecy with which absolutist regimes surrounded themselves, to generate a basis of fact for public debate.[36]

Facts, however, were only one side of the coin; political reflection was the other. Events such as the American War of Independence, the French Revolution, and the collapse of the Holy Roman Empire necessarily provoked an examination of fundamental constitutional issues. As a result, ideas such as popular sovereignty, the rights of man and the social contract were taken up by political journals during the Enlightenment and the Napoleonic period. In this process, two factors reinforced each other:

first, political literature became less academic, overstepping 'the bounds of its subject in the direction of political journalism';[37] and second, these themes became popular because their significance increasingly made them spill over into non-specialist organs.[38] Added to this was the nitty-gritty of everyday politics: plans to reform the education system, the debate on the guilds, the problem of serfdom, reflections on the criminal justice system, thoughts on poor relief and suggestions for improving industry and agriculture.

However, it was not only these overtly political journals that pushed forward the process of politicisation. Enlightened journals in general had the same effect. Thus, literary magazines such as Wieland's *Teutscher Merkur* (*German Mercury*) increasingly discussed political subjects. An attempt has been made to analyse the topics dealt with by the most important German journals of the late eighteenth century.[39] The results of this project, based on a computer analysis of 70,000 articles in about 160 periodicals published between 1750 and 1800, are as follows: 23.4 per cent were on the natural sciences; 15.7 per cent on contemporary society; 9 per cent on medicine; 8.9 per cent on the arts and humanities; 8.5 per cent on economics; 7.5 per cent on theology and religion; 7.1 per cent on politics; 6 per cent on law and jurisprudence; 5.6 per cent on philosophy; 4.2 per cent on education and schooling; and 4.0 per cent on history. Of course, such general categories are problematic. Nor do these figures show how the relative importance of individual topic areas changed during the second half of the century. But it is quite clear that politics, society, law and economics played an important part in the discourse of German enlightened society.

Originally, then, journals had concentrated on giving their readers facts, and had provided the raw material for political discourse. Increasingly, however, writers become more willing to take sides. The most obvious expression of this change was that controversies began between individual journals. According to Bödeker:

> The transition of the journal from its role as provider of material for political discourse to that of simultaneous bearer and representative of that discourse took place primarily in the latter third of the eighteenth century. At this time the press grew into its new function as an institution of public reflection and representative of public opinion. Journalists, and almost every learned German, spent at least some of their time writing for journals, on affairs they considered to be of public import and which they felt would be occupying the thoughts of others like them.[40]

Like journals, newspapers had a long history in Germany, having developed out of the so-called *Messrelationen* around 1600. In the period under discussion here, they were therefore a firmly established medium, indeed, the most important one as far as politics were concerned. During the eighteenth century, their numbers tripled. With its 200 newspapers, Germany was 'the country with the most newspapers in the world'.[41] Most of them probably had an average circulation of around 600 to 700, although some boasted much higher figures. As early as 1757 the *Reichspostreuter* (*Imperial Postal Messenger*), published in Altona, had a circulation of 11,000, while between 1741 and 1768 that of the *Real-Zeitung* (*Fact sheet*) from Erlangen was as high as 18,000. The rapid burst of politicisation which German society went through in response to the French Revolution and subsequent events seems to have stimulated the German newspaper market. In any case, by the end of the eighteenth century, a number of newspapers had achieved considerable circulation figures. Thus the *Neuwieder Zeitung* (*Neuwied News*) had 14,000 subscribers in 1792; the Augsburg *Ordinari Post-Zeitung* (*General Postal News*) had about 10,000 readers in 1800; and the Berlin *Vossische Zeitung* (*Vosses Newspaper*) had a circulation of 7,000 in 1798.[42] By far the largest figures, however, were achieved by the *Hamburgische Unpartheyische Correspondent* (*Hamburg Impartial Correspondent*), which published no fewer than 36,000 copies at the turn of the nineteenth century, before Hamburg was occupied by French troops: a number of sources even suggest the extraordinary figure of over 50,000.[43] Estimates indicate that by 1800 the German daily press sold considerably more than 300,000 copies per week: a figure which could be matched by no other contemporary printed material except the Bible and devotional literature.[44]

Two factors were involved in newspapers becoming a 'mass' medium in the German-language area during the second half of the eighteenth century: first, the contents of newspapers changed. Austere lists of events were increasingly replaced by argument and reflection. The French Revolution, above all, had a politicising and polarising effect, forcing many newspaper editors to adopt a position which in turn influenced the reading public.[45] This points to the second important aspect, namely, the new forms of reception that had become established. Parallel to the reading societies in which the educated urban upper classes assembled to read demanding material together, subscription clubs emerged among the urban and rural lower classes, giving their members cheaper access to newspapers, which they purchased collectively. This collective form of consumption was an expression of a growing curiosity and an increased need for entertainment among circles outside the enlightened elite. In addition to subscription clubs, pubs, coffee houses and taverns were places in which newspapers were read. Often teachers or clergy would organise reading circles in these places, which not only provided an opportunity for communal reading, but also served as forums for discussion.[46] All of these institutions frequently involved illiterate people, who gained access to the contents of newspapers when others read them aloud.

In the eighteenth century, most newspapers came out two to four times per week. As a rule, they consisted of four to eight quarto pages, printed in one or two columns. Daily newspapers were not the norm until the first third of the nineteenth century. Prior to this, most newspapers did not give articles headlines: only the place of origin and the date of the announcement were mentioned. In the early nineteenth century it became common to organise articles according to subject or geographical headings. Political reportage formed the bulk of newspaper contents, and war reports, court reports and official announcements and promulgations clearly dominated. By comparison with reporting on foreign affairs, domestic political news from the paper's home territory and neighbouring states of the Holy Roman Empire took a back seat: first, because news from France and England, for instance, was more easily available, and second, because there were political reasons why supra-regional newspapers in Germany had to be very careful when reporting the politics of neighbouring German states.[47]

Among the many newspapers that were published in the late eighteenth and early nineteenth centuries, a few stand out. These include the above-mentioned *Sta[a]ts- und Gelehrte Zeitung des Hamburgischen Unpartheyischen Correspondenten*, commonly known as the *Hamburgische Correspondent*.[48] Published since 1731, the paper profited from Hamburg's comparatively liberal press policy.[49] It was read by people from all over the Reich, and even from abroad, for example, Scandinavia. Contemporaries judged the *Hamburgische Correspondent* to be not only the biggest, but also the best newspaper at the turn of the century. By that time its reporting was already based on stories filed by its own correspondents.[50] The occupation of Hamburg by Napoleonic troops put an end to the *Hamburgische Correspondent*'s pioneering role as the most influential supra-regional newspaper in the German-language area. Its place was to some extent taken by the *Allgemeine Zeitung (General News)*, founded by the publisher Johann Friedrich Cotta in 1798.[51] Published first in Stuttgart and then moving to Ulm before settling in Augsburg in 1810, the *Allgemeine Zeitung* was the most influential organ of the German press in the first half of the nineteenth century thanks to its comprehensive and balanced reporting. At this time, it undeniably had a European range. 'Completeness', 'truthfulness' and 'impartiality' were its guidelines, laid down when the newspaper was founded, and followed over the years under Cotta's influence.[52] This pragmatic and clever publisher was able to combine political caution, economic benefit and a differentiated, but sometimes somewhat featureless, journalism.[53] The *Allgemeine Zeitung* was one of the first newspapers to be produced by a full-time, professional editor. Initially, Cotta tried to engage the poet and historian Friedrich Schiller as editor, but then the well-known historical-political writer and Baden professor Ernst Ludwig Posselt accepted the job. Posselt received an annual salary of 2,196 Gulden, plus half of the profit from every copy over 1,250 sold.[54] Cotta paid particular attention to building up a unique network of correspondents, which cost him 5,500 Gulden a year. He himself maintained contacts with a wide range of influential, well-informed and high-ranking political decision-makers. This strategy undoubtedly increased the standing of his newspaper, but it also meant that it was occasionally subjected to the state's propaganda measures.[55]

Finally, pamphlets were a fourth medium of the emerging public sphere.[56] They were easy to produce, if necessary clandestinely, and could be distributed quickly and in a targeted way. Especially at times of political unrest, they represented a welcome means of communication because of their flexibility. State propagandists used them for their press campaigns, as did revolutionary journalists, who produced anonymous pamphlets that were illegally distributed. Napoleon, for example, always took a portable printing press with him on his campaigns in order to accompany his military activities with up-to-date bulletins – a strategy that the Prussian generals adopted in the 1813–14 wars of liberation.[57] That period saw the peak of German pamphleteering, when the uncrowned king of the medium was Ernst Moritz Arndt, whose anti-Napoleonic pamphlets were published in print-runs of four to five, and sometimes even six, figures.[58]

The development of a political public which such print activity demonstrates could not be ignored by the state authorities. Indeed, they soon developed comprehensive mechanisms to handle the press. Yet the fragility of the late Enlightenment administrations, to which recent research has drawn our attention,[59] was reflected in the manner and effectiveness with which the press was controlled.[60] As Kiesel and Münch note of German censorship as a whole:

It was based on a whole series of legal regulations; it was applied by numerous censorship colleges and an army of censors; in sum, it was an immense and monstrous institution, which could be understood only in terms of its historical genesis in a Germany that was territorially and confessionally fragmented after the Reformation.[61]

The general legal framework for censorship came from the legislation of the Holy Roman Empire, whose roots went back into the sixteenth century and whose leitmotif was the integrity of the religious, political and moral orders in their traditional form. Both the Reich's censorship authorities (including the imperial book commission, which supervised the holding of fairs in Frankfurt-on-Main) and the censorship authorities of the individual territories had to conform to this legislation, although the territories supplemented imperial legislation with their own laws.[62] Just as the conditions governing the legislative framework in individual territories varied widely, so too did the organisation of the institutions which were set up to exercise censorship and to hunt down and confiscate deviant writing. There was not only a difference between spiritual and secular territories; even within secular territories the structure of censorship authorities varied considerably. Added to this was the fact that these institutions were frequently reorganised during the late eighteenth century, not least because the demands made of censorship changed constantly in response to the dynamic of the literary market. Given all this, it is not surprising that the practice of censorship varied widely in different territories, and that next to states which attempted to maintain a rigid censorship regime there were more liberal ones. Authors in particular exploited this situation. Thus, the book market could be only partially controlled, since if a publication was banned in one place, its author could find another. Looking back to the late eighteenth century, the Hamburg bookseller Friedrich Perthes wrote to his Weimar colleague Friedrich Justin Bertusch in 1814:

Germany always had the most complete freedom of the press, in fact and in deed, because anything that was banned in Prussia could be printed in Württemberg, anything that was banned in Hamburg could be printed ten steps away in Altona. No book remained unprinted and undistributed.[63]

Frederician Prussia – the state that is often seen as the model for harsh regimes – particularly demonstrated how inefficient censorship could be in the German territorial states of the eighteenth century. Frederick the Great undoubtedly had the will to bring the press under his control, and during his 46-year reign, he passed forty-three censorship laws.[64] These laws, however, were generally meaningless, for on the whole, Prussian censorship in the second half of the eighteenth century was extremely chaotic.[65] There was no central censorship authority. Instead, numerous institutions, offices and individuals were involved in censoring the different genres of contemporary literature. Those who acted as censors were not specialists, but pursued this activity in addition to their main work. For long periods during the second half of the eighteenth century, the Prussian censorship system was based on close co-operation between censors, publishers and authors. Moreover, roles were not clearly distributed between these three groups:

Many publishers were no mere businessmen, but were proud of their prestige in the Republic of Letters and sometimes wrote books and edited journals themselves. Authors only rarely made a living by their pens; they were often civil servants or members of the clergy. Last, but not least, censors were in most cases *hommes des lettres*.[66]

Given these circumstances, it is obvious that censorship under Frederick the Great was not a particularly efficient instrument of repression, and occasionally, censorship was more of a threat to the supporters of tradition than to enlightened writers.

This cosy arrangement between authors, publishers and the state seems to have changed during the late 1780s. Frederick William II, who had succeeded Frederick the Great in 1786 and was an advocate of orthodox Protestantism, made a number of attempts to eliminate the moderate, liberal climate that had previously dominated Prussia. The measures he took included introducing more stringent censorship regulations. Yet attempts at repression could still misfire.[67] In any case, most German territories responded to the French Revolution and to the more intense political debate it inspired in Germany by passing tougher censorship regulations early in the 1790s. Thus, among others, Austria and Württemberg introduced new censorship laws in 1791, and Prussia tightened up its existing censorship regulations during the 1790s.[68] Control of the press was placed on an entirely new footing again by the French occupation, and the imposition of the Napoleonic system of censorship and control of the press.[69] In concrete terms this meant that loopholes in the German censorship system were closed, while at the same time the French authorities made sure that the press in allied or subject German states toed the political line dictated by the *Moniteur*.[70] In conquered Prussia, for example, French troops marching into Berlin immediately began to monitor the press. The editors of the *Vossische Zeitung* and the *Spenersher Zeitung* (*Speners Newspaper*) were obliged to print French army bulletins, paeans of praise for Napoleon and articles satirising Prussia's military and its royal couple. A French-led office checked all newspapers before publication, and well-known public figures were put under surveillance.[71]

Prussia was no exception. Similar conditions existed in the other German territories. In Bavaria, a French ally, the government successively tightened its control over the press from 1806.[72] This was in part the result of French intervention, but some measures were a form of pre-emptive obedience, designed to prevent Napoleon from intervening in ways that would threaten Bavarian sovereignty. The government also placed more stress on its right to interpret what was 'useful truth'. On 1 January 1807, the editors of both 'state newspapers' were ordered not to print any news that they had not received from the Minister of Foreign

Affairs. In 1808, the government, under pressure from the French, had to ban the *Bamberger Zeitung* (*Bamberg News*). Even before this, a decree had been issued dictating that from now on no 'risky' news was to pass the censors, and that only information from official or already censored papers was to be published. Soon, even domestic news was subjected to censorship. The guidelines were always so vague that the government was able to make arbitrary decisions, making the work of editors, but also of censors, very difficult. Censorship of the press was supplemented by an elaborate system of public opinion polling and surveillance, which went from checking letters to deploying spies in pubs and public places. The government attempted to shape opinions based on the belief that if it was informed early enough about renegades and malcontents, it could counter dangerous tendencies by putting forward 'rational' arguments or issuing prohibitions. Such methods were typical of the enlightened-didactic, absolutist style of government of these years, which could also be found in other German states.[73]

Under such circumstances, it is not surprising that the number of newspapers, books and other material printed in Germany fell, and that the political content of the papers was sharply reduced. The rigorous tutelage in which the press was kept 'not only did not tolerate any word that offended the ruling power, or any phrase that could be turned against it; one already attracted the punishing attention of the police if one neglected, at every opportunity, to praise the government in extravagant language', complained the Württemberg country parson and publisher Johann Gottfried Pahl, whose *National-Chronik der Teutschen* (*National German Chronicle*) was banned by the Stuttgart government in 1809.[74] In cases of doubt, the French authorities did not shrink from drastic interventions: in 1806 the Nuremberg bookseller Palm was sentenced to death and shot for distributing an anonymously written pamphlet, *Deutschland in seiner tiefen Erniedrigung* (*Germany in its Deep Humiliation*).[75] Not until Napoleonic rule in Germany came to an end did the pressure of censorship on political journalism briefly lift. The wars of liberation brought about 'total confusion in large parts of Germany, and even caused orderly censorship to collapse'.[76]

The development of modern state propaganda in Germany following Napoleon's defeat was still closely related to the Napoleonic model. Napoleon's intention 'to conquer Europe not only with troops, but also with propaganda' had a lasting impact on German governments.[77] Napoleon's masterly control of the public sphere inspired his opponents in Germany – initially Austria and Prussia – to change their press policies. The Austrian government felt compelled to give up its traditional attitude of secrecy,[78] without, however, abandoning its claim to control the public sphere absolutely. One of the leading players in this change was Metternich, who, during his time as ambassador in Paris between 1806 and 1809, had become familiar with Napoleon's policy for controlling public opinion.[79] Metternich wrote numerous memoranda to his superiors in Vienna, trying to convince them of the value of an offensive press campaign. In 1809, when he took over government in Austria, he used his experience to try to beat Napoleon on the propaganda field using his own weapons.[80] In the case of Prussia, too, the confrontation with Napoleon, especially the crushing defeat of 1806–7, triggered the development of modern propaganda techniques. State Chancellor Hardenberg, who had already recognised the value of 'public opinion' at the beginning of his career, pursued this policy decisively.[81] With Metternich, he was one of the first German statesmen to recognise the danger posed by Napoleonic propaganda. Like the Austrian minister, he advocated new ways of dealing with the public and referred directly to the example set by the French leader.

The appeal to 'public opinion', therefore, was an integral part of Prussia's struggle against Napoleonic France. In the opinion of Baron Karl vom und zum Stein, 'this wicked nation [France]' must 'succumb to public opinion, if it is stirred up in the right way'.[82] At the same time, press policy, like all reforms of that period, was intended to have an impact at home: to awaken public spirit and encourage the whole nation to take part in the polity in order to renew it. Reformers addressed previously neglected social groups,[83] and 'public opinion' was promoted into a legitimating authority, though one based on duty and reason, rather than direct political participation on the part of the people. In the process, a sense of Prussian national identity emerged.[84] Former Minister Stein's vision of a once only *'levée en masse'* against Napoleon was not shared, however, by Hardenberg, who was more cautious and tended to favour direction by the authorities.[85] Yet even he supported a wide-reaching press campaign when the revolt began in 1813. Particularly in the area of foreign policy, the Prussian press was given new freedoms and opportunities which broke with existing rules. Thus, numerous pamphlets, proclamations and newspaper and journal articles were published, aiming to 'stimulate and encourage patriotic, Prussian, truly German sentiments'.[86] Although the emotional-patriotic tone of this campaign was primarily directed at Prussia, it could easily expand into the notion of a Prussian-dominated German nation, particularly since it sometimes cultivated an excessive Francophobia, and a disastrous 'delusion of [national] superiority'.[87] The enthusiasm of leading Prussian generals for propaganda and publicity could also be problematic. Feeling unencumbered by diplomatic considerations, they frequently came into conflict with the more cautious political leadership.[88]

The Prussian leadership used the publicity, staff and techniques of the war-time propaganda campaign in the post-war conflict concerning the new German order, when during the Congress of Vienna, a press war broke out with Bavaria. The government of Bavaria, under Maximilian von Montgelas, also had an imposing propaganda apparatus.[89] The Prussians opened their press offensive at the end of 1814, when Bavaria, because of its strict insistence on sovereignty at the Congress of Vienna, had become the main target of an excited campaign in which Prussian power politics, rising German national emotions and traditional views of the Reich combined and reinforced each other. In response, the Bavarian authorities decided to mount an offensive against the Prussian-German movement. As a result, Bavaria became the most important state protagonist, after Prussia and Austria, of the propaganda struggle surrounding the post-war 'German question', and at times, the most virulent opponent – as expressed in the press – of the German national movement. The main organ of this campaign was the journal *Allemannia*, which was founded in 1815 and published anonymously. It has been called 'an experiment, completely unique in the history of the German press, in state-directed clandestine journalism'.[90]

In assessing the propaganda policy of these three German governments, four main points stand out: first, the unmistakable influence of Napoleonic press policy. Second, that propaganda was intended to close the gap between 'public opinion' and the views of the government in favour of the official view. The press, therefore, was to serve the political interests of the state, and was closely controlled by the authorities. Yet the reaction to the campaigns showed that they were successful because officially endorsed opinion already had some support among a public which merely had to be mobilised. This was the case, for example, in Prussia during the wars of liberation. The third point that stands out is that propaganda campaigns were conducted overwhelmingly by servants of the state. On the one hand, this was an expression of rulers' desire to direct opinion, but it also reflected the large part played by officials in the political and journalistic discourse of the times. In Bavaria, for example, the editor-in-chief of the *Allemannia* was a Foreign Ministry official, the authors were also mostly high-ranking officials or professors, and there was only one professional journalist among them. In Austria the picture was similar, and only Prussia's government succeeded in gaining the services of a number of independent journalists. The fourth, and final, point which emerges is that the propaganda campaigns of the governments in Berlin, Vienna and Munich were limited to a very brief period: they began during the wars of liberation and ended soon after the Congress of Vienna, when, in the course of the restoration, official policy concerning public debate began to change throughout Germany. Metternich, in particular, and conservative circles within the Prussian bureaucracy wanted to restrict public debate about politics, and limit it to cabinet level again. In this attempt they used the time-honoured instruments of censorship and repression. The Carlsbad Decrees of 1819 and the strong censorship practice of the *Vormärz* (pre-March) period were the result of this reversal.

The development of German print culture was accompanied by intense discussion about the freedom of the press, which unfolded during the final decades of the eighteenth century.[91] Numerous voices spoke out against the existing censorship regime. Frequently, the reform of existing censorship laws was advocated for quite pragmatic reasons. People were aware that regulations were difficult, if not impossible, to enforce, and that this could damage the credibility of the state. Criticism also grew because of the subjective nature of censorship, which depended on the decisions of individual censors. As a way out of this situation, it was recommended that the British model of legislation should be adopted: 'The English ... arrangement whereby every author or printer has to be named, and if necessary, has to take responsibility, seems to me to be the only natural one.'[92] In addition, arguments were made concerning individual rights. This was the basis of remarks made by the philanthropist Carl Friedrich Bahrdt in 1787.[93] For him, 'the freedom to think and to judge' was 'the most holy, most important and most inviolate right of humankind'. Bahrdt believed that this freedom included the opportunity to exchange opinions unimpeded by the state: 'The freedom to communicate one's insights and judgements, in spoken or written form, is simply, like the freedom to think, a holy and inviolate right of humanity which, as a general human right, is above all prince's law.'[94] Other writers argued in similar vein, and consistently questioned the existing form of press control. In addition, it was also thought that the press should function as a means of controlling political power, and that journalism was a way of legitimating contact between subjects and the authorities.[95]

Such thoughts fit easily into Habermas's concept of the structural transformation of the public sphere. However, the question remains as to how typical they were of the debate over the freedom of the press that took place in German enlightened society. For there was also another, quite different, strain of argument.[96] A substantial number of contemporaries from the enlightened milieu believed that restrictions were necessary, and declared censorship to be a legitimate means of state policy. This argument was based on the assumption that most people lacked insight and reason. Truth and enlightenment could not, therefore, be fully bestowed upon them. Consequently, the authorities had to protect them from certain insights – above all, in the interests of preserving political and social cohesion. This was the line taken in 1804 by Johann Friedrich Zöllner, a typical figure in Prussia's enlightened Church bureaucracy:

> reading books is indisputably one of the most effective means of promoting moral and intellectual education. But it is also well known that it has to be selective, planned, and carefully prepared if it is not to be disadvantageous. Apart from the Bible, the hymnal, and one or two devotional tracts suitable for them [the masses], there is little that can be given directly to them... The other printed material in which the masses take delight largely corrupts their reason and their moral feeling. This is why I argue... that all works which are written specifically for the common people should be subject to the strictest and most vigilant censorship.[97]

Such doubts about the rationality of the people were taken even further. The dichotomy between the enlightened elite and the 'immature' masses was seen as fundamental to the problem of freedom of press and opinion. The enlightened elite, in its own interests, was to have the right to unimpeded public discourse, while the masses were to be subjected to intervention by the authorities. Thus, Ernst Ferdinand Klein, one of Prussia's leading legal thinkers and reformers, argued that while the learned world should have freedom for 'philosophical discourse', control should be exercised over 'what the masses read'. In practice, this meant that 'almanacs, the catechism, weekly newspapers and other works intended for the masses are subject to censorship'.[98] Another contemporary wrote:

> General principles do not apply to censorship and freedom of the press. I advocate unrestricted freedom of publication for works intended only for that part of the nation which is already enlightened, and which only they will be able to read. For the reading matter of the common people, by contrast, I believe that a highly vigilant censorship is needed.[99]

Such sentiments were – to a large extent – the result of what the sociologist Hans Weil has described as elite withdrawal and separation on the part of the *Gebildeten* in the eighteenth century.[100] But something more lay behind it: a fear that society would be polarised by the contemporary press. The *Gebildeten* viewed the idea of free journalism acting in opposition to state authority with a degree of concern. The idea that public opinion could be a politically reasoning anti-governmental force lay beyond the intellectual horizons of many enlightened contemporaries. Instead, they opted for a moderate form of public criticism. They saw a suitable corrective to absolutist practice in a moderate 'press freedom', and 'modest judgements about the measures taken by the prince and his servants'.[101] The suggestion was made that recourse could be made to traditional, non-public ways of expressing criticism in the absolutist-bureaucratic state – for example, pleas, petitions and complaints. The aim, consequently, was not public debate as a means by which a broadly based will emerged, but a limited discussion of public affairs by informed, interested and loyal people who, 'unlike wilful boys', would not 'misuse their freedom'.[102] It is not surprising that contemporary writers took such a cautious position on the question of press freedom, for those who discussed this problem frequently held bureaucratic or semi-bureaucratic positions, and had little interest in challenging the political establishment of which they themselves were a part.

These reservations on the part of the *Gebildeten* point to a more general problem concerning a heuristic approach to the history of the press and the public in Germany in the late eighteenth and early nineteenth centuries. Is it really true to say, as Jürgen Habermas does, that private individuals, who had gathered as a public, set about forcing public power to legitimate itself to public opinion? At least some of the writings of the enlightened elite, as we have seen, give us reason to doubt this. In addition, we must remember that the history of the press and the public sphere in Germany ultimately remains unintelligible without reference to the state. Thus, the boom which journals experienced in the late eighteenth century was to a large extent due to authors and readers, who, as we have seen, were in the service of the state. In other words, those who thought about and discussed politics, society and the law were frequently themselves a part of the system that formed the focus for their debate. It therefore makes little sense to assume an opposition between public and state; a more appropriate image is that of a closed circle. This is true of not only the late eighteenth century, but to a certain extent, the early nineteenth century. For as the German states, following the Napoleonic model, tried to pursue an offensive press policy, a public sphere was formed that, to a considerable extent, was the product of official action. The 'structural transformation of the public sphere' that took place in Germany, therefore, was pushed on not only by the laws of commerce and consumption, but equally by the state and its agents.

NOTES

1 See Holger Böning (ed.), *Französische Revolution und deutsche Öffentlichkeit. Wandlungen in Presse und Alltagskultur am Ende des 18. Jahrhunderts* (Munich, 1992); Wolfgang Burgdorf, *Reichskonstitution und Nation. Verfassungsreformprojekte für das Heilige Römische Reich deutscher Nation im politischen Schrifttum von 1648 bis 1806* (Mainz, 1998).

2 Wolfram Siemann, 'Propaganda um Napoleon in Württemberg. Die Rheinbundära unter König Friedrich I. (1806–1813)', *Zeitschrift für Württembergische Landesgeschichte*, 47 (1988), 359–80. See also Roger Dufraisse, 'Témoignages sur le culte de Napoléon dans les pays de la rive gauche du Rhin (1797–1811)', *Jahrbuch für westdeutsche Landesgeschichte*, 2 (1976), 255–84; Antje Seimer, '"Moi, toujours moi, rien que moi" – Zu einigen Facetten des Napoleonbildes in der deutschen Publizistik', in Böning (ed.), *Französische Revolution*, 309–22.
3 Michael Stolleis, *Geschichte des öffentlichen Rechts*, vol. I: *Reichspublizistik und Policeywissenschaft 1600–1800* (Munich, 1988), p. 64.
4 Hans H. Gerth, *Bürgerliche Intelligenz um 1800. Zur Soziologie des deutschen Frühliberalismus* (Göttingen, 1976); Hans Erich Bödeker, 'Die "gebildeten Stände" im späten 18. und frühen 19. Jahrhundert: Zugehörigkeit und Abgrenzungen. Mentalitäten und Handlungspotentiale', in Jürgen Kocka (ed.), *Bildungsbürgertum im 19. Jahrhundert*, part IV (Stuttgart, 1989), 21–52.
5 Birgit Fratzke-Weiss, *Europäische und nationale Konzeptionen im Rheinbund. Politische Zeitschriften als Medien der politischen Öffentlichkeit* (Frankfurt-on-Main, 1998), esp. pp. 85–141.
6 Jörg Requate, *Journalismus als Beruf. Entstehung und Entwicklung des Journalistenberufs im 19. Jahrhundert. Deutschland im internationalen Vergleich* (Göttingen, 1995); James Retallack, 'From pariah to professional? The journalist in German society and politics, from the late Enlightenment to the rise of Hitler', *German Studies Review*, 16 (1993), 175–223.
7 Johann Goldfriedrich, *Geschichte des Deutschen Buchhandels vom Beginn der klassischen Litteraturperiode bis zum Beginn der Fremdherrschaft (1740–1804)*, 3 (Leipzig, 1909), p. 249.
8 Requate, *Journalismus als Beruf*, pp. 126ff; Retallack, 'From pariah to professional?', pp. 184ff.
9 Gerth, *Bürgerliche Intelligenz*, pp. 63f.
10 Joseph Görres, 'Die teutschen Zeitungen', *Rheinischer Merkur*, 80 (1 July 1814).
11 Quotations from C[hristoph] M[artin] Wieland, *Gespräche unter vier Augen* (Leipzig, 1799), Gespräch no. 9: 'Über die öffentliche Meinung', 304–46, pp. 315 and 345. Quoted by Karl Heinz Schäfer, *Ernst Moritz Arundt als politischer Publizist. Studien zu Publizistik, Presspolitik und kollektivem Bewusstsein in frühen 19. Jahrhundert* (Bonn, 1974), p. 31. See also Franz Schneider, *Pressefreiheit und politische Öffentlichkeit: Studien zur politischen Geschichte Deutschlands bis 1848* (Berlin, 1966), pp. 108–10.
12 Reinhard Wittmann, 'Der lesende Landmann. Zur Rezeption aufklärerischer Bemühungen durch die bäuerliche Bevölkerung im 18. Jahrhundert', in Wittmann, *Buchmarkt und Lektüre im 18. und 19. Jahrhundert. Beiträge zum literarischen Leben 1750–1880* (Tübingen, 1982), 1–45.
13 Martina Graf, 'Buch und Lesekultur in der Residenzstadt Braunschweig zur Zeit der Spätaufklärung unter Herzog Karl Wilhelm Ferdinand (1770–1806)', *Archiv für Geschichte des Buchwesens*, 42 (1994), 1–317, p. 228.
14 Theodor Bitterauf, 'Zur Geschichte der öffentlichen Meinung im Königreich Bayern im Jahre 1813 bis zum Abschluss des Vertrages von Ried', *Archiv für Kulturgeschichte*, 11 (1913–14), 31–69, p. 56
15 Rudolf Schenda, *Volk ohne Buch. Studien zur Sozialgeschichte der populären Lesestoffe 1770–1910* (Frankfurt-on-Main, 1970), p. 444.

16 Rolf Engelsing, *Der Bürger als Leser. Lesergeschichte in Deutschland 1500–1800* (Stuttgart, 1974); Reinhard Wittmaun, *Geschichte des deutschen Buchhandels. Ein Überblick* (Munich, 1991), pp. 172–9.
17 Goldfriedrich, *Geschichte des deutschen Buchhandels*, p. 250. Dominik von König, 'Lesesucht und Lesewut', in Herbert G. Göpfert (ed.), *Buch und Leser. Vorträge des ersten Jahrestreffens des Wolfenbütteler Arbeitskreises für Geschichte des Buchwesens 13. und 14. Mai 1976* (Hamburg, 1977), pp. 89–112; Schenda, *Volk ohne Buch*, p. 88; Silke Schlichtmann, *Geschlechterdifferenz in der Literaturrezeption um 1800? Zu zeitgenössischen Goethe-Lektüren* (Tübingen, 2001).
18 See Rolf Engelsing, *Analphabetentum und Lektüre* (Stuttgart, 1973), pp. 54–68; Engelsing, *Bürger als Leser*; Schenda, *Volk ohne Buch*; Erich Schön, *Der Verlust der Sinnlichkeit oder Die Verwandlung des Lesers. Mentalitätswandel um 1800* (Stuttgart, 1987), pp. 298–300.
19 See the comments on 'gemeinsames Rezipieren' (reading in common) in Schön, *Der Verlust der Sinnlichkeit*, pp. 177–222.
20 Otto Dann (ed.), *Lesegesellschaften und bürgerliche Emanzipation. Ein europäischer Vergleich* (Munich, 1981); Georg Jäger and Jörg Schönert (eds.), *Die Leihbibliothek als Institution des literarischen Lebens im 18. und 19. Jahrhundert. Organisationsformen, Bestände und Publikum* (Hamburg, 1980).
21 Helmuth Kiesel and Paul Münch, *Gesellschaft und Literatur im 18. Jahrhundert. Voraussetzungen und Entstehung des literarischen Marktes in Deutschland* (Munich, 1977), p. 181.
22 Goldfriedrich, *Geschichte des Deutschen Buchhandels*, p. 557.
23 See Wittmann, *Geschichte des deutschen Buchhandels*, pp. 112ff.
24 Hans Erich Bödeker, 'Journals and public opinion. The politicisation of the German Enlightenment in the second half of the eighteenth century', in Eckhart Hellmuth (ed.), *The Transformation of Political Culture. England and Germany in the Late Eighteenth Century* (Oxford, 1990), 423–46, pp. 427ff. See also Paul Hocks and Peter Schmidt, *Literarische und politische Zeitschriften 1789–1805* (Stuttgart, 1975); Margot Lindemann, *Deutsche Presse bis 1815* (Berlin, 1969), pp. 180–247; Joachim Kirchner (ed.), *Bibliographie der Zeitschriften des deutschen Sprachgebiets bis 1900*, 4 vols. (Stuttgart, 1969–89), vol. I: *Die Zeitschriften des deutschen Sprachgebiets von den Anfängen bis 1830* (Stuttgart, 1969).
25 Joachim Kirchner, *Die Grundlagen des deutschen Zeitschriftenwesens. Mit einer Gesamtbibliographie der deutschen Zeitschriften bis zum Jahre 1790*, 2 vols. (Leipzig, 1928/31), vol. I: *Bibliographische und buchhandelsgeschichtliche Untersuchungen* (Leipzig, 1928), 38–55, esp. pp. 49ff and p. 54.
26 See Ulrike Weckel, *Zwischen Häuslichkeit und Öffentlichkeit. Die ersten deutschen Frauenzeitschriften im späten 18. Jahrhundert und ihr Publikum* (Tübingen, 1998).
27 See Daniel L. Purdy, *The Tyranny of Elegance. Consumer Cosmopolitanism in the Era of Goethe* (Baltimore, MD, 1998).
28 Wolfgang Martens, *Botschaft der Tugend. Die Aufklärung im Spiegel der deutschen Moralischen Wochenschriften* (Stuttgart, 1968).
29 See, for example, Bödeker, 'Journals and public opinion', p. 430.
30 See Holger Böning, *Das Intelligenzblatt. Dokumentation zu einer literarisch-publizistischen Gattung der deutschen Aufklärung* (Bremen, 1991); Thomas

Kempf, *Aufklärung als Disziplinierung*. *Studien zum Diskurs des Wissens in den Intelligenzblättern und gelehrten Blättern der zweiten Hälfte des 18. Jahrhunderts* (Munich, 1991).
31 Holger Böning, 'Aufklärung und Presse im 18. Jahrhundert', in Hans-Wolf Jäger (ed.), *'Öffentlichkeit' im 18. Jahrhundert* (Göttingen, 1997), 151–63, pp. 158 and 160.
32 Fratzke-Weiss, *Europäische und nationale Konzeptionen*, pp. 35ff.
33 On the *Berlinische Monatsschrift* see Norbert Hinske (ed.), *Was ist Aufklärung? Beiträge aus der Berlinischen Monatsschrift*, 4th edn (Darmstadt, 1990); P. Weber (ed.), *Berlinische Monatsschrift (1783–1796)* (Leipzig, 1986).
34 See Elmar Wadle and Gerhard Sauder (eds.), *Georg Friedrich Rebmann (1768–1824). Autor, Jakobiner, Richter* (Sigmaringen, 1997).
35 See Bödeker, 'Journals and public opinion', pp. 430ff.
36 Gerhard Schuck, *Rheinbundpatriotismus und politische Öffentlichkeit zwischen Aufklärung und Frühliberalismus. Kontinuitätsdenken und Diskontinuitätserfahrung in den Staatsrechts- und Verfassungsdebatten der Rheinbundpublizistik* (Stuttgart, 1994), pp. 55–63.
37 Stolleis, *Geschichte des öffentlichen Rechts*, vol. I, p. 320.
38 Schuck, *Rheinbundpatriotismus*, pp. 22ff.
39 See Bödeker, 'Journals and public opinion', pp. 435ff.
40 Ibid., p. 441.
41 Böning, 'Aufklärung und Presse', p. 152. Figures from Martin Welke, 'Zeitung und Öffentlichkeit im 18. Jahrhundert. Betrachtungen zur Reichweite und Funktion der periodischen deutschen Tagespublizistik', in Elger Blühm (ed.), *Presse und Geschichte*, vol. I: *Beiträge zur historischen Kommunikationsforschung* (Munich, 1977), 71–99. See also Brigitte Tolkemit, *Der Hamburgische Correspondent. Zur öffentlichen Vorbereitung der Aufklärung in Deutschland* (Tübingen, 1995), pp. 2–8.
42 Welke, 'Zeitung und Öffentlichkeit im 18. Jahrhundert'.
43 Tolkemit, *Der Hamburgische Correspondent*, pp. 30ff.
44 Welke, 'Zeitung und Öffentlichkeit im 18. Jahrhundert', p. 79.
45 Holger Böning, 'Zeitungen für das "Volk". Ein Beitrag zur Entstehung periodischer Schriften für einfache Leser und zur Politisierung der deutschen Öffentlichkeit nach der Französischen Revolution', in Böning (ed.), *Französische Revolution*, 467–526.
46 Welke, 'Zeitung und Öffentlichkeit im 18. Jahrhundert', pp. 80ff.
47 For Bavaria, see Theodor Bitterauf, 'Die Zensur der politischen Zeitungen in Bayern 1799–1825', in Karl A. von Müller (ed.), *Riezler-Festschrift. Beiträge zur bayerischen Geschichte* (Gotha, 1913), 305–51.
48 See Tolkemit, *Der Hamburgische Correspondent;* Lindemann, *Deutsche Presse*, pp. 162–5.
49 Tolkemit, *Der Hamburgische Correspondent*, pp. 46–52.
50 Ibid., pp. 10ff.
51 See Michaela Breil, *Die Augsburger 'Allgemeine Zeitung' und die Pressepolitik Bayerns. Ein Verlagsunternehmen zwischen 1815 und 1848* (Tübingen, 1996). Also Eduard Heyck, *Die Allgemeine Zeitung 1798–1898. Beiträge zur Geschichte der deutschen Presse* (Munich, 1898).

52 Breil, *Augsburger 'Allgemeine Zeitung'*, pp. 42ff.
53 Daniel Moran, *Toward the Century of Words. Johann Cotta and the Politics of the Public Sphere in Germany, 1795–1832* (Berkeley, CA, 1990); Retallack, 'From pariah to professional?', p. 183; Monika Neugebauer-Wölk, *Revolution und Constitution. Die Brüder Cotta. Eine biographische Studie zum Zeitalter der Französischen Revolution und des Vormärz* (Berlin, 1989).
54 Michael von Rintelen, *Zwischen Revolution und Restauration. Die Allgemeine Zeitung 1798–1823* (Frankfurt-on-Main, 1994), pp. 29ff.
55 Wolfgang Piereth, *Bayerns Pressepolitik und die Neuordnung Deutschlands nach den Befreiungskriegen* (Munich, 1999), pp. 165–70; Andrea Hofmeister-Hunger, *Pressepolitik und Staatsreform. Die Institutionalisierung staatlicher Öffentlichkeitsarbeit bei Karl August von Hardenberg (1792–1822)* (Göttingen, 1994), pp. 310–28.
56 Gert Hagelweide, 'Flugblatt und Flugschrift', in *Handbuch der Publizistik*, vol. III, pp. 39–48; Karl Schottenloher, *Flugblatt und Zeitung. Ein Wegweiser durch das gedruckte Tagesschrifttum* (Berlin, 1922).
57 Hofmeister-Hunger, *Pressepolitik und Staatsreform*, pp. 264–73.
58 Schäfer, *Arndt*, pp. 256ff.
59 See John Brewer and Eckhart Hellmuth (eds.), *Rethinking Leviathan. The Eighteenth-Century State in Britain and Germany* (Oxford, 1999).
60 See Kiesel and Münch, *Gesellschaft und Literatur im 18. Jahrhundert*, pp. 104ff.
61 Ibid., p. 106.
62 Ulrich Eisenhardt, *Die kaiserliche Aufsicht über Buchdruck, Buchhandel und Presse im Heiligen Römischen Reich Deutscher Nation (1496–1806). Ein Beitrag zur Geschichte der Bücher- und Pressezensur* (Karlsruhe, 1970).
63 Quoted from Ludwig Geiger (ed.), 'Buchhändlerbriefe von 1786 bis 1816', *Archiv für die Geschichte des Deutschen Buchhandels*, 8 (1883), p. 323.
64 I owe this reference to Klaus Berndl.
65 Eduardo Tortarola, 'Censorship and the conception of the public in late eighteenth-century Germany: or, are censorship and public opinion mutually exclusive', in Dario Castiglione and Lesley Sharp (eds.), *Shifting the Boundaries. Transformation of the Languages of Public and Private in the Eighteenth Century* (Exeter, 1995), 131–50.
66 Ibid., p. 135.
67 See Klaus Berndl, 'Neues zur Biographie von Ernst Ferdinand Klein', in Eckhart Hellmuth, Immo Meenken and Michael Trauth (eds.), *Zeitenwende? Preußen um 1800* (Stuttgart, 1999), 139–81, esp. pp. 161ff.
68 Lindemann, *Deutsche Presse*, p. 256; Ulrike Schömig, *Politik und Öffentlichkeit in Preußen. Entwicklung der Zensur und Pressepolitik zwischen 1740 und 1819* (Würzburg, 1988).
69 Rüdiger Busch, *Die Aufsicht über das Bücher- und Pressewesen in den Rheinbundstaaten Berg, Westfalen und Frankfurt* (Karlsruhe, 1970); Karlheinz Fuchs, *Bürgerliches Räsonnement und Staatsräson. Zensur als Instrument des Despotismus. Dargestellt am Beispiel des rheinbündischen Württemberg (1806–1813)* (Göppingen, 1975); Heribert Gisch, '"Preßfreiheit" – "Preßfrechheit". Zum Problem der Presseaufsicht in napoleonischer Zeit (1806–1818)', in Heinz-Dietrich Fischer (ed.), *Deutsche Kommunikationskontrolle des 15. bis 20. Jahrhunderts* (Munich, 1982), 56–74; Schneider, *Pressefreiheit*, pp. 173–7.

70 Schäfer, *Arndt*, p. 58. See also Gisch, '"Preßfreiheit" – "Preßfrechheit"'.
71 Hofmeister-Hunger, *Pressepolitik und Staatsreform*, p. 187.
72 Piereth, *Bayerns Pressepolitik*, pp. 50–7.
73 Wolfram Siemann, '*Deutschlands Ruhe, Sicherheit und Ordnung.*' *Die Anfänge der politischen Polizei 1806–1866* (Tübingen, 1985), pp. 48–71.
74 Schäfer, *Arndt*, p. 59. On Pahl and the *National-Chronik*: Schuck, *Rheinbundpatriotismus*, pp. 31–5.
75 Otto Tschirch, 'Die Flugschrift "Deutschland in seiner tiefen Erniedrigung" und ihr Verfasser', *Historische Zeitschrift*, 165 (1942), 47–71.
76 Schäfer, *Arndt*, p. 59.
77 Schneider, *Pressefreiheit*, pp. 173–7, quotation at p. 173. André Cabanis, *La presse sous le Consulat et l'Empire (1799–1814)* (Paris, 1975).
78 Schneider, *Pressefreiheit*, pp. 55–66.
79 Wolfgang Piereth, 'Propaganda im 19. Jahrhundert. Die Anfänge aktiver staatlicher Pressepolitik in Deutschland (1800–1871)', in Ute Daniel and Wolfram Siemann (eds.), *Propaganda. Meinungskampf, Verführung und politische Sinnstiftung 1789–1989* (Frankfurt-on-Main, 1994), 21–43, pp. 23–6; Schneider, *Pressefreiheit*, pp. 177–83.
80 See Metternich's letter to Stadion, 3 April 1809: Metternich-Winneburg (ed.), *Aus Metternichs nachgelassenen Papieren*, vol. II, p. 295.
81 Hofmeister-Hunger, *Pressepolitik und Staatsreform*, pp. 25–145; Thomas Stamm-Kuhlmann, '"Man vertraue doch der Administration!" Staatsverständnis und Regierungshandeln des preußischen Staatskanzlers Karl August von Hardenberg', *Historische Zeitschrift*, 264 (1997), 613–54, esp. pp. 629–33.
82 Stein to Friedrich Wilhelm Count von Götzen; 8 June 1809: in Georg Heinrich Pertz, *Das Leben des Feldmarschalls Grafen Neithardt von Gneisenau* (Berlin, 1864), vol. I, p. 502; Dieter Riesenberger, 'Freiherr vom Stein. Öffentliche Meinung, Kriegsmobilisierung und politische Neuordnung', in Jost Dülffer (ed.), *Kriegsbereitschaft und Friedensordnung in Deutschland 1800–1814* (Münster and Hamburg, 1995), 57–75.
83 Schneider, *Pressefreiheit*, p. 179.
84 Ruth Flad, *Studien zur politischen Begriffsbildung in Deutschland während der preußischen Reformen. Der Begriff der öffentlichen Meinung bei Stein, Arndt und Humboldt* (Berlin and Leipzig, 1929), p. 4.
85 Hofmeister-Hunger, *Pressepolitik und Staatsreform*, pp. 202ff.
86 Instructions from August Count v. d. Goltz, dated 24 June 1813: Paul Czygan, *Zur Geschichte der Tagesliteratur während der Freiheitskriege*, 2 vols., vol. I: *Einführung in die Aktenstücke*; vol. II: *Aktenstücke in zwei Abteilungen* (Leipzig 1909–11), vol. II, part 1, p. 120.
87 Thomas Stamm-Kuhlmann, 'Humanitätsidee und Überwertigkeitswahn in der Entstehungsphase des deutschen Nationalismus. Auffällige Gemeinsamkeiten bei Johann Gottlieb Fichte, Ernst Moritz Arndt und Friedrich Ludwig Jahn', *Historische Mitteilungen*, 4 (1991), 161–71.
88 See, for example, Gerhard Johann David von Scharnhorst's urging of Hardenberg in March 1813, before the foundation of the *Preußische Correspondent*: Czygan, *Freiheitskriege*, vol. II, part 1, pp. 64–6.
89 See Piereth, *Bayerns Pressepolitik*; and Piereth, 'Propaganda im 19. Jahrhundert', pp. 27–32.

90 Karl D'Ester, 'Der Rheinische Merkur von Joseph Görres im Kampf der Meinungen seiner Zeit. (Nach handschriftlichen Quellen)', *Görres-Beiträge. Festgabe zur Jubiläumstagung der Görres-Gesellschaft* (Koblenz, 1926), 63–87, p. 70.

91 See, for example, Eckhart Hellmuth, 'Zur Diskussion um Presse- und Meinungsfreiheit in England, Frankreich und Preußen im Zeitalter der Französischen Revolution', in Günter Birtsch (ed.), *Grund- und Freiheitsrechte im Wandel von Gesellschaft und Geschichte. Beiträge zur Geschichte der Grund- und Freiheitsrechte vom Ausgang des Mittelalters bis zur Revolution von 1848* (Göttingen, 1981), 205–26; Hellmuth, 'Enlightenment and freedom of the press: the debate in the Berlin Mittwochsgesellschaft, 1783–1784', *History*, 83 (1998), 420–44; Franz Schneider, 'Presse, Pressefreiheit, Zensur', in Otto Brunner, Werner Conze and Reinhart Koselleck (eds.), *Geschichtliche Grundbegriffe. Historisches Lexikon zur politisch-sozialen Sprache in Deutschland*, vol. IV (Stuttgart, 1978), 899–927; Schneider, *Pressefreiheit*, pp. 101–45.

92 Anon., 'Censur und Press-Freiheit', in August Schlötzer, *Stats-Anzeigen*, vol. IV (Göttingen, 1783), 420–23, p. 422.

93 John Christian Laursen, 'Literatures of publicity and the right to freedom of the press in late eighteenth-century Germany: the case of Karl Friedrich Bardt', in Castiglione and Sharp (eds.), *Shifting the Boundaries*, 105–30; Hellmuth, 'Zur Diskussion um Presse- und Meinungsfreiheit', pp. 215–16.

94 Carl Friedrich Bahrdt, *Ueber Pressfreiheit und deren Gränzen. Zur Beherzigung für Regenten, Censoren und Schriftsteller* (Züllichau, 1787), pp. 44–5.

95 Bödeker, 'Journals and public opinion', pp. 442ff.

96 See Hellmuth, 'Zur Diskussion um Presse- und Meinungsfreiheit', esp. pp. 210ff.

97 Johann Friedrich Zöllner, *Ideen über Nationalerziehung* (Berlin, 1804), pp. 278–80.

98 Hellmuth, 'Enlightenment and freedom of the press', p. 431.

99 Ibid.

100 Hans Weil, *Die Entstehung des deutschen Bildungsprinzips*, 2nd edn (Bonn, 1967).

101 Ernst Ferdinand Klein, 'Über Denk- und Druckfreiheit. An Fürsten, Minister und Schriftsteller', *Berlinische Monatsschrift*, 3 (1784), 312–30, at p. 328. For evidence that Klein was the author, see Hinske (ed.), *Was ist Aufklärung?*, p. 517.

102 Klein, 'Über Denk- und Druckfreiheit', p. 329.

4 England, 1760–1815

Hannah Barker

This chapter covers an important period in the history of the English press. It begins at the accession of George III in 1760 – often seen as heralding a new phase in the development of popular politics and print culture – and ends in 1815, with the cessation of hostilities against France which had lasted almost twenty-five years. Historians of England have long associated the press with changes in the way the political world operated in the eighteenth century. For John Brewer, it formed a central component of an 'alternative structure of politics' which emerged in the 1760s and which spawned a series of radical movements.[1] For earlier Whig historians, the emergence of the press – and the newspaper press in particular – was part of the inexorable rise of accountable government and democratic society.[2] Although such a Whiggish teleology is misleading on several counts – not least because it ignores the role of the conservative press in combating reform – it is true that from the early eighteenth century newspapers (taken in the widest sense to include most types of serial publication, which included 'news') encouraged the wider population to take an interest, and even to play a part, in political life.

Compared to some of its continental counterparts, the English newspaper press was intensely political and fiercely outspoken. Moreover, English newspapers did not limit their coverage to national or international affairs and – again in contrast to much of the rest of Europe – the press in England provided a consistent and often critical commentary on local events as well. English newspapers would also have appeared unusual to a European readership as they tended to be larger than papers produced elsewhere, contained more text and displayed more varied contents. In addition to news concerning parliament, the court, elections, local government and foreign relations, advertising constituted an important part of a newspaper's make-up, as did information on crime, trade, fashion, theatre, racing and shipping. Both the breadth and depth of coverage displayed by the English newspaper press suggest that it catered for a unique form of public sphere and political arena.

The political views and information that the English newspaper press imparted, coupled with the intense debate which it engendered, helped to bring politics in England out of the restricted arena of the political and social elite to a much wider public. Moreover, through the promotion of certain concepts of liberty, in particular the belief that Britons were all free citizens living in a free state, newspapers encouraged the public to believe they had not just the opportunity, but the right, to involve themselves in the nation's political life, and to protest when they disapproved of government action. Indeed, the press itself was to become the principle medium to articulate and disseminate protests against the government, as well as playing a crucial role in the political education and politicisation of the English people. Bob Harris has further claimed that the press encouraged a greater sense of national consciousness in the eighteenth century.[3] Thus, newspapers helped not just to create public opinion, but also gave it a distinctly national character.

The rise to prominence of 'public opinion' in English political life during the eighteenth century was widely commented upon at the time. Quite who produced public opinion, though, was hotly debated throughout the period, and contemporaries could not agree concerning the identity of 'the public'. For some it described those whose constitutional standing, education or wealth gave them a legitimate say in the nation's affairs; for others, the term was synonymous with the mob. But many understood that it was access to print which secured membership of the public, since politicisation and the growth of print culture were seen to go hand-in-hand. Newspapers themselves encouraged readers to believe that they had a close relationship with each other, and most papers claimed to represent public opinion in some way, particularly by the nineteenth century. Using terms such as 'the people' and 'the public' from the mid-eighteenth century onwards, newspapers increasingly addressed much wider (and less easily definable) sections of the population, rather than presuming to speak only to freeholders, voters or the rich.

In addition to proclaiming their allegiance to public opinion, newspapers also used more subtle methods to encourage their readers that they spoke with 'the voice of the people'. Letter-writers used pseudonyms to suggest that an individual was speaking not for him or herself, but as the representative of a wider social group, or even of the public as a whole. Martin Smith has noted that the signatures of letters published by the *Manchester Herald* and *Manchester Gazette* suggest a 'proletarian' readership: for example, 'one of the common people', 'a plebeian' and numerous letters signed by weavers and spinners.[4] This, in turn, suggests a public which extended fairly low down the social scale. Rather than alienating readers, the anonymity of many newspaper contributions served to promote both newspapers and the political world which they described as inclusive and accessible.

A Prussian traveller, Johann Wilhelm von Archenholz, noted in 1791 how highly the public prized the ability to write anonymously for newspapers. He described the method by which articles and letters could be delivered secretly to printers by means of a special post-box, and claimed that 'if you chose to make yourself known to the printer, he is obliged to observe secrecy. Nothing can force him to violate this, for were he to do so, he would not only lose his business, but also have his house exposed to the fury of the populace.'[5] Many letters consisted of attacks on individual public figures. Newspapers offered the unique opportunity to utter a tirade against, or to appeal to, those individuals – like politicians, ministers, bishops, or even the King – who would normally have been at too great a social distance. As 'John Bull' noted in a letter addressed to the King in 1781, 'it is the Birth-right of all free Britons to study public affairs, it is their duty to lay the result of their enquiries with candour and impartiality before your Majesty, and even the Public, when their views are laudable to your Royal interest, and the Good of their Fellow Citizens'.[6]

Indeed, such was the degree to which the newspaper audience was presumed to be able to involve itself in the nation's political affairs that the modern separation of 'high' and 'low' politics appears artificial and inadequate to describe the complexities of political life, particularly in the capital. Newspapers encouraged their readers to believe that they could participate in the world of politics in a variety of ways: most clearly, in the letters which appeared to allow individuals to address important figures, or the public en masse, and which also gave the opportunity to contribute to public debate in its truest sense. In addition, the familiarity with which those in 'high' politics were described, flattered in its assumption that the well-informed newspaper-reader was politically 'in-the-know', rather than just a passive observer of political life.

As towns across England witnessed a growth in population, newspapers helped promote a new political culture which encouraged individuals outside the political elite to form independent political organisations and to develop further notions of their own rights and liberties. Over time, criticism of central government gave rise to full-scale national movements that aimed to change the way in which society was run. Newspapers both represented and helped to further such movements in crucial ways. Although newspapers in the eighteenth and early nineteenth centuries did not – as a rule – dictate to individual politicians or governments, nor effect policy changes on a day-to-day basis, a fundamental acknowledgement that government was based on consent meant that successive administrations were neither unaffected by newspapers, nor unbending in the face of popular protest. The political elite became increasingly sensitive to the tenor of extra-parliamentary politics and on certain occasions, particularly during periods of political crisis, the press played an important role in altering or promoting existing governmental policy. Moreover, as speeches made in parliament, at election hustings and in public meetings became more commonly reported, speakers at such events were increasingly aware that their message would be conveyed to a much wider audience, and as a result, often modified what was said.[7]

The frequency with which newspapers influenced political decision-making, and the degree of impact that the press had on the general political climate became more marked during the eighteenth century. Such influence was evident during the 1760s, when a press war forced the Prime Minister, the earl of Bute, into the political wilderness, and helped secure both fame and power for one of his main critics, the radical politician John Wilkes. The press helped Wilkes to create a popular movement on a national scale, as his success at capturing much of public opinion outside the ruling elite was given clear expression in the country's newspapers.[8] Wilkes's struggle with the government clearly represented wider political issues for English men and women. Throughout the country newspaper readers were kept apprised of events surrounding him at the same time that they were informed about the war with America.[9] During the 1780s, the newspaper press buttressed the cause of the King and his Prime Minister, William Pitt, against a hostile campaign by supporters of the defunct government of Lord North and Charles James Fox,[10] and in the following decade, newspapers helped promote and define the increasingly polarised nature of English popular politics, whilst the radical press acted as a constant irritant and source of alarm for the government.[11]

The growing role of the newspaper press in British politics was related to the increased prominence of print culture as a whole. However, the place of newspapers in the hierarchy of political print also changed significantly during our period. The essay paper was in decline after the 1760s, and although pamphlets were still hugely important during the American War, they were being slowly eclipsed by newspapers, which increasingly not only provided their readers with the most up-to-date news, but also produced their own commentary on events. Moreover, the extensive publication of letters meant that the relationship between readers and the political opinions espoused by newspapers appeared particularly close: a fact that made them more attractive to their audience. By the 1780s, newspapers had emerged as a force to rival all other forms of political print. Their dominance of the popular political sphere was reinforced by the part they played in several nationally based extra-parliamentary campaigns in the 1780s and 1790s, in particular the parliamentary reform and anti-slavery movements, and in the role of the press in the fierce political arguments surrounding the French Revolution. From this point on, newspapers increasingly dominated public debate: a situation that was not to change until the twentieth century.

Not surprisingly, it was at times of particular political unrest that the newspaper press could appear most influential, and even a source of threat to politicians. In the later part of the eighteenth century, such fears were marked. During the wars with revolutionary France, the writer and politician Edmund Burke charged newspapers with deliberately subverting the moral and social order in France and threatening to do the same in Britain.[12] The end of hostilities with the French in 1815 did little to allay such fears, and the early nineteenth century saw increasing levels of anxiety amongst a ruling class facing growing demands for reform, and, on occasion, believing the country to be on the brink of revolution. Robert Southey, erstwhile reformer, turned defender of the establishment, traced contemporary popular unrest in the 1810s directly to those 'weekly apostles of sedition' which found their way 'to the pot-house in town, and the ale-house in the country, inflaming the turbulent temper of the manufacturer, and disturbing the quiet attachment of the peasant to those institutions under which he and his fathers have dwelt in peace'.[13]

Despite the alarm shown by members of the ruling elite at radical and 'seditious' publications, however, state action against the press was limited. No doubt many shared the view of the politician Henry Bankes that the press was 'a tremendous engine in the hands of mischievous men',[14] but the country's rulers either felt unwilling or unable to counteract any but the most extreme of publications. One reason for this was the ambivalence with which many politicians viewed the press. It was true that a hostile press was a thorn in any government's side, but it was equally the case that a supportive press could prove a great advantage. Moreover, and more importantly, despite the loud declamations made about the threat to constitutional stability posed by newspapers, few, if any, politicians would have believed that the press on its own could either initiate radical change in the way in which society was governed, or dictate the identity of the party in power.

Despite the existence of a series of sweeping laws in the eighteenth and early nineteenth centuries, the press in England was rarely subject to a system of organised government or legal repression, and it certainly never experienced the kind of rigorous censorship which occurred in parts of Continental Europe (providing a source of much comment by foreign visitors).[15] This is not to say that English newspapers were free from governmental constraints, and the eighteenth and early nineteenth centuries witnessed the enactment of a variety of controlling and containing measures. One of these was taxation, although government policy in this area seems to have been driven largely (although not wholly) by the revenue needs of the state, rather than by a desire to keep the press within certain limits. Thus, newspaper taxation, like many other forms of taxation, was at its height at the end of the war with Napoleonic France in 1815, after two decades during which government expenditure had been driven steadily upwards by a war effort unprecedented in its proportions.[16] Enforcement of the taxation laws could be haphazard, though, and an unstamped press thrived from the early eighteenth century, and was especially active in the early nineteenth century. The producers of unstamped papers could rely in the main on bureaucratic inefficiency or the unwillingness of government to prosecute, coupled with their own attempts at evading detection.

Alongside the pressures imposed by taxation, another important restriction on press freedom came from the seditious libel law. This was sweeping in both its reach – in terms of who could be prosecuted – and in its definition of sedition. For almost all of the period under discussion, truth was not a defence, and for much of the eighteenth century the role of the jury was only to determine the fact of publication and the identity of the subject. It was the judge who decided whether the act had been done with criminal intent and if the material concerned did indeed constitute seditious libel. The power which this conferred on the judiciary was a cause of much discontent, and was the motivation for Fox's Libel Act of 1792, which gave juries the right to bring in general verdicts and reduced the part played by judges. However, this change in the law may well have made little difference at the time, since the climate of the 1790s probably encouraged more convictions than previously.[17]

Despite the bulk of legislation concerning the press appearing particularly harsh, royal proclamations were still used throughout the eighteenth century to exhort magistrates to unearth and prosecute the authors and publishers of seditious material at times of political crisis. This suggests the inefficiency with which the law was enforced the rest of the time. Of course, as the amount of political printed matter produced expanded on a dramatic scale, rigorous control of the press became increasingly impractical, even if the government had been sufficiently motivated to try to enact it. Instances of government repression were more than balanced by the amount of anti-administration material that was able to flourish. Even in the midst of the anti-revolutionary paranoia of the 1790s, for example, the state did not attempt a systematic clamping-down on press freedoms (or any other freedoms come to that), and the machinery of repression in England changed very little in the 1790s in comparison with the rest of the eighteenth century.[18]

This is not to say that Pitt's government made no moves against the press, and radical newspapers in particular were often harassed both by central and local apparatuses of the state. The editor of the radical London daily the *Argus*, for example, was forced to flee the country in 1792 to escape a prosecution for seditious libel.[19] The government also made use of *ex officio* informations to combat radical newspapers. This was a legal move which dispensed with the intermediate step of a grand jury and allowed the government to prosecute for libel more or less at will.[20] Very few *ex officio* informations were filed against publishers and printers, but there is no doubt that they served to intimidate the printing community in general. Such action resulted in the destruction of both the *Leicester Chronicle* and the *Manchester Herald* in 1793.[21] In the case of the *Herald*, the government brought as many as thirteen informations and indictments against the paper within a matter of months.[22]

Whilst governments might bully certain sections of the press, the state also conceded some of its powers following legal battles in the 1760s and 1770s, when politicians lost their ability to issue general warrants and to prevent the publication of parliamentary debates.[23] The results of government action against the press were piecemeal and scarcely uniform in their impact, particularly outside London. Thus, in 1794, a friend of the political reformer Christopher Wyvill recommended Solomon Hodgson's *Newcastle Chronicle* to him, as it was run by 'a man ... very firm to the cause of liberty & reform & ... not to be dismay'd at the threats that are constantly made to intimidate him'.[24] In addition, some of the London newspapers, most notably the *Morning Chronicle* and the *Morning Post*, also opposed the government throughout the 1790s. Some years later, during the wars with Napoleonic France, the lack of an official or even a voluntary form of press censorship caused the government alarm on several occasions as sensitive military information was divulged which – it was claimed – the enemy might have used to its advantage. Whilst commanding in the Peninsula, the Duke of Wellington often had cause to complain of the freedom with which the press discussed the military situation. In March 1812, he wrote to his brother, Lord Wellesley, that the next campaign should prove a success 'unless those admirably useful institutions, the English newspapers, should have given Bonaparte the alarm, and should have induced him to order his marshals to assemble their troops to oppose me'.[25]

In addition to the enactment of legal restraints, the press was subject to more subtle means of 'high' political interference. The payment of 'subsidies' or bribes during the eighteenth century became a dominant theme for many historians of the press. Perhaps the most influential of these was Arthur Aspinall, whose work depicts eighteenth-century newspapers as victims of the supposedly rampant and pervasive corruption of the period.[26] Aspinall's views were based largely on politicians' correspondence and government papers, and the resultant 'high' political vision is too narrow to show fully the relationship between newspapers and the wider political world. He asserted that the sale of newspapers in the eighteenth century was too restricted to make them self-supporting, and that they were therefore dependent for their survival on political subsidy. Yet this was unlikely to have been the case, since newspapers were increasingly profitable during this period, whilst levels of bribery appear to have been relatively low. In the early 1780s, the *Morning Post*, for example, paid out dividends of £1,500 and made returns for its owners of 18 per cent,[27] whilst in 1788, a third share in the *World* was worth £4,000.[28] Christie has shown that by the 1810s a successful paper such as the *Morning Chronicle* could make annual profits of £12,000.[29] Indeed, Aspinall himself argued that by around 1815 newspapers were becoming so profitable, and governments so poor by comparison, that full-scale 'corruption' was no longer an option. As Lord Liverpool wrote to Castlereagh in that year,

> no paper that has any character, and consequently an established sale, will accept money from the Government; and, indeed, their profits are so enormous in all critical times, when their support is most necessary, that no pecuniary assistance that Government could offer would really be worth their acceptance.[30]

But newspapers were not wholly, or even largely, open to control by political subsidy even before the nineteenth century. The relationship between politicians and newspapers throughout the period under discussion was a complex one, but by and large, subsidy was not the controlling force in newspaper politics. For the most part newspapers depended on advertising revenue and, more importantly, sales, to make money. Newspapers in England were, above all, commercial enterprises. Given the basis of newspaper profitability, newspapermen concentrated on increasing readership and advertising revenue as the means to ensure financial security, rather than chasing relatively small political bribes.[31] It was the profitability of newspapers, not the availability of politicians' money, which led to an increase in titles as the period progressed. This development was not, of course, limited to London, and the provincial press also grew prolifically (with less question here of political subsidy, at least in the eighteenth century). There is no doubt that political 'corruption' was not uncommon. What we need to remember is that the relationship between newspapers and politicians was complicated: that politically inspired plans often failed or even backfired, and that for every 'corrupt' paper sold, many others which were opposed to the government (the main briber of newspapers) were consumed by the public.

As public opinion, rather than political manipulation, was the driving force behind newspaper politics, the Earl of Bute's famous attempt to influence the public mood by rigging press coverage in the 1760s largely backfired. Although he hired a gang of journalists to sing the Administration's praises, their efforts made little difference in the face of hugely popular papers such as the *North Briton* and the *Monitor*.[32] Government Secret Service accounts show that several thousand pounds were given to newspapers and writers during the early 1780s, yet both North's ministry, and that of the Rockingham Whigs which followed it, proved singularly unsuccessful at arranging support from a majority of London newspapers.[33] Despite the existence of political backers, newspapers struggled if they did not attract readers. In 1811, for example, the *National Adviser* was started in London with the support of some politically motivated 'gentlemen of respectability' who were eager to counter 'Jacobinical principles'. However, as the editor was to relate to Lord Sidmouth in 1813, low sales meant the paper proved too expensive to continue on the basis of only 'the most distinguished and flattering support from a highly respectable, it not a numerous body of readers'.[34] Outside London, the gentlemen of Kendal who joined together in 1818 hoping to counteract the 'vile effects' upon the 'lower orders' of the established *Kendal Chronicle*, found that their paper, the *Westmorland Gazette*, was never a great success.[35]

When trying to suppress or influence newspapers, politicians came up against powerful ideological opposition stemming from a belief in the sanctity of the liberty of the press. For much of our period, the majority of commentators argued – *contra* Edmund Burke – that the press was not a threat to the constitution, but its main form of protection. The 'liberty of the press' was a powerful rhetorical concept, and was seen as a means of defending the country against corrupt government, by publicising the actions of its rulers in its role as a public watchdog. Even the conservative lawyer William Blackstone defended a free press, arguing that 'the liberty of the press is indeed essential to the nature of a free state ... Every man has an undoubted right to lay what sentiment he pleases before the public; to forbid this, is to destroy the freedom of the press.'[36] Although the press was not depicted as a 'fourth estate' until the 1820s, the foreign commentator Jean de Lolme described censorial power in England as resting with the people, supported by a free press, as early as 1771.[37] In his view, the liberty of the press provided the 'extreme security' of the constitution:

it is the public notoriety of all things, that constitutes the supplemental power, or check, which ... is so useful to remedy the unavoidable insufficiency of the laws, and keep within their respective bounds all those persons who enjoy any share of public authority.[38]

For some, then, the liberty of the press was a central pillar of the constitution. 'Against venal Lords, Commons, or juries', claimed the Whig politician, Richard Brinsley Sheridan, 'against despotism of any kind or in any shape – let me but array a free Press, and the liberties of England will stand unshaken.'[39] Such arguments were increasingly used in the nineteenth century not just to promote the proper functioning of the existing constitution, but also to campaign for a greater say amongst the population at large in how the country was run. Crucial to this development was the use of the press as a source of information and a form of political education. Thus, a writer in *Lloyd's Evening Post* noted in 1780: 'Without newspapers ... our Country Villager, the Curate, and the Blacksmith, would lose the self-satisfaction of being as wise [as] our First Minister of State.'[40] Knowledge was seen by many as a crucial weapon for the common man in the fight against unfair government. The Manchester radical Thomas Cooper informed Edmund Burke in 1792 that 'ignorance was the ally of the courts, and information was the ally of the people'.[41] Newspapers themselves increasingly encouraged such interpretations of their role. Many used symbols such as Hermes, messenger of the Gods, and the all-seeing eye with the motto '*nunquam dormio*' (I never sleep). Titles such as the 'Sun', the 'Star', the 'Comet' and the 'Lantern' suggested the enlightening effects which the newspaper press bestowed on society, while its supposed guiding and protecting properties were apparent in titles such as 'Champion', 'Moderator', 'Vindicator' and 'Sentinel'.[42]

Yet despite the general enthusiasm shown for the enlightening effects of print, throughout our period a few commentators who supported a free press still warned of its propensity to delude the public if used corruptly. The Whig writer Vicesimus Knox was convinced of the potential for harm. In 1795 he wrote:

Perhaps there is nothing which contributes so much to diffuse the spirit of despotism as venal newspapers, hired by the possessors of power, for the purpose of defending and prolonging their possession. The more ignorant classes have a wonderful propensity to be credulous in all that they see in print, and will obstinately continue to believe a newspaper, to which they have been accustomed, even when notorious facts give it the lie.[43]

Not only could the proper role of the press be perverted, but some conservative commentators denied that the public had any right to know about, or comment on, politics at all. In particular, they attacked the legitimacy of popular sovereignty implied by the concept of the liberty of the press. The MP William Windham, who blamed parliamentary reporting for the naval riots of 1797, argued that the press was changing the relationship between the people and the House of Commons, since it gave

> the People an opportunity of sitting in judgement every day on the measures under discussion in that House, tumultuously to express its disapprobation or approbation – and favoured the propensity of all vulgar minds, perhaps also of minds of no mean endowments, to form premature or intemperate decisions upon the whole matter, long before the details of its parts and the character of its principles could be discussed and unfolded by the Legislature.[44]

But protests such as this were increasingly swimming against the tide, as newspapers became yet more entrenched in English politics at all levels and championing the liberty of the press ceased to be the preserve of radicals and reformers. The potency of ideas about press freedom and the degree to which print became an accepted part of everyday life was such that many nineteenth-century conservative commentators also began to argue for the positive effects of the press.[45]

As the increasingly high profile of the press in English society suggests, there was a dramatic increase in the number of newspapers produced in England during the eighteenth and nineteenth centuries. By 1760, newspapers were established in most of the major towns of England. A surge in the last two decades of the eighteenth century meant that by 1800 over seventy provincial newspapers were published each week.[46] A lack of records makes it difficult to give newspaper circulation figures, at least before the 1830s, with any degree of certainty. However, the survival of some taxation records means we know that 9.4 million newspaper stamps (a stamp appearing on each legitimately produced paper as a record of the tax paid) were issued in 1760 and 12.6 million in 1775. In 1801, 7 million stamps were issued for London papers and 9.4 million for those produced in the provinces (or 16.4 million in total); by 1816 the total sale of stamps had reached over 22 million.[47]

It is likely that individual London papers had circulations of between 2,000 and 5,000 in the 1780s, and that despite the rise in overall circulation, the sales of individual papers did not increase dramatically in the early years of the nineteenth century. According to government estimates in 1811, seven London papers had circulations of around 3,000, with the *Courier*, the *Times* and the *Evening Mail* enjoying sales of over 5,000.[48] Outside London, despite the boom in the number of titles, sales of individual papers were generally lower. In the second half of the eighteenth century most papers would have sold 1,000–2,000 copies.[49] A trend of slow growth continued into the nineteenth century. Based partly on Stamp Office records, Wadsworth estimated that a majority of provincial newspapers produced fewer than 2,000 copies per week before 1850 – although there were some notable exceptions.[50]

Despite the relatively slow growth in the circulation of individual titles, throughout the eighteenth and early nineteenth centuries newspaper production as a whole grew at a much faster rate than did the country's population. The period also witnessed unprecedented levels of urban growth. This development had great implications for the expansion of the newspaper press. It was in towns where newspapers were not only produced, but also largely consumed. Here the newspaper press could thrive, surrounded as it was by a large and accessible market and other features of urban development which encouraged the popularity and circulation of newspapers, such as inns, shops, book clubs, coffee houses and, most importantly, a vigorous and active local political culture whose participants demanded a steady source of news, information and debate. Whilst these may seem like the perfect ingredients for Habermas's bourgeois public sphere, this new arena – like the press which it supported – was not restricted to the middle classes.

This lack of social limitation on the part of newspapers was evident despite the fact that their price (at least in the case of the 'legitimate', tax-paying press) was kept high by government taxation. The average 1757 price of $2\frac{1}{2}$d, for example, constituted about 5 per cent of a London labourer's total weekly wage, and almost 10 per cent of one working in the countryside. The highest price of 7d, reached in 1815, appears to have constituted a lower percentage of some workers' pay. For London artisans, the cost of a newspaper was about 2 per cent of their weekly wage, but it was still between 6 and 12 per cent of the money received by labourers outside London, such as pitmen on the Tyne and Wear and lead miners in the Pennines.[51] It was the constant complaint of newspaper publishers that advertising and sales taxes threatened to ruin their businesses, and the success of unstamped newspapers at various points suggests that a cheap press could ensure a larger market than could more expensive, stamped papers.

Yet high prices did not necessarily mean low or socially restricted readerships between 1760 and 1815, as relatively few papers would have been read by just one person. Whilst estimates of the degree of multiple readership which took place have varied a good deal, there is little doubt that the proportion of newspaper readers was higher in the capital than anywhere else during the eighteenth and early nineteenth centuries. In the late eighteenth century, the political agent Dennis O'Bryen believed that there were 250,000 newspaper readers in the capital, an estimate of ten readers for each paper.[52] O'Bryen's figure constitutes one-third of the London population. Looking back even earlier, Michael Harris has calculated that by the middle of the eighteenth century there were 100,000 newspapers sold there every week,[53] or about 16,500 per day (Monday–Saturday). Using the same multiplier of ten, this suggests that one-quarter of the capital's residents read a newspaper in 1750, compared with a third in the 1780s. This proportion does not appear to have increased much by the turn of the century, although readership seems to have increased steeply by 1840 to as much as five-sixths of the London population.[54]

Estimating the number of newspaper readers in the provinces is equally problematic and speculative. In 1750, there were at least forty provincial newspapers produced in England. If we assume a weekly print-run of 1,000 copies for each, this means that an estimated 40,000 copies of provincial newspapers appeared every week. The number of people who read each paper was probably lower in the provinces than in the capital, so if we use a multiplier of five, then the estimated size of the provincial newspaper readership is 200,000, or about 4 per cent of the population in England outside London. By 1780, this figure had probably doubled to 8 per cent; and by the 1830s it may have been 16 per cent.[55] This suggests a much lower level of readership than in the capital, but one that was growing quickly. However, these calculations do not take into account the degree of penetration by London newspapers in the provinces, nor do they show the undoubted importance of regional variation and, in particular, the difference between urban and rural readerships. It was almost certainly the case that a far greater proportion of provincial newspaper readers came from towns and their immediate environs, and that readership was spread more thinly in rural areas.

The correspondence, diaries and memoirs of the upper classes in the eighteenth and early nineteenth centuries leave us in no doubt that newspapers provided a constant source of information, debate and concern for the ruling elite throughout our period. However, since this group was both small and changed very little in size, its members are unlikely to explain the rise in newspaper sales. The pattern of newspaper proliferation during the eighteenth and early nineteenth centuries makes it tempting to link the growth in newspaper readership to the expanding middle classes: the mostly urban, consuming and socially ambitious men and women who have recently received much historical attention. Yet the boom in newspaper circulation outstripped the growth of the middle classes, and other evidence indicates a more extensive broadening of the newspaper-reading public during the eighteenth century.[56]

In both London and the provinces, there is much anecdotal evidence that suggests that those fairly low on the social scale might have had access to newspapers, although more stress was laid on this phenomenon by those commenting on the metropolis. In 1758 Dr Johnson noted that 'all foreigners remark, that the knowledge of the common people of England is greater that that of any other vulgar. This superiority we undoubtedly owe to the rivulets of intelligence, which are continually trickling among us, which every one may catch, and of which every one partakes.'[57] One such foreign writer, Johann Wilhelm von Archenholz, described reading the daily papers to be 'actually an epidemical passion among the English', and noted that 'sometimes a politician will insert an essay on a subject which concerns the welfare of the whole nation, and every body, even a fish-woman, is able to comprehend it. It is not at all uncommon to observe such persons reading and commentating on the public prints.'[58]

Literacy was also thought to be on the increase. In 1791, the London publisher James Lackington described reading amongst 'the poorer sort of farmers, and even the poor country people in general... in short, all ranks and degrees now READ'.[59] This contemporary perception is not necessarily supported by modern historical research, which suggests that even by the mid-nineteenth century, half of the English population could not write (with women less likely to be literate than men).[60] Of course, judging literacy levels amongst any social group is notoriously difficult, particularly as the ability to read was not dependent upon the ability to write.[61] Moreover, the audience for newspapers was not limited to those who could read, since papers could be, and often were, read aloud. David Vincent's work on literacy and popular culture in England between 1750 and 1914 has shown how familial and community networks ensured that most illiterate people knew others who were literate. Vincent argues that 'the skill of reading... was at once a personal and a collective possession':[62] in other words, that those who could read were expected to read aloud to those who could not.

By the late eighteenth century, reading newspapers aloud was common amongst radical groups such as the London Corresponding Society and the Manchester Reformation Society.[63] In 1817, Southey complained to Lord Liverpool that newspapers such as *Cobbett's Register* and *Hone's Register* were 'read aloud in every ale-house' and wherever soldiers met together.[64] In addition to reading papers aloud, sharing newspapers appears to have become increasingly common during our period. In Tiverton in 1799, the radical London *Courier* was reportedly circulated amongst a surgeon, Congregational minister, druggist, undermaster of a local school and a French émigré, before being passed on to a sergemaker and then to 'the common people'. Another copy was said to have been passed around fifteen pairs of hands, and was finally sold to a

Parson Lewis of Clayhanger, according to a hostile observer, 'to poison the honest countrymen'.[65]

For those without the opportunity or inclination to organise the shared purchase of a newspaper, other options still existed which were cheaper than bearing the whole costs alone. For the price of a drink, coffee and public houses provided access to newspapers for those who could not afford to buy their own. It should be noted, however, that many coffee houses had a more select clientele than other venues in terms of social class, and that they were also likely to be male-dominated spaces, unlike alehouses and taverns, where the company was more mixed.[66] A writer in *Lloyd's Evening Post* in 1780 commented that 'Without newspapers our Coffee-houses, Ale-houses, and Barber shops would undergo a change next to depopulation.'[67] According to Cobbett, newspapers were an even bigger draw for publicans than the beer they served:

Ask the landlord why he takes the newspapers. He'll tell you that it attracts the people to his house, and in many cases its attractions are much stronger than those of the liquor there drunk, thousands upon thousands of men having become sots through the attraction of these vehicles of novelty and falsehood.[68]

Godwin was less critical of pubs, which he described as the labourer's university, a place where men were educated into citizenship.[69]

The eighteenth century also witnessed the rise of libraries and subscription reading rooms, where members paid a fee to gain access to several newspapers. As John Brewer has pointed out, early libraries were not cheap to join, and their cost probably restricted membership to the 'gentle and professional or merchant classes',[70] but this situation was to change somewhat in the nineteenth century. Aspinall notes that by the early 1800s, every large, and many small, towns had their own subscription reading rooms, usually charging a guinea a year.[71] For those less well off, there were smaller scale penny-a-week subscription rooms, generally run by radicals, such as the Union Rooms in Prescot, or the shops of men such as the Manchester brushmaker Joseph Johnson, who was using his establishment as a working-class reading room at the end of the Napoleonic Wars.[72] Poorer readers could also hire newspapers for a fraction of the cover price from hawkers who would then return the papers to the publishers as unsold. Although this practice was made illegal in 1789, it appears to have continued unchecked.[73]

For some historians, the key to discovering the identity of newspaper readers lies not in the accounts of contemporary observers, or in evidence of the population's access to print, but in the newspapers themselves. Text-based approaches assume that what appears to be a paper's targeted audience and what constituted its actual readership are closely related. Schweizer and Klein have used this method in a study of London newspaper advertisements in the early 1790s. From this they have concluded that newspapers were 'a vehicle for the expression of the sentiments of the new moneyed class who comprised a vital segment of the reading public'.[74] It is true that for much of the eighteenth and early nineteenth centuries, newspapers carried a range of advertisements which appear to support the thesis linking them to a growing commercial, consumerist 'middle class'. Thus, for example, one finds a concentration of advertisements for goods and services at the 'luxury' end of the market. But whilst an examination of newspaper advertisements does suggest a certain type of reader, it is an approach which places great weight upon the ability of advertisers to gauge the effectiveness of advertising, and, more importantly, it assumes that advertisers catered for the bulk of newspaper readers. Both assumptions are open to question, and there is evidence to suggest that eighteenth-century advertisers intended to appeal to only a select and richer proportion of newspaper readers.[75]

It has also been argued that other newspaper content betrayed a particularly bourgeois tone and perspective.[76] However, the press in England increasingly addressed a more socially diverse audience. Newspapers have also been linked to the middle classes because of their interest in the world of trade and commerce.[77] But once again, we should be wary of assuming that newspaper interests solely reflected the concerns of the growing commercial classes, since foreign news had occupied a prominent place in English newspapers throughout the eighteenth century. In addition, news from abroad would have appealed to more than just those interested in its economic repercussions. Richard Wilson has also cast doubt on the importance of newspapers to traders and manufacturers, and has argued that although the amount of specifically business- and trade-orientated news in papers increased from around 1760, other sources of information, and particularly correspondence with suppliers, agents and customers, continued to be more important until the development of trade journals in the late nineteenth century.[78]

English newspapers between 1760 and 1815 were not, then, the preserve of the middling sorts, nor of the elites. Whilst it would be a mistake to describe them as truly popular – in the sense that they were read by everybody – they were certainly read by increasing numbers, and by individuals from across the social spectrum. Moreover, whatever the social or numerical limitations of its readership, the press was certainly populist. It appealed to the English people en masse, presuming to speak both to them and for them, and in facilitating the exchange of information and ideas and providing a new institutional context for political action, it was instrumental in the development of public opinion and, with it, the political public sphere.

NOTES

1 John Brewer, *Party Ideology and Popular Politics at the Accession of George III* (Cambridge, 1976).
2 See, for example, F. K. Hunt, *The Fourth Estate: Contributions Towards a History of Newspapers, and the Liberty of the Press* (London, 1850); Alexander Andrews, *The History of British Journalism*, 2 vols. (London, 1859); Charles Pebody, *English Journalism, and the Men who have Made it* (London, 1882); H. R. Fox Bourne, *English Newspapers: Chapters in the History of Journalism*, 2 vols. (London, 1887).
3 Bob Harris, *Politics and the Rise of the Press: Britain and France, 1620–1800* (London, 1996), pp. 43, 82ff.
4 M. J. Smith, 'English radical newspapers in the French Revolutionary era, 1790–1803', Ph.D. thesis, University of London (1979), p. 169.
5 J. W. von Archenholz, *A Picture of England* (Dublin, 1791), pp. 39–40.
6 *Public Advertiser*, 14 July 1781.
7 See, for example, the discussion of Edmund Burke's speeches on American taxation in 1774 and on Conciliation in 1775 in Hannah Barker, *Newspapers, Politics, and Public Opinion in Late Eighteenth-Century England* (Oxford, 1998), p. 16, n. 30.
8 Brewer, *Party Ideology and Popular Politics at the Accession of George III*; R. R. Rea, *The English Press in Politics, 1760–1774* (Lincoln, NE, 1963).
9 Kathleen Wilson, *The Sense of the People: Politics, Culture and Imperialism in England, 1715–1785* (Cambridge, 1995), p. 232; Solomon Lutnick, *The American Revolution and the British Press 1775–1783* (Colombia, MO, 1967); H. T. Dickinson, *The Politics of the People in Eighteenth-Century Britain* (Basingstoke, 1995).
10 Barker, *Newspapers, Politics, and Public Opinion*.
11 Dickinson, *Politics of the People*; M. J. Smith, 'English radical newspapers'.
12 T. W. Copeland (ed.), *The Correspondence of Edmund Burke*, 10 vols. (Cambridge, 1958–78), vol. VI, p. 242; vol. VII, pp. 216, 229, 260.
13 K. Gilmartin, *Print Politics: The Press and Radical Opposition in Early Nineteenth-Century England* (Cambridge, 1996), p. 74.
14 Arthur Aspinall, *Politics and the Press, c. 1780–1850* (London, 1949), p. 1.
15 See, for example, J. L. de Lolme, *The Constitution of England, Or an Account of the English Government* (London, 1784); Archenholz, *A Picture of England*.
16 Patrick K. O'Brien, 'The political economy of British taxation, 1660–1815', *Economic History Review*, 2nd series, 41, 1 (1988), 1–32.
17 H. M. Lubasz, 'Public opinion comes of age: reform of the libel law in the eighteenth century', *History Today*, 8 (1958), 453–61.
18 Clive Emsley, 'An aspect of Pitt's "Terror": prosecutions for sedition during the 1790s', *Social History*, 6, 2 (1981), 155–84; Emsley, 'Repression, "terror" and the rule of law in England during the decade of the French Revolution', *English Historical Review*, 100 (1985), 801–25.
19 Smith, 'English radical newspapers', p. 8.

20 Emsley, 'An aspect of Pitt's "Terror"', p. 168.
21 Harris, *Politics and the Rise of the Press*, p. 44.
22 Smith, 'English radical newspapers', pp. 229–30.
23 P. D. G. Thomas, *John Wilkes: A Friend to Liberty* (Oxford, 1996), ch. 5; Thomas, 'John Wilkes and the freedom of the press (1771)', *Bulletin of the Institute of Historical Research* (1960), 86–98.
24 J. E. Cookson, *The Friends of Peace: Anti-War Liberalism in England, 1793–1815* (Cambridge, 1982), p. 133.
25 Aspinall, *Politics and the Press*, pp. 34–5.
26 Ibid., p. v.
27 Ibid., p. 72.
28 Ibid.
29 I. R. Christie, 'British newspapers in the later Georgian Age', in Christie (ed.), *Myth and Reality in Late Eighteenth-Century British Politics* (London, 1970), 311–33, pp. 318–22.
30 Cited in Tom Morley, '"The Times" and the concept of the fourth estate: theory and practice in mid-nineteenth century Britain', *Journal of Newspaper and Periodical History*, 1, 3 (1985), 11–23, pp. 12–13.
31 Barker, *Newspapers, Politics, and Public Opinion*, ch. 2.
32 John Brewer, 'The misfortunes of Lord Bute: a case-study in eighteenth-century political argument and public opinion', *Historical Journal*, 16, 1 (1973), 3–43.
33 Barker, *Newspapers, Politics, and Public Opinion*.
34 Aspinall, *Politics and the Press*, p. 89.
35 Ibid., pp. 356–63.
36 Dickinson, *Politics of the People*, p. 169.
37 J. A. W. Gunn, *Beyond Liberty and Property: The Process of Self-Recognition in Eighteenth-Century Political Thought* (Kingston, Ont., 1983), p. 90.
38 De Lolme, *The Constitution of England*, pp. 299–300.
39 Aspinall, *Politics and the Press*, p. 33.
40 Lutnick, *The American Revolution and the British Press*, p. 1.
41 Smith, 'English radical newspapers', p. 151.
42 Aled Jones, *Powers of the Press: Newspapers, Power and the Public in Nineteenth-Century England* (Aldershot, 1996), pp. 31–3.
43 Vicesimus Knox, *The Works of Vicesimus Knox*, 7 vols. (London, 1824), vol. v, p. 174.
44 Jeremy Black, 'Politicisation and the press in Hanoverian England', in Robin Myers and Michael Harris (eds.), *Serials and Their Readers, 1620–1914* (Winchester, 1993), 63–82, p. 75.
45 Hannah Barker, *Newspapers, Politics and English Society 1695–1855* (Harlow, 2000), pp. 20–21.
46 Barker, *Newspapers, Politics, and Public Opinion*, p. 111; A. P. Wadsworth, 'Newpaper circulations, 1800–1954', *Transactions of the Manchester Statistical Society* (1955), 1–41, p. 16.
47 Jeremy Black, *The English Press in the Eighteenth Century* (Beckenham, 1987), pp. 104–5; Christie, 'British newpapers', p. 313.
48 Christie, 'British newpapers', p. 323.

49 Barker, *Newspapers, Politics, and Public Opinion*, p. 114.
50 Wadsworth, 'Newpaper circulations, 1800–1954', pp. 16–17.
51 John Rule, *Albion's People: English Society, 1714–1815* (Harlow, 1992), pp. 168 and 182–4.
52 Dennis O'Bryen to Edmund Burke, March 1782, Wentworth Woodhouse Muniments, Sheffield City Archives, BK1/1557.
53 Michael Harris, *London Newspapers in the Age of Walpole: A Study in the Origins of the Modern English Press* (London, 1987), p. 190.
54 On population, see C. M. Law, 'Some notes on the urban population of England and Wales in the eighteenth century', *Local Historian*, 10 (1972), 13–26, p. 24; B. R. Mitchell, *British Historical Statistics* (Cambridge, 1988), p. 30. On the growth of the newspaper press, see Barker, *Newspapers, Politics and English Society*, ch. 2.
55 On population see E. A. Wrigley and R. S. Schofield, *The Population History of England 1541–1871: A Reconstruction* (Cambridge, 1989), pp. 333–5 and appendix 3; Law, 'Some notes on the urban population', pp. 22 and 24; Mitchell, *British Historical Statistics*, pp. 15, 25–7 and 30. On the growth of the newspaper press, see Barker, *Newspapers, Politics and English Society*, ch. 2.
56 Barker, *Newspapers, Politics, and Public Opinion*, pp. 22–42.
57 M. Harris, *London Newspapers in the Age of Walpole*, p. 195.
58 Archenholz, *A Picture of England*, pp. 44 and 39.
59 James Lackington, *Memoirs of the First Forty-Five Years of the Life of James Lackington* (London, 1792), p. 254.
60 Roger Schofield, 'Dimensions of illiteracy in England 1750–1850', in H. J. Graff (ed.), *Literacy and Social Development in the West* (Cambridge, 1981) 201–13, p. 207; L. Stone, 'Literacy and education in England 1640–1900', *Past and Present*, 42 (1969), 69–139, p. 105; David Vincent, *Literacy and Popular Culture: England 1750–1914* (Cambridge, 1989), pp. 22–4. But see Margaret Spufford, *Small Books and Pleasant Histories: Popular Fiction and its Readership in Seventeenth-Century England* (London, 1981) for evidence of a large and 'humble' reading public from the seventeenth century; also D. Cressy, *Literacy and the Social Order* (London, 1975).
61 Margaret Spufford, 'First Steps in literacy: the reading and writing experiences of the humblest seventeenth-century spiritual autobiographies', *Social History*, 4 (1979), 407–35.
62 Vincent, *Literacy and Popular Culture*, pp. 23 and 49.
63 Arthur Aspinall, 'The circulation of newspapers in the early nineteenth century', *Review of English Studies*, 22, 85 (1946), 29–43, p. 34.
64 Aspinall, *Politics and the Press*, p. 29.
65 Smith, 'English radical newspapers', p. 165.
66 Brewer, *Party Ideology and Popular Politics*, pp. 148–50; Wilson, *The Sense of the People*, p. 47. See also Aytoun Ellis, *The Penny Universities* (London, 1956); Bryant Lillywhite, *London Coffee Houses* (London, 1963).
67 Cited in Lutnick, *The American Revolution and the British Press*, p. 1.
68 Cited in Aspinall, *Politics and the Press*, p. 11.
69 Cited in Aspinall, 'The circulation of newspapers in the early nineteenth century', p. 38.

70 Paul Kaufman, *Libraries and Their Users* (London, 1969), p. 192; Brewer, *Party Ideology and Popular Politics*, p. 151.
71 Aspinall, 'The circulation of newspapers in the early nineteenth century', p. 30.
72 Ibid., pp. 25–31.
73 [Stanley Morison], *The History of the Times*, vol. 1: '*The Thunderer*' *in the Making: 1785–1841* (London, 1935), p. 435.
74 K. Schweizer and R. Klein, 'The French Revolution and the developments in the London daily press to 1793', *Publishing History*, 18 (1985), 85–97.
75 Barker, *Newspapers, Politics, and Public Opinion*, pp. 32–3.
76 Stephen Botein, Jack R. Censer and Harriet Ritvo, 'The periodical press in eighteenth century English and French society: a cross-cultural approach', *Comparative Studies in Society and History*, 23 (1981), 464–90. Cf. B. Harris, *Politics and the Rise of the Press*, pp. 94–6.
77 John Brewer, *Sinews of Power: War, Money and the English State, 1688–1783* (London, 1989), p. xxi.
78 Richard Wilson, 'Newspapers and industry: the export of wool controversy in the 1780s', in Michael Harris and Alan Lee (eds.), *The Press in English Society From the Seventeenth to the Nineteenth Centuries* (London, 1986), 80–104, p. 82.

5 Ireland, 1760–1820s

Douglas Simes

In its earliest years, perhaps through to 1760, the Irish newspaper was in many respects close to the model propounded by Jürgen Habermas.[1] Intimately associated with learned societies and debating clubs on the one side, and with coffee shops, booksellers and other commercial enterprises on the other, it was inextricably linked to the literary and political spheres.[2] As well as philosophical and moral essays it contained practical disquisitions on developmental issues, verse and *belles lettres*, and occasionally political polemic. Jonathan Swift, Dean of St Patrick's, who was a leading politician and propagandist, as well as a literary lion, and who patronised and utilised the press and maintained close ties to it, was a symbol of its aspirations, if not, perhaps, of its achievements. A century and more later, when, in 1833, the foundation of the *Dublin University Magazine* again brought together many of Ireland's best intellects in both the literary and political spheres, much of the early promise remained unrealised. The Irish newspaper press was not a failure, and indeed even in its darkest hours retained a vigour and freedom which would have been found astonishing in many parts of Europe. It was rather that it had developed less than might have been anticipated. It was still dominated by small-scale family enterprises of marginal profitability and tenuous viability. Its influence, in the political sphere, which admittedly had changed markedly, was still limited and uneven. Above all, it had moved away from rational-critical discourse, to reflect the sectarian divisions of an increasingly polarised society.

This outcome has often been explained in terms of national struggle and political repression, with special attention being given to the activities of the executive at Dublin Castle, and the adverse impact of the Act of Union in 1800. The seminal and detailed work of R. R. Madden, with its intense romantic and nationalist bias, has cast a long shadow,[3] and continues to exert an influence. Yet, while it would be foolish to deny any validity to the factors Madden identifies, they do not constitute an entire explanation of the unusual trajectory of the Irish press. It was clear long before the Union, and indeed almost from the outset, that a volatile mixture of sectarian division, ideological fragmentation, commercial aims and frustrations and governmental ineptitude, inconsistency and high-handedness was likely to produce an idiosyncratic outcome.

The Irish press developed a political tone, even if it was not a prevalent one, virtually from the beginning.[4] Moreover, party politics intersected with sectarian divisions between Catholics and Protestants. An observer noted in 1745,

> It is amazing how zealously our Roman Catholics are affected with the success of the French in Flanders. *Pues [Occurrences]* is their paper, the Protestants prefer *Faulkners [Dublin Journal]* ... and it is diverting how they fight each other with their different intelligences ...[5]

The polemic rapidly became what Robert Peel, the Irish Secretary between 1812 and 1818, was later to describe as 'high-seasoned'.[6] Given a literate population often raised on morality and action tales[7] such as *The History of Rogues and Raparees* and *The Seven Champions of Christendom*, a little sensationalism probably met a market need. Certainly it rapidly attached itself to the in-fighting of the political elites, as well as becoming a staple of content generally. This was not uniquely Irish. In Ireland, however, the political and sectarian divisions were very deep, and only a very little scurrility or vitriol was necessary to excite antagonisms.

While the newspapers developed an enthusiasm for politics, intermittently at first and then as a staple of content, it was not their main imperative. The majority of newspapers, from their outset, existed to make money for their proprietors. The owners were usually middle-class families, or limited partnerships of small to medium businessmen. It was a risky business, and many more enterprises failed than succeeded.[8] Readership was limited by high illiteracy and Irish-speaking, and by cost, difficulties of distribution and inescapable sectarian orientations.[9] It was a highly competitive market, and any perceived advantage was sedulously pursued by someone. Popular politics was one way of attracting subscribers and advertisers, and so ensuring survival. It was certainly not the only way. Indeed, it may well not have been the most effective or characteristic way. Many of the prints that adopted that strategy proved financially unprofitable, or, like the initially lucrative radical *Northern Star*, ephemeral. Newspapers which eschewed political comment virtually altogether, like the specialist advertising journals, and those dedicated to London and foreign news, frequently produced better returns and endured much longer. The same was often true of those which espoused elite or sectarian politics, like the *Dublin Evening Mail*, or which advocated the governmental viewpoint and received subsidies, such as the prints associated with Francis Higgins. In broad terms the Irish press was shaped by its limited market, and the resultant commercial pressures which made the competition intense. In this context the potential attractions and advantages of highly seasoned sectarian and ideological popular politics were readily apparent. Not surprisingly, successive governments, only too aware of the tensions beneath the veneer of Irish society, sought by recurrent bouts of intervention to offset, influence or control what they regarded as a dangerous tendency. Precisely how these interacting factors impacted on the evolution of the press varied from decade to decade.

By the 1760s Ireland's newspaper press was already well established, at least in Dublin and Belfast, and had taken on many of the features that were to persist well into the following century.[10] It had grown, and to a degree prospered, in a largely free environment.[11] There was no censorship, no effective guild control, no special taxation and only occasional government interference. The newspapers were small-scale commercial enterprises usually owned by families or friends, drawn from within a narrow circle of printers, booksellers and coffee-house proprietors. They were often an ancillary rather than a primary source of income. Generally they had 400 to 800 subscribers, though one or two reached 1,800 or even 2,000.[12] Income was largely generated by advertising, although the subscribers list was important, both in itself and for attracting potential advertisers. The standardised format of the papers,[13] which were usually two-leaf, four-page folios, 12 or 18 inches by 11, and devoid of large type or illustration, was dictated by the need to maximise advertising space while keeping the cost of production low. Content was also shaped by advertising. An issue of *Pue's Occurrences*, for example, might have nine columns of advertising compared with two and a half of news. *The Belfast News-Letter* might have seven of its twelve columns in advertising. *Saunders News-Letter*, which was primarily mercantile, had as many as ten and a half columns of advertisements out of a total of twelve.[14]

The key to survival and expansion, in an increasingly competitive industry, lay in attracting new subscribers and advertisers. Given the difficulties in communications, coupled with the high levels of illiteracy and Irish-speaking already mentioned,[15] there was a limit to what could be achieved in the provinces, especially Connaught and Munster. As a result, it was necessary to maximise appeal to the anglophones of Ulster and Leinster.[16] While it was possible to reach the English-speaking Catholics, they remained wary of sectarian bias.[17] Among the English-speaking Protestants, the community to whom newspapers primarily appealed, there were significant numbers who were illiterate or unable to pay. In this competition for the residual potential market, various strategies were adopted: including, on one occasion at least, 'fair-sexing' a newspaper (by making it more attractive to women readers).[18] More characteristic was linking the newspaper to a supportive business such as a coffee house, where copies could be made available to the clientele. Dick's Coffee House, 'a rendez-vous for literary people, wits, politicians and writers', was owned by Richard Pue of *Pue's Occurrences* and was also home to *The Flying Post*.[19] A related strategy was specifically to target the literary market.[20] James Carson of the *Dublin Weekly Journal* was closely associated with Lord Molesworth's philosophical circle, and published the poetry of Henry Parnell. Richard Reilly and the *Weekly Oracle* had the backing of the erudite and influential Dublin Society. Richard Faulkner of the *Dublin Journal* was not only Swift's printer, but also a friend of Chesterfield and Berkeley. A rich man, his lavish dinner parties became an important feature of Dublin political and literary life.

Politics played a limited part in the search for new readers in this formative period through to the early 1760s and were to be handled cautiously, especially since the government had occasional but recurrent bouts of utilising parliamentary privilege or the law of seditious libel to harass newspapers.[21] In such endeavours both parliament and the judiciary proved enthusiastic partners. The intense party politics of the 1720s, and especially of the period when Sir Constantine Phipps was rallying opposition to the Whigs, effectively wrecked the Tory part of the press.[22] The first phase of Dr Charles Lucas's controversial journalistic and political career in the 1740s, which ended with a writ of outlawry, also produced casualties.[23] Nevertheless it is a mistake to assume that politics were not frequently present, and intermittently important. The careful selection of the foreign news and the emphasis given to it often indicate political sympathy: stress on the persecution of Polish Protestants, for example.[24] More obviously, the fiery anti-Catholic diatribes of *Whalley's News Letter* or the implicitly anti-English debate about the causes of famine in 1729, displayed a willingness to appeal to public feeling on at least an occasional basis.[25] It remained safer and easier, however, to attract new customers by obtaining the most recent British and Continental news, by improving distribution networks, or publishing some literary or philosophical 'lion'. In the late 1760s and early 1770s, this situation changed. The rise of a Wilkes-style charismatic politician – in the shape of Charles Lucas – willing to appeal to the public by means of the newspaper press, coincided with the tenure in office of a Lord-Lieutenant, Lord Townshend, whose policies offended much of the politically significant population. Politics in the press moved from being occasional and slightly peripheral to being a central and continual concern.

Contrary to his intentions, Lord Townshend did much to facilitate the politicisation of the press. In many respects an 'enlightened minister', he wanted to make government more efficient, cost-effective, equitable and tolerant. But his policies, such as proposing to tax absentee landowners, and his perceived softness on Roman Catholics and agrarian agitators, antagonised major sections of the elite. His dismissal of the 'undertakers', or traditional parliamentary managers, deprived him of their skills, and alienated some of the great families. His concession of the Octennial Act meant that the disaffected had a better hope of making their opposition tell, since an election would occur now every eight years, not just at the death of the monarch. At much the same time, Charles Lucas, a political outsider, was showing that charisma, a critical approach to government and a warm espousal of popular Protestantism could, when backed by close contact with the press, break down many of the traditional barriers.[26] His control and utilisation of the *Freeman's Journal* pointed a message, which was lost neither on the government, nor on aspiring opposition politicians such as Henry Flood and Henry Grattan. If Lucas could arouse public opinion and forward political and personal goals with his newspaper interest, what might an opposition Patriot who was also a 'social insider' not achieve? Although Lucas died in 1771, and Townshend went home in 1772, the changes they had catalysed gathered momentum. The opposition had learnt valuable lessons from a political master. It was not about to forget them. The imposition of the first stamp tax on newspapers in 1774 suggests that the government had learned something too: specifically that there were more subtle ways of limiting the impact of hostile newspapers than prosecutions and writs of outlawry.

The period from the late 1770s to the Rebellion of 1798 and its aftermath was one of continuing and intense political ferment. This was the zenith of the landowning Protestant hegemony usually known as the Ascendancy, its moment of fullest freedom and maturity. Initially at least, it appeared that through enlightened debate it would evolve into a tolerant elite guiding a prosperous and progressive society. In salons, debating societies, Masonic lodges and coffee shops, the elite, and indeed the literate generally, exchanged new ideas and mapped out strategies. The latest British ideas and fads appeared in the newspapers weekly. French ideas, frequently filtered through the Huguenot community, were also influential.[27] Dublin purchased as many copies of the *Encyclopédie* as London.[28] Cultured politicians brought both classical and new ideas into play in parliament, and politics more generally. Charlemont translated Petrarch and Catullus, as well as leading the Volunteers. Henry Flood translated Homer and Desmosthenes, in addition to propagating freer trade and constitutional amendment.[29] Catholics and Protestants mixed and exchanged ideas in fashionable venues and societies, and not least in Masonic lodges, the Grand Lodge having at one point a Catholic majority.[30] Even Lord Charlemont, an enthusiast for decorating the statue of the Protestant hero, King William, believed 'the spirit of toleration has gone abroad'.[31]

It was not to last, and the signs were apparent almost from the outset. For all the elegant turns of polished debate, it was the threat of force by the Volunteers which produced the Renunciation Act. Despite the talk of toleration by the Ascendancy at its most relaxed and complacent, sectarianism was on the rise from the 1770s. Both Flood and Charlemont soon reasserted their anti-Catholic convictions.[32] The enfranchisement of Catholics in 1793 led to Catholic triumphalism and acute Protestant anxiety. In Protestant circles talk of the massacres of 1641 being renewed became commonplace. In 1795, as an overspill from unaddressed agrarian problems, and the resultant rise of the secretive peasant-based and violent Catholic Defenders, the militant Protestant Orange Order, also originally peasant-based, was founded. It spread rapidly, and was widely perceived by Catholics as expressing the attitudes of Protestants more generally. It was not a large step, as was to be soon proved, from Volunteer threats of force to yeomanry employing pitch-caps, nor from sectarian rhetoric by Patriot politicians and radical newspapers to the 1798 anti-Protestant cleansing by pike at the Bridge of Wexford, or by fire at the Barn of Scullabogue.[33]

Throughout the successive phases of Ireland's development in this period, the newspapers were to play a vital part. In their differing ways they sought to discern, articulate, arouse and exploit what Edmund Burke described as 'general opinion', and what in common usage became known as 'public opinion'.[34] The specialist reporter was almost unknown at this period, but proprietors or editors often haunted coffee and alehouses and places of fashionable resort to learn how people felt, as well as to drum up custom.[35] Frequently, they accepted the input of leading literary or political figures as expressing public opinion, as well as arousing it. Henry Flood, for example, in his *Philadelphus Letters* and *Syndercombe Letters* in the *Freeman's Journal* fulfilled such a dual role.[36] By the 1780s, there were already signs that some newspapers were actively manipulating the public response. In the struggle over the Prime Minister Pitt's commercial propositions in 1788, for example, the newspapers played 'a vital part in fomenting public discontent'.[37] They did not do this by well-informed rational-critical discussion. Rather, to offset 'the general bankruptcy of their analysis', 'the emotional content ... was kept high'.[38] By the 1790s, matters were clearly worse. The 'paranoid fantasies' by which at least one journal sought to arouse Catholic fears were to have tragic consequences in outbreaks of 'sectarian cleansing'.[39]

For all their pretensions, though, most newspapers were not driven primarily by ideologies or high political exigencies, but by the need to return a reasonable profit to their marginally middle-class, and frequently struggling, proprietors. This was not a simple task. In the 1780s, perhaps 50 per cent of Ulstermen – the most literate – had the necessary basic reading skills to comprehend newsprint. Among the young, this figure may have reached 67 per cent in Ulster, and 59 per cent in Leinster.[40] Both literacy and English-language knowledge were increasing, the latter quite rapidly.[41] Moreover, Catholic anglophones may have been more ready to subscribe than previously, given the spread of more tolerant attitudes in some parts of the press, and the emergence of Catholic proprietors.[42] However, even if the pool of potential readers was increasing, it could not be fully tapped. The costs of production remained high, given the need to import most presses, type and paper,[43] and hence the price per copy was prohibitive for many poorer literates. While a titan like the *Dublin Evening Post* might claim a circulation of 4,000 as early as 1781, many Dublin newspapers, and virtually all of the rapidly multiplying provincials, sold fewer than 1,000 copies.[44] Competition for the subscribers and advertising needed to sustain so many marginal enterprises remained intense.

As a consequence of the competition, various strategies were devised for survival and expansion. *Saunders News-Letter* successfully introduced the daily.[45] *Finn's Leinster Journal* took great care with its subscription list and distribution network.[46] The *Drogheda News-Letter* introduced a kind of leading article.[47] Others concentrated on specialist advertising, improved presentation, or obtaining the most recent news from London. Whilst some strategies were determinedly apolitical, most probably contained an element of political targeting. Financially, it made sense to please some defined segment of a rather narrowly composed 'public', the government, or a political patron or organisation. These were all sources of supplementary advertising revenue or other funding. Of course, there were significant concomitant risks. The *Belfast News-Letter*, one of the oldest and most strongly based newspapers in Ireland, lost one-fifth of its subscribers by a single miscalculation of the Ulster mood, when it blamed the death of a loyalist tradesman on the citizens of Belfast.[48] The passage of time and governmental initiatives increased the pressures to accept the risks of an explicit political line. In 1774, stamp duty was imposed at $^{1}/_{2}$d per copy, and advertisement tax at 2d. In 1785 stamp duty was raised to 1d and the advertisement tax to 1 shilling. In an arguably punitive measure of 1798, stamp duty reached 2d, and a tax was imposed on both home-produced and imported newsprint. Advertisements fell sharply as early as 1785, when the *General Evening Post* lost four columns, and the *Volunteer's Journal* two of its four sheets.[49] As a result, the price of newspapers continued to be forced up. By 1798, the *Dublin Evening Post* had reached 4d, a prohibitive cost for many.[50] While taxes across the Irish Sea were both earlier and heavier, they were almost certainly more easily absorbed in the larger, more dynamic and more prosperous English market.

Of the possible political strategies available to newspapers, perhaps the safest was to become part of the emergent governmental press interest. This could entail control, but more frequently involved acceptance of some degree of influence. Government newspapers were rarely popular, at least judged by copies sold:[51] though to some extent this may reflect a lack of interest in the hard work of pursuing subscribers and advertisers, given a secure income. By either choice or necessity, their income was largely derived from government advertising, and subventions from such sources as the Secret Service Fund. Proprietors and editors might also be in receipt of places and pensions. Government-influenced journals were most frequently recipients of government Proclamations, although occasional use was made of other kinds of funding or privileged access to information. It was possible to ensure a prolonged existence for a journal, and a very satisfactory income for its proprietor or editor, by adopting this strategy. During the closing decades of the eighteenth century, John Giffard of the *Dublin Journal* was receiving £1,600 per annum for journalism alone, as well as holding a lucrative place in Customs and the captaincy of a Militia troop.[52] Francis Higgins of the *Freeman's Journal*, who doubled as a kind of spymaster, may well have fared even better. In addition to the journalistic subsidy of £1,500 per annum, he had a £300 pension, special payments as an agent, and as much as £500 per annum from gambling tables at his coffee house, an abuse in which authority connived.[53] Higgins was rich enough to be able to assemble around himself a kind of intellectual 'court', not unlike that of Faulkner in an earlier period. It was characteristic of the milieu that the 'court poet' was Leonard McNally, a zealous Protestant, who was informing on the United Irishmen.[54] Support of government was not a risk-free strategy. The newspapers involved often lost subscribers, and their owners and editors were subject to vitriolic character attacks by opposition, and especially radical, journals.[55] Government support was often unforthcoming or unreliable.[56] Journals frequently dwindled into total dependence or failed outright. Popular, if not always spontaneous, pressure could wreck businesses and lives.[57] Several members of John Giffard's family were murdered in the Rising of '98, including a son and son-in-law. George Gordon of the *Belfast News-Letter* had to flee under the pressure of reiterated death threats. Henry Morgan of the *Cork Herald* was forced to abandon his native city, and W. P. Carey of the *General Evening Post* sought refuge for himself and his family in England.

In the 1780s, at least, a moderate opposition stance was a widely preferred alternative strategy. The Patriot programme, in both its Whiggish (Grattan) and anti-Catholic (Flood) variants, had a broad-based appeal. There was genuine enthusiasm in many quarters for improved trading arrangements, more honest government, a reformed parliament and less restrictive constitutional ties to Britain. The *Dublin Evening Post*, which met this market best, and appealed to Roman Catholics with its religious tolerance as well, became the largest and most lucrative of Irish newspapers for some years.[58] The Whiggish *Hibernian Journal* seems to have prospered on a similar basis.[59] Newspapers of this kind, as well as attracting enhanced subscriptions and increased advertising, were also to an extent subvented by paid communications from organisations such as the Volunteers.[60] A moderate opposition strategy was also not without its hazards. On occasion, the law officers of the crown, the judiciary, and the parliament all demonstrated a good deal of ingenuity and determination in harassing temperate opponents. The lurid allegations against Francis Higgins, made by John Magee, the admittedly erratic proprietor of the *Dublin Evening Post*, involved him in an on-going feud not just with Higgins and his protégés, but with Lord Clonmell, the most redoubtable judge of the Court of King's Bench. The curious legal antics which ensued were disruptive for the newspaper, and ultimately disastrous for Magee's personal life and mental stability.[61] Nor was it necessary to be John Magee, with his abrasive edge, to encounter trouble. The bland and cautious *Saunders News-Letter* had its problems, with one proprietor being horse-whipped by John Giffard, and his successor being held in custody and reprimanded by the House of Commons.[62]

It is quite possible that the moderate journals relished a little controversy and harassment as good for business. They had to bear in mind, to a degree in the 1780s, and pre-eminently in the 1790s, the need to compete with more radical and sensational prints for public attention. The more restrained radical publications, and most notably the *Northern Star*, did manage to wed commercial aims to ideological imperatives. The *Northern Star* may have had little literary merit, and been overly full of undigested and indigestible details of the French Revolution, but it met, at least briefly, a market demand. It attained a circulation estimated as high as 4,000,[63] and copies turned up as far south as Waterford. Its more racy feature articles, such as 'Billy Bluff and Squire Firebrand', may have played a part in this, as may the fact that it was initially run by shrewd Belfast businessmen. It is more difficult to discern any realisable commercial goals in the more flamboyant radical prints. The *Volunteer's Journal*, which advocated tarring and feathering, and possibly lynching, of unpopular members of government,[64] the aristocratically owned *Press* which deliberately and calculatedly set out to arouse Catholic fears of genocide with elaborate fantasies of Orange plots,[65] and above all the *Union Star* which galvanised its readers with assassination lists and dreadful revolutionary verse,[66] cannot really have expected conventional returns on money invested. Perhaps they were genuinely expecting a quick revolutionary triumph and the endorsement of a grateful people? It is just possible that tenuous links with revolutionary governments may also hold part of the answer.[67]

Whatever the motivation of their proprietors, the government had no patience with newspapers which advocated violence, especially aimed at its own members. Nor was it inclined to tolerate pro-French newspapers in war-time. The full panoply of the law, and occasionally of extra-legal measures, descended on offenders. The *Volunteer's Journal* claimed in 1794 it had faced two informations *ex officio*, three motions to show cause, two indictments for misdemeanours, and four indictments for high treason, in nine months.[68] A long series of legal manoeuvres against the proprietors of the *Northern Star*, which persuaded most of them to abandon it, only ended with the physical destruction of the press by soldiers.[69] In December 1797, the conductor of the *Press*, Peter Finnerty, found guilty of seditious libel, was imprisoned for two years, fined £20, and obliged to give security of £1,000 for good behaviour on his release. The true proprietor, Arthur O'Connor, was tried for high treason a few months later.[70]

By the later 1790s, the parameters of acceptable political debate in Ireland had tightened noticeably. This was not just the result of the extension of governmental control and influence through the consistent use of governmental resources. It was also a sign of changing attitudes among the newspaper-owning and reading elite as the French Revolution descended into Terror, and Europe was embroiled in war. Edmund Burke was not alone among Whigs in denouncing revolutionary excess and falling in behind the government. In Ireland Henry Grattan, the Whig leader, fiercely denounced newspapers that encouraged assassination.[71] Moderate liberal journals such as *Finn's Leinster Journal* and the *Waterford Herald* decided the time had come to make terms with government.[72] The difference between a governmental strategy and a moderate opposition one eroded, at least to a degree. The radical strategy ceased to be viable, doomed by its own inherent weakness and folly as well as by governmental repression and elite hostility. The *Northern Star* was forced out of business in 1797, and the *Press* and *Harp of Erin* were extinguished in 1798.[73]

The rebellion of '98, and the ensuing Act of Union, are usually regarded, and not without some justification, as ushering in an especially bleak period of Irish press history. Newspapers struggled to survive, often for financial reasons, in an environment in which the government had largely set the parameters of debate and monitored them closely. Still, it is necessary to keep a sense of perspective. Much of the cautious conservatism was dictated not by government, but by the changed expectations of readers, especially in the powerful and wealthy Protestant community. Moreover, there remained a surprising amount of freedom given that the country had experienced large-scale internal bloodshed, and was involved in a major international conflict. By contemporary European standards, and indeed by twentieth-century war-time standards, the Irish newspapers had considerable latitude for debate. Highly important, and contentious, issues such as the Union and Catholic Emancipation were discussed in depth,[74] and with some asperity. There remained a sturdy independent or lightly influenced press which was quite willing to ask questions, and engage in critical debate. Even the government-controlled press, with its internecine disputes, its sectarian animosities, and its occasional assertions of independence, was frequently a challenge and an irritant to the politicians who nominally directed it.[75]

Although an unmitigatedly gloomy assessment of the status of the Irish press in this period is inappropriate, it remains true that it lacked the confidence, vigour and occasional ferocity of the preceding period. No doubt the Union with Britain in 1800 played some part in this. It reduced Dublin to a regional city, albeit an important and distinctive one, and deprived it of a parliament readily at hand to be influenced or pressured. The politicians departed for Westminster, and in their wake so did hostesses such as Lady Charleville and the Countess of Blessington,[76] and newspapermen such as the Ultra Tories S. L. Giffard and William Maginn of the *Standard* and *St James Chronicle* and the liberal Alexander Wood of the *Traveller*.[77] It took some years for those who remained Dublin-based to realise that there were ways in which they might utilise the London Irish to influence the British parliament and media.

Probably more important than the Union, at least in the short term, were the systematic press policies of the more dynamic Lords-Lieutenant and Chief Secretaries. Faced with rising sectarian tensions, and the exigencies of long-continuing warfare, as well as periods of economic contraction, Dublin Castle instituted legal proceedings as and when it felt necessary. The Protestant mood ensured that it could usually do so with confidence, even when juries were involved.[78] Especially relentless was the very young and highly organised Robert Peel, whose prosecution of the *Dublin Evening Post* in 1813/14 brought it, and the Magee family who owned it, to heel. The most popular paper in Ireland, although never a governmental paper as such, became 'Castle Catholic'.[79] Prosecution was, however, only a part of the more systematic press management by government, and not, in general, the most effective part. Increased taxation rendered more papers amenable to government's favours. In 1810 the advertisement duty was raised to 2 shillings, and in 1815/16 to 3 shillings. While this level was attained in Britain earlier, its impact was less far-reaching because of the generally stronger economy. In 1810, the *Evening Post* lost ten of its sixteen columns of advertisements in a week.[80] By 1820, even *Saunders News-Letter*, which 'specialised in advertising', was suffering a decline.[81] The income from the duty, indicative of the falling volume of advertisements, and also of dwindling returns to newspaper owners, continued to slide: in 1813, it was £21,000; by 1829, it was £15,000.[82] By the latter date even the *Evening Mail*, Ireland's most successful newspaper, was encountering problems.[83]

Although literacy rates were continuing to rise, and English-language usage to spread,[84] the price of newspapers was a discouragement to purchase especially in the post-war years. At 5d to 7d per copy for most prints it was difficult to attract new readers, or even to retain old ones such as the formerly prosperous agrarian 'middlemen' of the war period.[85] No amount of hireage or group reading provided comfort to those who needed to make a reasonable profit. It was possible to an extent to attract readers and gain ground against competitors by technical innovations. The quality of presentation, in matters such as paper and type, improved. Journalism became more professional, and direct reportage more common.[86] The editorial was developed and spread rapidly. Distribution networks were often enhanced. Only for the very fortunate few did such innovations suffice in themselves. For most the lure of some measure of governmental assistance, especially if accompanied by only limited interference, was irresistible. The government, when it kept within budget, spent approximately £20,000 per annum. About £15,000 of this came from the Proclamation Fund, money set aside for official government notices. Most of the rest came from the Secret Service Fund.[87] Pension, places and privileged access to information were occasionally used as supplements. Much of the money went to sustain the government-initiated and -controlled newspapers. *The Patriot*, for example, with its modest readership of 750, was given at least £1,760 in 1816, including £500 from the Secret Service Fund and £400 in Proclamations.[88] A hostile source suspected that the true figure, including pensions, was as high as £2,640.[89] The more successful *Correspondent*, and the declining and ineffectual *Hibernian Journal* and *Dublin Journal*, were also lavishly endowed.[90] Much smaller, but still significant, amounts were bestowed on friendly, but largely independent, publications, such as the *Dublin Evening Post* and the *Freeman's Journal*.

The government was frequently restive about the results of its investment. Wellesley Pole, who was Chief Secretary 1809–12, observed, during what was theoretically one of the high points of repressive control, that 'the government has been assailed from all quarters, particularly by the factious prints, with the grossest abuse'.[91] It still had to cope with the scurrilities and horror stories of the *Irish Magazine*, complete with 'Goyaesque illustrations', and the 'disguised near-pornographic libels' of the *Dublin Satirist*.[92] More significantly, the government had also to accept the offsetting influence of highly organised pressure groups with a shrewd press sense. For example, the Catholic Board, a pressure group seeking Catholic emancipation, helped sustain *The Messenger*.[93] Daniel O'Connell, the most dynamic Catholic political leader, bestowed favours on such Proclamation-accepting newspapers as the *Dublin Evening Post* and the *Freeman's Journal*, which reciprocated.[94] The Orange Order made clear to its members which journals it favoured,[95] and encouraged a degree of Protestant zeal in otherwise reliable prints which was a recurrent embarrassment. Except perhaps during Robert Peel's tenure of office as Irish Secretary, opposition influence, of various kinds, seems to have been almost as characteristic as governmental.

Governmental policies may have succeeded to an extent in damping down sensationalism, controversy and sectarianism during the crucial war years, but it was a very limited and incomplete achievement. Once the war was over, governmental consensus about managing the press began to disintegrate.[96] Robert Peel, who was alarmed at the subversive potential of militant Catholicism, did not hesitate to prosecute the *Chronicle* in 1816, as he had the *Evening Post* in 1813. His views were not, however, shared by later office-holders such as Wellesley and Grant. Governmental press policy very quickly lost focus and continuity. The punishment of the editor of the *Chronicle*, who received six months' imprisonment and a fine of £100 for a 'trifling and insignificant' libel, was no doubt significant as a last manifestation of the rigorous Peelite approach to the press.[97] More importantly, though, it showed the direction in which a less managed press would probably evolve. In response to the prosecution the newspaper 'published a list of the religions of all those involved in the case. The entire panel for both grand and petty juries, the court officers, the clerks – even the bailiffs sent round to arrest MacDonnell – were Protestants.' This small outburst of sectarianism was a harbinger of things to come.[98]

The nadir of the Irish press, as far as confidence and vigour of debate were concerned, was probably about 1817, and to some extent there was a revival in the 1820s. By 1824, Dublin had twelve metropolitan newspapers, not including the weeklies,[99] and there was a network of provincial papers which covered virtually the entire country. Literacy was continuing to increase slowly in the two more prosperous provinces, and both literacy and English-speaking were spreading rapidly in Connaught and Munster.[100] Subscription rates, and almost certainly readership, remained limited, however, with levels below that of 1800.[101]

Commercial viability was a real problem during the 1820s. The average circulation of an Irish newspaper was 547 copies per issue.[102] Admittedly this concealed significant disparities. The *Ballina Impartial* predictably enough sold many fewer copies than the average, and the *Dublin Evening Mail* rather more. Still, even the latter sold only a little over 3,000 copies.[103] The average for all English newspapers, in contrast, was 3,260.[104] Returns from advertisements were also low and falling. By this stage the number of advertisements per issue had fallen to an average of sixteen.[105] Even a prominent paper like the *Freeman's Journal* might have only two to three columns of largely institutional advertising.[106] While this to some extent was probably a reflection of economic stagnation, it was also a by product of continuing high taxation. With relatively high production costs, limited elasticity of demand, and severe taxation, the price of newspapers was high, generally ranging from 5d to 7d, which was a deterrent even for the marginally middle-class literate. Hired newspapers, public readings, and coffee and alehouse copies may have expanded readership beyond sales figures,[107] but did little to help finances. It is significant that by the early 1830s a special subscription was necessary to rescue the country's best-selling journal.

The hitherto successful strategy of boosting income by accepting some form of government subvention was no longer an easy way out of commercial dilemmas. The end of the Napoleonic Wars removed a major incentive to government intervention. Whig criticism, and a general post-war mood that favoured economy and retrenchment, discouraged free spending on projects of debatable worth. Checking Catholic militancy, which some Chief Secretaries thought justified a continuation of expenditure, never commanded the same support, even in governmental ranks, as resisting French influence and Jacobin ideas. Funds became more limited and were more sparingly bestowed. Monies from the Proclamation Fund fell from £9,500 in 1821 to £6,000 in 1826 and £3,750 in 1829.[108] Money for advertisements from government departments fell from £1,873 in 1816 to £1,077 in 1821, and continued to erode thereafter.[109] The impact on the government-controlled journals, not all of which were entirely contemptible, was dramatic. The *Hibernian Journal* ceased publication in 1822, the *Dublin Journal* in 1826, and the more successful *Patriot*, which was also hit by the rise of a direct competitor, in 1829. Only the *Correspondent*, renovated as the *Evening Packet*, survived – and it reasserted its independence.

The impact of governmental retrenchment went well beyond the controlled newspapers, and necessitated new approaches to sustain flagging finances. Rapid production of copy, better reporting and social targeting were all tried. The Ultra Tory *Dublin Evening Mail* was the trend-setter.[110] Although owned by Roman Catholics, it aimed at, and was loyal to, the High Protestant party. Its formula of scathing editorials, sensational snippets and enlivening woodcuts, alongside thorough and detailed reporting, soon won it a large and steady circulation. The financial difficulties it was to encounter in the 1830s demonstrated with great clarity the problems of successful newspaper ownership even given a shrewd market strategy. In this kind of environment, and driven, as always, by the commercial imperative, newspapers naturally turned to the major available source of patronage and of subscribers and advertisers, namely the powerful and well-endowed pressure groups which had evolved since the 1790s, but more especially in the 1820s. These were invariably sectarian. It was a peculiarity of these organisations that, while they were designed primarily to influence decision-making in London, they often displayed nostalgia for the lost Irish legislature. A wide range of Irish issues were brought forward and discussed, usually in a quasi-parliamentary fashion, by men who thought of themselves as, in some measure at least, representative. However, the discussions were 'intra-communal', and while in theory inclusive, were in practice usually rigidly sectarian.

The sectarian pressure groups, increasingly strident, high-profile, powerful and salient to the political process, were both a manifestation of heightened religious tension and a catalyst to its on-going intensification. They steadily accrued strength in a society where the major religious fault-line, always significant, was steadily widening, probably from the 1770s, and certainly from the late 1790s. The final phase of this process encompassed the whole of the 1820s, especially the last rancorous years of the Catholic Question and its immediate aftermath.

While moderate opinion endured and was occasionally influential in these years, it was increasingly eroded and forced onto the defensive. Within all the major Churches compromisers, ecumenicists, liberals and advocates of toleration were being outflanked by those of narrower and more intense convictions:[111] followers of the 'Old Light', Evangelicals and New Reformationists, Anti-Vetoists and Ultramontanes. At much the same time the Masonic Order, hitherto a cross-sectarian meeting ground for those of a liberal cast of mind, was ceasing to fulfil that role. Following Leo XII's denunciation of it in the 1820s, Catholics largely withdrew.[112] Daniel O'Connell, once an enthusiastic adherent, became a vehement antagonist,[113] placing it on a par with Orangeism.

The tendency towards polarisation was apparent throughout society. Sectarian antagonism was obvious in corporations, Grand Juries, guilds, charities and schools. Calls for exclusive dealing extended it to the business sector.[114] Sectarian competition on the land, already acute, was exacerbated by organisations such as the Protestant Colonisation Society, which called for exclusive settlements and one-faith tenantry.[115] Nor were intellectual and educational institutions immune. Angry Trinity Protestants rejected J. W. Croker, a confidant of Wellington and Peel, as too moderate! Zealous Catholics successfully purged a Dublin library of obnoxious publications of the opposite persuasion.[116] Although there is a paucity of evidence, there is really no reason to believe that such a pervasive process would not also have had an impact on coffee houses and tavern reading rooms.

By the late 1820s, polarisation was far advanced. R. L. Sheil, the prominent Catholic Association leader and orator, observed in 1829, 'the division between Catholic and Protestant is widening. They were before parted, they are now rent asunder.'[117] This was true, except perhaps in the far west, at local as well as national level. County Longford, for example, was 'a cauldron of sectarian animosity'.[118] In Cork 'the positions adopted were ... starkly sectarian'.[119] In effect, and increasingly, there were two separated communities and political public spheres. There is some variation of opinion about just how important the role of the press was in facilitating this process. Theodore Hoppen's suggestion that it was the 'creator of tribal political loyalties and identities'[120] is worthy of serious consideration, but appears to overstate both its penetration and influence. Few would disagree, however, that the press reinforced and exacerbated old animosities. The sectarian organisations had money to spend, and numerous adherents with purchasing power. The temptation to accept their support for commercially driven journals with low profit margins, and scant prospect of alternative subsidies, was frequently overwhelming.

On the Catholic side, Daniel O'Connell talked openly in the late 1820s of spending £15,000 of Association money on the press.[121] While that sum may not, in fact, have been expended, it is quite certain that significant amounts were spent on advertising,[122] and that favours were extended to newspapers and proprietors. Angry Protestants charged that O'Connell had suborned most of the Dublin press.[123] While this was something of an exaggeration, it is nonetheless true that O'Connell put considerable effort into influencing the newspapers. Had he been a little less arbitrary, and more diplomatic, he would have been truly formidable. As it was he did not maximise his influence, especially after his open commitment to the *Pilot*,[124] which he facilitated, directed and defended, impinged on relationships with rival Catholic journals.

To some extent, especially at key moments, the Catholic Church was also important in reinforcing sectarian proclivities in the press. The *Freeman's Journal*, for example, in 1829-30, was heavily dependent on the advertising of the Church and its agencies.[125] The *Weekly Register* prospered for a time on the close identification of Church and Association.

Among the duties of the Church Warden was to receive copies of the *Weekly Register*, containing detailed reports of the Catholic Association in Dublin, which they were to make available to their fellow parishioners, and to read outside Catholic churches on Sunday mornings. At the peak of the agitation 6,000 copies of the Register were being distributed in this manner each week.[126]

Later, the *Comet* had a brief incandescence by linking O'Connellite politics to attacks on the Church of Ireland.[127]

On the other side of the chasm, the more militant Protestants were also setting the tone and pace. The Orange Order, with very limited funds, at least until the 1830s, had nevertheless targeted its advertising to friendly journals, which were also indicated to the faithful as suitable reading matter.[128] The Protestant Conservative Association, which was better funded, had a mutually advantageous relationship with both the *Evening Mail* and the *Warder*. The Brunswick movement, set up to oppose Catholic emancipation, may have had as much as £100,000 in its coffers.[129] It could certainly afford to assist the specially created *Star of Brunswick* and to buy up thousands of copies for distribution in England.[130] It could also afford to transmit money to the expatriate editor of the *Standard*, S. L. Giffard, and to promise the purchase of multiple copies of English Ultra Tory papers.[131] There was very close liaison between the Ultra press on both sides of the water and hardline politicians. The Sheehans of the *Evening Mail* visited Lord Farnham for consultations.[132] The Reverend Charles Boyton, dubbed by one historian 'the Protestant O'Connell',[133] wrote leaders for more than one newspaper in Dublin, and had a working relationship with at least two London journals.[134]

By the late 1820s the intellectual equivalent of 'exclusive dealing' was well established in political and newspaper circles. Advertising from Churches and their agencies, and from sectarian organisations, invariably turned up in appropriate prints. Advice was provided so that readers might seek out papers of the right sort. The *Warder* drew attention to reliable Protestant prints in the metropolis.[135] The *Wexford Herald* attempted a comprehensive list for the provinces.[136] Efforts were made to obscure internecine competition and tension in the interests of solidarity. There were also occasional endeavours to censor or exclude the opposing viewpoint. Daniel O'Connell, for example, was in the forefront of a successful attempt to exclude the *Dublin Evening Mail*, Ireland's most widely read paper, from the city library in 1823. 'We kicked out the Mail by 227 to 147,' he observed. 'It was truly one of the most extraordinary political days I have seen in my time.'[137] Such a strategy brought together the strands of sectarian animosity and commercial rivalry very neatly, but did little to facilitate rational discussion.

Cross-sectarian debate atrophied throughout the 1820s and 1830s, becoming more contracted in scope and content, and confrontational in tone. It was hallmarked by such symbolic obsessions[138] as the massacres of 1641 and St Bartholomew's Day, the Treaty of Limerick, and the supposed indecencies of the theology of Peter Dens. Priestly politics boded large, as did the moral obliquities of parsons. The general tone can be well-enough gauged from the public letter addressed 'To the Protestants of Ireland' by Ireland's most powerful politician, Daniel O'Connell, in 1830. Ostensibly conciliatory in its intent, it contained numerous well-seasoned remarks on such subjects as masonic 'orgies', the 'Janissaries' of the yeomanry, and Orange bigotry. It was rounded out with a full-blooded onslaught on the 'Orange press', 'which subsists on Protestant patronage', in its totality, including its proprietors and journalists, its motivation and conduct.[139] This feeling was heartily reciprocated, in scathing contempt for 'leading demagogues and their press'. Not surprisingly, rational debate about major issues grew increasingly 'intra-communal'.[140] The prevailing milieu was not one in which mild-mannered middle-roaders found it easy to compete successfully. The word 'impartial' had long been suspect, and 'conciliatory' now joined it.[141] Latter-day interventions in the press, by both Tory and Whig governments, tended to be mediatorial and to aim at being conciliatory or even-handed. They usually resulted in intended beneficiaries being despised by majorities in both camps. The moderate Protestant *Patriot* collapsed as readers deserted it for the more hardline *Warder, Antidote* and *Evening Mail*. The moderate Catholic *Dublin Evening Post* went into decline, despite being conducted by the immensely competent F. W. Conway.

The extent to which the communities and their respective presses had diverged by the end of the second decade of the nineteenth century was symbolised in 1833 with the emergence of Ireland's first successful magazine, the *Dublin University Magazine*.[142] This periodical was aimed at the intellectual and social elite, at those who might have been expected preeminently to favour inclusive rational-critical debate. It attracted a galaxy of literary talent, including Carleton, Lever, Lover, Le Fanu, Mangan and Fergusson. It also attracted vigorous and well-informed controversialists, and expert writers on technical subjects. On subjects as varied as emigration, investment, land, folklore and the Irish language, it was at 'the cutting edge'. Yet it was determinedly and almost totally exclusivist, Protestant and Tory. It made manifest at the highest level of literary and cultural endeavour, the separation which had been increasingly apparent in the popular press. In Ireland religion was functioning in a way similar to, though not identical with, class in the Habermas model.

Historical discussion of Irish newspapers has tended to concentrate upon their relationship to Enlightenment thought, especially in its more radical manifestations, and on their contribution to the evolution of romantic nationalism. As a corollary a good deal of attention has been devoted to the recurrent attempts by government to limit their freedom and restrict their influence. A simple truth is thereby obscured. The Irish press was not generally cowed or silenced by its various travails. By the 1820s, it was, by most standards, remarkably (and indeed bloody-mindedly) free. It could be relied upon to be highly critical in its scrutiny of government and established institutions. It was never backward in transmitting its own trenchant, and usually contradictory, perceptions of popular opinion to those in authority. It was rarely reluctant to influence and shape, and occasionally inflame, the public mind.

Its vigour was also apparent in other ways. It was innovative in its attempts to meet the demands of a somewhat sluggish market. It experimented with improved paper and format, more rapid production, enhanced distribution strategies, weeklies, Sunday papers, specialist prints and magazines. It was too, inclusive in its own particular way. Right from the beginning women had played a significant role as proprietors and contributors, and this continued.[143] It was a rare political or religious minority that could not gain access to print. The press provided a career open to at least a fortunate few among the literate poor. The classic example is William Carleton, perhaps the greatest of nineteenth-century Irish novelists. For all its strengths, however, the Irish press was far removed from the Habermasian model. At the outset, and indeed well into the eighteenth century, it had conformed quite closely. From the 1760s, it progressively diverged. The keys to its idiosyncratic development were the commercial imperative, sectarianism, governmental intervention and their fluctuating interaction. With a few exceptions Irish newspapers existed primarily to make a profit for the families and limited partnerships of small businessmen which owned them. In the largely unrestricted early years some were quite lucrative, and men like Faulkner became rich and influential. Later, the market became very much more competitive, and the prospect of minimal profits, or outright failure, quite high. Government taxation, designed initially perhaps for revenue, but later intended to drive the price of newspapers up to limit their influence, was an important factor. It was not, however, the only one. Throughout the period considered by this book, population was increasing rapidly, as were literacy rates and English-language-speaking. Despite this the press notably failed to penetrate much of the potential market. The number of newspapers increased, but the number of copies sold remained limited. The best-selling newspaper in 1831 sold fewer copies than the best-selling newspaper in the 1770s or 1790s.[144] The geographical spread was very uneven, judging by the number of stamps issued by the Treasury. The city and county of Dublin, with 380,000 people, accounted for 2,262,315 stamps in 1830/31.[145] Even allowing for the national circulation of the major metropolitan papers, this was disproportionate. Moreover, of the 1,691,000 stamps issued in the rest of the country, almost a million went to just four counties: Antrim, Cork, Londonderry and Waterford. On the other hand the four western counties of Clare, Galway, Roscommon and Sligo, with a combined population of 1,095,000, absorbed just 78,356 stamps. In 1831, as a century before, newspapers tended to reach Protestant rather than Catholic, Pale rather than Gael, and urban rather than rural. The old barriers might have eroded a little, but they had certainly not been broken down. Because Irish newspapers remained small enterprises seeking profits in a limited market, they were often easily susceptible to the blandishments of whoever had resources to bestow, in terms of subscribers, advertisers, or favours. They responded both to the public mood, albeit of a restricted 'public', and to the overtures of pressure groups, as well as to the douceurs and threats of successive governments.

In the heyday of Protestant Ascendancy, and until the complacency of the minority began to wane in the face of Catholic renewal, there was a ready market for what might be loosely described as Enlightenment ideas. Patriot, and later United Irish newspapers, attained wide circulations. There was significant latent sectarianism, but it was masked, to a considerable degree, by widespread consensus on constitutional reform and freer trade, and by a growing awareness of the need to reach some sort of accommodation between Catholics and Protestants. Widespread elite support for change, as well as the press input of such groups as the Volunteers, and later the United Irishmen, effectively counteracted intermittent and frequently inept attempts at control by government.

The 1790s saw the pattern changing. The progress of the French Revolution may have delighted and galvanised some elements of Irish society, but it certainly alarmed others. A more determined government, faced with war as well as revolution, intervened more vigorously and decisively. It had the backing of an increasing proportion of the elite, and of Protestants more generally. The traumatic year of 1798, which at the same time demonstrated the futility of the radical agenda, and the continuing potential for social jacquerie and sectarian cleansing, hastened the process. It was a crucial turning point. With the government and much of public opinion of the same conservative mind many of the newspapers swung around. Some were subverted, or massively bribed, but many were quite happy to accept a limited degree of influence in return for a modest amount in subsidy. Radical and pro-French newspapers were suppressed, and more moderate papers which resisted were harassed. However, government control, even under the redoubtable Robert Peel towards the end of the Napoleonic Wars, was never complete or secure, and never precluded significant debate on issues such as the Union and Catholic emancipation.

The end of the war ushered in a period of progressive, though never complete, government disengagement. The mood was for retrenchment and financial accountability, and there was less consensus on the legitimacy of intervention, when the apparent enemy was the Catholics rather than the French and their would-be collaborators. Successive governments sought to disburden themselves of financial commitments, and to strictly regulate those which remained. The end result was a disjointed and increasingly enfeebled Irish press policy, apparently intended to be mediatorial and moderating. Apart from its taxation component, which kept newspaper prices high and their subscribers elite, it was generally ineffectual. The retreat of government opened the way, not for a return to Enlightenment ideals, or rational-critical debate, but for the full emergence and intensification of sectarian disputation. The Irish press was still limited by governmental policies which kept prices high. It had failed to break through the barriers which would have enabled it to tap the rapidly growing market of poorer anglophone literates. Deprived of the supplement of governmental subsidy, it turned to the easy available alternative, the well-funded and widely supported sectarian pressure groups of the 1820s and 1830s. Their rancorous antagonisms came to set the tone of much of the press. The press did not create the sectarianism, but it certainly did much to propagate and enhance it. By the middle 1830s it was clear that even at the highest levels of political reflection and literary endeavour there was sectarian polarisation. The *Dublin University Magazine* was an ornament of Irish culture, but its religious and party politics were exclusive and vehement. It symbolised a press in which Laodiceanism and enlightened scepticism, not to mention rational inter-community debate, had become heavily discounted. Newspapers which preached moderation, conciliation and detachment still existed, but they rarely reflected the popular mood even among those affluent enough to be purchasers. It was the militants who were at 'the leading edge' of the Irish press, and they set the predominant tone.

The Irish public political sphere was apparently polarised by religion rather than fragmented by class, and the press both reflected and facilitated this process. In effect two largely separate and antagonistic communities evolved, each with its own press interest which helped sustain both internal cohesion and external animosity. This may well have always been the most likely outcome of the interaction of deep-seated, if at times latent, sectarianism, and intense commercial rivalries in a restricted market. The main role of governmental intervention, which was the major variable, may simply have been to influence the timing of the process and the degree of animosity. In the present state of historical research most conclusions are of necessity tentative, since there are significant imbalances and lacunae in much of the discussion, especially for the later periods. When we know as much about the long-lasting and influential *Dublin Evening Post* and *Dublin Evening Mail* as we do about the short-lived and aberrant *Northern Star*, as much about the working relationship of the sectarian organisations with the press as about the manipulative endeavours of Robert Peel, and as much about the Sheehans and the 1820s as about Sam Neilson and the 1790s, it will be possible to address the complex issues involved with more authority and certainty.

NOTES

1 Jürgen Habermas, *The Structural Transformation of the Public Sphere: An Inquiry into a Category of Bourgeois Society*, trans. T. Burger (Cambridge, MA, 1989); 'Further reflections on the public sphere', trans. T. Burger, in Craig Colhoun (ed.), *Habermas and the Public Sphere* (Cambridge, MA, 1993), 421–60.
2 Robert Munter, *The History of the Irish Newspaper 1685–1760* (Cambridge, 1967), esp. pp. 157–88.
3 R. R. Madden, *The History of Irish Periodical Literature, from the End of the 17th to the Middle of the 19th Century, its Origin, Progress and Results*, 2 vols. (London, 1867).
4 Munter, *Irish Newspaper*, pp. 6–7, 119–30, 131–4, 153–6.
5 Richard Edwards to Francis Price, 4 August 1745, HMC, Puleston MSS, p. 333.
6 C. S. Parker (ed.), *Sir Robert Peel, from his Private Papers*, 3 vols. (London, 1891–9), vol. I, pp. 134–5.
7 Niall O'Ciosain, *Print and Popular Culture in Ireland 1750–1850* (London and New York, 1997), pp. 50–51.
8 Munter, *Irish Newspaper*, p. 62.
9 Ibid., pp. 68–70.
10 Ibid., pp. 155–6, 185.
11 Ibid., pp. 39, 67, 189.
12 Ibid., p. 89.
13 Ibid., pp. 58–9.
14 Madden, *Irish Periodical Literature*, vol. II, pp. 210, 230, 257.

15 There was no Irish-language newspaper throughout the entire period up to 1833.
16 Munter, *Irish Newspaper*, p. 90.
17 Ibid., p. 69.
18 Ibid., p. 162: 'Through a feature column, "Martha Love-Rule", the Journal contributed advice to the lovelorn and responded to female queries'.
19 Madden, *Irish Periodical Literature*, vol. I, p. 226.
20 Munter, *Irish Newspaper*, pp. 161–8; Madden, *Irish Periodical Literature*, vol. II, pp. 35–6.
21 Munter, *Irish Newspaper*, pp. 189–91.
22 Ibid., pp. 125–9.
23 Ibid., pp. 186–7.
24 *Dublin Journal*, 27 March 1725.
25 Madden, *Irish Periodical Literature*, vol. I, p. 239; Munter, *Irish Newspaper*, pp. 153–6.
26 James Lydon, *The Making of Ireland: From Ancient Times to the Present* (London and New York, 1998), p. 240.
27 Madden, *Irish Periodical Literature*, vol. I, p. 239; Munter, *Irish Newspaper*, pp. 153–6.
28 Lydon, *The Making of Ireland*, p. 253.
29 James Kelly, *Henry Flood: Patriots and Politics in Eighteenth-Century Ireland* (Dublin, 1998), p. 175.
30 Lydon, *The Making of Ireland*, p. 251.
31 Ibid., p. 253.
32 Marianne Elliott, *Wolfe Tone: Prophet of Irish Independence* (New Haven and London, 1999), pp. 113, 115, 157; Kelly, *Henry Flood*, pp. 196, 304–6, 379.
33 Nancy J. Curtin, *The United Irishmen: Popular Politics in Ulster and Dublin 1791–1798* (Oxford, 1994), p. 220.
34 Habermas, *The Public Sphere*, pp. 94–5.
35 Munter, *Irish Newspaper*, pp. 50, 81, 109; W. P. Carey, *Appeal to the People of Ireland* (Dublin, 1795), p. 11.
36 Kelly, *Henry Flood*, pp. 122–5, 137–8.
37 James Kelly, *Prelude to Union: Anglo-Irish Politics in the 1780s* (Cork, 1992), p. 199.
38 Ibid., p. 154.
39 Curtin, *United Irishmen*, p. 220.
40 O'Ciosain, *Print and Popular Culture*, pp. 32–8.
41 Ibid., pp. 154–69.
42 Madden, *Irish Periocial Literature*, vol. II, pp. 37, 170, 181, 236–9, 242.
43 Munter, *Irish Newspaper*, pp. 47–8.
44 Madden, *Irish Periodical Literature*, vol. II, p. 297.
45 Ibid., vol. II, pp. 255–6.
46 Ibid., vol. II, pp. 237–8.
47 Ibid., vol. II, p. 249.
48 Brian Inglis, *The Freedom of the Press in Ireland 1784–1841* (London, 1954), pp. 69–70.
49 Ibid., pp. 45–6.

50 Ibid., p. 110.
51 Ibid., pp. 177, 234.
52 Ibid., p. 60.
53 Ibid., p. 57; *General Evening Post*, 1 May 1781.
54 R. B. MacDowell, *Ireland in the Age of Imperialism and Revolution* (Oxford, 1979), pp. 529–30.
55 Madden, *Irish Periodical Literature*, vol. II, pp. 110, 126, 152–5, 300–301, 309, 338.
56 A. Aspinall, *Politics and the Press 1780–1850* (Brighton, 1949), p. 136; Inglis, *Freedom of the Press*, pp. 70–72.
57 Madden, *Irish Periodical Literature*, vol. II, p. 124; Aspinall, *Politics and the Press*, pp. 110–17.
58 Inglis, *Freedom of the Press*, p. 75.
59 Kelly, *Henry Flood*, pp. 230, 339; Inglis, *Freedom of the Press*, pp. 82–5.
60 Charlemont to Halliday, February 1787, HMC, Charlemont MSS, pp. 47–8. Charlemont to Halliday, 3 August 1790, ibid., pp. 128–9.
61 Inglis, *Freedom of the Press*, pp. 75–80; Madden, *Irish Periodical Literature*, vol. II, pp. 347, 367.
62 Inglis, *Freedom of the Press*, pp. 84–5.
63 Ibid., p. 94; Lydon, *The Making of Ireland*, p. 267, claims 5,000; Madden, *Irish Periodical Literature*, vol. II, p. 233, gives a relatively detached view of its style and content.
64 Inglis, *Freedom of the Press*, pp. 23, 44; A. P. W. Malcolmson, *John Foster: The Politics of the Anglo-Irish Ascendancy* (Oxford, 1978), p. 49.
65 Curtin, *United Irishmen*, p. 220.
66 Inglis, *Freedom of the Press*, pp. 89–91.
67 The French spy Duckett was closely associated with the *Northern Star*, and a friend of Benjamin Franklin's with the *Volunteer's Journal*.
68 Inglis, *Freedom of the Press*, p. 30.
69 Ibid., pp. 92–8.
70 Ibid., pp. 98–104.
71 *Irish Parliamentary Register*, vol. III, p. 166 (12 April 1784).
72 Inglis, *Freedom of the Press*, pp. 70–72.
73 MacDowell, *Imperialism and Revolution*, pp. 594–8.
74 Inglis, *Freedom of the Press*, pp. 111–12; Aspinall, *Politics and the Press*, pp. 317–25.
75 Inglis, *Freedom of the Press*, pp. 126, 151–3, 162–3, 165–6, 181.
76 *The Literary Life and Correspondence of the Countess of Blessington*, 3 vols. (London, 1855), vol. I, pp. 166–7.
77 John Bric to Daniel O'Connell, 9/11 November 1820: Maurice O'Connell (ed.), *The Correspondence of Daniel O'Connell*, 7 vols. (Shannon, 1977), vol. II, pp. 303–5; Aspinall, *Politics and the Press*, pp. 327, 335–40.
78 Inglis, *Freedom of the Press*, p. 142.
79 Ibid., pp. 138–41.
80 *Dublin Chronicle*, 24 May 1816.
81 Inglis, *Freedom of the Press*, p. 175.
82 Ibid., p. 190.

Ireland 1760–1820

83 National Library of Ireland, Farnham MSS, 18612(15), Copy of Agreement of 12 April 1832.
84 O'Ciosain, *Print and Popular Culture*, pp. 38, 154–69.
85 Inglis, *Freedom of the Press*, p. 191.
86 Ibid., p. 168.
87 Inglis, *Freedom of the Press*, p. 149. The official amount in the Proclamation Fund was £10,500 but this was habitually overspent. Under the Grenville ministry as much as £18,000 p.a. was drawn from this source.
88 Ibid., p. 146.
89 Ibid., p. 145.
90 Ibid., pp. 145–6.
91 Ibid., p. 130.
92 Ibid., p. 123.
93 Ibid., p. 122.
94 O. MacDonagh, 'Ideas and Institutions 1830–1845', in T. W. Moody, F. X. Martin and F. J. Byrne (eds.), *A New History of Ireland*, 9 vols. (Cambridge, 1976–96), vol. v, *Ireland under the Union I*, ed. W. Vaughan, 218–41.
95 Aspinall, *Politics and the Press*, pp. 345–9.
96 Inglis, *Freedom of the Press*, pp. 164–89.
97 Ibid., p. 142.
98 *Dublin Chronicle*, 24 May 1816.
99 Inglis, *Freedom of the Press*, p. 174.
100 O'Ciosain, *Print and Popular Culture*, pp. 38, 154–69.
101 Inglis, *Freedom of the Press*, p. 190.
102 Ibid., p. 193.
103 Ibid., p. 175.
104 Ibid., p. 193.
105 Ibid.
106 For example, *Freeman's Journal*, 1, 2, 4, 5 January 1830. Very rarely did it much exceed four columns.
107 O'Ciosain, *Print and Popular Culture*, pp. 187–9.
108 Aspinall, *Politics and the Press*, p. 145.
109 Inglis, *Freedom of the Press*, p. 179.
110 Ibid., pp. 170–71.
111 Desmond Bowen, *The History and Shaping of Irish Protestantism* (New York, 1995), pp. 194–222.
112 W. J. McCormack (ed.), *The Blackwell Companion to Modern Irish Culture* (Oxford, 1999), p. 236.
113 *Freeman's Journal*, 5 January 1830.
114 *Star of Brunswick*, 13 December 1828.
115 *Transactions of the Protestant Colonisation Society of Ireland* (Dublin, n.d.).
116 John O'Connell (ed.), *The Select Speeches of Daniel O'Connell MP*, Second Series (Dublin, 1828), vol. II, pp. 242–3.
117 *Warder*, 3 September 1828.
118 Liam Kenney, Kerby A. Miller and Mark Graham, 'The Long Retreat: Protestants, Economy and Society 1660–1926', in Raymond Gillespie and Gerard Moran (eds.), *Longford Essays on County History* (Dublin, 1991).

119 Ian d'Alton, *Protestant Society and Politics in Cork 1812–1844* (Cork, 1980), pp. 36, 201.
120 K. Theodore Hoppen, *Elections, Politics, and Society in Ireland 1832–1885* (Oxford, 1994), p. 458.
121 Aspinall, *Politics and the Press*, p. 320.
122 Ibid., pp. 319–24.
123 *Warder*, 2 August 1828.
124 Inglis, *Freedom of the Press*, pp. 220–24.
125 See, for example, 5 September 1828, 7 January and 12 April 1830.
126 Sir Thomas Wyse, *Historical Sketch of the Late Catholic Association of Ireland*, 2 vols. (London, 1829), vol. I, pp. 338–40.
127 Inglis, *Freedom of the Press*, pp. 197–8; *Cork Constitution*, 28 January 1832.
128 Aspinall, *Politics and the Press*, pp. 345–9.
129 *Bath and Cheltenham Gazette*, 13 November 1828. For reasons which are unclear this newspaper was unusually well informed about Irish affairs.
130 National Library of Ireland (NLI), Farnham MSS 18610(1), Captain Cottingham to Farnham, 6 February 1829; 18610(2), J. S. Cotterell to Farnham, 9 January 1829.
131 NLI, Farnham MSS 18604(4), D. H. Kelly (Secretary of Brunswick Constitutional Club of Ireland), 6 February 1829; 18609(1), Reverend Charles Boyton to Farnham, 5 February 1829.
132 NLI, Farnham MSS 18610(4), Captain Cottingham to Farnham, 18 July 1831.
133 d'Alton, *Protestant Society and Politics in Cork*, p. 166.
134 NLI, Farnham MSS 18609(1), Boyton to Farnham, 5 February 1829; Boyton to Farnham, 20 March 1830; Boyton to Farnham, 4 December 1830; 18609(2), Boyton to Farnham, 14 December 1830.
135 *Warder*, 2 August 1828.
136 *Standard*, 14 October 1828 (*Standard* attributes it incorrectly to the *Warder*).
137 O'Connell to his wife, 2 December 1823: M. O'Connell, *Correspondence of Daniel O'Connell*, vol. II, pp. 521–2.
138 See, for example, *Warder*, 16, 19 and 26 July 1828; *Star of Brunswick*, 29 November 1828; *Freeman's Journal*, 1 and 15 January 1830; Inglis, *Freedom of the Press*, p. 198; T. M. Madden (ed.), *Irish Periodical Literature; Reminiscences from 1798 to 1856: Being the Memoirs (Chiefly Autobiographical) of Richard Robert Madden* (New York, 1891), pp. 307–8.
139 *Freeman's Journal*, 5 January 1830.
140 *Warder*, 3 September 1828.
141 Inglis, *Freedom of the Press*, p. 34; *Warder*, 16 July 1828.
142 D. G. S. Simes, 'A Voice for Irish Conservatism: the *Dublin University Magazine* 1833–41', in J. Wilkes (ed.), *Conference Papers of the Australasian Victorian Studies Association (1993)* (Auckland, 1993); Wayne E. Hall, *Dialogues in the Margin: a Study of the Dublin University Magazine* (Washington, 2000) was not available at the time of writing.
143 Munter, *Irish Newspaper*, p. 34. Madden, *Irish Periodical Literature*, vol. II, pp. 172–8, 230; T. M. Madden, *Reminiscences of Richard Robert Madden*, pp. 307–8.

144 Inglis, *Freedom of the Press*, pp. 94, 175; Madden, *Irish Periodical Literature*, vol. II, p. 292.
145 All figures are derived from the Stamp Tax returns: HC 1829 (164) xxii. 273, 1830 (119) xxv. 365, 1830 (549) xxv. 349 and 1831–2 (242) xxxiv. 123. Population statistics are derived from B. R. Mitchell, *British Historical Statistics* (Cambridge, 1986), p. 32.

6   America, 1750–1820

David Copeland

Between 1750 and 1820 America underwent a series of extensive political upheavals in which the press played a pivotal role. Beginning as colonies of Great Britain, America declared its independence in 1776 following a tumultuous ten years of protest against British laws and taxes. After eight years of revolution, Britain agreed to a peace that allowed the newly formed United States to develop its unique governmental system. From the end of the Revolution through to the first two decades of the nineteenth century, Americans transformed their country from a loosely organised confederation of states into a nation with a strong central government and a powerful constitution. In all these developments, a fast-growing newspaper press acted both as witness to events and as an active participant in the political process. As America's public sphere developed and the voice of public opinion became more dominant, the press played a crucial role in shaping this new political world.

On 1 January 1799, Judge Alexander Addison warned in Boston's *Columbian Centinel*, 'Give to any set of men the command of the press, and you give them the command of the country, for you give them the command of public opinion, which commands everything.' Addison wrote his letter to the Federalist newspaper at a time when America's two main political ideologies – Federalism and Republicanism – vied for control of the United States, itself scarcely a decade old. Addison's Federalist party, which favoured a strong, central government and controlled the presidency, was locked in battle with the Republicans, who wanted less centralisation and more power for individual states. Whilst politicians debated the issues, however, arguably the most important debate took place in America's press, since, as one writer remarked, '[W]ithout political knowledge the people cannot secure their liberties, and this necessary information they receive by the medium of News-Papers.'[1]

Six months before Addison wrote his letter to the *Centinel*, President John Adams sponsored a series of new laws collectively known as the Alien and Sedition Acts. At the heart of this measure was an attempt to silence newspapers opposed to the Federalist Administration. Anyone who wrote, uttered, printed or published any false, scandalous or malicious comments against the government was to be punished by fine and imprisonment. The Alien and Sedition Acts appeared to be a direct violation of America's First Amendment, which stated, 'Congress shall make no law... abridging the freedom of speech, or of the press.' That Adams and the Federalists felt this law was necessary tells us much about the importance of newspapers in influencing American society during the late eighteenth and early nineteenth centuries. It also explains the comments of the Republican printer William Duane, who was as keen as many politicians to influence opinion. 'The fact is', Duane wrote, 'that my pen and press are the only formidable weapons I have ever used.'[2]

The prominence of newspapers and other forms of print reflected both the breadth of popular involvement in public debate and the widespread use of the press to facilitate and promote this process. But it was not just the backcountry farmer, middle-class merchant or elite, educated planters, lawyers and politicians who had access to, and used the public forum afforded by, the press.[3] High literacy rates in America, which exceeded 90 per cent in some regions by 1800, meant that even the poor were more often literate than not,[4] and ensured that access to the public sphere was restricted neither by gender nor race. Thus people of colour and women could also voice their opinions and shape the public sphere to some degree, as could those who were motivated solely by religious beliefs.[5] Although voting and other forms of formal political involvement was limited to white males, women were active in shaping society and had been for decades. America's female population had always been literate, and by the nineteenth century, literacy rates between the sexes were nearly identical.[6] When one also considers the subscription penetration of newspapers, and factors such as women's role as educators of children in the home, there seems little doubt that they were avid readers of newspapers and would have discussed their contents.[7]

Whilst newspapers had a wide audience, determining how many Americans actively contributed to press debate is difficult, particularly because of the use of pseudonyms and common absence of any form of signature on essays and letters. Especially in the colonial period and the era before the repeal of the Alien and Sedition Acts in 1802, many writers avoided using their real names. Anonymity protected them from libel charges and allowed them to be more vituperative in their assaults. But it served another purpose, too. Anonymity also reflected a commitment to a particular cause or argument, rather than an appeal to personal authority. Thus, John Dickinson's 'Letters from a Farmer in Pennsylvania' of 1767 and 1768 represented the mass of hardworking colonials – farmers, merchants, shippers – not the elite of society from which he came. His arguments concerning a boycott of British goods in an effort to influence British tax policies were of more importance than the true identity of the writer, despite the fact that Dickinson, as a well-known and influential Philadelphia lawyer, had a certain amount of individual status. Similarly, in the pivotal years of 1787 and 1788, discussion of the direction which the new Republic should take captured significant space in the newspaper press, as Federalists and Anti-Federalists debated the philosophical basis for the new nation. Some of America's greatest and best-known thinkers – Alexander Hamilton, James Madison and John Jay – penned *The Federalist Papers*. Seventy-seven of the eighty-five essays appeared in newspapers throughout America under the pseudonyms 'a Citizen of New York' and 'Publius'.

Yet despite a lack of evidence concerning both the readers and writers of newspapers, it seems likely that the public sphere in America was broader than that of most European nations, and that the American press was particularly powerful. As one Vermont writer stated, 'All ranks and descriptions of men, read, study, and endeavour to comprehend the intelligence they [newspapers] convey... as if they were sanctioned by irrefragable authority.'[8] In common with European states, however, the American public sphere was not owned solely by a bourgeois class,[9] nor was it narrowly devoted to any form of 'rational-critical debate', since Americans cleverly mixed the emotion that surrounded the volatile issues of independence and nationhood with Enlightenment rationalism in the writings that appeared in the public prints.[10] According to Michael Schudson, America did not fit into Habermas's model of a rational-critical sphere where public debate shaped political policy because there was little political involvement by the press or by the populace at this time, whilst papers only reacted in times of political crisis.[11] He notes that few people with the franchise chose to vote during the first forty years of the United States' existence, and cites the work of Stephen Botein, which claims that printers were reluctant to take sides during America's formation, and only did so when forced.[12] Schudson believes that news was chosen to avoid controversy, and that printers sought to present material that was a safe alternative to political debate. For eighteenth-century printers, he argues, the more remote the news was and the less local connection there was, the better.[13]

This approach, however, misses the intricacies of news dissemination in eighteenth-century America. As Richard D. Brown has pointed out, America's naturally pluralistic society produced a complicated system for sharing information. Brown notes that word of mouth, public ceremony and address, coupled with printing, all combined to shape society.[14] Newspapers throughout the eighteenth century, and even into the nineteenth, sometimes found it less necessary to discuss local issues than those with more holistic implications because of alternative local oral networks and ceremonies. This did not mean, however, that print – and specifically newspapers – played a secondary role to the oral dissemination of information throughout our period. Nor does it mean that local issues were not discussed in newspapers. Thus, the events of the 1750s surrounding the French and Indian War (America's name for its part in the Seven Years War) propelled newspapers to a position of prominence in terms of the spread of information because local, trans-colonial and international events all had the potential for direct repercussions throughout America.

Although the French and Indian War proved a significant turning point for American newspapers, the written dissemination of news had begun to increase in prominence much earlier. Handwritten newsletters in the late seventeenth and early eighteenth centuries which were circulated among the clergy, merchants and others set the stage for the introduction of public prints. Benjamin Harris stated that he was beginning *Publick Occurrences* in 1690, in part, so 'That people every where may better understand the Circumstances of Publique Affairs, both abroad and at home' and to stop the 'many false reports' being spread by New England's oral network.[15] Even though John Campbell's *Boston News-Letter*, begun in 1704, often published news up to a year old, it assumed a growing importance in the information-dispersal network of New England. One letter-writer from Harvard in 1714, for example, simply mentioned reading about the news rather than commenting on it because both he and his father subscribed to Boston's newspaper and were 'informed by this weeks Newsletter' of the events.[16]

As the number of newspapers grew in specific locales during the 1730s and 1740s, print culture began to do more than supplement oral traditions. In towns with multiple newspapers, such as Boston, New York and Philadelphia, printers offered readers a wide range of topics and issues. Moreover, they began to provide a forum for debate, such as that surrounding the itinerant preacher George Whitefield in 1739. Newspapers, rather than the oral communication network, stimulated discussion and sustained it, even though print did not supplant oral communication altogether.[17] When newspapers were delivered to specific communities, according to a New Jersey account, 'one subscriber would read it [the newspaper] on the evening of its arrival and pass it over to his neighbor the next morning'.[18] Similarly, people would go to taverns to borrow newspapers once they arrived in a town or listen there as the paper was read aloud, as the growing ties between regions in colonial America heightened the population's interest in both local and national affairs.[19]

Gradually, local news became an important part of shared information, both because its appearance in a paper gave the news legitimacy and provided a way to disseminate it to other regions through the exchange of newspapers by printers and because the issues being discussed on local levels had national repercussions.[20]

To say, as Schudson does, that the press was not involved in political dialogue unless dragged there is therefore unlikely. America's printers included controversial information in their newspapers, which is why *Publick Occurrences* lasted just one issue in 1690 (falling victim to administrative censorship), and why printers and editors in the eighteenth century believed their publications needed to stimulate debate within the public sphere. As William Cobbett said in his *Porcupine's Gazette and Daily Advertiser* in 1797, 'Professions of impartiality I shall make none,' adding that any editor that did not actively involve his newspaper in the political issues of the day was 'a poor passive fool, and not an editor'.[21] Philip Freneau declared in the same decade that 'public opinion sets the bounds to every government, and is the real sovereign of every free one.'[22] And a host of printers from 1754 until the Revolution agreed with Benjamin Franklin's famous woodcut, 'JOIN, or DIE', and promoted the unity of the colonies and colonials in the French and Indian War, the Stamp Act crisis, and the prelude to the Revolution itself.

It has been argued that because eighteenth-century assemblies conducted much of their business in secret – only occasionally publishing their proceedings in an official journal – America's public sphere was limited and its openness questionable.[23] Yet there is little to indicate that such attempts at secrecy had much impact on the press's discussion of political proceedings. Although delegates to the Constitutional Congress in Philadelphia in 1787 voted 'That nothing spoken in the House be printed, or otherwise published or communicated without leave',[24] newspapers discussed the delegates attending the convention, the significance of what was taking place, the election of George Washington as President, the form the new government might take, and the weaknesses of the old government under the Articles of Confederation during the convention.[25] In the same year, Congress authorised the Secretary of State to select newspapers to publish the laws and resolutions it passed. Congress subsequently expanded the number of papers that published its proceedings and even added a German-language edition to the authorised list. By 1799, it mandated that at least one newspaper in each state – more if needed – would be selected to publish legislature.[26] Newspapers were therefore able to both report and comment on proceedings with relative freedom. They thus allowed individuals at all levels to become part of the public sphere and 'join in debate of issues bearing on state authority'.[27]

The fact that voting numbers were low, therefore, is of less importance to the existence of a public sphere than the degree and nature of public debate that took place in other arenas. In this respect, America can be seen as sharing many similarities with several of the European countries examined in this volume, and England in particular.

Indeed, it was because America developed as a group of British colonies that its newspapers followed the pattern and practice of newspapers there in other respects too. The first American effort at producing a newspaper, Boston's *Publick Occurrences Both Forreign and Domestick*, came eighty-three years after initial British colonisation in 1607. Benjamin Harris's paper officially fell victim to licensing, as the Governor's Council of Massachusetts Bay invoked the instructions given to it by parliament in 1686. 'Forasmuch as great inconvenience may arise by liberty of printing within our said territory under your government,' the directive issued to all colonial governors until 1730 stated, 'you are to provide by all necessary orders that no person keep any printing-press for printing, nor that any book, pamphlet or other matter whatsoever be printed without your especial leave and license first obtained.'[28] Parliament allowed licensing to lapse in England in 1695, but American newspapers operated under the official shackles of licensing for the first three decades of the eighteenth century. Until that time, the phrase 'Printed by Authority' in the paper's nameplate indicated that its licence to print news had the approval of the colonial government. While licensing affected newspaper publication when there was only one newspaper in America, the practice never truly stopped printers from printing what they wanted once competition for readers began in the 1720s. Printers quickly followed English practices of layout and emulated the essays of Trenchard, Gordon, and others.

The subject matter of opinion pieces in newspapers varied, but before the middle of the eighteenth century, most dealt with education, medicine, religion, and issues concerning correct social behaviour, including marriage. As America grew more populous and economically independent, political issues became the central focus of opinion in newspapers, especially in the twenty-five years before the Revolution. But politics also played a role in many of the issues surrounding education, medicine and religion. As early as 1721, for example, a smallpox epidemic spurred a medical debate with political and religious overtones in Boston. Competing factions used letters and essays to discuss the validity of inoculation, and their debates also included the control of the colony's government and religious establishments.[29] War was a more pressing topic of debate from the mid-eighteenth century onwards. From 1754, newspapers printed nearly every obtainable piece of information about the fighting in America, and did the same with news concerning battles between Britain and France in any part of the world during the Seven Years War. American newspapers presented a comprehensive national and international picture of events for all who read the papers or heard their contents discussed in public places.[30] Moreover, the press sought to influence the country's managing of its international affairs. Printers in 1754 and 1755, for example, pushed for acceptance of the Albany Plan of Union. Newspapers published speeches from colonial assemblies and essays from anonymous writers detailing the horrors of what would happen to America if the French and Indians were not stopped. Creating a universal voice that opposed French aggression in America was not difficult, but printers were doing more than this, even if they did not realise it. They were making the press indispensable to public debate through practices such as verifying sources of news, supporting causes and urging adoption of political action. Events in the 1750s thus paved the way for the press's growing role in shaping public debate and popular politics in America for years to come.[31]

By 1773, Patriot leaders realised that the national agenda could be shaped by what appeared in the press, which is why John Adams described the work of the printers of the *Boston Gazette* as 'a curious employment, cooking up paragraphs, articles, occurrences, &c., working the political engine'.[32] By this point, printers were also more conscious of their influence. *The New-York Journal* printer, John Holt, wrote to Samuel Adams in the early days of 1776 that 'It was by means of News papers that we receiv'd and spread the Notice of the tyrannical designs formed against America and kindled a spirit that has been sufficient to repel them.'[33] The press, therefore, was widely acknowledged as a shaper of political culture and an agenda-setter for public debate. As John Adams wrote to Thomas Jefferson in 1815:

What do we mean by the Revolution? The war? That was no part of the Revolution; it was only an effect and consequence of it. The Revolution was in the hearts and minds of the people... The records of the thirteen legislatures, the pamphlets, newspapers in all the colonies, ought to be consulted during that period to ascertain the steps by which the public opinion was enlightened and informed concerning the authority of Parliament over the colonies.[34]

One sees some proof of Adams' observation by examining coverage of the Boston Massacre of 1770. Coloured woodcuts by Paul Revere depicting Red Coats firing into an innocent crowd of Bostonians printed in a handbill, coupled with inflammatory descriptions of the massacre in the *Boston Gazette*, transformed an event provoked by Bostonians into an act of aggression by British troops. As time passed, the Boston Massacre took on a meaning of its own thanks to the press. Isaiah Thomas of the

Massachusetts Spy, for example, published remembrances of the massacre yearly.³⁵ The entire event was slowly transformed into part of America's cultural fabric, taking on new meaning as issues changed. In 1887, for example, Crispus Attucks, an African American and one of those killed in the King Street confrontation, became a symbol for civil rights.³⁶

Not surprisingly, participation in the public sphere increased as America made the transition from colony to nation. In political battles between Federalists and Anti-Federalists, for example, Saul Cornell has noted that Anti-Federalists from all social and economic strata participated in the printed debate over the form of government the United States should adopt.³⁷ While this is true, it did not necessarily mean active involvement by all Americans as correspondents, letter-writers or essayists – rather, that the press was at least *presumed* to be open to all. Benjamin Franklin, along with most other American printers, realised this early on. Franklin acknowledged that printers were the sole proprietors of their presses, but he said, 'they willingly allow, that any one is entitled to the Use of it, who thinks it necessary to offer his Sentiments on disputable Point to the Publick'.³⁸ He also believed that when issues of public importance were at stake, 'both Sides ought equally to have the Advantage of being heard by the Publick'. Franklin believed if that happened, then truth – by which he meant the general good – would always win out.³⁹ In 1770, the anonymous BRITANNICUS reiterated Franklin's ideas when he wrote in a New York essay, '*Public grievances* can never be redressed but by *public complaints*; and they cannot well be made *without the* PRESS.'⁴⁰

The relationship between the press and the public sphere was clearly a symbiotic one. Discussion of the issues of the day took place in coffee houses, taverns and even on public streets. But the catalyst for debate was almost always the printed word in newspapers, which according to James Carey was key to the formation of the public sphere in America.⁴¹ Increasingly, after the French and Indian War, the press assumed a major role in shaping public debate. As a French diplomat pointed out in 1783, 'They [Americans] have printed news at once; they [newspapers] are read avidly in the Circles, the taverns and public places. They dispute the articles; they examine from all sides, since all the individuals without exception take part in public affairs and are naturally talkers and questioners.'⁴² Whilst other forms of printed material such as pamphlets and broadsides remained important, much of what appeared in them ended up shared throughout America in the newspaper press. This was especially true in the case of pamphlets. Thomas Paine's *Common Sense*, for example, was enormously successful in this form, but it still found its way into newspapers as a way to disseminate the pamphlet's main points quickly.⁴³ Paine's other influential writing of the Revolution, *The Crisis*, appeared first in the

Pennsylvania Journal in three instalments before becoming a pamphlet. The same is true of *The Federalist Papers*, which were expanded slightly into pamphlet form in 1788, but were introduced to Americans via New York newspapers and reprints of the essays in the papers of other states. As the number of daily newspapers in America increased, it became more easy and efficient to use newspapers to shape opinion rather than other printed matter. The use of pamphlets and broadsides did not end, but they – like their readers – were increasingly dependent on newspapers. Thus, when Federalists in Albany, New York, wanted to promote their candidates for election in 1799, they produced a broadside listing their candidates that referred its readers back to the *Albany Gazette* for more in-depth information.[44]

As part of the colonial inheritance, ownership of newspapers followed British tradition from their emergence in the late seventeenth century: they were run by printers, postmasters or influential individuals who contracted the paper's production to a printer. Most vied for the royal printing contracts of their respective colonies. The competition for this business often produced odd results. In Virginia, for example, the assembly decreed all printing would go to the *Virginia Gazette*. As a result, every paper published in the colony before the Revolution was named *Virginia Gazette*, with several versions sometimes in direct competition and distinguished only by the name of the printer. By 1760, increases in sales meant that printers did not necessarily need a government contract to produce a profitable newspaper. Printers generally expected a weekly circulation of between 500 and 600 papers, and larger cities produced more than one newspaper. Boston, for example, had four newspapers in 1754, with a combined circulation of 2,400. This means that the population-to-newspaper-issue ratio was seven to one.[45] Newspaper penetration into society may have been even greater in the 1760s and later, however, as Americans shared their newspapers and read and discussed them at public houses. One New York writer explained that newspapers were 'borrowed one to another to the distance perhaps of twenty miles', while another said America had become 'a nation of newspaper readers'.[46]

As has been noted, the growth of newspapers from the middle of the eighteenth century coincided with increased public interest in political issues, first prompted by the French and Indian War. By the time France surrendered Canada in 1760, the colonies' English-language papers had grown from eleven to nineteen, an increase of 73 per cent and a growth rate twice that of the population from 1750 to 1760.[47] Following the war, the number of newspapers grew steadily to the beginning of the Revolution in 1775, when forty papers were published in America. That number fell to thirty-five by 1783. Newspaper production quickly rebounded, however, with a daily newspaper appearing for the first time in 1783. In colonial America, most papers appeared weekly, although printers attempted more frequent publication as early as 1720. For the most part, these attempts failed, probably for a number of reasons including scarcity of paper and news, coupled with a lack of financial resources. However, printers did issue multiple weekly issues on occasion, when they felt the news of the day warranted additional production (such as during the French and Indian War and again in the 1770s).

The political debate surrounding the adoption of the Constitution and Bill of Rights between 1787 and 1791 helped spur the growth of newspapers further, with ninety-one being regularly published in 1790. That number included eight dailies and produced a total circulation of about 50,000. Following the Revolution, Americans moved westward, filling the territory between the Appalachian Mountains and Mississippi River. This migrant population was accompanied by newspaper printers who set up presses when new communities were founded. By 1800, the number of newspapers increased to 234 with twenty-four dailies and a total circulation of 145,000. Before the Revolution, American newspapers were located along the Atlantic seaboard in towns with water access to the Atlantic Ocean. Water access remained important to the spread of news after the war, but twenty-one newspapers were published west of the mountains in 1800. By 1808, newspaper production crossed the Mississippi River,[48] and in 1815, 413 papers were printed in America, increasing to 512 in 1820 with some printing 4,000 copies per issue: a number that would jump to more than 25,000 in less than six years.[49] 'In no other country on earth,' wrote the editor Noah Webster in 1793, 'not even in Great-Britain, are newspapers so generally circulated among the body of people, as in America.'[50]

As the number of newspapers grew during the early nineteenth century, so, too, did the level of political affiliation shown by the press. In 1808, for example, all but fifty-six of the 329 newspapers in the United States were openly aligned with a political party. The politicisation of the press and its role in shaping policy changed radically during our period because of political upheaval, war and the developing government of the United States. In the early eighteenth century, newspaper printers usually advocated impartiality and were generally united in their outlook on the American situation. By 1770, however, printers began to develop fierce loyalties and commonly became openly partisan. Following the Revolution, and as the party system grew, both politicians and newspaper printers started new papers to support specific political agenda and to sway public opinion. In the decade following the constitution's ratification, the country witnessed a battle of competing political ideologies. The principal formulators of these principles were the Republican Thomas Jefferson and the Federalist Andrew Hamilton. Again following a British lead, newspapers began to support and promote the emerging parties and their chief spokesmen. The resulting partisan press, while not specifically owned by the political parties, certainly advocated and promoted what their respective party leaders said. The political system of the day also ensured that the party in power could reward its loyal editors by granting them government printing contracts and political office. Patronage meant considerable income for the newspaperman. John Fenno, for example, received up to $2,500 as printer to the Senate thanks to Hamilton. The same privileges were granted at all levels in America: from the presidency to local councils.[51]

But the American press was not simply showered with gifts in an attempt to control its contents – it could also be subject to harsher measures. Until 4 July 1776, America operated officially under British law. As a result, British libel laws technically controlled anything that the press printed. Still, few charges of seditious libel were brought against newspaper printers from 1735 – the year of the famous libel trial of New York printer John Peter Zenger – to the Revolution. As colonial legislatures gained more power, however, they did use libel laws in an attempt to control criticism in the volatile post-Stamp Act years of the 1765–6.[52] When James Parker published a handbill entitled 'To the Betrayed Inhabitants of New York' in 1770, the assembly took Parker and his apprentices into custody, where one of the apprentices revealed that Alexander McDougall, a member of the Sons of Liberty, had been in the shop. McDougall was promptly arrested for seditious libel, but though he spent time in gaol, he was not convicted, since the only one who could actually say McDougall wrote the handbill – Parker – died before the trial. After that, the assembly attempted to punish McDougall and even threatened him with *peine forte et dure*, a form of torture designed to make a suspect enter a plea in a case. McDougall resisted, and the torture threat was abandoned. Finally, the assembly's common-law charges against him were dropped.[53] In Boston, where radical Americans were even more fervent in their attacks on the British government and constantly used the Patriot press to slander officials, Governor Francis Bernard, Chief Justice Thomas Hutchinson and the Governor's Council all failed to get a grand jury to indict any writer or printer for the *Boston Gazette* on charges of seditious libel, which has led Leonard Levy to conclude that 'The law of seditious libel simply had no meaning any longer.'[54]

Yet though colonial governments were unable to control the press to any great extent between 1760 and 1776, factional groups outside government had greater success. Threats could follow printers' refusals to publish Patriot articles. '[I]f you cannot find room for such things,' a Georgia

Committee of Correspondence wrote to Savannah printer James Johnston concerning Patriot activities in Boston, 'we are determined to find one that will, and soon.'[55] Patriots also used coercion and assault in certain instances. When Boston printer John Mein referred to the Boston Massacre of 1770, somewhat mildly, as 'a most unfortunate affair', an economic boycott of his paper ensued, putting him out of business in four months. He returned to Britain in fear for his life. In New York, James Rivington refused to discontinue printing Tory views in his *New-York Gazetteer*. As a result, outraged Patriots hanged the printer in effigy in April 1775. Within a month, following the Battles of Lexington and Concord, his print shop was mobbed and Rivington taken into custody, where he was forced to sign an oath of allegiance to the American cause (although he ignored it and continued with his pro-British printing). In November, Patriots again entered Rivington's shop. This time, they demolished his press, and Rivington, like Mein, fled to Britain.[56]

Tighter governmental and legislative control of the press was apparent in the post-revolutionary period, when the new government of America felt under particular threat. In 1794, Jay's Treaty with Great Britain averted another war, but this, in turn, angered France, which had supported the United States since the struggle for independence and believed – since the Republicans endorsed the French Revolution – that they could rely on American support. As a result, France began raids on American ships. In 1797, President Adams tried to negotiate in secret with the French, but their agents demanded extortion money and hinted that America might be ripe for a bloody revolution along French lines. During what became known as the XYZ affair, Republican papers publicised these clandestine activities while angry Federalist news-sheets responded by associating the Republicans with French revolutionary violence, and accused them of being traitors. In an effort to silence opposition voices they feared were out to destroy the constitution, Federalists in Congress passed the Alien and Sedition Acts to clamp down on the press. Harrison Gray Otis justified the Acts in a speech in Congress: 'Every independent Government has a right to preserve and defend itself against injuries and outrages which endanger its existence.'[57] Outside government, a Boston writer stated, 'It is patriotism to write in favor of our government, it is sedition to write against it.'[58] About twenty-five people were arrested, with fourteen indictments handed down during the Acts' duration.[59] They were repealed in 1802, and for the most part, attempts at federal control of the press ended, although some states continued to charge editors with libel.

The relative weakness of governmental press controls in America compared to those in Europe may have been due in part to an ideological reluctance to stifle public opinion. At the same time that Patriots were bullying the Tory printers of revolutionary America, they espoused freedom for America's presses in their official documents. As early as 1774, the Continental Congress, in an attempt to gain Canadian support for its efforts to establish a new North American government, explained the significance of a free press:

> The last right we shall mention, regards the freedom of the press. The importance of this consists, besides the advancement of truth, science, morality, and arts in general, in its diffusion of liberal sentiments on the administration of Government, its ready communication of thoughts between subjects, and its consequential promotion of union among them, whereby oppressive officers are shamed or intimidated, into more honourable and just modes of conducting affairs.[60]

In addition, numerous states followed the lead of Virginia in 1776, where delegates adopted the Declaration of Rights, penned by George Mason, which stated, 'That the freedom of the press is one of the great bulwarks of liberty, and can never be restrained but by despotick governments.'[61]

After the Revolution, the United States operated under the Articles of Confederation, which did not mention press freedom. The concept, however, could be found in the constitutions of nine of the thirteen original states, yet when delegates met in Philadelphia in the summer of 1787 to draft a new plan of government, freedom of the press was again omitted. This, and other civil liberties, became the focal point of state ratification of the constitution, and the subject of much discussion. Mason complained that there 'is no declaration of any kind for preserving the liberty of the press'. He maintained that without a statement on press freedom and a press to keep government in check, despotic administrations might place restrictions on all liberties.[62] Perhaps the fullest debate on the freedom of the press took place in Massachusetts between John Adams and William Cushing. Cushing wrote that 'This liberty of publishing truth can never effectually injure a good government, or honest administrators,' while Adams believed 'The liberty of the press is essential to the security of freedom in a state: it ought not, therefore, to be restrained in this Commonwealth.'[63] The result of such debates was the Bill of Rights and the First Amendment, which guaranteed the right to free speech and a free press in 1791.

The fact that neither Tories, Republicans nor any dissenting political voice could ever be completely silenced reinforces the complex nature of the public sphere in America. Not all Americans were opposed to British colonial status and taxes from 1773 to 1776; not all Americans believed that the ideas of Republicans were libellous or harmful to the

United States from 1798 to 1800. And, after the demise of the Federalist party during 'the era of good feeling' – the term coined by editor Benjamin Russell to describe the eight-year period that began with the 1816 election[64] – not all Americans felt that a unified political consensus existed in America. Such beliefs were evident in the papers, and even the minority voice, which many attempted to suppress, remained alive in the public sphere. Yet such independent voices were under increasing attack in the nineteenth century. Although Alexis de Tocqueville remarked that in America the power of the press 'causes political life to circulate through all the parts of that vast country... It rallies the interests of the community round certain principles and draws up the creed of every party...', he also noted that 'When many organs of the press adopt the same line of conduct, their influence in the long run becomes irresistible, and public opinion, perpetually assailed from the same side, eventually yields to the attack.'[65]

This point was not lost on Thomas Jefferson when he wrote to fellow Republican James Madison that 'The engine is the press' in the months before the crucial 1800 election.[66] Jefferson, and the Republicans elected after him, enlarged the political patronage system, which became invaluable in the promotion of Republican ideals. Republicans voted in 1804 to add to the list of newspapers that could publish governmental proceedings, and Madison – when he was elected in 1808 – rewarded newspapers that had worked to elect both Jefferson and himself with government printing contracts.[67] The Republicans realised all too well that the party that best controlled the press – or had the greatest number of newspapers supporting its cause – would ultimately – to use Tocqueville's terminology – 'be irresistible'. As a result of the Republicans' ability to dominate public debate in the early nineteenth century, the two-party system was temporarily suspended on a national level. The Federalists could only muster electoral votes from New England in 1816, whilst they were labelled 'the enemies of the country' in Republican newspapers.[68] In 1820, the Federalists did not even put forward a presidential candidate. Still, the Republican victory was neither total nor long-lasting, and in 1819 the editor of the West Chester, Pennsylvania, *Village Record* commented that 'parties exist, and as much zeal is exhibited [in Pennsylvania], as in any state where the old party names still prevail'.[69]

Whatever the outcome of such inter-party battles, what was clear was the powerful role that the press had assumed in American society. This was evident to Isaiah Thomas, variously an apprentice, printer and editor from 1756 until 1802, who published *The History of Printing in America*, the nation's first media history, in 1810. Thomas observed that newspapers have become the vehicles of discussion, in which the principles of government, the interest of nations, the spirit and tendency of public measures... are all arraigned, tried and decided. Instead, therefore, of being considered now, as they once were, of small moment in society, they have become the welfare of the state, and deeply involving both its peace and prosperity... The general circulation of *Gazettes* forms an important era... in the political world. By means of this powerful instrument, impressions on the public mind may be made with a celerity, and to an extent, of which cannot but give rise to the most important consequences in society. Never was there given to man a political engine of greater power....[70]

Just as Habermas has suggested, the public sphere in America grew out of coffee houses, clubs, and other gatherings where public discussion took place. In such arenas, the newspaper increasingly served as the primary catalyst for debate from the French and Indian War period onwards. Americans did not abandon pamphlets, broadsides or public oration; they realised, however, that the public prints afforded them the best and quickest method of entering into public debate. To be sure, speeches under liberty trees and poles in communities throughout America in the 1760s and 1770s shaped local public opinion, but those speeches would have had little effect elsewhere had it not been for those enterprising printers who published them. Because most of the issues affecting America from the 1750s onwards encompassed all colonies, and subsequently all states, newspapers became the easiest means of sharing information. The New York printer James Parker noted in 1750, 'This Taste, we Englishmen, have for News, is a very odd one; yet it must be fed... it is an Amusement we can't be without.'[71] Virginian David Roper, proposing a new publication for Richmond, echoed these comments seventy-five years later when he noted that 'A thirst for newspaper reading prevails among all ranks of society throughout our country'.[72] Whilst the population's appetite for news was evident from an early date, the role of the newspaper in American society was to change over time. With the politics of revolution, Americans increasingly turned to newspapers as a way to influence public opinion. By the ratification of the constitution, America's leaders were keenly aware of this fact and sought ways to control opinion through patronage.[73] In this new political world, the engine of motivation for shaping colonies into a nation, for creating revolution, for forging a government and for effecting political change was the newspaper press.

NOTES

1 *Worcester* (MA) *Magazine*, third week in May 1786.
2 William Duane to Stephen R. Bradley, 10 November 1808, quoted in Richard N. Rosenfeld, *American Aurora: A Democratic-Republican Returns* (New York, 1997), p. 3.

3 See Saul Cornell, *The Other Founders: Anti-Federalism & the Dissenting Tradition in America, 1788–1828* (Chapel Hill, NC, 1999), pp. 26, 84–5.
4 Richard D. Brown, *Knowledge Is Power: The Diffusion of Information in Early America, 1700–1865* (New York and London, 1989), p. 12.
5 See, for example, Mary Beth Norton, *Founding Mothers & Fathers: Gendered Power and the Forming of American Society* (New York, 1996); Mary P. Ryan, *Civic Wars: Democracy and Public Life in the American City during the Nineteenth Century* (Berkeley, CA, 1997); Gary B. Nash, *Forging Freedom: The Formation of Philadelphia's Black Community 1720–1840* (Cambridge, MA, 1988); and Carol Sue Humphrey, *The Press of the Young Republic, 1783–1833* (Westport, CT, 1996), pp. 141–3. By 1850, for example, nearly 200 religious newspapers were printed in America. They were identical in most respects to secular papers except for publishing denomination-specific information. See, for example, David Copeland, 'Preserving a Denomination: The Promotion of Women by the North Carolina Antebellum Baptist Press', in David Sachsman (ed.), *The Press and the Civil War* (New Brunswick, NJ, 2000), 123–36.
6 Brown, *Knowledge Is Power*, p. 12.
7 A twentieth-century study, George Gallup, 'A Scientific Method for Determining Readership-Interest,' *Journalism Quarterly*, 7 (1930), 1–13, discovered that women were just as interested in political news as men. The same may be assumed for our time period, since most women were literate and the political affairs of the time affected them as well. Women also actively engaged in political activities during this period. One example is the Edenton Tea Party, where fifty-one North Carolina women entered into an agreement to boycott British-imported tea in 1774: see David Copeland, *Debating the Issues in Colonial Newspapers* (Greenwood, CT, 2000), pp. 316–18.
8 *Green Mountain Patriot* (Peacham, VT), 1 June 1798.
9 See Jürgen Habermas, 'Further Reflections on the Public Sphere', in Craig Calhoun (ed.), *Habermas and the Public Sphere* (Cambridge, MA, 1992), 421–61. For a similar view of the public sphere see, for example, David Waldstreicher, *In the Midst of Perpetual Fetes: The Making of American Nationalism, 1776–1820* (Chapel Hill, NC, 1997); Geoff Eley, 'Nations, Publics, and Political Cultures: Placing Habermas in the Nineteenth Century', in Craig Calhoun (ed.), *Habermas and the Public Sphere*, 289–339; Ryan, *Civic Wars*.
10 David S. Shields, *Civil Tongues and Polite Letters in British America* (Chapel Hill, NC, 1997), pp. xv–xvi.
11 Michael Schudson, 'Was There Ever a Public Sphere? If So, When? Reflections on the American Case', in Calhoun (ed.), *Habermas and the Public Sphere*, 143–63.
12 Stephen Botein, '"Meer Mechanics" and an Open Press: The Business and Political Strategies of Colonial American Printers', in Donald Fleming and Bernard Bailyn (eds.), *Perspectives in American History*, IX (Cambridge, MA, 1975), 127–225.
13 Schudson, 'Was There Ever a Public Sphere?', p. 153.
14 Brown, *Knowledge Is Power*, p. 292.
15 *Publick Occurrences Both Forreign and Domestick* (Boston), 25 September 1690.
16 John Legg to Rev. Rowland Cotton, 1716, quoted in Sheila McIntyre, '"I Heare it so Variously Reported": News-letters, Newspapers and the

Ministerial Network in New England, 1670–1730', unpublished paper, American Journalism Historians Association Annual Convention, London, Ontario, October 1996.
17 Charles E. Clark, *The Public Prints: The Newspaper in Anglo-American Culture, 1665–1740* (New York, 1994), pp. 169–70.
18 Quoted in Richard B. Kielbowicz, *News in the Mail: The Press, Post Office, and Public Information, 1700–1860s* (Westport, CT, 1989), p. 26.
19 John B. McMaster, *History of People of the United States*, 8 vols. (New York, 1883–1913), vol. I, p. 42, quoted in Kielbowicz, *News in the Mail*.
20 David Copeland, *Colonial American Newspapers: Character and Content* (Newark, DE, 1997), pp. 271–3.
21 *Porcupine's Gazette* (Philadelphia, PA), 5 March 1797.
22 *National Gazette* (Philadelphia, PA), 19 December 1791.
23 Schudson, 'Was There Ever a Public Sphere?', p. 154.
24 Max Ferrand (ed.), *The Records of the Federal Convention of 1787*, rev. edn, 4 vols. (New Haven, CT, 1937), vol. I, p. 15.
25 Carol Sue Humphrey, '"Little Ado about Much": Philadelphia Newspapers and the Constitutional Convention', *American Journalism*, 5 (1988), 63–80.
26 Culver H. Smith, *The Press, Politics, and Patronage: The American Government's Use of Newspapers 1789–1875* (Athens, GA, 1977), pp. 39–41.
27 Craig Calhoun, 'Introduction: Habermas and the Public Sphere', in Calhoun (ed.), *Habermas and the Public Sphere*, 1–48, p. 7.
28 'Licensing of Printing Presses and Printing', in Leonard W. Labaree (ed.), *Royal Instructions to British Colonial Governors 1670–1776*, 2 vols. (New York, 1935), vol. II, p. 495.
29 See William David Sloan, 'The *New-Britain Courant*: Voice of Anglicanism', *American Journalism*, 8 (1991), 108–41.
30 See Warren B. Johnson, 'The Content of American Colonial Newspapers Relative to International Affairs, 1704–1763', Ph.D. thesis, University of Washington (1962), p. 451.
31 See David Copeland, '"JOIN, or DIE": America's Press during the French and Indian War', *Journalism History*, 24 (1998), 112–21, pp. 112–19. It has been argued that America's press began shaping the public sphere earlier: see Michael Warner, *The Letters of the Republic: Publication and the Public Sphere in Eighteenth-Century America* (Cambridge, MA, 1990). Usually, however, scholars place the beginning of the operation of the public sphere, and the press's role in it, later – see, for example, Schudson, 'Was There Ever a Public Sphere?'; Waldstreicher, *In the Midst of Perpetual Fetes*; Ryan, *Civic Wars*; Cornell, *The Other Founders*; and John L. Brooke, 'Ancient Lodges and Self-Created Societies: Voluntary Association and the Public Sphere in the Early Republic', in Ronald Hoffman and Peter J. Albert (eds.), *Launching the 'Extended Republic': The Federalist Era* (Charlottesville, VA, 1996), 273–380.
32 John Adams, *The Works of John Adams, with a Life of the Author, Notes and Illustrations*, ed. C. F. Adams, 10 vols. (Boston, MA, 1850–1856), vol. II, p. 219, quoted in Philip Davidson, *Propaganda and the American Revolution, 1763–1783* (Chapel Hill, NC, 1941), p. 227.

33 John Holt to Samuel Adams, 29 January 1776, quoted in Schlesinger, *Prelude to Independence: The Newspaper War in Britain 1764–1776* (New York, 1957), p. 284.
34 John Adams to Thomas Jefferson, 1815, quoted in Bernard Bailyn, *The Ideological Origins of the American Revolution* (Cambridge, MA, 1967), p. 1.
35 See, for example, *Massachusetts Spy* (Boston), 5 March 1772 and 10 March 1774.
36 *Boston Daily Advertiser*, 3 June 1887.
37 Cornell, *The Other Founders*, pp. 81ff.
38 *Pennsylvania Gazette* (Philadelphia), 24 July 1740.
39 Ibid., 10 June 1731.
40 *New-York Journal; or, the General Advertiser*, 15 March 1770.
41 James W. Carey, 'The Press, Public Opinion, and Public Discourse', in Theodore L. Glasser and Charles T. Salmon (eds.), *Public Opinion and the Communication of Consent* (New York, 1995), 373–402, p. 381.
42 Quoted in ibid., p. 380.
43 See, for example, *Virginia Gazette* (Williamsburg, Pinkney), 3 February 1776.
44 Michael Schudson, *The Good Citizen: A History of American Civic Life* (New York, 1998), p. 78.
45 Figures based on Arthur M. Schlesinger, *Prelude to Independence*, p. 303; and Sidney Kobre, *Development of American Journalism* (Dubuque, IA, 1969), p. 28.
46 *New York Journal*, 24 February 1795; *Port Folio Magazine*, quoted in William David Sloan and James D. Startt (eds.), *The Media in America: A History*, 4th edn (Northport, AK, 1999), p. 70.
47 Copeland, 'JOIN, or DIE', p. 118. Newspaper numbers exclude any German-language newspapers that were printed in the colonies during this period.
48 America's press technically reached the Mississippi River with the Louisiana Purchase in 1803, since two French-language newspapers were published in New Orleans: the *Moniteur de la Louisiane*, which began printing in 1794, and the *Telegraphe*, which was founded days after the purchase went through.
49 Numbers of newspapers included in this section are based on personal research; Alfred McClung Lee, *The Daily Newspaper in America* (New York, 1972); Humphrey, *The Press of the Young Republic*; and Edwin Emery and Michael Emery, *The Press and America*, 6th edn (Englewood Cliffs, NJ, 1988), p. 104.
50 *American Minerva* (New York), 9 December 1793.
51 Smith, *The Press, Politics, and Patronage*, pp. 17–23.
52 Jeffery A. Smith, *Printers and Press Freedom: The Ideology of Early American Journalists* (New York and Oxford, 1988), p. 83.
53 Leonard W. Levy, *Emergence of a Free Press* (New York and Oxford, 1985), pp. 76–81.
54 Ibid., p. 67.
55 *Georgia Gazette* (Savannah), 26 October 1774.
56 Francis G. Wallett, *Patriots, Loyalists & Printers* (Worcester, MA, 1976), pp. 36–7.

57 *Annals of Congress*, US House of Representatives, 5th Congress, 2nd Session (Washington, DC, 1834), 8:2164.
58 *Columbian Centinel* (Boston, MA), 5 October 1798.
59 James Morton Smith, *Freedom's Fetters: The Alien and Sedition Laws and American Civil Liberties* (Ithaca, NY, 1956), pp. 185–7.
60 'To the Inhabitants of the Province of Quebec', 24 October 1774, in Chauncey Ford, et al. (eds.), *Journals of the Continental Congress, 1774–1789* (Washington, DC, 1904–1937), 1–108.
61 *Virginia Gazette* (Williamsburg, Purdie), 14 June 1776, postscript.
62 Quoted in Bernard Schwartz, *The Bill of Rights: A Documentary History*, 2 vols. (New York, 1971), vol. I, p. 450.
63 Quoted in Levy, *Emergence of a Free Press*, pp. 198–9.
64 Ibid., 12 July 1817.
65 Alexis de Tocqueville, *Democracy in America*, 2 vols. (New York, 1946), vol. I, pp. 186–8.
66 Jefferson to Madison, 5 February 1799, in Paul L. Ford, *The Works of Thomas Jefferson*, 10 vols. (New York, 1892–9), vol. VII, p. 344.
67 Smith, *The Press, Politics, and Patronage*, pp. 42–3.
68 *American Watchman and Delaware Republican*, 21 October 1815, quoted in Sloan and Startt (eds.), *The Media in America*, p. 82.
69 *Village Record* (West Chester, PA), 10 November 1819.
70 Isaiah Thomas, *The History of Printing in America* (1810; reprint, New York, 1970), pp. 18–19. Thomas quoted directly from Samuel Miller, *A Brief Retrospect of the Eighteenth Century*, 2 vols. (New York, 1803), vol. II, 251–5.
71 *New-York Gazette Revived in the Weekly Post-Boy*, 22 January 1750.
72 Prospectus for *Christian Journal* (Richmond, VA), published in *Family Visitor* (Richmond, VA), 8 October 1825.
73 Schudson, *The Good Citizen*, p. 113.

7 France, 1750–89[1]

Jack Censer

By 1789, educated Frenchmen and women had gained wide experience of reading periodicals, even though a half-century earlier, periodicals featured little even in the lives of the elite.[2] Although many other kinds of periodicals served the general public – primarily advertisers and literary journals – newspapers attracted the most interest. French eighteenth-century readers, who understood the politics of culture extremely well and tended to see cultural politics as that arena left open when politics was censored or obscured, saw newspapers, with their political emphasis, as the most significant of all serial publications. Perhaps future analysts might find gender or class or regional differences played a part in the public's assessment, but it does appear that, for the educated, politics, narrowly conceived, trumped cultural and other disputes. For these reasons, and because the chapter by Simon Burrows on 'The Cosmopolitan Press' above has already given considerable information on the business, structure and control of the French press, this chapter concentrates on the political messages circulating in the press inside ancien regime France.

The French political press originated in 1631 when Théophraste Renaudot, under the aegis of Cardinal Richelieu, founded the *Gazette de France*. Closely tied to the government, this newspaper depended on and reflected royal policy. While handbills, fliers and manuscript materials abounded, the government squashed any effort to begin alternative serial publications because it had guaranteed a monopoly to Renaudot.[3] Nonetheless, within fifteen years, new Francophone organs established themselves across the border to address the French market and other readers throughout Europe. By the mid-eighteenth century, this political press consisted of the *Gazette de France* and several extra-territorial gazettes, though only a few were allowed to enter France. An alteration of policy in the late 1750s opened the borders to about a dozen more periodicals.[4] The six most important were based in four Dutch cities (The Hague, Amsterdam, Leiden and Utrecht), Avignon and Germany (the *Courier du Bas-Rhin*, founded in 1767).[5] Along with the *Gazette de France*, these papers shared a sombre style and comprehensive coverage, though they differed over the treatment of non-political fare. Whatever their similarities in appearance, all extra-territorial papers enjoyed an independence from France totally unavailable to the *Gazette*.

Throughout the period 1745 to early 1787, the *Gazette de France* and its relatives provided the lion's share of political information to contemporary readers. Nevertheless, several journalists experimented with alternative approaches, including a handful of adventurers who produced the published equivalent of the gossipy *nouvelles à la main*.[6] But after 1770, some really important innovations appeared. In 1772, the government accepted a proposal by the press tsar Charles-Joseph Panckoucke to publish a paper under its guidance – the *Journal de Genève* – that would claim a foreign provenance but actually be based in France. Two years later, he added a literary section, which also appeared in another of his papers, the *Journal de Bruxelles*. By 1778 the political sections of both papers had also become identical. In the same year, Panckoucke's widely read *Mercure de France* added the political portion of the Brussels sheet to its pages.[7] These two French organs differed from other newspapers because they were clearly – at least to twentieth-century observers – published in France, yet claimed a foreign origin. Although their copy resembled that of the foreign papers, the government had more direct levers of control. In contrast to older papers they also adopted a magazine-like appearance, with fewer and longer articles than their predecessors. In the mid-1770s, yet another type of news organ emerged, when the Foreign Minister, the Count de Vergennes, to further his policy of supporting the American revolutionaries against the British, established then subsidised the *Affaires de l'Angleterre et de l'Amerique*. From its inception in 1776, the *Affaires de l'Angleterre et de l'Amerique* was distinguished by a far more analytic style than that of any other political paper.[8] This strategy had been tried earlier, in the mid-1750s, but without major effect.[9] The London-based *Courier de l'Europe*, which had begun in 1776 like other foreign gazettes, also became a heavily controlled organ to support French foreign policy. Although these papers enjoyed a mixture of independence and dependence which was seemingly little different to Panckoucke's journals, the government was playing a risky game in hoping this controlled medium would damage the more independent competitors.

The assortment of political periodicals emerging in the 1770s also included the *Annales politiques, civiles et littéraires du dix-huitième siècle*, begun in 1777 by Simon-Nicolas-Henri Linguet. Linguet's journal resembled the foreign gazettes in that it was a privately run journal published abroad, but the comparison ends there. Like the *Affaires de l'Angleterre et de l'Amerique*, the *Annales* was a journal with a focus, in this case the opinions of Linguet. And his views were possibly the most extreme published prior to the Revolution.[10]

Newspapers experienced repression across a wide spectrum as the government sought to insulate the monarchy from criticism. The case studies that follow show both how policy and effectiveness varied and fluctuated with circumstance, and how individual journals could experience specific ministerial interventions. Despite this shifting governmental framework, the number of papers increased over time, from five in the 1740s to a dozen in the late 1750s and nineteen by the end of the ancien regime – and these totals only include papers that lasted at least three years and circulated legally. The papers' readership also apparently increased, from a combined weekly circulation of 12,300 during the War of Austrian Succession to 44,000 during the American Revolution, and this figure does not include Linguet's wildly popular *Annales*, which appeared spasmodically. In peace these numbers sagged considerably, probably at least by one-half, if the experience of the *Courrier d'Avignon* after the Seven Years War is typical. In France, the readers seemingly came from the educated elite and almost half of them were nobles. Given the small proportion of nobles in the overall population, they constituted a huge proportion of the newspapers' clients.

Within the constraints imposed by the government, this panoply of print organs competed for the attention of the French public. The rest of this chapter assesses how problematic this was for the Bourbon government, focusing narrowly, and thus sharply, on politics. This allows us to address the audience's understanding of the French government, surely the most significant question for French people. But concentrating on France does not mean we should ignore foreign news, both because foreign developments had implications for France and because readers, recognising that the government influenced the press, hoped to learn about their own land through a variety of portals.

The conservative end of the ancien regime political spectrum was generally marked by royal self-justifications about the monarch's divine right to rule. The polar opposite is more difficult to fix, as it lay in contested ground, for, while never envisioning a revolution, many contemporaries scorned, and some even vilified, both Louis XV and Louis XVI.[11] Although some scholars have placed the press close to the conservative pole,[12] a few historians claim to have identified an evolution toward radicalism.[13] The most conservative political journal under the ancien regime was the monarch's own *Gazette de France*.[14] Although this periodical shared much stylistically with the other gazettes, its unique role as the representative of the royal viewpoint gave it a certain distinctiveness. The paper presented events in an opaque manner, but made its overall viewpoint apparent through endless repetition, as well as occasional exemplary coverage and injections of opinion. In the absence of editorial comment, its position was not forcefully presented but reasonably clear. To understand the results of this approach, it is necessary to examine first domestic, then foreign, affairs. When directly covering France, the *Gazette*'s editors tried to bolster the image of the monarchy and monarch, by emphasising the king in his ceremonial and familial role. The other institutions of state and prominent individuals appeared only as they circulated through the royal domain. The mysteries of state – a term referring to monarchical habits whose actual practice was reserved to the king and shrouded from the public – remained absolutely safe in the hands of the *Gazette*.

In its coverage of France's foreign policy, however, this government organ produced a more mixed picture. As a paper of record, the *Gazette de France*'s reports generally accorded with how an unfettered educated elite would have interpreted events. As such, the domestic and military failures of France's allies and successes of her enemies would eventually surface. The same was true of France's own military ventures. In this way, royal policies came under scrutiny. But one should not overemphasise this openness, because the government occasionally imposed a certain propagandistic angle, or more often simply omitted problems, though they frequently resurfaced later in a rather distorted manner. Moreover, many events reinforced French policy and the *Gazette* swiftly reported them.[15] However, over the course of the century, in presenting the domestic political structures of other countries, the *Gazette de France* developed a more challenging coverage of France. To explore this evolution requires examining the *Gazette*'s reporting. In the 1740s and early 1750s the *Gazette*'s reporting of the affairs of other countries emphasised the role of the primary political authority. When the countries covered were monarchies, personal rule and the ruler's intervention into daily affairs received attention, as it did in coverage of France. But by the end of the ancien regime, the paper reported, at least obliquely, much more conflict and stressed the actions of competing elites rather than that of the rulers themselves. Perhaps this point is best demonstrated by contrasting two issues of the *Gazette*: one from 1751, the other from 1782.

In 1751, the *Gazette de France* published a twelve-page weekly edition. The number of 24 July 1751 was no different from usual. Of the sixty-three news bulletins on foreign matters in this issue, one covered armed conflict, and the remainder related the internal political situations of many European countries – including Scandinavian, German and Italian states, Great Britain and Spain. Regardless of the country described, the only significant place for political contestation implicitly lay within the ruling elite, since the *Gazette* reported not only on sovereigns, but on ministers, diets, parliaments and significant personages at court. This coverage paid no attention to problems between these elites and their rulers but tacitly recognised divided authority. Whatever potential tensions the *Gazette*'s pattern of reporting implied tended to be nullified by the enthusiasm the paper manifested toward each country's leader. Twenty-seven of the sixty-three articles exclusively described the sovereign and consort, and the attitudes expressed supplemented this volume of attention. While the *Gazette* routinely noted the intermediate bodies and courtiers, it only concentrated on the rulers of state. Thus the lead article in the issue of 24 July praised the resolution and diligence shown by the Swedish king in rebuilding fire-ravaged Stockholm. Even more significant, these encomiums merely reinforced the yet stronger plaudits of the preceding week's description of the actual fire. The *Gazette* noted that 'the wind was blowing directly on the port, the storehouses and artillery depot; it is only by the presence of the Monarch and by the admirable dispositions that His Majesty ordered, that these depots, so precious to the defence of the state, have been saved'. Other monarchs were similarly praised in the same issue for apparently crucial interventions of their own.

By the 1780s, the *Gazette de France* published four pages twice weekly in far smaller print. The issue dated 19 November 1782 resembles any other, and includes material from Warsaw, Madrid, Vienna, Naples, London, The Hague and Versailles. But if physical changes in the paper over the preceding thirty years had been slight, there had been significant, if subtle, alterations in content. There had been little shift in its coverage of conflict between the ruling elite and the population at large: democratic revolutions abroad and local, more 'social' insurgencies scarcely received notice. Yet, the coverage of politically constituted entities did undergo a significant change. Only four articles directly concerned the monarch. Now, the *Gazette*'s portrayal of the elite showed a variety of elements without any one pre-eminent. For the most part, articles simply recounted how various officials and courtiers performed their political and social duties. But this disintegration of monarchical leadership could also suggest limits to sovereign authority. The manifesto promulgated by the Polish Grand Chancellor before a meeting of the Diet and published as the lead story on 19 November provides an excellent example. Instead of leading, the Chancellor was pleading. Rather than commanding, the official 'strongly recommended', 'reiterated', and 'wished'. Of course, Polish officials had always approached the Diet that way, but this case was hardly unique in the *Gazette* at this time, and in general the paper now envisaged authority as shared.

A wide reading in the *Gazette* of the late 1740s and early 1750s and the late 1770s and early 1780s, though inevitably impressionistic, further validates this pattern. To be sure, coverage of military campaigns in both periods, despite the appearance of officers and generals, usually seems implicitly to focus on kings. Military affairs were, after all, emanations of royal power. But in other spheres of political activity, one sees the predicted paradigm. During the earlier period, even the reports of internal crises centred on the King's government. For example, one report from London in 1751 stated: 'As contraband is always proceeding despite the measures taken by the government, and since the Isle of Man, by its location, contributes much to illicit commerce, the government would like to unite this island with Great Britain.'[16] Similarly, reports of uprisings or disturbances, especially in European colonies, typically concluded by announcing the resumption of order.[17] The implicit assumption behind the phrasing of these reports was that government had a single leader. And the *Gazette* always placed great emphasis on the sovereign's leadership: it even viewed George III, the constitutional monarch of Britain, as an absolutist.[18]

From the late 1770s, important exceptions can be found to the common reportorial tendencies of the *Gazette*. Under the influence of Vergennes, some positive reporting of the Americans and their Revolution filtered into the paper, although it never printed the text of the Declaration of Independence.[19] Moreover, sometimes the paper presented monarchic actions as responses to unavoidable moral *dicta* and hence treated monarchs as something less than free agents, acting according to ethical constraints.[20] While this did not overturn the *Gazette*'s view of ancien regime governance as the rule of competing bodies, it did modify even further the paper's emphasis on personal rule.

This transformation in the *Gazette*'s portrayal of internal politics occurred seamlessly over time. Gradually the paper paid less attention to monarchical authority and gave more space to competition, at least with other constituted powers, and especially during the democratic revolutions towards the end of the century. A new view, not of subordinate political organs and individuals, but of the monarchy, primarily characterised the change. Indeed, one simply finds fewer items about the sovereign. The reasons for this glacial shift in the *Gazette*'s representation of monarchy are unclear, but whatever the cause, such a general tendency posed difficulties, at least in theory, for the French state. Envisioning foreign governments as functioning through competing bodies and divided authority undermined the royal administration's officially sanctioned absolutist view of French governance. In fact, the practice of Bourbon government was more flexible than the theory, and the public, which already believed in contestation with the crown, was only too willing to accept this new vision. Readers could juxtapose articles about foreign governments against those concerning France, permitting them to perceive the latter stories as unrepresentative and less realistic. Of course, the resultant contrast between French and foreign governments provided at most an indirect critique, and in all probability the government permitted the *Gazette* to take an implicitly positive view of alternative political structures only because of the mildness of the threat. Probably, this new reporting mainly reflected a shift in political structures (or understanding about these structures) which the government simply ignored.[21] Yet if problematic news seeped out even in the government sponsored *Gazette*, the extra-territorial gazettes posed far greater difficulties.

For a variety of reasons, but above all the relative influence of the French state, the foreign gazettes published a wide range of opinion on France. This diversity becomes apparent if we contrast the reporting of two of them, one among the most, the other the least, adventurous in their views of France. Least pointed was the *Courrier d'Avignon*, which was published in a Papal enclave surrounded by France. It generally appeared bi-weekly in a four-page edition with sporadic supplements until its demise in 1794 and was priced at 18 livres for an annual subscription. The *Courrier d'Avignon* was founded in 1733 by François Morénas, a local writer, and the Giroud family, established Avignon publishers, and survived until 1794. In 1742, the Girouds gained complete control, but by 1750 Morénas was once again serving as their editor. This arrangement lasted until 1768, when the French, in a dispute with the Pope over Gallicanism, occupied Avignon. The Bourbon monarchy, which customarily allowed only the *Gazette de France* to publish news within its borders, outlawed the *Courrier d'Avignon*. Morénas immediately requested and received permission to continue the newspaper from Monaco, another Papal territory. In late 1774, when the French evacuated Avignon, Morénas had just died. Even though anonymous editors successfully maintained the *Courrier de Monaco* for six months in 1775, Bourbon officials had always perceived Monaco as a temporary solution and insisted that the *Courrier de Monaco* resume in Avignon. Joachim Le Blanc, an important French official there, received the privilege to publish in 1775 and when he died, in 1782, his widow assumed control and operated it until 1792. The Le Blancs hired as their editors successively the abbé Roubaud (1775–6), Jean-Baptiste Artaud (1776–83) and finally Sabin Tournal, who would achieve fame in the Revolution.[22] The Bourbon invasion of Avignon and the forced relocation of its newspaper reveal clearly the ultimate and exceptional power the French possessed over both the city and the *Courrier d'Avignon*. To promote their own policies, the French authorities occasionally intervened in news reporting. On the whole, they limited themselves to minor adjustments, but from time to time they sought to influence news about individual countries more systematically. In addition to such sporadic coercive measures, the French issued a stream of propaganda promoting their own view of politics.[23]

In this restrictive environment, the *Courrier d'Avignon*'s coverage of France was much less challenging than that of the Dutch gazettes; yet it nevertheless enjoyed some independence.[24] The portrayal of the domestic politics of foreign countries went well beyond that in the *Gazette* and yielded a stronger critique. Little changed in its portrayal of how traditional bodies functioned – whether sharing or monopolising authority – across our period. But as democratic movements emerged, they were treated dispassionately, often favourably, suggesting a world with many choices. Although the *Courrier d'Avignon* downplayed, or even omitted, reference to rioters (as in the case of London's Gordon Riots in 1780), thus differentiating them from revolutionaries, its coverage admitted the existence of both conflicting elites and political upheavals.[25] The implicit contrast with static absolutism made this coverage more challenging than that in the *Gazette de France*. All this provided the possibility of contemplating absolutism critically; coverage of large-scale changes suggested major alternatives.

The *Courrier d'Avignon* also embarked on a different tack from the *Gazette de France* by sustained reporting of potential aspersions on France's friends or by ennobling her enemies. For example, the paper's treatment of British politics from mid-1778 to late 1780 under a London dateline was clearly contrary to French governmental interests. In this period, the French were at war with their traditional rival; yet the *Courrier d'Avignon* praised the British authorities and downplayed any opposition to them. The paper persisted in praising George III explicitly and implicitly for his performance as chief executive, his paternal relationship with parliament and the people, and his position in a brilliant court.[26] It admiringly chronicled the King's activities as commander-in-chief of the military forces, and one report noted that the royal example inspired the war effort of the entire nation.[27] This and similar encomiums reflected the *Courrier d'Avignon*'s favourable view of the British military engagement.

While this example shows how the *Courrier d'Avignon* could pursue a line relatively independent of French interests, it would be unfair to regard its treatment of foreign affairs as uniformly or generally inimical to France. From the late 1740s until the resumption of hostilities in the mid-1750s, the *Courrier d'Avignon* rendered little judgement on France's foreign policy. But treatment of the Seven Years War (1756–63), a very difficult conflict for the Bourbon government, proved far less favourable to France. The support offered during the previous conflict was replaced by a muddle of coverage that surely would have displeased authorities in Versailles. Thereafter, from the mid-1750s until the mid-1770s, with peace more or less the order of the day, the *Courrier d'Avignon* commented little on French foreign policy, either explicitly or implicitly. Yet during the American Revolution, an avalanche of praise for the Bourbons outweighed the substantial endorsement, noted above, of Hanoverian policy in the London section of the paper. This commitment to French foreign policy endured almost into the mid-1780s, when the treatment of problems elsewhere in Europe reduced its positive edge.

An overview of the *Courrier d'Avignon*'s treatment of French policy during the American Revolution casts light on its ambiguous approach to foreign reporting. Britain – as France's main antagonist – was so important in French foreign policy considerations that examining the former throws much light on the latter. As earlier noted, from mid-1778 to 1780, the British government was treated positively in reports from London. Indeed, the paper singled out Lord North for favourable attention, and one report was particularly sympathetic. After describing an attack by Charles James Fox that condemned the entire North ministry, the periodical summarised the conclusion of the debate:

This bloody diatribe was finished with nothing resolved. The minister constitutionally obliged to listen to all sorts of indignities, Lord N—H responded sensitively to the many reproaches. He is accused of having betrayed his country and having accumulated emoluments and offices. He offers to resign what the king has given him. Attacked for his love for his family, he sheds tears at the memory of the death of a recently deceased son; numerous legislators, thinking that a good father cannot be dishonest, defend him.[28]

To a society brimming with a new sentimentality, such phrases translated into a strong endorsement of North.

Juxtaposed against such positive assessments, which also predominate in reports from Britain in the years preceding the Boston Tea Party, were many contrary views. From 1774 to 1778 and again after 1780 assaults on their government originated from various British provenances. While the king fared reasonably well, ministers received strong criticism. In the earlier period the *Courrier d'Avignon* adopted a strong anti-war stance, a position directly contradicting the executive's policy. Before the outbreak of hostilities, the paper merely urged compromise with the Americans,[29] but once the Revolution erupted, it highlighted British atrocities. One article in effect labelled British actions a crime, describing a soldier who preferred to resign his commission rather than 'adopt the horrible alternative of stifling his humane impulses and bathing his hands in the blood of his relatives, his comrades, and his compatriots'.[30] The *Courrier d'Avignon* also concentrated on failures in battle. Even reviews of British military successes were likely to point out the temporary and inconclusive nature of such victories.[31] The newspaper also applauded the motives of the colonists and thus implicitly criticised ministers who tried to suppress such noble people. In the paper's view, the Americans possessed wisdom, moderation and firmness.[32] Although such positions might also tarnish the monarch, the *Courrier d'Avignon*'s direct criticism of ministers made them appear the principal target.[33]

The London reports in the *Courrier d'Avignon* openly accused ministers of carrying out poor policies and immoral plans in violation of historic liberties. The journal attacked an array of ministerial efforts, including proposals for reorganising the East India Company,[34] but its criticism focused mainly on their 'tyrannical', 'despotic', and 'arbitrary' actions against the Americans.[35] Such efforts, which were designed to reduce the Americans to 'slavery', would gain nothing and lead to a heavy loss of British 'blood' and 'treasure'.[36] The newspaper also linked attacks on the Americans' freedom to a similar assault on the rightful liberties of Englishmen.[37] Another article assailed the ministry for failing to allow the king to receive the just complaints of the City of London in a suitably decorous manner, and argued that such errors might lead to a loss of confidence in the crown and difficulty for the succession of the royal line.[38] This threat contained some criticism of George III, but the *Courrier d'Avignon*, at least on the surface, fired its salvos at the government for standing between the people and the throne.

After 1780, the *Courrier d'Avignon*'s coverage resumed its diatribes against the British ministry. The paper depicted the chief failing of ministers to be their role in the armed struggle, accusing them of persisting in the war against all reason, ruthlessly seeking to dominate the whole of Europe, and misleading the nation about the chances for peace.[39] A new tone characterised the paper's coverage of the government. It began to scrutinise its activities far more closely, and reports consistently revealed a group of men motivated by opportunism and necessity rather than political principle.[40] The *Courrier d'Avignon* reiterated its view that greed led ministers to their evil deeds,[41] and the fall of the North ministry in March 1782 (reported on 12 April) strongly reinforced this criticism, since it suggested the fate awaiting such politicians.

The British ministry was castigated both in the high volume of critical reports from Britain and the much more negative reports that filled the *Courrier d'Avignon*'s American and Continental columns. Most reports from America between 1774 and 1778 clamoured for British resistance and decried the executive. They brutally assaulted the motives and character of both the monarch and his advisors.[42] Only a single report sought to justify the King, and none admired his ministers.[43] Reports dramatically proclaimed support for popular sovereignty in Britain, reflecting the thinking of many Americans who wished to justify both their own behaviour and the activities of their radical supporters in London.[44] As American news about Britain tapered off in 1778, the paper began to print reports supposedly penned on the Continent. These reports assailed George III and his advisors without reservation. According to the paper's columns with Continental bylines, the King and his ministers set out to dominate the seas in order to secure British economic and political preeminence: France and her allies had confronted the oppressor simply to preserve the freedom of the seas. Suffering great losses in war and much disruption at home, Britain was supposedly unable to realise her goals. No polite praise for an adversary muted this attack.[45] Nor did these reports view either parliament or the opposition party positively. The overall picture reflected the prevalent European opinion that Britain's bellicosity was a function of the greed, corruption and cynicism of George III and his ministers.[46]

This analysis of British coverage in the *Courrier d'Avignon* gives texture and resolution to the points made regarding foreign reporting and shows the complicated messages available. It also reveals, especially in its praise for the North ministry from 1778 to 1780, how the *Courrier d'Avignon* could be more critical than the *Gazette de France*. However, without precisely mimicking the *Gazette*, the *Courrier d'Avignon* could also treat French foreign policy positively and did so impressively in the years running up to the Revolution.

At the other end of the spectrum of gazettes to the *Courrier d'Avignon* was the *Gazette de Leyde*, a paper whose view of French domestic politics illuminates the editorial policy of its Avignon-based rival. Using the *Gazette de Leyde* poses a difficulty, since the French government forbade its legal circulation, apparently successfully, from 1745 to the late 1750s. Nonetheless, this paper, though among the most aggressive, generally came close enough to others of its type to justify it as a reasonable selection. Among the most adventurous gazettes, the *Gazette de Leyde* held many extra valuable resources. True, it was somewhat reticent, common to publications of its type, and the French government tried hard to fetter sources so as to restrict access to news even among the most independent foreign journalists. Even when the government could not actually bury damaging material, it tried to limit the problem by subsidising and thus controlling Pascal Boyer, who ran a Paris news bureau that supplied the non-French journals during the 1780s.[47] Conversely, all Dutch publications could count on a home environment that was willing to tolerate critical reporting. And the local government, unlike the pliant Papal authorities, had no desire to assist the exercise of Bourbon hegemony. The *Gazette de Leyde* held additional particular advantages. Founded before 1677 by the French Huguenot family the De la Fonts, the *Gazette de Leyde*, or, as it was formally known, the *Nouvelles extraordinaires de divers endroits*, lasted until 1811 with only a brief suppression in 1798. By the end of the eighteenth century, subscribers received the newspaper, normally eight densely printed pages, twice weekly at a cost of 36 livres annually, much higher than either the *Courrier d'Avignon* or the *Gazette de France*. Another Protestant family, the Luzacs, had bought the paper as a family business in 1738. Etienne Luzac acted as publisher until 1772, when his nephew Jean assumed control. Under their aegis, the *Gazette de Leyde* became the most informative Francophone newspaper of its day,[48] and the diversity of its audience, spread throughout Francophone Europe, helped to insulate the paper from any specific French demands. In short, the fragmented nature of the Leiden paper's potential readership gave its editors substantial leeway in setting policy.

Not only were fewer outside forces brought to bear on the Leiden journalists than on their colleagues in Avignon, but the former also appeared much more likely to resist them. The publishers, the Luzac clan, were closely involved in running the paper and doubtless possessed a great commitment to it, not only as a business. Perhaps a sense of purpose among these Dutch-based Huguenots made them less profit-minded and more concerned about their paper's content? Certainly the *Gazette de Leyde*'s last publisher of the ancien regime, Jean Luzac, specifically believed both in liberty in the abstract and the American Revolution in particular, helping John Adams gain Dutch recognition of the United States. He also aided the Polish and later Dutch freedom movements. A man with such commitments would likely wish his paper to illustrate his own point of view. Other family members also seem to have resolved to use their paper in a similar manner within the constraints common to all gazettes.[49]

The Luzacs' presentation of the structure of foreign countries' political systems was at least as problematic for the Versailles government as that of the *Courrier d'Avignon*. The paper treated politics as consisting both of contestations among formal bodies and revolts from below. Although the *Gazette de Leyde* generally omitted or deprecated social upheavals, such as the Gordon Riots, the Luzacs went further than the *Courrier d'Avignon* by systematically favouring democratic rebellions that seemed to aspire to political rather than social change.[50] In taking this position, the *Gazette de Leyde* confronted royal absolutism, albeit on theoretical grounds. Likewise the *Gazette de Leyde* seems to have followed the broad outline of the *Courrier d'Avignon*'s treatment of French foreign policy. But the Leiden news-sheet went further than its more constricted relative. During the Seven Years War (coverage of which lasted from the mid-1750s to the mid-1760s), the *Gazette de Leyde* portrayed French folly far more explicitly than did its Avignon cousin. In fact, the French authorities, who worried about the press a great deal, particularly the Dutch gazettes, found the Leiden paper the most troublesome.[51] This negative coverage made the *Gazette de Leyde*'s positive treatment of French foreign policy during the American Revolution[52] particularly welcome.

While the relative independence of the gazettes in general, and the *Gazette de Leyde* in particular, permitted a broader consideration of French domestic news than in the *Gazette de France*, the extent of the difference varied over time. This is exemplified by a comparison of the *Gazette de Leyde*'s bold announcement of the Maupeou reorganisation of the judiciary in 1771 with the coverage of France in 1782, when the French Foreign Minister Vergennes was repressing reporting. Between 9 and 19 July 1782 the *Gazette de Leyde* included twenty brief articles on France, which collectively show a smoothly functioning government. There is scarcely a hint of the country's fiscal problems and the long history of deadlock between monarch and *parlements*. To be sure, the paper mentioned a tax increase and the Paris *parlement*'s consequent remonstrance. Yet, according to the *Gazette de Leyde*, the principal problem with this tax was that the judiciary did not wish it to be extended more than three years beyond the war with Britain. Such coverage scarcely hinted at the potential resistance of the magistrates. Another article suggested political divisions when it reported on a council of war held in Brest that because of conflicting information was unable to determine the fate of the Indian fleet. Nonetheless, such problematic reports contrasted with the general tenor of the remaining seventeen bulletins. These discussed municipalities donating cannons to the King, the presentation of individuals at court, the travels of the royal family, the construction and departure of ships and the capture of enemy vessels. One release typifying this genre of reporting appeared in the issue of 19 July. It noted: 'Since the departure of M. the Count d'Artois, the royal family has dispersed: the King remains alone at Versailles; the Queen and Madame Elizabeth occupy the Trianon; Monsieur, Madame, and Madame the Countess d'Artois have returned to Brunoy where they plan to rest a month; the Aunts of the King are at Bellevue and will return from there to their property of Louvois.' Such reports on the daily life of royalty both presumed and proclaimed its importance.

A sharp contrast to such reports can be found in the *Gazette de Leyde* of 15 March 1771. True, this issue was even less restrained than usual, but it is valuable precisely because it represents an extreme, both stylistically and substantively. Although it concentrated on just four separate questions regarding France, these reports occupied about 65 per cent of the paper's columns. One article, to be sure, resembled reporting on those occasions when the French government forced the press into virtual silence, dutifully noting the Marquis of Noailles's leave-taking from the King and the royal family in order to assume the position of ambassador to The Hague. However, the remainder of the paper revealed a France racked by controversy. One article discussed parlementary resistance to ministerial pressure for taxes, another revealed difficulties in the army. But not surprisingly, the controversy over Maupeou's reforms, which ultimately sought the destruction of the *parlements* and their replacement by more reticent courts, provided the centrepiece. In fact, the editors devoted 60 per cent of the issue to this subject, including reports clarifying the position of the government and the reactions to it from *parlements* in Bordeaux and Besançon, the Paris Chambre des Comptes and an anonymous writer.

The reporting of the Maupeou coup also reveals that the Luzacs wished to accomplish more than showing France as a society in conflict. Through the arrangement of the story, the paper indicated not only that the Bourbons were not as dominant as they might wish, but they ought not to be so powerful. The *Gazette de Leyde* introduced its account by labelling the alterations a 'total change in the form of administration'. The paper then summarised these changes and a large part of the decree that authorised them. However, the one page devoted to this material was dwarfed by the reporting of objections. The many complaints took a variety of tacks, but almost all labelled the Maupeou reforms as radical, immoderate and disruptive to the peace of the nation. Typical of these objections was the discussion of the Besançon *parlement*, which begged the King to:

continue to reign by love, by justice, and by observation of the rules and forms wisely established, in consequence to abolish even from memory an edict destructive of *French* liberty, and to remove himself from the authors of counsels as contrary to his interests and his glory as pernicious for his People, and to reestablish his *parlement* of Paris, &c.

By selecting and publishing many such documents, the *Gazette de Leyde* positioned itself firmly among those who wished to limit monarchical authority and raised the theory of parlementary constitutionalism. In essence, this theory held that the ancient law of France guaranteed individuals and corps particular rights or privileges, and, above all, that the *parlement* held the office of its magistracy by right, and therefore efforts by monarchs to alter this were despotic. To Frenchmen, who understood the efforts of the monarchy to control the press, the mere publication of these views constituted their advocacy, but the *Gazette de Leyde* often went further. In contrast, upheavals of the *peuple* received little or negative attention, with Damiens's assassination attempt on Louis XV drawing a particularly virulent blast.[53]

Other periods existed when such aggressiveness scarcely entered the Leiden newspaper. Indeed, from late 1771 to 1774, and again from 1776 to 1784, the King was portrayed as virtually the sole significant vector of political activity in France. During these periods, with a few exceptions, the monarchy occupied the same central place in the *Gazette de Leyde* as in the *Gazette de France*. Clearly, the efforts of the Maupeou government and Vergennes to repress negative reporting on France had yielded results.[54]

The behaviour of the *Gazette de Leyde* helps explain the domestic reporting of the *Courrier d'Avignon* and other French-language newspapers. While the Avignon paper was certainly no different from the more aggressive foreign papers, it shared their general trajectory in a muted fashion. When others described various degrees of resistance, the *Courrier d'Avignon* at least managed to envisage France as a country with competing interests and thus collaborated in undermining absolutist claims. Not surprisingly, when her relatives remained quiet, she followed suit. If the *Gazette de Leyde* and the *Courrier d'Avignon* represented opposite ends of the press spectrum, what can be concluded generally about the treatment of France in the foreign political press? As the century wore on, its reporting of foreign countries provided an indirect rebuke to Versailles by reinforcing and expanding the *Gazette de France*'s own tendency to treat a range of political actors beyond monarchs. As such, the gazettes were indicating not so much a specific alternative to, but the possibility of difference from, absolutism. The bigger the difference, the more the imagined alternatives might grow. Revolutions made this still clearer. The audience, restless under absolutism, would have been likely to pay attention to the critique.[55] The foreign gazettes also covered France's difficulties in foreign policy in a sustained manner. Interestingly, here it was the 1750s and 1760s that contrasted with the generally positive treatment during the American Revolution.

As this summary suggests, over time there were important changes in the gazettes. Crudely speaking, one might use 1772 to divide the entire period. Fairly harsh domestic critiques of the monarchy during the Seven Years War, which continued until 1772, were followed by near silence thereafter. This change paralleled an improved treatment of foreign policy and an evaluation of non-absolutist arrangements that yielded oblique criticism. While not relishing these latter critiques, government found them easier to stomach than the direct blasts on domestic and foreign efforts that they had to endure in the early period. Surprisingly then, the overall treatment improved, although eventually, after 1784, the glow of French successes during the American Revolution faded.

A closer look at the final decades of the ancien regime reveals interesting details. The new organs that emerged during this more quiescent period provide the subject for the remainder of this essay. While the content of Panckoucke's widely read periodicals remains generally unstudied, available research suggests their view of France was little different to the foreign gazettes. From 1778, when the *Journal de Bruxelles* (whose political coverage was merged with the *Journal de Genève*) became the political part of the *Mercure de France*, its reporting on the American Revolution fell under the sway of Vergennes, who wanted to use the press to bolster support for French policy. This influence manifested itself by largely favourable reporting of American and British opposition to George III's policies.[56] In general, this reporting helped to lessen whatever criticism there was of French foreign policy. The consistency of reporting was sufficient that readers might imagine, like readers of the *Gazette de France*, that other countries behaved according to French dictates. While readers of the foreign gazettes might believe the world outside France behaved autonomously, in the *Mercure* the actions of other countries appeared less independent. While this shift primarily affected only Britain and America, it was important enough to influence the entire perspective. Naturally, it reduced the volume of criticism of the French government; but by slanting coverage so far toward the British opposition and American revolutionaries the paper simultaneously emphasised the existence of political orders very different from the French. Certainly, such reports were not a textbook for revolution, but as a suggestion of the limits of absolutism and the possibilities for major change, they were potentially problematic. In sum, although the vicissitudes in political coverage diluted these messages, such reporting both favoured French foreign policy and ran inadvertent political risks. By associating French foreign policy with popular colonial rebellion, the government scored one of its relatively rare unqualified successes with public opinion, but allowing a positive drum roll for American ideology raised the spectre of alternative approaches to government. With the benefit of hindsight, this seems an uneven swap, but contemporaries appear to have been more impressed by their government's success than by alternative ideals.[57] Following the lead of the *Gazette de Leyde* and its comrades, which had taken advantage of government relaxation of controls under Turgot (1774–6), after 1784 Panckoucke's papers also began to display a little more spark. However, although they criticised domestic politics, they did so less often and with greater circumspection than the Leiden paper.[58]

Vergennes extended an influence similar to that which he enjoyed temporarily over the *Journal de Bruxelles* in the case of his purposely designed propaganda organ the *Affaires de l'Angleterre et de l'Amerique* and from 1778 to 1784 with the *Courier de l'Europe*. When under French domination, the *Courier de l'Europe*, like the *Affaires de l'Angleterre et de l'Amerique*, reflected royal policy by systematically printing favourable reports about George III's domestic critics and his adversaries across the Atlantic. However, the different emphases of the two papers had contrasting but complementary influences. More than any other journal, the *Affaires de l'Angleterre*'s incautious pro-American propaganda released the poisons of problematic political forms, whereas the *Courier de l'Europe* did the most to spread notions of the British system of liberal politics. Simultaneously, like the *Journal de Bruxelles*, these periodicals produced many articles tacitly supporting foreign policy while indirectly questioning France's governmental arrangements. This same propaganda, by glorifying the American and British opponents of George III, lent support to the Ministry of Foreign Affairs, and this surely was the reason for Vergennes's support. Thus, overall, like the foreign gazettes and Panckoucke's organs, these papers both appear sympathetic to the monarchy as their endorsement of liberal regimes was more than offset by praise for foreign policy.[59]

In contrast, Linguet's *Annales* was unlike any other periodical. It was extremely idiosyncratic, and its targets are often unclear. In the short term Linguet was an advocate of absolute monarchy as the best course open to the French people, but he reached this conclusion through a radical attack on the social structure and every minister serving Louis XVI.[60] Despite this rather confused viewpoint, the *Annales* was extremely popular, as the large numbers of pirate editions pay witness. Although the size of its press-run remains uncertain, it eclipsed all other papers whenever it appeared, and this popularity perhaps provided Linguet with the liberty to reshape the form of the political information he supplied, emphasising opinion above information.[61] Nonetheless, the *Annales* did not offer a view of France that was fundamentally different to that found in other papers for a number of reasons. Much of what Linguet had to say was quite abstract. He rarely discussed particular policies or developments and his commentary on France was unusually open to multiple interpretations. Thus, his critiques were no more direct than the gazettes' treatment of British and American politics.

Even though the *Annales*' arguments did not significantly change the course of the French press, Linguet remains very important. It would not be an exaggeration to see him as an early celebrity, a social phenomenon more common in later centuries. As such, the public appeared more impressed by his language and his courage than his specific viewpoint. In fact, from the beginning of Linguet's journalistic career, these two elements – personality and the willingness to shock – are the clues to understanding him. He first came to public attention for his outspoken confrontations with the Enlightenment establishment, particularly the Académie française, which he attacked as unworthy on a number of grounds. But in the debate over the Académie, the reasoned arguments pale into insignificance compared to the clash of personalities involved.[62] Linguet's impact is further illuminated by a later confrontation with Vergennes, when the minister complained about the journalist's strong language rather than his arguments. Indeed, the minister recommended that the 'employee' (i.e. Linguet) who wrote the piece for one of Panckoucke's journals ought to be fired. In reply, Linguet justified neither his reasons nor his language, but instead relied on his individual rights, declaring: 'One speaks here of the employed person as a lackey who may be let go when one is discontented with him.' But, continued Linguet:

> The one called here a person... would never have agreed to be humiliated as a placeholder only dependent on the caprices of a publisher. The only way this can happen is if at the bar of literature all the rights of a citizen are removed without reservation and if the publishers and the lawyers are above the laws and the courts.

Significantly, Linguet closed by demanding his rights and refusing to sacrifice his honour.[63] This battle, like much of Linguet's career, can be reduced to a conflict, not over differing viewpoints, but over exaggerated language and Linguet's personal claims.

While it was Linguet himself who raised his rights in this dispute, his mere existence was in some ways problematic for an absolutist conception of politics. For his readers' construction of Linguet as a combatant implied some criticism of ancien regime government. In Linguet they saw a man standing for individual rights and vociferously defending his position. Yet this, even when combined with the biting but largely abstract prose of his paper, remained only another oblique attack on France. When one combines his tangential critique with the paper's irregular schedule of publication, the critical power of the *Annales* appears much reduced. The *Annales* had a very short run in France, permitted to enter only from 1777 to 1780, although much smuggling occurred in other periods.[64] It may have been officially restored after 1784 but was denuded of much of its most radical material.[55] Even when it was allowed to circulate, Linguet's erratic work habits resulted in only sporadic publication.[66] All told, then, the *Annales*' power remained somewhat limited. Surely the paper was far less significant than Linguet himself, who took centre stage far more consistently than he could issue the *Annales*, successfully using other means to portray himself as an embattled hero thwarting unfair authorities. Nevertheless, the reputation of the *Annales* grew during the Revolution, because its example became all the more significant in the maelstrom after 1789. In its own times, however, it would be wise not to overrate its importance.[67]

This assessment of Linguet reinforces the view that the new entries on the journalistic scene in the 1770s and 1780s did not fundamentally alter the impression of politics given in the foreign gazettes. Although the new journals shifted the content and shape of reporting, mainly by increasing support for foreign policies and deepening the praise for alternative political structures, they did not sharply change the overall outlook on the French government. But they did add nuances to the vision of France articulated by the gazettes.

Having plotted the view of France in the political press, it is time to assess how problematic this medium proved to be. The press before 1772 certainly contained a spate of news challenging the monarchy and paraded French domestic difficulties. While a lack of research dictates limited commentary on the coverage of foreign affairs, reviewing the *Courrier d'Avignon* and the *Gazette de Leyde* indicates confusion. If anything stands out, it is criticism. But this is not the entire story. Prior to the late 1750s, the government severely restricted the circulation of all the foreign gazettes except the *Courrier d'Avignon*. Against this depleted field and circumspect periodical stood the totally statist *Gazette de France*, whose circulation likely overwhelmed the opposition. Only in the very late 1750s and 1760s would the full challenge posed by the press manifest itself. In this period – the lead-up to the Maupeou coup – periodicals truly were problematic, at worst spreading parlementary constitutionalism throughout the kingdom. But the last years of the ancien regime witnessed a far less troublesome press, even a supportive one during the American Revolution, despite Linguet's intervention. Although on the eve of Revolution the press surely awoke, this analysis attests that the content of the press from 1772 until 1785 hardly amounted to a rising, sustained criticism of the government. But neither does it completely endorse Jürgen Habermas's view of the French political press, which he sees as quiescent until the Revolution. For him, only the literary journals proved contestatory.[68] Clearly, the political periodical did have 'politics' and important ones, especially in the late 1750s and 1760s. But a more important question surely is whether the trajectory of ideas in the French press has anything to contribute to the historiography of the French Revolution. Whatever the debates among scholars, most regard the outbreak of revolution as all but inevitable. However, the improved reporting on the King in the press suggests that as late as the American Revolution, the monarch's position was not lost. One must explain how the King, buoyed by a positive image during the American Revolution, and generally in the early stages of the French Revolution, too, found his political capital so quickly dissipated.[69] Thus, study of the political press encourages closer scrutiny of the monarch's continuing strength and the events of the late 1780s and early 1790s that cost Louis XVI so dearly.

NOTES

1 This article is a revised and adapted version of Jack R. Censer, *The French Press in the Age of Enlightenment* (London and New York, 1994), pp. 15–17, 33–52.
2 See Censer, *The French Press*, pp. 10–12.
3 Howard Solomon, *Public Welfare, Science, and Propaganda in Seventeenth Century France: The Innovations of Théophraste Renaudot* (Princeton, NJ, 1972), pp. 100–122.
4 Gilles Feyel, 'La Diffusion des gazettes étrangères en France et la révolution postale des années 1750', in Henri Duranton, Claude Lebrosse and Pierre Rétat (eds.), *Les Gazettes européennes de langue française (XVIIe–XVIIIe siècles)* (Saint-Etienne, 1992), 89–98. See also Simon Burrows's chapter above.
5 Claude Bellanger, Jacques Godechot, Pierre Guiral and Fernand Terrou (eds.), *Histoire générale de la presse française*, vol. I, Jacques Godechot (ed.), *Des Origines à 1814* (Paris, 1969), pp. 143–57 and 285–98.
6 See Gilles Feyel, 'Nouvelles du Temps', in Jean Sgard (ed.), *Dictionnaire des journaux (1600–1789)* (Paris, 1991), p. 950. For a very strong statement on behalf of the *nouvelles*, see François Moureau (ed.), *De Bonne Main. La Communication manuscrite au XVIIIe siècle* (Paris, 1993).
7 For the definitive work on this subject see Suzanne Tucoo-Chala, *Charles-Joseph Panckoucke et la librairie française, 1736–1798* (Paris, 1975), pp. 191–251.
8 For superb essays on these two journals see Peter Ascoli, 'The French press and the American Revolution: the Battle of Saratoga', in Joyce Duncan Falk (ed.), *Proceedings of the 5th Annual Meeting of the Western Society for French History* (Santa Barbara, CA, 1977), 46–55, and Ascoli, 'American Propaganda in the French Language Press during the American Revolution', in *La Révolution américaine et l'Europe* (Paris, 1979), 291–305.
9 On earlier efforts by the Foreign Minister Choiseul, consult Madelaine Fabre, 'Edme-Jacques Genet', in Anne Marie Choillet and François Moureau (eds.), *Dictionnaire des journalistes (1600–1789)*, Supplement II (Grenoble, 1983), pp. 80–86.
10 There exists a substantial bibliography on Linguet but my analysis here depends on Darline Gay Levy, *The Ideas and Careers of Simon-Nicolas-Henri Linguet: A Study in Eighteenth Century French Politics* (Urbana, IL, 1980), pp. 172–224, and Jeremy D. Popkin, 'The Pre-Revolutionary Origins of Political Journalism', in Keith Michael Baker, François Furet and Colin Lucas (eds.), *The French Revolution and the Creation of Modern Political Culture*, vol. I,

France 1750–89   179

Keith Michael Baker (ed.), *The Political Culture of the Old Regime* (Oxford, 1987), pp. 203–23.
11 Censer, *The French Press*, passim.
12 Those who have found the political press to be conservative have generally not considered the circulation of the foreign press: see Robert Darnton, *The Literary Underground of the Old Regime* (Cambridge, MA, 1982), p. 113. But the profession as a whole, by searching for the roots of the Revolution without ever consulting the periodical press, has largely rendered implicitly its view of the conservative nature of eighteenth-century journalism.
13 For two hypotheses in that very direction, see Jack R. Censer, 'Die Presse des Ancien Régime im Übergang – eine Skizze', in Reinhard Kosseleck and Rolf Reichardt (eds.), *Die Französische Revolution als Bruch des gesellschaftlichen Bewusstseins* (Munich, 1988), pp. 127–52, and Popkin, 'Pre-Revolutionary Origins of Political Journalism'.
14 For a long discussion of this subject, see Christopher Todd, *Political Bias, Censorship and the Dissolution of the 'Official' Press in Eighteenth-Century France* (Lewistown, NY, 1991), pp. 261–308.
15 The history of the suppression of problems is long. For a 1711 case, see ibid., p. 5.
16 5 June 1751.
17 See, for a typical example, 19 June 1751.
18 17 July 1751.
19 Cited in Peter Ascoli, 'American Propaganda in the French language press during the American Revolution', in *La Révolution américaine et L'Europe* (Paris, 1979), 291–305 and Durand Echeverria, *Mirage in the West: A History of the French Image of American Society to 1815* (New York, 1960), pp. 36–7.
20 For example, see 18 October 1782 and especially 8 November 1782, concerning Florence.
21 See this tendency tracked in Hans Rosenberg, *Bureaucracy, Aristocracy, and Autocracy: The Prussian Experience, 1660–1815* (Boston, MA, 1958).
22 René Moulinas, *L'Imprimerie, la librairie et la presse à Avignon au XVIIIe siècle* (Grenoble, 1974), pp. 300–345. On the *Courrier d'Avignon*, see also Charles F. Hinds, 'The *Courrier d'Avignon* in the reign of Louis XVI', M.A. thesis, University of Kentucky (1958).
23 Moulinas, *L'Imprimerie*, pp. 372–9; and Censer, *The French Press*, ch. 5.
24 On the content of the *Courrier d'Avignon* see René Moulinas, 'Du Role de la poste royale comme moyen de controle financier sur la diffusion des gazettes en France au XVIIIe siècle', in P. Deyon (ed.), *Modèles et moyens de la réflexion politique au XVIIIe siècle*, 3 vols. (Lille, 1977), vol. I, 383–95, p. 394.
25 Echeverria, *Mirage in the West*, p. 43 n; and Bernard Faÿ, *The Revolutionary Spirit in France and America*, trans. Ramon Guthrie (New York, 1927), p. 54.
26 *Courrier d'Avignon*, 17 December 1779.
27 Ibid., 21 September 1779.
28 Ibid., 13 July 1779.
29 See for example, ibid., 21 March 1775.
30 Ibid., 17 May 1776.
31 Ibid., 8 November 1776.

32 Ibid., 4 July 1775.
33 For an exceptional criticism of the monarch, consult ibid., 9 May 1777.
34 Ibid., 26 December 1777.
35 Ibid., 28 July 1775
36 Ibid., 14 November 1775; 29 November 1776.
37 Ibid., 24 October 1775.
38 Ibid., 14 July 1775.
39 Ibid., 12 June and 10 July 1781.
40 Ibid., 5 November 1782.
41 Ibid., 8 January 1782.
42 For typical reporting from America, see ibid., 8 September 1775.
43 For the exceptional report on the monarch, see ibid., 7 January 1777.
44 To understand the American view of the British constitution, see Caroline Robbins, *The Eighteenth-Century Commonwealthman* (Cambridge, MA, 1959), especially pp. 356–77 and 385–6; Bernard Bailyn, *The Ideological Origins of the American Revolution* (Cambridge, MA, 1967).
45 Supplement to the *Courrier d'Avignon*, 23 July 1779.
46 Frances Acomb, *Anglophobia in France, 1763–1789* (Durham, NC, 1950), pp. 51–68.
47 Jeremy D. Popkin, 'The *Gazette de Leyde* and French Politics under Louis XVI', in Jack R. Censer and Jeremy D. Popkin (eds.), *Press and Politics in Pre-Revolutionary France* (Berkeley, CA, 1987), 75–132, p. 82.
48 Jeremy D. Popkin, *News and Politics in the Age of Revolution: Jean Luzac's Gazette de Leyde* (Ithaca, NY, and London, 1989).
49 Popkin, *News and Politics*, pp. 137–87.
50 Ibid.
51 Pierre Rétat, 'Les Gazetiers de Holland et les puissances politiques: une difficile collaboration', *Dix-huitième siècle*, 25 (1993), 319–35. For another comparative treatment which envisions the *Gazette de Leyde* as a very aggressive paper but only slightly more so than several others, see Pierre Rétat (ed.), *L'Attentat de Damiens. Discours sur l'événement au XVIIIe siècle* (Paris, 1979), pp. 15–46.
52 Popkin, *News and Politics*, pp. 137–57.
53 For the general reaction of the press regarding this attempt on Louis XV, consult Rétat (ed.), *L'Attentat de Damiens*, pp. 15–46.
54 Popkin, *News and Politics*, pp. 139–40 and 149–50. For more detail on government strategies for control see Simon Burrows' chapter above.
55 For an excellent comparative account, consult Jean-Louis Lecercle, 'L'Amerique et la guerre d'independance', in Paule Jansen et al., *L'Année 1778 à travers la presse traitée par ordinateur* (Paris, 1982), 17–42.
56 Ascoli, 'American Propaganda', and 'The French press and the American Revolution'.
57 Frances Acomb, *Mallet du Pan (1749–1800): A Career in Political Journalism* (Durham, NC, 1973), pp. 158–209.
58 Tucoo-Chala, *Panckoucke*, pp. 205–6; Acomb, *Mallet du Pan*, pp. 158–209.
59 These views on the *Affaires d'Angleterre et de l'Amerique* depend heavily on Sgard, *Dictionnaire des journaux*, pp. 7–10. For the *Courier de l'Europe*, my assessment follows the magisterial study by Gunnar and Mavis von Proschwitz,

Beaumarchais et le Courier de l'Europe: *documents inédits ou peu connus*, 2 vols. (Oxford, 1990). The von Proschwitzs see a school for the French in the coverage of the British opposition. However, Keith Baker, 'Politics and public opinion under the Old Regime: some reflections', in Censer and Popkin, *Press and Politics*, 204–46, questions this possibility, as he says the French were especially wary of their across-the-Channel neighbours. My own view is that such caution surely affected the use of the British system as a blueprint, but not the suggestion that the Bourbon monarchy needed radical overhaul. The French admired enough about the British surely to see their political structure as a rebuke to absolutism and as a tool for speculating about a better government.

60 Levy, *Linguet*, pp. 172–80.
61 Popkin, *News and Politics*, pp. 62–3.
62 François Metra, *Correspondance secrète, politique, et littéraire: ou mémoires pour servir à l'histoire des cours, des sociétés et de la littérature en France, depuis la mort de Louis XV*, 16 vols. (London, 1787–90), vol. III, p. 276.
63 Ibid.
64 Levy, *Linguet*, pp. 172–225; and Jeremy D. Popkin, 'Un Journaliste face au marché des périodiques à la fin du dix-huitième siècle: Linguet et ses *Annales politiques*', in Hans Bots (ed.), *La Diffusion et la lecture des journaux de langue française sous l'Ancien Régime* (Amsterdam, 1988), 11–19.
65 Louis Petit de Bachaumont (attrib.), *Mémoires secrets pour servir à l'histoire de la république des lettres en France, depuis 1762 jusqu'à nos jours, ou journal d'un observateur*, 36 vols. (London, 1777–87), XXV, p. 95.
66 Popkin, *News and Politics*, p. 62.
67 Miriam Yardeni, 'Paradoxes politiques et persuasion dans les *Annales* de Linguet', in Harvey Chisick (ed.), *The Press in the French Revolution: Studies on Voltaire and the Eighteenth Century*, vol. 287 (Oxford, 1991), 211–19, comes to largely similar conclusions.
68 Jürgen Habermas, *The Structural Transformation of the Public Sphere: An Inquiry into a Category of Bourgeois Society*, trans. Thomas Burger (Cambridge, MA, 1991), pp. 151–6.
69 See, for example, the successes of the administration in Harold T. Parker, *The Bureau of Commerce in 1781 and Its Policies with Respect to French Industry* (Durham, NC, 1979).

8 The French revolutionary press

Hugh Gough

Any analysis of the French press during the Revolution is made difficult by the contrast between the brevity of the period and the volume of the material. If we take Napoleon's accession to power in 1799 as the end of the Revolution – and it is just one of many possibilities – then the event lasted around ten years. During that short time, over 2,000 newspapers were published, together with some 13,000 political pamphlets and posters. But it was the newspapers that caught the eye of contemporaries. The author and journalist Louis-Sébastien Mercier noted: 'there is no street without a newspaper print shop and three journalists in the attics, writing – or rather doing a scissors and paste job on – their newspaper columns'.[1] Not all the newspapers have survived, but those that have still leave a daunting amount of text to analyse. The nature of this text was new too, as literature and books, which had dominated the reading habits of the nobility and bourgeoisie under the ancien regime, now took second place to newspapers and pamphlets. Charles de Lameth remarked to the National Assembly on 16 January 1790 that most Parisian printers had, of necessity, made the switch from quality to quantity, from books to newspapers.[2] Most of their customers had too, and although many of the newspapers that they read were ephemeral, a significant number were impressively durable, lasting for months and even years. That durability was in turn the result of a radical change in editorial and publication habits, as speed became the order of the day, replacing the more sedate rhythm of the ancien regime. Journalists had to adapt to the condensed format of newspapers, which imposed severe constraints on length and style. Writers used to the leisurely literary cadences of formal style had to learn how to summarise at speed and how to phrase their articles in a manner that would attract readers and their subscriptions.[3] The change was difficult, yet those who succeeded found themselves in a new and influential profession which carried a political weight that even the Enlightenment *philosophes* had never enjoyed. A new role, new styles, new vocabularies and new production habits therefore transformed the French press in the revolutionary decade.

The French revolutionary press 183

Because of the density of the printed material, all histories of the revolutionary press have had to navigate uneasily between detailed monograph and impressionistic survey. Two of the most substantial and durable surveys were published in the mid-nineteenth century, by Léonard Gallois and Eugène Hatin, at a time when journalism was closely linked to the fortunes of political liberalism.[4] Gallois's two-volume history, after a brief introductory chronological summary, concentrates on the most prominent journalists and the major newspapers. Hatin's eight-volume history, published fifteen years later, begins well before the Revolution but devotes most of its attention to the period 1789 to 1799, concentrating like Gallois on both personalities and titles. Both are concerned mainly with the emergence of the Parisian press and pay little attention to developments outside the capital. Several other general histories were published in the late nineteenth and early twentieth centuries, but the first significant advance on the groundwork done by Gallois and Hatin appeared only in the late 1960s, with the publication of a five-volume history of the French press in which the revolutionary period was covered by Jacques Godechot. A well-respected political historian of the Revolution, Godechot substantially updated Hatin's approach, linking the fortunes of the press to the politics of the Revolution and incorporating research carried out during the intervening 100 years, some of it by his own research students.[5] Since 1969, other books and articles have both extended our knowledge of the press and transformed our understanding of its role.[6]

Little of this research has made any overt attempt to link in with Habermas's views on the relationship between social change and the emergence of public space. Habermas's path-breaking book first appeared in French translation in 1978, sixteen years after its initial publication and eleven years before its appearance in English.[7] For much of the forty years that have elapsed since its initial publication, the traditional historian's suspicion of sociology combined with scepticism over Habermas's Marxist approach has ensured that his work was largely ignored, except by historians of ancien regime public opinion.[8] Among the latter, two historians of the press, Jack Censer and Jeremy Popkin, because of their interests in the links between ancien regime and Revolution, have related parts of their research to Habermas's ideas on the growth of an autonomous 'public sphere'.[9] In a recent study of the ancien regime press, Censer has stressed the important role played by articles in the advertising journals, or *Affiches*, in articulating the themes of a Habermas-style bourgeois civil society. However, he also notes their relative failure in airing political issues and controversy.[10]

Nevertheless the political press that appeared in France in 1789 did not emerge overnight. Despite the persistence until 1789 of pre-publication censorship and licensing control, the press had expanded during the eighteenth century and over forty provincial, and almost as many Parisian, journals were being published at the beginning of 1789. In addition, several foreign newspapers such as the *Gazette de Leyde* and the *Courrier d'Avignon* were allowed to circulate relatively freely.[11] However, except in periods of instability or factional division at court, the political content of the domestic press was carefully controlled, and articles on French politics were scarce and conformist. Readers interested in subversive commentary on court politics were better catered for in the underground pamphlet press, which was better equipped to evade censorship and paint a lurid picture of a court allegedly embroiled in sexual and financial scandal.[12] Nevertheless, as Jeremy Popkin has argued, some developments anticipated the transformation of 1789. Certain editors developed the technique of analytical narrative that their revolutionary counterparts were later to perfect, blending chronological detail with ideological commentary. In addition, Simon-Nicolas-Henri Linguet's mixture of personalised polemic and conspiracy theory, in his *Annales politiques, civiles et littéraires*, anticipated the sensationalist style that Marat, Hébert and others were to exploit with devastating success. Above all, several of the foreign journals developed techniques of political narrative which built up anticipation and uncertainty in the mind of the reader in a way that revolutionary journalists were later to do.[13]

These developments were straws in the wind, but until 1789 radically changed the context of press activity, that wind was really only a breeze. Then, in May 1789, during the early days of the meetings of the Estates General, Mirabeau defied government censorship by producing a newspaper under the guise of a published form of correspondence with his constituents in Provence. Several other newspapers followed suit, providing accounts of the crucial Assembly debates of May and June, before the fall of the Bastille threw the floodgates open in July. By the end of the year, 194 new journals had appeared in Paris and thirty-five in the provinces.[14] During 1790 and 1791, more than 300 new journals appeared each year, and this number dipped only slightly in 1792. Even during the Terror, at a time when censorship and the guillotine were powerful disincentives, new journals appeared at a rate of almost ten per month.[15] The rate climbed again after Thermidor, with the collapse of the Terror, and only during the latter years of the Directory, when censorship became draconian, did it decline again.[16] Many of these newspapers were extremely short-lived, yet others like the *Révolutions de Paris*, the *Patriote françois* or the *Ami du roi* stayed in production for several years and wielded significant political influence. Some even survived into the nineteenth century. The *Gazette universelle*, for example, was launched in the autumn of 1789 and defended constitutional royalism through no less than three major title changes until its closure in 1810. The *Moniteur*, launched in the dying weeks of 1789, was even more durable, lasting in various guises until the German invasion of 1940.

This kind of growth was made possible by the collapse of censorship in the summer of 1789. The principle of press freedom was written into article XI of the Declaration of the Rights of Man in August 1789, with the explicit understanding that subsequent legislation would define its legal limits: 'The free communication of thoughts and opinions is one of the most precious rights of man; every citizen can therefore speak, write and print freely, except to answer for abuse of this freedom in cases laid down by the law.' Yet drafting a definition of 'abuse' and establishing a legal mechanism for its control was not easy in a time of such rapid political change, and debates in the National Assembly over the next two years revealed deep divisions between deputies over the relative advantages of freedom and control. Few were prepared to defend the ancien regime practice of prior censorship, but many of the centre and right wanted to ensure that editors guilty of publishing libellous or seditious articles would be prosecuted. Defining libel and sedition, however, was the stumbling block as there was no consensus on the issue. However much the majority of deputies was appalled by the excesses of Marat's *Ami du peuple* or Camille Desmoulins's *Révolutions de France et de Brabant*, they were wary of passing legislation that might be exploited to suppress all radical criticism. Indeed, a minority on the left, led by Robespierre and Pétion, opposed any specific press legislation at all and argued that the laws of libel were sufficient protection. As a result, it was only in late August 1791 that two constitutional articles were finally passed, defining a number of press 'offences' (including the incitement to commit an illegal act and the discrediting of public officials) and providing for trials to be held before a jury. Yet they were to prove ineffective and vanished with the constitution a year later.[17]

In the debate between 1789 and 1791 the right argued consistently that social order and stable government required press restraint, while the left replied that a free press was essential for the development of an enlightened public opinion. Those arguments changed sides, however, in the summer of 1792, as war led to Republic and Terror. Several right-wing journals were closed down in the aftermath of Louis XVI's removal on 10 August, and although many reappeared with new titles and a conservative republican editorial policy, the Convention declared support for monarchy a capital offence before the end of the year. Legislation in the spring of 1793 added support for counter-revolution to the list of capital offences and the law of suspects of 17 September 1793 widened the net still further. The Jacobin left that had opposed censorship in 1789 now defended it as a political necessity. Leading Girondin newspapers were closed down, their editors and printers imprisoned and guillotined, and dissident Jacobin journalists suffered the same fate. Among them were prominent political personalities such as Camille Desmoulins, editor of the *Vieux Cordelier*, and Jacques-René Hébert, whose *Père Duchêne* had an enthusiastic following among the Parisian *sans-culottes* and the Cordeliers club. The Jacobin attitude to the press was perhaps best expressed by a secretary of the Committee of General Security, Momory, sent to supervise the arrest of a journalist, Jean-Charles Laveaux, in Paris in the spring of 1794. When Laveaux protested at the impounding of his press along with his papers, Momory merely replied: 'a printing press is a piece of property with which one can do a great deal of harm'.[18]

After Robespierre's fall in the summer of 1794 Jacobin policies were reversed and press freedom became a Thermidorean symbol for resistance to the Terror. A lively press sprang up which was virulently anti-Jacobin, outspokenly conservative and frequently royalist. This prompted legislation against the right-wing press in the spring of 1795, and further legislation in the spring of 1796, directed against both the extreme left and the extreme right. Yet both were ineffective, as juries simply refused to convict because they considered the penalties too harsh. Effective action only came with the Fructidor coup d'état of September 1797, when over seventy newspapers were closed and the Directors empowered to ban any newspaper considered a threat to political stability. A stamp tax was introduced weeks later, which raised production costs significantly and sent many of the smaller papers to the wall. These draconian powers were renewed in the following year and used against both royalist and Jacobin journals, until the Brumaire coup of 1799 brought Napoleon to power. He rapidly refined the Directory's arsenal of repression and, by its final years, the First Empire had created a censorship regime that made that of the ancien regime seem mild in comparison.[19]

Press freedom, therefore, thrived between 1789 and 1792, then again between 1794 and 1797. The periods of the Terror and the Second Directory (1797–99) were more restrictive. Yet law was not the only means open to governments for press control. Money was too, and almost every revolutionary regime attempted to buy favourable press coverage. Louis XVI subsidised royalist titles, and the Girondin ministry which succeeded the monarchy in August 1792 set up a propaganda *bureau* under the control of Jean-Marie Roland at the Ministry of the Interior, which subsidised a range of pro-Girondin journalists and pamphleteers to encourage Roland's brand of moderate republicanism. Although Jacobin protests forced the *bureau*'s closure in January 1793, the Jacobins themselves used the same methods. Once in power, they used government subsidies to bolster up a range of radical newspapers, including the *Feuille de salut public*, which the Committee of Public Safety established as its own mouthpiece in the autumn of 1793. Jacobin clubs in Paris and the provinces also subsidised their own newspapers.[20] The practice of government subsidies continued after Thermidor and, although galloping inflation and state penury reduced the Directory's resources, it provided intermittent press subsidies between 1795 and 1799, and financed its own newspaper, the *Rédacteur*, from the winter of 1795–6 onwards.

Although censorship and patronage affected the conditions under which journalists worked, the business structures of journalism remained relatively unchanged during the Revolution. Methods remained artisanal, with small workshops using hand-operated wooden presses that had changed very little for over three centuries. Large enterprises existed, but they were rare. During the last years of the ancien regime, Charles-Joseph Panckoucke had emerged as a press baron in Paris, controlling major titles such as *Gazette de France*, the *Mercure* and the *Journal de Bruxelles*. Aware that the collapse of privilege threatened his dominance, Panckoucke launched the *Moniteur* in the late autumn of 1789. Committed to extensive news coverage and to detailed reports of Assembly debates, the *Moniteur* rapidly established itself as an authoritative daily journal of record. At the height of its success, along with Panckoucke's other newspapers, it kept twenty-seven presses busy and employed ninety-one workers. Others shared Panckoucke's approach. Louis-Marie Prudhomme was a minor bookseller before the Revolution, but in July of 1789 he reprinted someone else's pamphlet on the fall of the Bastille, which was an immediate commercial success. He promptly relaunched it as a weekly newspaper, the *Révolutions de Paris*, which was to last until the early spring of 1794 and generated enough profits to enable him to buy his own presses and print shop. At the height of his success, Prudhomme owned fourteen presses and employed a team of journalists, a press manager, a sales manager, numerous print workers and several hundred part-time assistants.[21] Elsewhere in Paris the *Gazette universelle* occupied eight presses in 1792, with daily sales of 11,000 copies and the *Journal du soir* used five presses for its 10,000 daily copies, employing sixty print workers and up to 200 street vendors.[22]

Yet these large-scale enterprises were atypical and most revolutionary newspapers were small-scale operations with a rudimentary business structure. An editor wrote his text and contracted with a printer to print and distribute it. He then either paid the printer out of his subscription revenue, and pocketed the rest as profit, or entered into a shared arrangement for the distribution of costs and profits. The well-documented case of Ferréol de Beaugeard, owner and editor of the *Journal de Marseille* for fourteen years between 1783 and 1797, is just one of dozens of this kind of operation.[23] Alternatively, printers who wanted to maximise the use of their presses did as many had already done for the ancien regime *Affiches*, by employing a writer or political activist to write the text of a newspaper in return for a salary. The highly successful *Courrier de Strasbourg*, published between 1791 and 1793, was owned by the bookseller and printer Jean-Georges Treuttel. He employed a writer and Jacobin activist, Jean-Charles Laveaux, as his editor, paying him an annual salary and retaining the profits for himself. There were variants on both these models and, as the Revolution progressed, the money involved in a successful newspaper led to increasingly complex contracts. Yet the basic structures remained the same, because social and economic conditions made them viable. On the editorial side there was no lack of potential journalists with political ambition looking for work, while on the production side the collapse of controls on the printing trade and the minimal costs involved in setting up a press led to a massive growth in printers.[24] The wooden hand-press may have struggled to produce 300 printed sheets an hour, but it had the advantage of being cheap to build, buy and run. Editors rarely had a problem finding a printer, except in the more sleepy provincial towns, and many bought their own press and ran the entire operation themselves. That was how Marat began his *Ami du peuple* in the autumn of 1789, before he opted to use printers who paid him a cash sum for his text.[25]

Who were the journalists who provided much of the dynamism behind press growth? No one has attempted detailed prosopographical analysis for the Revolution to match the dictionary of ancien regime journalists produced by Jean Sgard, although William J. Murray has carried out a partial analysis for the early years.[26] This shows that journalists could be either young – in their twenties – or relatively old – in their forties or fifties. They also came from a wide social spectrum of literate society, from the sons of artisans at the lower end of the scale to the nobility at the top. A significant number were former nobles, such as Condorcet or Mirabeau, while priests were prominent too, with non-jurors such as the abbé Royou and constitutional priests such as Claude Fauchet or Euloge Schneider. Lawyers were ubiquitous, but a range of other occupations is represented too, including doctors (Marat), minor *philosophes* (Carra and Gorsas), actors (Aristide Valcour) and printers too numerous to mention. Like André Malraux's Gaullists, the Revolution's journalists came from the eighteenth-century equivalent of the Paris Metro.

Yet wherever they came from, journalists entered an occupation which was increasingly being considered a distinct profession with its own rules and its own status. The word '*journaliste*' was already in use in 1789, but journalism as an occupation was held in low regard, because of the prestige of 'serious' literature and the requirement for journalists to accept the constraints of censorship. The pre-Revolution of 1787–8 did little to change this, as protests against Calonne's and Brienne's reforms were largely voiced in pamphlets, which were better equipped than newspapers to avoid censorship. However, the government's collapse in 1789 ensured that journalism became an integral part of the new political culture. Assembly debates created a voracious demand for regular reporting in the capital and the emergence of elected administrative structures at departmental, district and municipal level in the provinces created a new political arena for the provincial journalist too. Pamphlets were still published in substantial quantities, but they were unable to provide the continuous updates of news and comment, circulated to a national audience, that newspapers could. As Brissot claimed, in a plea for press freedom in the summer of 1789: 'But a newspaper penetrates everywhere instantly. It is read everywhere and even by the less well off. A hundred thousand people have read a newspaper by the time barely a hundred have read a pamphlet.'[27] Journalism became an essential cog in the wheel of politics, newspapers a daily necessity and journalists politically important for the first time in French history. Readers needed

this rapid and secure communication that only periodicals can offer, to circulate opinion and enlightenment from the centre to the periphery and to bring them constantly together from each point of the opposing extremes, just as in the biological world the fluids necessary for life carry the essentials of survival to all parts of the human and vegetable body.[28]

The new status of journalists was best summed up in the words of a 1797 pamphlet:

Certainly it is a trade, and a very lucrative one from what I hear. Those who work in it have no other form of work, and would not have the time for two such jobs. Previously a news writer produced a paper a week, and it could hardly be called a full time profession. Today that is no longer the case. Our newspaper editors are real *journalists*; every day, and often twice a day, they write, print and sell what they know about and what they don't know about, what they have been ordered to print, what they have been told, and whatever is passing through their head. And it is certainly a well organised business, with directors, treasurers, office workers, foremen, wholesale and retail sales, by the year, by the month, by single number – the whole workshop is organised for the purpose. And what would anyone who denies this say to a policeman who asked for his profession? He could reply 'man of letters', but he would reply that that was all very well, but rather vague, so how do you earn a living? You would then have to admit what you are now denying, and to reply 'journalist'.[29]

If journalists enjoyed a new status, they also acquired a new role.[30] During the ancien regime journalists frequently compared themselves to historians, gathering information, differentiating between truth from error and presenting a reliable account of events for readers to use to come to their own conclusions. This was how Mallet du Pan defined his role as editor of the *Journal de Bruxelles*, differentiating himself from a mere 'chronicler' who listed events and gossip without analysis of commentary.[31] For Mallet a journalist needed to show detachment and analytical ability, particularly in his handling of foreign news, as censorship precluded domestic political comment. During the Revolution, some journalists remained attached to Mallet's ideal, particularly in the serious dailies which concentrated exclusively on the reporting of Assembly debates. Etienne Feuillant, in his *Journal du soir* in July 1790, promised his readers: 'Accuracy, speed, the exact wording of every decree and no commentary; news occasionally, but only when it is absolutely authentic: those are my obligations.'[32] Even journalists who followed Feuillant's example had to cope with the production speed required of a daily newspaper, had to understand the new world of political ideology, had to follow debates in the poor acoustics and procedural chaos of the Salle du Manège and had to learn to take notes accurately and swiftly.[33] Yet none of these problems was insuperable and serious dailies such as the *Moniteur* or the *Journal des débats* quickly found a sizeable and loyal readership.

Most journalists, however, saw their role in a different light and catered for a different kind of reader. Not content to be mere chroniclers, they claimed for themselves the role of political mentors, interpreting events from a particular viewpoint and rallying their readers behind a political cause. They called their newspapers 'orators', 'patriots', 'friends of the people' or 'friends of the King', 'sentinels' or 'publicists' to symbolise this new role, and abandoned Mallet's ideals of detachment and analysis in favour of a partisan and campaigning role.[34] One of the earliest definitions of this 'new' journalism was given by Brissot in his 1789 pamphlet on press freedom. Citing both revolutionary America and Britain to show its benefits, Brissot claimed press freedom as a natural right, which would lead to the improvement of human society, and a property right, which would enable individuals to claim ownership of the ideas that they had created. Yet he went on to claim freedom also as a prerequisite for democracy in a country as dispersed and rural as France, as it alone would encourage the circulation of ideas and information beyond the place in which they had been first conceived, enabling them to reach a national audience. Newspapers provided the kind of political information that could alone lead to the formation of an enlightened public opinion: 'To hinder press freedom is to interrupt this universal communication which is so essential in the context of an ignorant people confronted by a wily aristocracy, and so useful to an active and perceptive people which is full of energy.' He later returned to the same theme in an argument with Camille Desmoulins in the summer of 1791 over the respective roles of the press and political clubs, arguing that newspapers played a prime role in political education, for 'the tribune of public education must embrace the whole population, its words must reach the hearing of the largest number of people possible'.[35] It was an argument echoed by other journalists and commentators. The *Journal patriotique de la Dordogne*, for example, argued that press freedom allowed journalists a unique role as intermediaries between elected deputies and the sovereign people in a country whose size ruled out the possibility of direct contact between the two. It was a medium 'whose effect on the brain, operating at a level that the senses cannot appreciate, manages to guide them without any hint of force; a power which, if humanity could ever attain perfection, would be the only one used by rulers and tolerated by the governed'.[36] A speaker in the Council of Elders in 1799 argued that newspapers enabled readers to access accurate news and analysis that would otherwise have taken them days to acquire.[37]

The view that journalists were necessary intermediaries between legislators and people in the new democratic political culture was a predictably popular idea among journalists themselves. The editor of the Jacobin club's *Journal révolutionnaire de Toulouse* in the autumn of 1793 claimed that his role was to guide readers towards republican patriotism: 'the facts that he publishes must be seasoned with intriguing and judicious reflections, suitable for strengthening public spirit, fortifying patriotism and supporting liberty against the attacks of aristocrats and moderates'.[38] The *Courrier d'Avignon* stated the same in the following spring: 'The patriotic journalist must act as the conductor which transmits the sacred fire of the fatherland into the minds of his readers.'[39] Other concepts of the journalist's role supplemented this. Some argued that journalists encouraged national unity by providing a flow of news within departments and between the provinces and Paris. The *Journal du Lot* in 1796, for example, argued that accurate local information enabled citizens to assume their political responsibilities, while departmental journals acted as 'lighthouses' or 'mirrors' for central government, enabling it to keep in step with events at local level.[40] The *Journal patriotique de la Bourgogne* made a similar argument in a spirited attack on critics of press freedom:

But they do not seem to realise that the number [of newspapers] grows in proportion to the growth in interest for public affairs, and that in every country where opinion is not chained to the yoke of tyrants, the free circulation of thoughts is linked to the system of government and to progress in peoples' reason. They do not realise that, at a time when each department and town is acquiring the chance to administer itself publicly, all provinces must maintain frequent communication between themselves, and newspapers are the only way of doing that.[41]

The departmental authorities of the Ain, welcoming the establishment of a short-lived *Journal du département de l'Ain* in the spring of 1792, noted that 'this kind of work is indispensable for educating citizens about everything taking place within the confines of a *département*'.[42]

Another role that journalists claimed was that of surveillance of political leaders, local authorities and agencies.[43] Vigilance was one of the key themes of revolutionary politics, feeding on political suspicion and the fear of plots.[44] It was Marat's speciality in the *Ami du peuple*, but it was by no means confined to him alone, being shared in varying degrees by journalists on all sides of the political spectrum.[45] Moderates and counter-revolutionaries denounced it in the early years of the Revolution, arguing that it led to witch-hunts which enabled demagogues to slander the great and the good, driving talented people out of politics and continuing a regrettable tradition of libel current in the underground pamphlets of the ancien regime.[46] Yet radical journalists defended it as something that encouraged political transparency, exposed corruption and counter-revolution, and strengthened the standing of the unjustly accused. The editor of the *Journal constitutionnel du département du Gers* proclaimed:

I believe myself, sir, to be the natural watchdog of the administration. It is the right of an honest journalist and, I would even say, his duty... According to the constitution, censure of the acts of public authorities is allowed; the ministers of this censure, Sir, are journalists.[47]

Finally, several journals also stressed their commitment to providing a political education for the urban poor and the peasantry. Several radical Parisian newspapers actively sought out a popular audience from among the city's *sans-culottes*. The best known genre for this was the figure of the *Père Duchêne*, an imaginary stove merchant who delivered a monologue on current affairs, spiced with colourful *argot* and swear words. It was first used in the autumn of 1790, with rival versions produced by two journalists, Jean René Hébert and Jean Charles Jumel. Hébert's version proved more durable and appealed to a sizeable *sans-culotte* audience in the summer and autumn of 1793, enabling Hébert to push his own political agenda onto the Committee of Public Safety.[48] Yet he was not alone, and public readings on streets, in cafés or in political clubs made it possible for other radical journalists to reach a *sans-culotte* audience. Rural readers were not forgotten either. The weekly *Feuille villageoise* was launched in September 1790 by the abbé Cérutti to explain the principles of the Revolution and its constitution to the peasantry.[49] It was aimed mainly at wealthier peasants and at priests, who were expected to spread its ideas in their local village. But others tried to reach further down the rural social scale, either by using a local dialect or by trying to explain the advantages that change had brought to the rural population in the style of a Catholic catechism.[50] Several general newspapers also tried to cater for peasant demands. Philippeaux, editor of the *Défenseur de la vérité* in Le Mans, referred to his paper as a *'cours d'instruction'* which he intended continuing until 'enlightenment has re-energised the countryside, there is an educational [i.e. political] club in every village, and all good cultivators of the soil have ceased being dependent on, and subordinate to, more educated men'.[51]

This positive view of the press's role was far from universally accepted. From the outset, right-wing journals attacked press freedom for unleashing a horde of 'venomous insects' or 'voracious and hideous caterpillars' who fomented hatred and whipped up political instability. Newspapers were too trivial a medium for serious political debate, and a threshold of literacy and wealth needed to be established to ensure that demagogues were kept out.[52] What the political right claimed in the early Revolution later spread to all parts of the political spectrum. Girondins accused Jacobin journalists of royalism, Jacobins accused *Enragé* journalists of treason, and both left-wing and right-wing republicans during the Directory denounced journalists of the other side as anarchist or royalist. Journalists were even likened to prostitutes, selling their services to the highest bidder, but with the distinctly non-carnal aim of creating anarchy.[53] Mercier and Louvet, both moderate republican journalists themselves early in the Revolution, accused their colleagues in the mid-1790s of betraying their mission as political educators because of their extremism and corruption. Journalists were now 'Egyptian locusts' who had betrayed the ideals of the Enlightenment, undermined public morality and caused the Terror.[54] Talot denounced newspapers in the Council of Five Hundred as 'mobile clubs preaching revolt and disobedience to the law', while his colleague Bellegarde had expressed his feelings just a few days previously by striking Langlois, editor of the *Censeur des journaux*, in the corridor outside the debating chamber.[55]

Yet, if journalists had acquired a controversial reputation and status, who read the newspapers that they produced? The weakness of archival evidence rules out a comprehensive answer, but enough has survived to provide a general overview. Most revolutionary newspapers were sold by pre-paid subscription rather than on the street, although some in Paris used a combination of both. Subscriptions had advantages for both journalists and clients: journalists receiving their revenue in advance, which enabled them to cover their printing costs and to know their print-run, and subscribers enjoying the benefits of continuity and direct delivery. Editors normally published a prospectus, outlining their intentions and inviting subscriptions, and regular publication then followed within a matter of weeks if the response was encouraging. Excess numbers of the initial editions were often sent as unsolicited mail to prospective customers, in the hope of bringing them on board. In the words of the *Courrier de Villeneuve-lès-Avignon* in December 1789: 'To enable people to make a judgement on the *Courrier*, we are sending copies to people in every town [of the region], and in particular to public places where they will be seen.'[56]

The minimum number of subscribers required to cover costs was usually quite low, as a one-man editorial operation in which the editor worked alone and merely employed a printer for publication and distribution could break even with little more than 300 subscribers. Any newspaper with over 1,000 subscribers was in a position to make a reasonable profit, if efficiently managed, and the curve rose steeply for sales above that. In reality, most provincial newspapers appear to have survived on print-runs of less than 500 and only the most successful exceeded it. Ferréol de Beaugeard's *Journal de Marseille* survived with around 300 subscribers before the Revolution, but climbed to around 500 in the summer of 1795 when it resumed publication after enforced closure during the Terror, attracting a sizeable anti-Jacobin readership. The *Courrier de Strasbourg* was able to exploit widespread interest in news from the Rhine frontier during the run-up to war in the spring of 1792 to build up over 1,200 subscribers within months of its launch. The *Journal général de l'Orléanais* also had 1,200 subscribers in 1791, the *Feuille de Flandres* claimed 1,000 at the end of the same year and one or two of the newspapers published in Rouen in the early Revolution probably did as well.[57] The Parisian press did far better, however, because it could appeal to a national market. Many of the major newspapers had sales of between 3,000 and 5,000 and several sold substantially more. Prudhomme's *Révolutions de Paris* reputedly sold over 100,000 copies of its early numbers, although this probably includes reprints.[58] Some numbers of Hébert's *Père Duchêne* are said to have sold up to 40,000 copies and at the height of its success in the summer of 1793, its average print-run was around 9,000.[59] Estimates for Brissot's *Patriote françois* suggest sales of over 5,000 in the early Revolution, while the counter-revolutionary *Actes des apôtres* had a print run of 4,500 at a time when a counterfeit edition was selling over 3,000 more.[60] Another right-wing paper, the *Gazette de Paris*, had a print-run of over 5,000 in 1790–91 dropping to under 3,000 in the spring of 1792, while in 1797 the royalist *Abréviateur universel* had 6,000 subscribers.[61]

Tracing the identity and social background of subscribers again runs up against the problem of evidence. Journalists and printers, having spent their lives working with paper, showed little interest in preserving it for posterity, and historians have to rely instead on the archival debris left by the police who often confiscated records at the time of arrest. The ambiguity of eighteenth-century social terminology is an added complicating factor, for an occupational definition such as 'tailor' or 'cabinet-maker' could apply to a one-man operation as well as to a large-scale employer. Clearly, the cost of subscriptions ruled out the very poor, although some had access to collective reading sessions organised by their *curé* or by their local *société populaire*.[62] Hébert's *Père Duchêne* was certainly widely read in clubs in the south-west, such as Perpignan and Bayonne, in 1793 and newspaper readings were the staple diet of clubs elsewhere too.[63] The Jacobin club in Mayenne as early as 1791 had an article in its constitution that provided for subscriptions to be taken out to newspapers that would be read aloud between seven and nine each morning.[64] The club in Rouen subscribed to twenty-four newspapers in late 1792 and cafés also took out subscriptions for the benefit of their clientele.[65]

Nevertheless, the scant figures that we have suggest that nobles and the bourgeoisie provided the main market. The nobility certainly feature strongly among subscribers to the right-wing press of the early Revolution, taking out just over half of the subscriptions to the *Gazette de Paris* between 1789 and 1792. The majority were army officers, many of them from the ranks of the poorer sword nobility who despised the extravagance and privilege of court life of the ancien regime but whose military career and social status had nevertheless been ruined by the Revolution. A further 15 per cent came from the clergy, mostly from the upper clergy, who were hostile to the religious reforms of the National Assembly, and 13 per cent were from women.[66] There is evidence to suggest that the nobility and clergy also remained significant minority subscribers to several provincial newspapers, as they had been under the ancien regime, but they are much less evident among right-wing newspaper subscribers after the Terror because of emigration and the ban on noble titles. In the case of the Patriot press, middle-class and lower middle-class readership was more in evidence. Subscription lists for the Paris Jacobin club's *Journal de la Montagne* during the Terror show that over 30 per cent of its Parisian readership came from shopkeepers and tradesmen, 20 per cent from office workers and employees, and almost as many from politicians. Artisans, on the other hand, made up barely 13 per cent. In the provinces the proportions were even more weighted towards wealth, with proportionately more from the professions, trade and industry, and only a little over 16 per cent from artisans and peasants combined. Just over 4 per cent were women.[67] Babeuf's *Tribun du peuple* attracted a predictably more popular audience for its message of radical Jacobinism in the winter of 1795–6, with over 70 per cent of its Parisian readership made up of shopkeepers, retailers and artisans, but less than 30 per cent of its provincial subscribers from the same ranks. Among Parisian subscribers a third had been *sans culotte* activists during the Terror.[68]

If the French Revolution transformed the status of journalism in France, it did so by linking its activity to political liberty and constitutional politics. Between 1789 and 1799, newspapers became not only an essential channel for the rapid dissemination of political information, but also a focal point for the discussions and debates of rival ideological groups. Like political clubs, newspapers attracted people who shared their viewpoint on major issues. In the words of one contemporary:

> You become the pupil of your paper . . . you take it as your guide, you take on its tone, its language and its authority; you make it your representative, your champion, your voice, your commentator [and] your apologist; you make it a point of honour to ensure that its doctrines, likes and dislikes prevail.[69]

France was neither the first nor the last country to witness the politicisation of journalism, as it had already taken place more gradually in Britain, Ireland and the United States and was to extend to much of Continental Europe over the next half-century. Yet the difference in the French experience was the speed and the context in which it took place. For the press achieved its freedom in France in 1789 more rapidly than either its British or American counterpart had, and did so within the context of a more radical political culture which, as Habermas notes, rapidly codified rights which had remained unstated and customary in both Britain and America, because of the evolutionary nature of their political culture. Because of the way in which the ancien regime had collapsed, everything had to be redefined from scratch in 1789 and the press played a central role in the debate on that reconstruction. Newspapers reflected and articulated the varieties of political opinion within communities, departments and the country as a whole, supplementing the role played by Jacobin clubs, electoral politics and parliamentary debates. Press freedom was a consequence of political collapse but also one of the causes of the instability and fragmentation that followed it.

NOTES

1 L. S. Mercier, *Le Nouveau Paris*, 6 vols. (Paris, 1798), vol. III, p. 163.
2 R. Manévy, *La Révolution et la liberté de la presse* (Paris, 1964), p. 19, n.1. See also the reply of Didot, when asked by the *comité de police* of the district of Saint-Germain-des-Prés in April 1790 why so famous a printer as he printed

the counter-revolutionary *Actes des apôtres*: 'He replied that it was because of the lack of books [to print].' See H. Maspéro-Clerc, 'Vicissitudes des *Actes des apôtres*', *Annales historiques de la révolution française*, (hereinafter *AHRF*), 190 (1967), 481–9, p. 483.
3 J.-P. Bertaud, 'Histoire de la presse et révolution', *AHRF*, 285 (1991), 281–98, p. 286.
4 Léonard Gallois, *Histoire des journaux et journalistes de la révolution*, 2 vols. (Paris, 1845); Eugène Hatin, *Histoire politique et littéraire de la presse française*, 8 vols. (Paris, 1859–61).
5 Claude Bellanger, Jacques Godechot, Pierre Guiral and Fernand Terrou (eds.), *Histoire générale de la presse française*, vol. I, Jacques Godechot (ed.), *Des Origines à 1844* (Paris, 1969).
6 See among others Laurence Stoll, 'The Bureau Politique and the management of the popular press', Ph.D. thesis, University of Wisconsin (1975); Jeremy D. Popkin, *The Right-Wing Press in France 1792–1800* (Chapel Hill, NC, 1980); Jack R. Censer, *Prelude to Power: The Parisian Radical Press 1789–1791* (Baltimore, MD, and London, 1976); Hugh Gough, *The Newspaper Press in the French Revolution* (London, 1988); Jeremy D. Popkin, *Revolutionary News: The Press in France 1789–1799* (Durham, NC, and London, 1990).
7 Jürgen Habermas, *L'espace public. Archéologie de la publicité comme dimension constitutive de la société bourgeoise* (Paris, 1978).
8 Keith Michael Baker, 'Introduction', in Keith Michael Baker, François Furet and Colin Lucas (eds.), *The French Revolution and the Creation of Modern Political Culture*, vol. I, Keith Michael Baker (ed.), *The Political Culture of the Old Regime* (Oxford, 1987), p. xiv, and Mona Ozouf, 'L'Opinion publique', *Political Culture of the Old Regime*, p. 470.
9 Jeremy D. Popkin, 'The Prerevolutionary Origins of Political Journalism', in Baker et al. (eds.), *French Revolution*, 203–23. See also Benjamin Nathan, 'Habermas's public sphere in the era of the French Revolution', *French Historical Studies*, 16 (1990), 620–44.
10 Jack R. Censer, *The French Press in the Age of the Enlightenment* (London and New York, 1994), pp. 209–11.
11 Jeremy D. Popkin, *News and Politics in the Age of the Revolution: Jean Luzac's Gazette de Leyde* (Ithaca, NY, and London 1989).
12 Robert Darnton, 'Philosophy under the cloak', in Robert Darnton and Daniel Roche (eds.), *Revolution in Print: The Press in France 1775–1800* (Berkeley, CA, Los Angeles and London, 1989), 27–49.
13 Popkin, 'Prerevolutionary origins'.
14 Pierre Rétat, *Les Journaux de 1789. Bibliographie critique* (Paris, 1988).
15 Jean-Paul Bertaud, 'Histoire de la presse', p. 294.
16 Gough, *The Newspaper Press*, pp. 118–23, 135–43.
17 A. Søderjhelm, *Le Régime de la presse pendant la révolution française*, 2 vols. (Paris and Helsingfors, 1901), I, pp. 118ff.
18 F⁷ 4769 dossier 3, Archives Nationales, Paris.
19 Søderjhelm, *Le Régime de la presse*, passim; A. Cabanis, *La presse sous le Consulat et l'Empire* (Paris, 1985).
20 Pierre Caron, 'Les publications officieuses du Ministère de l'Intérieur en 1793 et 1794', *Revue d'histoire moderne et contemporaine*, 14 (1910), 5–43.

21 Pierre Rétat, 'Forme et discours d'un journal révolutionnaire. Les *Révolutions de Paris* en 1789', in Claude Labrosse and Pierre Rétat (eds.), *L'Instrument périodique. La fonction de la presse au XVIIIe siècle* (Lyon, 1985), pp. 141–2; G. Villacèque, '*Les Révolutions de Paris*: journal patriote, 1789–1790', D.E.S. thesis, University of Toulouse (1961), pp. 57–8.

22 Jeremy D. Popkin, 'Journals: The new face of news', in Darnton and Roche (eds.), *Revolution in Print*, 141–64, pp. 145–6.

23 René Gérard, *Un Journal de province sous la révolution. Le 'Journal de Marseille' de Ferréol de Beaugeard (1781–1797)* (Paris, 1964), pp. 39–40.

24 Eric Wauters, *Une Presse de province pendant la révolution française: journaux et journalistes normands (1785–1800)* (Paris, 1993), pp. 329–31.

25 Olivier Coquard, *Marat* (Paris, 1993), pp. 255–8.

26 J. Sgard, *Dictionnaire des journalistes* (Grenoble, 1976); William J. Murray, 'Journalism as a career choice in 1789', in Harvey Chisick (ed.), *The Press in the French Revolution: Studies on Voltaire and the Eighteenth Century*, vol. 287 (Oxford, 1991), 182–8.

27 Jacques-Pierre Brissot, *Mémoire aux Etats-Généraux sur la nécessité de rendre dès ce moment, la presse libre et surtout pour les journaux politiques* (Paris, 1789), pp. 5–8, 21.

28 J. P. F. Duplantier, *Opinion de J. P. F. Duplantier, député du département de la Gironde, sur la liberté de la presse. Séance du 22 prairial an VII* (Paris, 1799), p. 6.

29 *Lettres à certains journalistes, par Louis Bienvenue, citoyen français* (Paris, n.d.), pp. 21–2.

30 See the comments of Lacretelle, editor of the *Nouvelles politiques*, in the spring of 1796: 'I was a long way from glory and even further from fortune; but in my profession of journalist I enjoyed a certain consideration and I had then a greater reputation than I have ever acquired by more important, more literary works.' Cited in Jeremy D. Popkin, *The Right-Wing Press in France*, p. 39; see also J.-B. Lacretelle, *Dix Années d'épreuves pendant la révolution française* (Paris, 1842), p. 31: 'How flattering it was for me, a young provincial lad, to see great orators, whose voice then filled the universe, come to thank me for the accuracy, and sometimes for the skill or the verve with which I had published their speeches, or tell me in advance of the passages that I should highlight.'

31 Hatin, *Histoire de la presse*, vol. v, p. 58: 'The facts alone, recounted accurately and in an orderly manner, stripped of the long-windedness associated with the spoken word: that is what history will one day consult, what the public expects and what we owe to it.' See also S. Tucoo-Chala, 'Presse et vérité sous l'ancien régime', *Revue du Nord*, 66 (1984), 713–21; Pierre Rétat, 'L'Idée et la pratique de l'histoire dans les journaux de 1789', *Résonance. Revue de l'expression lyonnaise*, 36 (1988), 67–79.

32 *Journal du soir*, 5 November 1790. See also the claims of the *Spectateur national* in 1790: 'Equally distant from despotism and anarchy, situating ourselves always, with moderation, between all parties, with the intention and hope of focusing their attention on strict and reflective ideas of justice, the authors of the *Spectateur national* may have seemed indecisive to readers inclined to

make hasty judgements. But their moderation is far removed from indecision' (prospectus, p. 1).
33 *Avis pour l'année 1790*, in *Journal général de l'Orléanais* (1790), pp. 3–4; *Avis concernant le Journal du département année 1791*, bound in *Journal général de l'Orléanais* (1791). Copies of both exist in the collection of the paper in the Bibliothèque municipale d'Orléans.
34 See the comments of Bayard (AA14 no. 719, Archives Nationales), when proposing the launch of an official government journal: 'It is very difficult for academicians and men of letters not to try to flash around their wit over the most simple of issues and to restrain from making comments. For this reason it would not seem necessary to use them for the editing of this gazette; a great deal of organisation, a precise and clear style, capable of being understood by everybody, must be preferred to the learned and precious expressions that most writers use these days.'
35 Pierre Laborie, 'Etude sur le *Patriote françois*', D.E.S. thesis, University of Toulouse (1959–60), pp. 142–4; see the same argument in *Patriote françois*, 2 August 1791, p. 135.
36 *Journal patriotique de la Dordogne*, 17 April 1791, pp. 4–7.
37 *Opinion de P. C. Laussat, sur la liberté de la presse. Conseil des Anciens. Séance du 28 messidor an VII* (Paris, 1799), p. 4.
38 *Journal révolutionnaire de Toulouse*, 26 September 1793.
39 *Courrier d'Avignon*, 3 prairial II (22 May 1794), p. 112; see also *Journal de Toulouse ou l'observateur antiroyaliste*, 13 pluviôse IV (2 February 1796), which describes the functions of a journalist as 'sublime functions when they serve to make liberty and the fatherland loved'.
40 J.-J. Lebon, 'La Presse montalbanaise des origines au début du 19e siècle', D.E.S. thesis, University of Toulouse (1971), pp. 121–2; see also *Le Corréspondant* prospectus, p. 7.
41 *Journal patriotique de la Bourgogne* (1789), prospectus.
42 E. Dubois, *Histoire de la révolution dans l'Ain*, 2 vols. (Bourg, 1932), vol. II, p. 320; see also *Journal du département de Loir et Cher*, 20 April 1792, pp. 41–2: 'Everybody agrees about the usefulness of newspapers. It is by them, for the most part, that public opinion is created and controlled.'
43 Claude Labrosse and Pierre Rétat, *Naissance du journal révolutionnaire, 1789* (Lyon, 1989), p. 174ff.
44 F. Furet, *Penser La Révolution française* (Paris, 1978), pp. 75–87.
45 Coquard, *Marat*, p. 232.
46 Antoine de Baecque, 'La Dénonciation publique dans la presse et le pamphlet (1789–1791)', in Chisick (ed.), *The Press in the French Revolution*, 261–79.
47 G. Brégail, *La Presse périodique dans le Gers pendant la révolution* (Auch, 1922), pp. 10ff.
48 Ouzi Elyada, 'Les Récits de complot dans la presse populaire (1790–1791)', in Chisick (ed.), *The Press in the French Revolution*, 281–92.
49 Melvin Edelstein, *La Feuille villageoise: communication et modernisation dans les régions rurales pendant la révolution française* (Paris, 1977).
50 *Journal de l'armée des côtes de Cherbourg*, 2 brumaire II (23 October 1793).
51 *Défenseur de la vérité*, 13 September 1792, p. 259.

52 Jean-Pierre Gallais, *Extrait d'un Dictionnaire inutile, composé par une société en commandite et rédigé par un homme seul* (Paris, 1790), pp. 162–8; *Dénonciation des libelles par Ant. Estienne* (Paris, 1791), pp. 23–4; *Journal de la ville et des provinces, ou le Modérateur*, 16 March 1790, pp. 298–9.
53 Hatin, *Histoire de la presse*, vol. IV, pp. 123–4; Søderjhelm, *Le Régime de la presse*, vol. II, p. 109.
54 *Discours sur la nécessité de mettre actuellement à l'éxécution l'article 355 de la constitution, par J.-B. Louvet* (Paris, 1796), p. 5; P. Roger, 'Repentirs de la plume: l'échec du journalisme révolutionnaire selon Mercier et Louvet', *Revue d'histoire littéraire de la France*, 90 (1990), 592–5.
55 Hatin, *Histoire de la presse*, vol. IV, pp. 123–4.
56 *Courrier de Villeneuve-lès-Avignon*, 1 December 1789.
57 Gérard, *Journal de Marseille*, pp. 63–74; Gough, *The Newspaper Press*, pp. 209–10; Wauters, *Une Presse de province*, pp. 295ff.
58 L. Prudhomme, *Au Calomniateur G. L. Tallien, secrétaire du comité de sûreté générale, sur le no. 65 de l'Ami des citoyens* (Paris, 1793).
59 Laborie, *Etude sur le Patriote françois*, p. 20; J.-B.-C. Delisle de Salles, *Essai sur le journalisme depuis 1735 jusqu'à l'an 1800* (Paris, 1811), p. 76.
60 Maspéro-Clerc, 'Vicissitudes', p. 484.
61 L. Coudart, *La Gazette de Paris: un journal royaliste pendant la révolution française (1789–1792)* (Paris, 1995), pp. 103–5; Ms. 722, Bibliothèque historique de la ville de Paris.
62 *Journal des sociétés patriotiques*, 24 October 1790; M. Bruneau, *Les Débuts de la révolution dans les départements du Cher et de l'Indre* (Paris, 1902), p. 262.
63 Richard Cobb, *Les Armées révolutionnaires des départements du Midi* (Toulouse, 1955), pp. 49, 84.
64 L1631, Archives départementales de la Mayenne.
65 F. Clerémbray, *La Terreur à Rouen* (Rouen, 1900), pp. 100–101.
66 Coudart, *La Gazette de Paris*, p. 214.
67 H. Gough, 'Les Jacobins et la presse: Le Journal de la Montagne (juin 1793–brumaire an II)', in A. Soboul (ed.), *Actes du colloque Girondins et Montagnards* (Paris, 1980), 269–96, p. 295.
68 R. Monnier, 'De L'An III à l'an IX: les derniers sans-culottes. Résistance et répression à Paris sous le Directoire et au début du Consulat', *AHRF*, 257 (1984), 386–406, p. 395.
69 P. L. Roederer, *Oeuvres du comte P. L. Roederer, pair de France, membre de l'Institut, publiées par son fils*, 8 vols. (Paris, 1853–9), VII, pp. 256–7.

9 Italy, 1760–1815

Maurizio Isabella

Until the 1760s, the map of Italian political journalism, reflecting the complex political conditions of a peninsula divided into a mosaic of absolute states and ancient republics, still presented features which had been established very much earlier.[1] While Mantua, Bologna, Rimini, Modena, Parma, Florence, Venice and Foligno could boast the existence of newspapers whose circulation extended well beyond the limits of state boundaries, the capitals of absolute states like Milan, Naples and Rome only had their official publications, dry bulletins listing official events, decrees and news from foreign courts intended only for a small circle of civil servants. The success of gazettes printed in peripheral cities – the foundation of which, in some cases, dated back to the previous century – depended on the fact that their location enabled them both to collect information more quickly from across the borders and to escape the control of central governments. For this reason they enjoyed a broader readership and a wider circulation. Venice and Genoa were the two most important centres for the collection of international political news. News was collected by specialised agencies from diplomats resident in the cities where they operated, or brought from abroad, although the channels for the further transmission of international news and the networks established across the peninsula are still largely unknown.[2]

During the period between 1760 and 1790, the political press in the Italian peninsula underwent dramatic changes. The number of gazettes grew steadily, and their geographical distribution changed quite dramatically, as the centres of political journalism moved from outlying areas to the capital cities of the states where reforms were more vigorously implemented and in which a high degree of cultural tolerance was permitted.[3] Milan, the capital of Habsburg Lombardy, Venice and Florence became the three most important centres of information. In Milan there were no fewer than five gazettes published in Italian. The most important were the *Gazzetta enciclopedica*, started in 1780 and edited by the famous intellectual Francesco Soave, and the *Giornale enciclopedico di Milano*, which first appeared in 1782. Both newspapers coupled political information with literary matters. The most widely read newspaper was the *Gazzetta di Milano*, the semi-official voice of the Lombard government. This weekly *Gazzetta* came into being in 1769 to replace the *Ragguagli di vari paesi* thanks to the intervention of the Plenipotentiary Minister Count Firmian. Firmian appointed the famous poet Giuseppe Parini as its editor in order to improve the quality of what had been a badly written and dull collection of news. The Milanese public also had access to local translations of foreign newspapers, like the *Staffetta di Sciaffusa*, the *Staffetta del nord* and the *Estratto delle notizie di Vienna*, Italian versions respectively of a Swiss, German and Austrian gazette.[4] Milan effectively became the main centre of dissemination of news coming from the other side of the Alps. Couriers took ten days to get to Milan from Paris, travelling via Lyon, Chambery and Turin. From Milan it took fifteen to twenty days for international news to become available in Venice and Florence, and around twenty to twenty-five days for it to reach Rome and Naples.

Venice was the second most important centre of information in northern Italy. The oldest newspapers were the *Nuovo Postiglione*, published as early as 1741, and the *Storia dell'anno*, a yearly periodical launched in 1737, which attempted to put political information into a historical perspective by summarising the main events of the year. In the second half of the eighteenth century Venetian political journalism was dominated by the figure of Domenico Caminer, who wrote for the above-mentioned newspapers as well as for the *Nuova gazzetta veneta*, the daily *Diario veneto* and the *Prospetto degli affari attuali d'Europa*, a quarterly journal which first appeared in 1788 following the model of the *Storia dell'anno*. From 1788, the Tuscan *Notizie del Mondo* was reprinted in Venice by the printer Graziosi, but later, thanks to the journalist Giuseppe Compagnoni, the Venetian edition began publishing its own material and became a completely new and original newspaper.[5]

The Tuscan press became particularly lively in the 1780s, when Florence became a centre of attraction for gazetteers coming from other states. The Tuscan capital then boasted the important *Notizie del Mondo* and the *Gazzetta universale* for international information, together with the *Giornale fiorentino istorico-politico letterario* and the government-controlled *Gazzetta toscana* for local news.[6] As far as the rest of the peninsula is concerned, political information remained extremely scarce. In Turin, the political centre of the Savoy dynasty's territories, from 1780, the absolutist government allowed only one gazette, the *Journal de Turin et des provinces*, which was published both in French and Italian, and replaced by the *Giornale degli avvisi e notizie del Piemonte* in 1786. Sardinia had its own newspaper, the *Gazzettino ebdomadario della Sardegna*, which conveyed the opinion of the Piedmontese administration, while French newspapers circulated in the French-speaking region of Savoy.[7]

In Rome information was dominated by only two periodicals. The annual almanac *Notizie per l'anno* contained a list of the most important public events of the Papal court. The gazette, entitled *Diario ordinario di Roma*, was issued twice or three times a week from 1716 until 1775, when it was divided into two separate newspapers devoted respectively to foreign and internal affairs. Both newspapers represented the official voice of the Papal government and informed readers of official ceremonies, the life of the main aristocratic families of the city, foreign dynasties, wars and unusual events. The only semi-independent newspaper published in Rome was the *Notizie politiche*, inaugurated in 1788. Elsewhere in the Papal states, however, provincial papers could be found in cities like Bologna, Pesaro and Foligno.[8] In Naples the political press was even less developed: the twice-weekly *Gazzetta civica napoletana*, used by the government to publish official communications, was the only product of local journalism. Its diffusion was probably extremely limited outside the capital. In Sicily the first gazettes were printed only in 1793.[9]

However, alongside these local journalistic products, foreign gazettes circulated and competed. In northern Italy the most important of these was the *Nuove di diverse corti e paesi*, issued in Italian from 1746 in Lugano, a Swiss town near the Lombard border. The *Nuove*, which were circulated through thirty-six different centres of distribution across the peninsula, represented one of the most reliable sources of information about international affairs.[10] Some other foreign gazettes were reprinted in their original language, as was the case with the *Gazette de Leyde* in Milan and the *Gazette d'Amsterdam* and the *Courier du Bas-Rhin* in Venice. Although gazettes mainly circulated within the state boundaries, they sometimes reached neighbouring countries. In Naples in 1782, there were more than fifty subscribers to the *Gazette de Leyde* and to the Florentine *Gazzetta universale*.[11] The Milanese *Gazzetta enciclopedica di Milano* was distributed in Piedmont, Genoa, Venice and Verona, central Italy, Tuscany, Rome, Naples and Vienna.

Most of the above-mentioned newspapers appeared either weekly or two or three times a week. The first daily newspapers to appear in Italy were the Venetian urban gazettes *Diario veneto*, the *Giornale veneto* and the *Novellista veneto*, local news-sheets which were published respectively in 1765, 1766 and between 1775 and 1776. Otherwise the majority of newspapers paid far more attention to European rather than local events. Franco Venturi's masterly reconstruction of European and American events, based on the extensive use of Italian gazettes, allows us to fully appreciate the cosmopolitan nature of Italian political journalism. During the 1760s and 1770s Italian readers had a chance to follow closely all major international events, ranging from the Corsican revolution and the Bohemian peasant revolts to the Mediterranean expedition of Catherine II and the Greek revolt against the Ottoman Sultan. Gazettes like the *Notizie del Mondo* and the *Nuove di diverse corti e paesi* were also well informed regarding the partitioning of Poland, the Pugachev revolt in Russia and the first signs of revolution in America.[12]

To conclude this general survey, attention should be drawn to the existence of hand-written gazettes, in addition to the printed press, in Tuscany and Venetia and probably elsewhere. Producing manuscript gazettes long remained a profitable activity. In a recent study of a Venetian weekly manuscript gazette called *Europa*, Mario Infelise stresses that this gazette, which survived until 1780, was produced in the same way as its seventeenth-century counterparts. It was in fact a collection of news drawn from European gazettes, letters or dispatches delivered by couriers or provided by diplomats and civil servants and dictated to copyists. Interestingly, the transaction in 1758 between its last owner, the famous journalist Domenico Caminer, and his predecessor simply involved the purchase of lists of foreign correspondents and subscribers.[13] In Italy these traditional forms of information survived until almost the end of the ancien regime.

In pre-revolutionary Italy the publishing industry was regulated by the guilds, and this favoured the monopoly of a limited group of families who handed on the trade from father to son. Although this system was a constraint on the development of market-oriented information and was undergoing a period of crisis, it did not prevent a dynamic surge in the activities of printers after 1760. In Venice, for instance, where the large firms which had traditionally dominated the publishing trade and its guild, the *Università della Stampa*, were in decline, journalists instead turned to smaller booksellers and printers, the *matricolati minori* of the guild, to publish their gazettes. Given the low costs and the limited risks of publishing a newspaper – journalists generally had lists of subscribers to offer printers – these small entrepreneurs were keen to support journalistic initiatives.[14] Likewise, in Florence, small and medium-size printing houses tended to replace the great enterprises which had thrived until the 1750s thanks to the publication of works of erudition, and between 1767 and 1783, the number of Florentine printing houses rose from ten to eighteen. Although the general financial precariousness of the new firms remained a standard feature of the trade, their small size enabled them to adjust to market conditions while also benefiting from a stable and regular income derived from newspapers. Moreover, booksellers and printers used the gazettes to advertise the books they published.

Maria Augusta Timpanaro Morelli describes two successful examples of these medium-size businesses: the Florentine *Notizie del Mondo* and *Gazzetta universale*.[15] These newspapers ensured the survival of two printing shops, which in turn supported some ten or dozen families. In 1780, the office staff of the *Gazzetta universale* comprised ten people. One of the two proprietors edited the paper, while the other ran the administrative side of the business, each being aided by an assistant. Four more people were in charge of the dispatch of the gazette and two others charged with its distribution. In the same year the *Notizie del Mondo* was run by a single gazetteer with the aid of a copyist, who earned respectively 8 and 4 scudi.[16] A further 4 scudi were used to pay the printers. More commonly, however, gazetteers had to supplement their income with other editorial work and publications. The owners of the *Notizie* were eight associates who earned 15 scudi each per month. The newspaper produced a net yearly income of 800–1,000 lire. Thus, Antonio Graziosi's earnings of 8,000 ducati from the sale of the Venetian version of the *Notizie del Mondo* represented an exceptional commercial return.[17]

As Anna Maria Rao shows in a recent study, the conditions of journalism in Naples were remarkably different, even though the capital of the kingdom was one of the main centres of the publishing trade in the peninsula.[18] The publication of gazettes and public announcements or *avvisi* was tightly controlled by the state through the granting of a privilege, called *ius prohibendi*, to single families of *librai stampatori*. These families, who printed and distributed newspapers along with their primary activity as publishers and sellers of books, enjoyed the title of *regi impressori* – Royal Printers – and paid a fixed amount to the government for it. The heavy burden of government control, exerted by the *Segreteria di giustizia*, hindered the development of a local political journalism, but was unable to prevent the smuggling of foreign gazettes which, according to the law, only Royal Printers were entitled to republish locally.

In Italy gazettes generally broke even at 200 issues, and many of them printed no more than this number of copies. The *Notizie del Mondo* printed 1,700 copies, while the *Gazzetta universale* reached 2,500 copies. Ristori's *Giornale Fiorentino istorico-politico letterario* printed only 250 copies, but was distributed across northern Italy. The *Gazzetta urbana veneta* had 2,000 subscribers. The prices of newspapers were generally modest. Marina Formica supposes that, given its very affordable price of 24 paoli, the *Diario di Roma* had a wide circulation and may have reached the lower strata of the Roman population.[19] In the 1790s in Naples, the cost of a yearly subscription to a gazette was 3 ducati, which corresponded to an outlay of less than 1 grano per day, the minimum bet on the popular lottery.[20] Limited editions did not prevent gazettes from enjoying a wide circulation in ancien regime Italy: a single copy was read by several people in public venues – the *caffettieri* usually bought gazettes for their patrons – as well as in private spaces. Furthermore, the practice of reading newspapers aloud undoubtedly multiplied their impact. Nevertheless, in spite of the low prices, the high rate of illiteracy throughout the peninsula, particularly in the south and outside the main towns and cities, was a barrier to extended readership. For example, as late as 1808, 83 per cent of men and 94 per cent of women in the Marche region of the Papal states were unable to produce a signature; in comparison 70 per cent of men and 47 per cent of women in Milan were sufficiently literate to sign their names.[21]

The problem of the effective circulation of newspapers leads to the even trickier question of the social dimension of their readership.[22] Undoubtedly, between 1760 and 1780, Italy witnessed a revolution in reading practices – similar to the one taking place in other parts of Western Europe – characterised by an increased and more bourgeois readership consuming books and periodicals alike. Interestingly, the urban gazettes which appeared in the Republic of Venice in the 1760s and 1770s, such as the *Nuova Gazzetta veneta* and the *Diario veneto*, started to offer the publication of commercial adverts to tradesman, craftsmen or small manufacturers and explicitly pleaded for a public of professionals, physicians and pharmacists. Nonetheless the very limited success of this offer and the short life of these gazettes suggest that a solid bourgeois public was not yet ready to support a wider market for newspapers. As Infelise rightly concludes, Italian readership was extremely slow to 'expand downwards from the urban aristocratic and *haute bourgeois* milieus to the middle classes'.[23] Until the end of the century, the bulk of it was most probably confined to those 150,000 intellectuals who, in Ristori's words, 'represented the Italian educated class'.[24] The frequent advertisement of French publications in the gazettes bears witness to the elite public to which these periodicals were addressed. Assuming a certain homogeneity between readers and writers, and between readers of books and gazettes, it will be useful to observe that, in a sample of 219 Italian intellectuals born between 1720 and 1780, 37 per cent of men of letters were ecclesiastics and 27 per cent aristocrats, although these percentages steadily decreased across the period.[25]

As everywhere else in Europe, the circulation of newspapers was linked to the development of different forms of sociability, both institutionalised and informal. In Venice, for instance, there were 206 coffee houses or *botteghe da caffè* in 1759. According to contemporaries, after 1750, when patricians acquired the habit of discussing politics outside the senate, the '*conversazioni pubbliche*' became all the rage, involving new sectors of the population. As a result the government decided to control the number of coffee houses. While these were public venues open to a general public which was not exclusively aristocratic but shared an increasing interest in gazettes, the Venetian patricians met also in the *ridotti* or *casini*, private apartments used to gamble, read and discuss politics with their peers.[26] It is most probably in these contexts that journalism reached new groups of readers.

Nonetheless, generally speaking politics remained outside the domain of organised forms of civil society. Italian sociability was in fact still dominated by academies, where public opinion developed in its pre-political form, as a result of discussions on literary matters or practical and technical issues like agricultural or scientific questions, and the journalism they produced followed similar lines. In this setting the birth of the first reading societies, or *gabinetti di lettura*, in the early 1790s represented a real element of novelty. In the *gabinetti di lettura*, political discussions excluded from the *accademie* were considered normal activities, and newspapers were available. Indeed, like an increasing number of institutions that came into being after 1750, they were free associations which rejected the traditional structure of the old aristocratic academies, based on the idea of the aristocracy as a body or a corporation. They accepted members simply on the grounds of their common interests.[27] Yet, in spite of this 'bourgeois' spirit, aristocrats still represented an important, if not overwhelming element of their membership. Piero del Negro's study on the reading society of Padova, founded in 1790, which represents an interesting exception to an otherwise neglected field of historical research in Italy, shows that out of sixty-three members, thirty-seven were either local noblemen or Venetian patricians, and that these aristocrats exercised control over the association. Among the others, nineteen were churchmen, most of them professional intellectuals, others were lawyers, academics from the local university, writers and physicians; only two were tradesmen. The society subscribed to all the major Italian and international gazettes.[28] Similar institutions were set up in several other provincial cities in Venetia, like Udine, Brescia and Bergamo, and in Florence, thanks to a new passion for politics triggered off by the revolutionary events in France.[29] Sometimes, more rudimentary forms of reading societies were established by booksellers. For instance, in 1789, the bookseller Stecchi in Florence set up a small private library in the premises of his shop, where customers could read and borrow local and international gazettes and books in return for an annual subscription fee of 10 paoli.[30]

The existence of a public sphere where political information was discussed, and the increase in the circulation of the press, suggest that public opinion, however limited in size and geographical distribution, became a reality in the period between 1760 and 1790. Indeed, the term *opinione pubblica* first appeared in Italy in 1762 in the private correspondence between the Lombard intellectuals and brothers Pietro and Alessandro Verri.[31] Although often employed as a rhetorical device – an abstract term pointing to the existence of a superior rationality – by the 1780s *opinione* and *opinione pubblica* frequently referred to a real and influential force. In this context public opinion generally denoted a number of universal and commonly shared principles and beliefs regarding morality, law and justice rather than the open discussion of different ideas. Occasionally, public opinion had the negative connotation of the ingrained superstitious beliefs that prevented ordinary people from becoming enlightened – hence, for instance, Gaetano Filangieri's belief in the *Scienza della legislazione* (1780) that education and schools had a crucial role to play in the development of a reasonable and progressive opinion.[32] What seems clear is that in all cases Italian intellectuals perceived public opinion as a sort of common ground between state and subjects, which resulted from the positive effects of enlightened reason both on the ruled and the rulers. Any form of tension between the two was to be avoided, as it was apt to disrupt the functioning of society. Therefore, free discussion, which Italian intellectuals of the Enlightenment unanimously advocated, was ultimately geared to reaching this perfect cohesion between the sovereign and the people. Pietro Verri concisely summarised this conviction in his *Meditazioni sulla economia politica* (1771):

The liberal discussion of opinions on these subjects frequently produces excellent ideas, and out of a mass of dreams and ranting are generated ideas that contribute to the prosperity of the state. The more enlightened the public, the more it will appreciate the beneficial decisions of the throne.[33]

However, Genovesi, Filangieri and Verri stressed the fact that political authorities could be successful only if they had public opinion behind them.[34] In the development of public opinion, these intellectuals foresaw a crucial role for themselves. In Verri's words:

Philosophers, neglected, oppressed, persecuted when alive, ultimately determine opinion ... sovereigns are enlightened and find the mass of the subjects more reasonable and willing to accept unprotestingly those novelties which would have appeared as a threat in the shades of ignorance. Opinion governs power, and good books govern opinion, immortal queen of the world.[35]

This argument justified the role that intellectuals wanted and occasionally managed to play in Milan, Tuscany and, to a lesser extent, in Naples, in supporting and actively contributing to economic and administrative reforms as bureaucrats. In reality perfect harmony between public opinion, philosophers and state was never really achieved, and Verri's constant warning that it was impossible to rule against opinion in his late writings points to the tensions which arose from their collaboration with the state.[36]

From the 1760s, the press came to be seen as one of the foremost instruments in the development of public opinion. In an article entitled 'Of the Periodical Press', published in 1764 in the famous periodical *Il Caffè*, Cesare Beccaria unambiguously laid down the civic aims of journalism, designed to improve both private and public life. Although he was mainly referring to journalism relating to contemporary economic, scientific and literary debates – of which *Il Caffè* was to become the most illustrious example in Italy – rather surprisingly, he explicitly mentioned gazettes, 'not less useful although less brilliant than the former'. According to Beccaria these latter shaped and strengthened the cosmopolitan dimension of public opinion:

These news items make us citizens of Europe; they produce a continuous commerce among the different nations and destroy that diffidence and contempt with which isolated nations look on foreign ones. Everything in Europe tends to become closer and more similar, and there is a stronger tendency towards equality than in the past.[37]

In the 1760s, Beccaria's positive remarks about gazettes represented an exception, as high-brow intellectuals tended to dismiss political journalism as an inferior trade. Not surprisingly, therefore, the word *gazzettiere* often had negative, if not wilfully derogatory, connotations, linked as it was to the idea of gazettes as mere collections of second-hand and unreliable, if not completely invented or exaggerated, pieces of information. The word journalist referred only to literary journalism.[38] Nevertheless, during the 1780s some gazetteers began to renovate traditional gazettes and to underpin their activities with the same intellectual principles of enlightenment and professional awareness that characterised literary journalism. In gazette articles it was increasingly possible to detect the journalists' opinion and original interpretation. The distinction between gazetteer and journalist became increasingly blurred.

Journalists like Giuseppe Compagnoni and Giovanni Ristori, who had devoted their energies to literary journalism for most of their careers, turned to newspapers expressing the desire to fulfil an educational mission and to provide more accurate and reliable information. Compagnoni's *Notizie del Mondo* moved away from the traditional division of gazettes into sections defined by the geographical origin of the news and started to order stories according to their content, thus facilitating their analysis. Careful checks on the sources of information which, according to Compagnoni, were missing from other newspapers, made his gazette the most popular and appreciated newspaper among the educated classes.[39] On the eve of the revolutionary events in France, the Tuscan Giovanni Ristori founded a weekly newspaper, *Spezieria di Sondrio*, which aimed to combine political news with ideological debate. As Beccaria had done almost thirty years before, Ristori reaffirmed the role of the press in enlightening the public. However, his awareness of the political role of journalists in the formation of public opinion was something very new and already anticipated the features of political journalism of the Revolutionary Triennium: 'We are not gazetteers, we are a society of friends who use the current affairs of nations, new laws, revolutions of all kind, as a pretext to find truth and reason concerning matters which regard the universal wellbeing of peoples.'[40]

Government had a direct and crucial influence over the initial development of political journalism in the Italian states. The strengthening of state censorship at the expense of the ecclesiastical censorship exerted through the Holy Inquisition or the Catholic hierarchy greatly contributed to a freer circulation of ideas and political information in the second half of the eighteenth century. In Lombardy and Tuscany, the territories directly controlled by the Habsburgs, the struggle between Church and state for the ideological control over culture and society resulted in a freer and more tolerant atmosphere. This had been one of the aims of the wider programme of reforms implemented by Maria Theresa, Joseph II and Leopold II.[41] New laws tended to treat books and gazettes as commodities that needed protection and control like any other goods. In Lombardy the Giunta degli Studi, a branch of the central administration, was given charge of censorship in 1768 and both the Church and the aristocracy, represented by the Senate, excluded from exercising censorship of any sort. Among the censors appointed in Milan, the government chose some of the most progressive intellectuals who animated Lombard Enlightenment: Paolo Frisi, Alfonso Longo and Gianbattista Vasco. In Naples the Prime Minister Bernardo Tanucci preferred to consider information not as something to be repressed but as useful means of broadening consensus. In 1767, he wrote to the King: 'I have helped myself with the Gazette, and I think I have managed to keep the people on my side.'[42] In general, more open attitudes towards information did not entail the disappearance of repressive measures when state interest clashed with freedom of expression. To give just one example, in 1780 the journalist Giovanni Ristori was condemned to exile for publishing a satirical article in the *Giornale fiorentino*.[43] However, in the 1770s and 1780s, the same government, faced with foreign governments complaining about the information provided by Tuscan gazettes, would dismiss any direct responsibility and refuse to intervene.[44]

Gazettes benefited from this new atmosphere since they generally represented the most effective form of propaganda for those governments whose new policies could find the support of progressive enlightened men of letters – hence the critical comments of Milanese and Tuscan gazettes about the influence of Jesuits on society until their suppression, their approval of the abolition of monasteries and religious orders without philanthropic purposes and their open support for the religious tolerance and school reform implemented by Joseph II.[45] The *Gazzetta enciclopedica di Milano* and the *Gazzetta toscana* in Florence endorsed such government economic policies as the implementation of a land register, the legislative attempt to favour land redistribution, the liberalisation of the grain trade and the abolition of feudal rights. Furthermore, gazettes reviewed new works by major intellectuals like Verri and Beccaria and placed them in the context of intellectual and political debates in Italy and Europe.[46]

In the Republic of Venice a state censorship independent from the Church had been a reality much earlier than in other parts of the peninsula. On the whole, Venetian censorship, supervised by the Senate and by the *Riformatori dello Studio* of Padova, was quite tolerant. The system of printers' privileges for the publication of gazettes was easily bypassed by pretending to reprint foreign gazettes that were actually totally new.[47] This traditional tolerance, in the absence of any programme of reforms, enabled Venice to become one of the capitals of the Italian political press. In those states where no major reform had been implemented, where intellectual freedom was limited and where censorship was particularly strict, gazettes became a mere instrument of absolutism, employed to reinforce the image of the state. This was the case in Piedmont and Sardinia, and in the Papal states. In Rome, the creation of a separate series of the *Diario ordinario* for home affairs, accompanied by a new iconography on its title page – such as the Papal tiara and St Peter's keys – was the result of the new Pope Pius VI's desire to emphasise his role as head of the Church and as absolute sovereign. In Marina Formica's words, the *Diario* became part of the Pope's ideological strategy to promote the importance of the Catholic Church and reiterate its hegemony in the world.[48]

To sum up, in those territories with the most progressive governments, the strongest stimulus to the development of public opinion came from the governments themselves. As a consequence, the development of the public sphere did not take place in opposition to the established authorities, but rather under the tutelage of the state. However, it was only within a limited sphere of discussion, in which free information was legitimate as long as it supported or did not harm the government's activities, that the political press could contribute to shaping conflicting positions within public opinion. In countries like Piedmont, the Papal states or the

Kingdom of Naples, where political information was tightly controlled by the state, books and literary journals stimulated the development of public opinion mainly in its pre-political sense, as an intellectual debate.

The impact of the revolutionary events in France on the Italian public and the consequent reaction of Italian governments show the fragility of the relationship established between the public sphere, public opinion and governments, which became progressively more anxious about controlling the political press in order to prevent social unrest. The flood of information pouring into the peninsula triggered off heated debates, which show a growing interest in revolutionary events among the public. Italian political journalism, generally cautiously favourable to the Revolution at first, but after 1792 unanimously critical of its violent and radical trajectory, responded to these extraordinary events with a variety of interpretations and political or moral judgements.[49] This appears to indicate that just before the end of the ancien regime, political information was contributing to the creation of an independent public opinion. With typical revolutionary rhetoric the Jacobin Matteo Galdi was later to claim that:

> The institution of the gazettes has been one of the great blows to tyranny: at first they described the customs of the peoples, the behaviour of the governments, and they ended up trying to improve the former and the latter. The peoples of Europe in this way, got to know only in a few days the most interesting events in all nations and courts, the reasons for wars and peace and trade treaties, so that they dared to judge, prophesy, decide sovereignly about their destiny, seated at times in front of the fire or in the coffee house.[50]

The most striking aspect of the political press after the invasion of the French army in 1796 and the collapse of the old regimes was its sudden growth in size.[51] The number of new newspapers published during the so called Revolutionary Triennium (1796–9) reached a total of forty in Milan, the unrivalled capital of republican journalism, thanks partly to the concentration of exiles from the collapsed Republic of Naples, and ten in Venice, Naples and Rome. In Piedmont, where there had been no independent political journalism before the invasion and the republican government lasted only for five months, nine newspapers were published, although several had very short lives and were printed in limited editions. Although the most popular newspapers published up to 4,000 copies, the average number of copies per title remained substantially unchanged after 1796, as the majority did not go beyond a few hundred. Yet the sheer number of new journalistic undertakings, facilitated by the abolition of all monopolies and privileges, shows how the collapse of the ancien regime released an unprecedented expression of intellectual and political energies.

In contrast to pre-revolutionary gazettes, republican newspapers contained mainly local political news and comment on the reforms journalists expected from the new republican authorities. They directly publicised the discussions in the legislative assemblies and revolutionary societies. International affairs played only a secondary role and were almost exclusively confined to information regarding the war. The quality of comment, the regular publication of leading articles and sections devoted to special issues and the direct and explicit comments of journalists on current events made the Republican political press the first example of modern journalism in Italy. Republican journalism – if we allow some degree of simplification – reflected the positions of the two main 'parties': the democratic patriots on the one side, and the moderates on the other. The democrats went so far as to advocate universal suffrage, the establishment of direct democracy and a redistribution of wealth which would take special account of the needs of the poor. They challenged the poll tax and the excise duties and defended the traditional governmental food supply system. The moderates confined their demands for equality to equality before the law, linked political rights to land ownership and praised free trade. Last but not least, journalists intervened in the debate about the future of Italy, which for the first time was described as a nation, and they discussed whether the peninsula should become a unified state or a confederation of independent republics.[52]

Bonaparte's policy of gearing the existence of 'the sister republics' to the financial needs of the Directorial government and its army and giving them a moderate social and political character made life difficult for the most radical wing of republican journalism. Between 1796 and 1799, the French authorities closed down several newspapers, following the decision to impose stricter control over political opposition. For this reason, many newspapers exercised self-censorship to prevent government intervention. However, leaving aside the existence of a government-subsidised political press – composed of papers like the *Monitore cisalpino* in Milan – independent newspapers like the Lombard *Tribuno del popolo*, the *Monitore di Roma* and the *Monitore napoletano* managed to convey the feelings of dissatisfaction of the local supporters of the Revolution towards their governments or the French authorities, and even to complain about the gradual loss of the Italian republics' independence. For this reason the Revolutionary Triennium was the freest period for political journalism Italian states had ever enjoyed.

Although references to the existence of, and the need to influence, public opinion can still be found in newspapers after 1796, it was the idea of public mind (*spirito pubblico*), which became the key element in Italian revolutionary language. With this expression patriots referred to the fundamental political attitudes of the citizens and to their attachment to free institutions. The creation of the public mind was considered to be of crucial importance for the very survival of democracy and journalists believed that their activity would contribute to this result.[53] The *Monitore di Roma*, for instance, declared that 'our newspaper is geared to the formation of a public mind'.[54] However, this link between democracy and the public mind should not mislead the modern reader. According to Italian patriots, the ultimate goal of the development of a public spirit was to achieve uniformity of views and attitudes: as good republicans, they were harshly critical of faction and party, in true Rousseauian style. Political pluralism was considered a threat to stability, 'the only way to prevent disorders is a uniform way of thinking... which is called public mind'.[55]

In their concern for multiplying the effects of political information and widening their readership, republican journalists went beyond the general remarks about the educational purpose of periodicals that gazetteers were already making before the end of the ancien regime. Instead they linked their mission to the defeat of ignorance and the dissemination of republican principles among all ranks of the population, which was the primary objective of the 'republican revolutionary education'. Most newspapers had one section permanently devoted to this purpose. They realised that political messages had to be expressed in a simple and understandable language, and had to be read in public, if they were to reach the masses. Priests, as well as teachers and doctors, were seen as ideal intermediaries to disseminate the messages contained in the press and 'enlighten' the illiterate population. The Neapolitan patriot Eleonora Fonseca Pimentel, editor and journalist of the *Monitore napoletano*, even went so far as to advocate the publication of gazettes in local dialect rather than in literary Italian, which was understood by only a tiny minority of the population.[56] In 1799 in Naples, her suggestion was taken up by the friar and priest who edited a newspaper written in dialect called *La Repubbreca spiegata co' lo santo Evangelio* (*The Republic explained with the Holy Gospels*). The democrats in fact were aware of the influence of religion on the masses, and tried to reconcile it with their political principles in order to ensure popular support for the new regime. Likewise, the Milanese *Termometro politico* published a series of articles which provided the Lombard clergy with a model of preaching inspired by democratic beliefs.[57] In practice, despite their good intentions, the efforts of the patriots to reach the masses and broaden their readership were largely unsuccessful. Both the cultural gap between them and the overwhelming majority of the population, and the distance between the democratic propaganda and the reality of heavy taxation, inflation, military invasion and abolition of communal rights account for the anti-French uprisings and the general hostility of the masses towards the new regime.[58]

In addition, journalism remained an activity dominated by men: Eleonora Fonseca Pimentel's commitment represented a famous but rare exception in the revolutionary press, in the same way that the Venetian Elisabetta Caminer (1751–96) had been the only female journalist committed to serious civil discussions in pre-revolutionary Italy.[59] Nonetheless, the importance attached to the widening of readership was reflected in a new attention to women. The first Italian political newspaper explicitly addressed to women dates back to the revolutionary period. *La vera repubblicana*, written by male journalists, was published in Piedmont in 1799 and, given its high price and cultured language, certainly targeted an upper-middle-class public of well-educated women. Although in *Il Caffè* Cesare Beccaria had as early as 1764 stressed the importance for the press of attracting a female public, during the ancien regime an explicitly female press had been confined to magazines like Gioseffa Cornoldi Caminer's *La donna galante* (1786–8), which published novels and short articles on fashion or theatre and avoided any involvement in contemporary civil and philosophical debates. The journalists of *La vera repubblicana* proposed, instead, a model of the revolutionary woman which not only – in line with ideas already developed in enlightened debates – condemned frivolity and encouraged study, but also stressed their rights as citizens. The newspaper condemned female education in convents, advocated divorce and the participation of women in the assemblies of constitutional circles where they should speak in public and insisted on the need for a revolutionary education for them. Its articles sketched an image of revolutionary women who had a clear role in the public sphere: women had to use their position as mothers, wives and educators to advance republican ideas and defend them in public arenas. However, they were denied any hope of obtaining active and direct political rights as voters, as their sovereignty allegedly lay 'in the heart and in the exercise of social virtues'.[60]

The expansion of the political press was accompanied by an explosion in the activities of organised civil society. Constitutional clubs and other similar societies shared the same political and educational purposes as newspapers but differed in several ways from pre-revolutionary forms of sociability. According to their statutes, large audiences of non-members were not only allowed, but also encouraged, to attend their frequent meetings and public discussions. This openness confirms the patriots' determination to build a bridge between them and the rest of the population. Although the official purpose of the sessions of Patriotic Societies was to support the work of the government, in revolutionary clubs citizens also ended up monitoring the effectiveness of governments and criticised their decisions, often considered inadequate. It is therefore hardly surprising that governments suppressed most of them during the Triennium.[61]

Their membership also helps to explain the novel characteristics of the revolutionary public sphere. Thanks to the work of Stefano Nutini and Marco Meriggi, we have a precise idea of the composition of the Società di pubblica istruzione (January–July 1797) and the Circolo costituzionale (October 1797–October 1798), the main patriotic clubs set up in Milan, then capital of the Repubblica Cisalpina. Although the membership of the Società di pubblica istruzione included some members of the old Milanese social elite, the overwhelming majority of members of the Circolo were military officials, civil servants, lawyers and other professionals, whose activities were linked to the life of the republic. Patricians represented only 5 per cent of the *associati*. Another important element of novelty was the relatively young average age of members (thirty-eight for the Società di pubblica istruzione, but almost 50 per cent of the members were under thirty-five). This seems to substantiate the argument that Italian Jacobinism was the expression of a generation younger than that of the intellectuals and civil servants who had supported absolutism. It was, then, this new generation which produced and consumed the most progressive republican journalism, and constituted a public sphere which could be defined as bourgeois, if not always for its social composition – the aristocratic element being still considerable – then at least for the recognition by its constituents that only civil rights defined their position vis-à-vis the authorities.

After the brief Austrian restoration in 1800, the constitutional reforms which transformed the Repubblica Cisalpina into the authoritarian Italian Republic (1802) and Kingdom of Italy (1805) radically redesigned the political map of Italy and marked the end of any form of independent journalism. The intellectuals who had animated the political debates of the Triennium were swept up in the 'bureaucratisation of the intellectual elites' which represented one of the most important elements of Napoleon's policy to control and gain the support of the national intelligentsia. Several of the younger and formerly democratic journalists were absorbed by the state administration.[62] The founder of the first revolutionary newspaper in Milan, Giovanni Rasori, became a university professor; Pietro Custodi, former editor of the *Tribuno del popolo*, Secretary General of the Ministry of Finance; the journalist Matteo Galdi, a diplomat; while Giovanni Ristori worked at the Ministry of Justice. Deprived of any political role, intellectuals remained useful in so far as they could provide technical expertise, become good administrators or contribute to government propaganda. Napoleon attached great importance to controlling public opinion. Under his regime, political information was reduced to official gazettes that were subsidised by the government and survived artificially due to compulsory subscriptions from local administrations. In 1811, a decree stating that there could be no more than one newspaper per department ended up encouraging most prefects to publish such a newspaper. The Napoleonic press hence became a mixture of official documents, local information, articles extolling the virtues of Napoleon and his government and international news where England always featured prominently as a corrupt country on the verge of bankruptcy.

The *Giornale italiano*, published three times a week from 1803 to 1813 in Milan, was the mouthpiece of the Napoleonic government and, with an average of 3,000 subscribers per issue, one of the most widespread newspapers in the Republic and subsequently in the Kingdom. Its first editor and journalist, Vincenzo Cuoco, became the ideologue of the Napoleonic regime. In the *Programma* of the *Giornale*, Cuoco declared that the aim of the newspaper was to educate the Italians to form a 'public mind'.[63] Cuoco attributed the morally destitute conditions of Italy to its absence, or in other words to the lack of that 'national pride which is necessary for the economic and moral development of a country'.[64] In Cuoco's words, in Italy, after the revolutionary hiatus, 'the order of things' had been re-established 'by a single man' who had saved the homeland. Moreover, Cuoco believed that 'unity' was Italy's first and foremost need, while the 'present state of ideas and customs ... after such long division' prevented the establishment of a stable republic.[65] Cuoco left the *Giornale* in 1806, but continued his journalistic activity in the Kingdom of Naples, where he edited the *Corriere di Napoli*, inspired by similar principles.

Newspapers like the *Giornale italiano* contributed to creating a truly national, if not independent, public opinion, and were an important element of the nation-building process in Italy. The argument that the Napoleonic state was to shape an Italian national identity through its new institutions was shared both by part of those conservative elites who had been hostile to democracy, and by the former radical intellectuals, who had been disappointed by the political divisions of the patriots and by the hostility of the masses. The former democrats believed that the administration for which they were now working would promote the transformation of their country from a backward feudal society into one that was more advanced and politically cohesive. In this sense, it is undeniable, as Capra puts it, that in spite of the latent opposition by large sections of the nobility, during the Napoleonic regime convergence between government ideology and educated public opinion was successfully achieved according to a model which had first been theorised in the age of enlightened despotism but was systematically applied only during the Kingdom of Italy.[66]

To complete its control over public opinion, the *longa manus* of the state was prepared to invade and colonise all independent forms of sociability. The Napoleonic organised civil society was, in Meriggi's words, 'a sociability of civil servants', and an extension of the public administration.[67] After the closure of all independent clubs, the first Napoleonic associations like the Milanese *Accademia letteraria* and the *Società di incoraggiamento delle scienze e delle arti*, founded in 1800 and 1807, excluded politics from their interests. The government subsidised these organisations and, in the case of the *Accademia*, imposed the presence of a delegate, a government official whose job was to control the debates and report them back to the authorities. Although by law they were recognised only for their status as landowners, aristocrats regained influence in this state-controlled public sphere.

If the Napoleonic regime had denied all forms of freedom of expression to the intellectuals, with its large administration filled with competent and highly educated civil servants it contributed to creating a new bourgeois and national educated class.[68] It was this latter that, after 1815, stirred political opposition against the restored regimes, while searching for a political and intellectual role in leading public opinion which governments denied them, thus fostering anti-Austrian and national feeling.[69] However, although an extremely important and sophisticated journalism engaged in social, economic and literary matters thrived in Restoration Italy, free political journalism reappeared in the peninsula only after 1847.[70]

NOTES

1 The best general history of Italian journalism is the work of Giuseppe Ricuperati, 'Giornali e società nell'Italia dell'Ancien Régime', in Valerio Castronovo and Nicola Tranfaglia (eds.), *Storia della stampa italiana*, 6 vols. (1976–99), vol. I, Valerio Castronovo, Giuseppe Ricuperati and Carlo Capra, *La stampa italiana dal Cinquecento all'Ottocento* (Rome, 1976), 67–372. The book was republished in 1986 (with an updated bibliography) and in 1999. There is as yet no general work on the birth and development of political journalism, as Ricuperati is mainly concerned with literary journalism. Recent essays and articles on Italian newspapers are footnoted throughout this essay. Nothing on the subject has appeared in English.

2 Mario Infelise, 'Le Marché des informations à Venise au XVII siècle', in Henri Duranton and Pierre Rétat (eds.), *Gazettes et information politique sous l'ancien régime* (Saint Etienne, 1999), 117–28; Infelise, 'Professione reportista. Copisti e gazzettieri nella Venezia del '600', in Stefano Gasparri, Giovanni Levi and Pierandrea Moro (eds.), *Venezia. Itinerari per la storia della città* (Bologna, 1997), 183–209.

3 On the distribution of Italian gazettes see Franco Venturi, *The End of the Old Regime in Europe*, trans. R. Burr Litchfield, 2 vols. (Princeton, NJ, 1989–91); Marco Cuaz, *Le nuove di Francia. L'immagine della rivoluzione francese nella stampa periodica italiana (1787–1795)* (Turin, 1990), pp. 19–24.
4 Cuaz, *Le nuove*, pp. 19–21. The *Gazzetta di Milano* was republished by Arnaldo Bruni (ed.), *La Gazzetta di Milano (1769)*, 2 vols. (Milan, 1981).
5 Mario Infelise, *L'editoria veneziana nel '700* (Milan, 1991), pp. 345–9; Marino Berengo, *La società veneta alla fine del Settecento. Ricerche storiche* (Florence, 1956), pp. 156–61. Newspaper articles have been reprinted in Marino Berengo (ed.), *Giornali veneziani del Settecento* (Milan, 1962).
6 Maria Augusta Timpanaro Morelli, 'Legge sulla stampa e attività editoriale a Firenze nel secondo Settecento', in *Rassegna degli Archivi di Stato*, 29 (1969), 400–473; Morelli, 'Persone e momenti del giornalismo politico a Firenze fra il 1766 e il 1799 in alcuni documenti dell'Archivio di Stato di Firenze', *Rassegna degli Archivi di Stato*, 31 (1972), 613–700.
7 Ricuperati, 'La circulation des nouvelles politiques à Turin et dans l'état de Savoie à la fin de l'Ancien Régime' and Raffaella Buoso, 'La gazette de Nice et quatre gazettes piémontaises conservées à Turin', in Duranton and Rétat (eds.), *Gazettes et information*, 57–67, 69–75.
8 Marina Formica, 'Mutamenti politici e continuità editoriali: le gazzette della tipografia Chracas', in Marina Caffiero and Giuseppe Monsagrati (eds.), *Dall'erudizione alla politica. Giornali, giornalisti ed editori a Roma tra XVII e XX secolo* (Milan, 1997), 103–26; Formica, 'L'information politique à Rome au XVII et au XVIII siècle', in Duranton and Rétat (eds.), *Gazettes et information*, 33–48. On the *Notizie per l'anno* see Marina Formica, 'Tra cielo e terra. Gli almanacchi romani del XVII e XVIII secolo', *Studi settecenteschi*, 15 (1995), 115–62.
9 Nino Cortese, 'Gazzette napoletane del Sei e Settecento', in *Cultura e politica a Napoli dal Cinquecento al Settecento* (Naples, 1965), 163–84.
10 Augusto Gaggioni, 'Le vicende politiche della tipografia dei fratelli Agnelli 1745–1799', *Archivio Storico Ticinese*, 7 (1961), 317–40.
11 Anna Maria Rao, 'Mercato e privilegi: la stampa periodica', in Rao (ed.), *Editoria e cultura a Napoli nel XVIII secolo* (Naples, 1998), 173–99.
12 Piero del Negro, *Il mito americano nella Venezia del '700* (Padua, 1986); Franco Venturi, *The End of the Old Regime*, vol. II, passim. Important remarks about Venturi's use of gazettes are in Marino Berengo, 'Fonti e problemi di Settecento riformatore', *Annali della Fondazione Einaudi*, 19 (1985), 442–50.
13 Mario Infelise, '*Europa*. Una gazzetta manoscritta del '700', in *Non uno itinere. Studi offerti dagli allievi a Federico Seneca* (Venice, 1993), 221–39.
14 Infelise, *L'editoria veneziana*, pp. 345–7.
15 Morelli, 'Persone e momenti', pp. 441–2.
16 Italy had a range of different currencies in the eighteenth century. This chapter mentions those of Naples, Tuscany, Rome and Venice. Their currency systems were as follows. Naples: 1 ducato = 5 tarí = 100 grani. Tuscany: 1 ducato fiorentino or scudo di moneta = 20 soldi = 240 denarii. Rome: 1 scudo romano = 10 giuli or paoli = 50 quattrini = 100 denari. Venice: 1 ducato = 24 grossi (but a parallel system was also in use in which 1 lire veneziane = 20

soldi = 240 denari. There were seven of these lire in a ducato). In 1785, one pound sterling was worth approximately 6 Venetian Ducati, 8.7 Florentine ducati fiorentini, 6.36 Neapolitan ducati, or 7.68 Roman scudi. These values are calculated following Giuseppe Felloni, *Gli investimenti finanziari genovesi in Europa tra Seicento e la Restaurazione* (Milan, 1971).

17 Renato Pasta, *Editoria e cultura nel Settecento* (Florence, 1997).
18 Rao, 'Mercato e privilegi'.
19 Formica, 'Mutamenti politici', pp. 106–7.
20 Anna Maria Rao, 'Introduzione', in Rao (ed.), *Editoria e cultura*, pp. 50–51.
21 On southern Italy see Maria Rosaria Pelizzari (ed.), *Sulle vie della scrittura. Alfabetizzazione, cultura scritta e istituzioni in età moderna* (Naples, 1989); on central and northern Italy see Attilio Bartoli Langeli and Xenio Toscani (eds.), *Istruzione, alfabetismo, scrittura: saggi di storia dell'alfabetizzazione in Italia (sec. XV–XIX)* (Milan, 1991). The data on Milan is in Alberto Milanesi, 'Gruppi sociali a Milano in età napoleonica: problemi di alfabetizzazione', in Franco Della Peruta, Roberto Leydi and Angelo Stella (eds.), *Mondo popolare in Lombardia, Milano e il suo territorio*, 2 vols. (Milan, 1985), vol. I, 635–58.
22 Mario Infelise, 'L'utile e il piacevole. Alla ricerca dei lettori italiani del Secondo Settecento', in Maria Gioia Tavoni and Françoise Waquet (eds.), *Lo spazio del libro nell'Europa del XVIII secolo* (Bologna, 1997), 113–26; Brendan Dooley, 'Lettori e letture nel Settecento italiano', in Mario Infelise and Paola Marini (eds.), *L'editoria del '700 e i Remondini* (Bassano, 1992), 17–38; Renato Pasta, *Towards a Social History of Ideas: The Book and the Booktrade in Eighteenth-Century Italy*, in Hans Erich Bödeker (ed.), *Histoires du livre. Nouvelles Orientations* (Paris, 1995), 101–38.
23 Infelise, 'L'utile', p. 123.
24 Giovanni Ristori, 'Colpo d'occhio su lo stato presente della letteratura italiana', *Nuovo Giornale letterario* (1788), republished in Berengo (ed.), *Giornali veneziani*, 618–54. In 1800, according to Karl Julius Beloch, *Storia della popolazione d'Italia* (Florence, 1994), the estimated Italian population amounted to 17.794 million.
25 Claudio Colaiacomo, 'Crisi dell' "Ancien Régime": dall'uomo di lettere al letterato borghese', in Alberto Asor Rosa (ed.), *Letteratura Italiana*, vol. II, *Produzione e consumo* (Turin, 1983), 363–412.
26 Françoise Decroisette, *Venise au temps de Goldoni* (Paris, 1999), pp. 58–62.
27 Amedeo Quondam, 'L'Accademia', in Asor Rosa (ed.), *Letteratura Italiana*, vol. I, *Il letterato e le istituzioni* (Turin, 1982), 823–98; Gianfranco Torcellan, 'Un tema di ricerche: Le Accademie agrarie del Settecento', in Torcellan, *Settecento veneto e altri scritti storici* (Turin, 1969), 328–59; Maria Pia Donato, 'La sociabilità culturale a Roma alla fine del Settecento: studi e fonti', *Archivi e cultura*, 23–24 (1990–91), 63–77; Eric William Cochrane, *Tradition and Enlightenment in the Tuscan Academies, 1690–1800* (Chicago, 1961). On sociability and public opinion see Marco Meriggi, 'Associazionismo borghese tra '700 e '800. Sonderweg tedesco e caso francese', *Quaderni Storici*, 71 (1989), 589–627.
28 Piero del Negro, 'Una società "per la lettura di gazzette e giornali" nella Padova di fine Settecento', *Archivio Veneto*, 123 (1992), 31–59.

29 Mario Infelise, 'Gazzette e lettori nella Repubblica Veneta dopo l'ottantanove', in Renzo Zorzi (ed.), *L'eredità dell'ottantanove e Italia* (Florence, 1992), 307–50; Jean Boutier, 'Les imprimés révolutionnaires français en Toscane: paradoxe d'une liberté surveillée (1789–1792)', *Mélanges de l'Ecole Française de Rome: Italie et Méditerranée*, 102 (1990), 423–68.
30 Valentino Baldacci, *Filippo Stecchi. Un editore fiorentino del Settecento fra riformismo e rivoluzione* (Florence, 1989).
31 Edoardo Tortarolo, 'Opinione pubblica', in Vincenzo Ferrone and Daniel Roche (eds.), *L'Illuminismo. Dizionario storico* (Bari, 1997), 283–91; Alberto Postigliola (ed.), *Opinione lumi rivoluzione, Materiali della società italiana di studi sul secolo XVIII* (Rome, 1993); Anna Maria Rao, 'L'opinion publique en Italie au XVIIIe siècle', *Journal of the International Society for the Study of European Ideas*, 1 (1996), 200–206; Maria Luisa Perna, 'L'universo comunicativo di Antonio Genovesi', in Rao (ed.), *Editoria e cultura*, pp. 391–404.
32 'Gaetano Filangieri, *Scienza della legislazione*', republished in Franco Venturi (ed.), *Illuministi Italiani*, vol. V, *Riformatori Napoletani* (Milan, 1962), 749–54. Similar ideas appear in Antonio Genovesi, *Delle lezioni di commercio o sia di economia civile* (Naples, 1768–70). I have used the edition published under the title *Opere scelte di Antonio Genovesi*, 2 vols. (Milan, 1824), where the relevant passages are found in vol. I, pp. 87, 181.
33 Pietro Verri, *Meditazioni sulla economia politica*, ed. Renzo De Felice (Milan, 1998), p. 111.
34 Genovesi, *Delle lezioni*, vol. I, p. 361.
35 Pietro Verri, 'Memorie appartenenti alla vita ed agli studj di Paolo Frisi', in Giulio Carcano (ed.), *Scritti vari di Pietro Verri*, 2 vols. (Florence, 1854), vol. II, 305–66, pp. 313–14.
36 Carlo Capra, 'Gli intellettuali e il potere: i casi di Beccaria e di Verri', in Antonio Santucci (ed.), *L'età dei lumi. Saggi sulla cultura settecentesca* (Bologna, 1998), 211–30; Pietro Verri, 'Pensieri sullo stato politico del milanese nel 1790', in Carcano (ed.), *Scritti vari*, vol. II, 1–38, appendix, p. 11.
37 'De' fogli periodici', *Il Caffè*, Tomo II, foglio I (1765), republished in *Il Caffè*, ed. Gianni Francioni and Sergio Romagnoli (Turin, 1993), p. 417.
38 Gianfranco Folena, *L'italiano in Europa. Esperienze linguistiche del Settecento* (Turin, 1983), pp. 17–18.
39 Giuseppe Compagnoni, *Memorie autobiografiche per la prima volta edite* (Milan, 1927), pp. 120–21.
40 *Spezieria di Sondrio*, n. d. [1790], quoted in Carlo Capra, *Giovanni Ristori da illuminista a funzionario 1755–1830* (Florence, 1968), p. 113.
41 On the reforms see Dino Carpanetto and Giuseppe Ricuperati, *Italy in the Age of Reason* (London, 1987). On censorship Antonio Rotondò, 'La censura ecclesiastica e la cultura', in Ruggero Romano and Corrado Vivanti (eds.), *Storia d'Italia*, vol. V, *I documenti* (Turin, 1973), part 2, 1399–1492; Alcesti Tarchetti, 'Censura e censori di Sua Maestà Imperiale nella Lombardia Austriaca: 1740–1780', in Aldo De Maddalena, Ettore Rotelli and Gennaro Barbarisi (eds.), *Economia, istituzioni, cultura in Lombardia nell'età di Maria Teresa*, 3 vols. (Bologna, 1982), vol. II, 741–92; Lodovica Braida, 'L'affermazione della censura di stato in Piemonte. Dall'editto del 1648 alle Costituzioni per

l'Università del 1772', *Rivista Storica Italiana*, 102 (1990), 717–95; Maria Grazia Maiorini, 'Stato e editoria: controllo e propaganda politica durante la Reggenza', in Rao (ed.), *Editoria e cultura*, 405–26.
42 Quoted in Maiorini, 'Stato e editoria', p. 423; Sandro Landi, *Il governo delle opinioni. Censura e formazione del consenso nella Toscana del Settecento* (Bologna, 2000).
43 Capra, *Giovanni Ristori*, pp. 39–41.
44 Ricuperati, 'Giornali e società', p. 237.
45 Carlo Capra, 'Stato e Chiesa in Italia negli anni di Giuseppe II', in Helmut Reinalter (ed.), *Der Josephinismus* (Frankfurt-on-Main, 1993), 103–19.
46 Franco Venturi, 'La Rivoluzione di Corsica: Le grandi carestie degli anni sessanta. La Lombardia delle riforme', in *Settecento Riformatore*, vol. v, *L'Italia dei Lumi (1764–1790)* (Turin, 1987), part 1.
47 Infelise, *L'editoria veneziana*, pp. 62–131.
48 Formica, 'L'information politique à Rome'.
49 Cuaz, *Le nuove*; Paolo Alvazzi del Frate, 'Rivoluzione e giornalismo politico nello Stato Pontificio', *Mélanges de l'Ecole Française de Rome: Italie et Méditerranée*, 102 (1990), 410–22; Anna Maria Rao, 'Accueil et refus de la révolution française dans la presse napolitaine (1789–1796)', in Michelle Vovelle (ed.), *L'image de la révolution française* (Oxford, 1989), vol. I, 353–8.
50 Matteo Galdi, *Saggio d'istruzione pubblica rivoluzionaria* (1798), quoted by Infelise, 'Gazzette e lettori', p. 309.
51 Capra, 'Il giornalismo nell'età rivoluzionaria e napoleonica', in Castronovo, Ricuperati and Capra, *La stampa italiana*, 404–72; Renzo De Felice, *Il triennio giacobino in Italia (1796–1799)* (Rome, 1990). A selection of articles from the Italian press during this period have been reprinted in Renzo De Felice (ed.), *I giornali giacobini italiani* (Milan, 1962).
52 On the ideas of the Triennium see Massimo Salvadori and Nicola Tranfaglia (eds.), *Il modello politico giacobino e le rivoluzioni* (Florence, 1990), pp. 100–131; Luciano Guerci, *Mente coraggio virtù repubblicane. Educare il popolo nell'Italia in rivoluzione (1796–1799)* (Turin, 1992); Eluggero Pii, 'La ricerca di un modello politico durante il triennio rivoluzionario (1796–99) in Italia', in Vittor Ivo Comparato (ed.), *Modelli nella storia del pensiero politico*, 2 vols. (Florence, 1989), vol. II, 271–96; Daniela Donnini Macciò and Roberto Romani, 'All equally rich: economic knowledge in revolutionary Italy, 1796–1799', *Research in the History of Economic Thought and Methodology*, 14 (1996), 23–49.
53 Erasmo Leso, *Lingua e rivoluzione. Ricerche sul vocabolario politico italiano del triennio rivoluzionario 1796–1799* (Venice, 1991), pp. 120 and ff.
54 Marina Formica, '"Vox populi, vox dei?" Tentativi di formazione dell'opinione pubblica a Roma', in Postigliola (ed.), *Opinione lumi rivoluzione*, p. 121.
55 Introduction to the *Giornale delle Guardie Nazionali*, in Luciano Guerci, 'I giornali repubblicani nel Piemonte dell'anno VII', *Rivista Storica Italiana*, 102 (1990), 375–421, p. 378.
56 Mario Battaglini (ed.), '*Il Monitore napoletano*'. *1799* (Naples, 1974).
57 Vittorio Criscuolo, 'Introduzione' to Criscuolo (ed.), *Termometro politico della Lombardia* (Rome, 1989), p. 19.
58 Carlo Zaghi, *L'Italia di Napoleone* (Turin, 1989), pp. 334–9.

59 Cesare de Michelis, 'Elisabetta Caminer', in *Dizionario biografico degli Italiani*, vol. XVII (Rome, 1974), 236–41.
60 Elisa Strumia, 'Un giornale per le donne nel Piemonte del 1799: "La vera repubblicana"', *Studi Storici*, 30 (1989), 917–46. On the image of women in eighteenth-century Italy see Fiamma Lussana, 'Misoginia e adulazione: ambiguità dell'immagine femminile nel secolo dei lumi', *Studi Storici*, 25 (1984), 547–58.
61 Marco Meriggi, *Milano borghese* (Milan, 1992), pp. 3–50; Marina Formica, 'Forme di sociabilità politica nella repubblica romana del 1798', *Dimensioni e problemi della ricerca storica*, 1 (1992), 73–88; Stefano Nutini, 'La Società di pubblica istruzione di Milano', *Studi Storici*, 30 (1989), 891–916; Umberto Marcelli (ed.), *Il gran circolo costituzionale e il 'Genio Democratico'* (Bologna, 1797–1798), 3 vols. (Bologna, 1986); Anna Maria Rao, 'Popular Societies in the Neapolitan Republic of 1799', *Journal of Modern Italian Studies*, 4 (1999), 358–66.
62 Carlo Capra, 'La condizione degli intellettuali negli anni della Repubblica Italiana e del Regno Italico, 1802–1814', *Quaderni Storici*, 23 (1973), 471–90.
63 On Cuoco see Giulio Bollati, *L'Italiano*, in Ruggero Romano and Corrado Vivanti (eds.), *Storia d'Italia*, vol. I, *I caratteri originali* (Turin, 1972), 949–1,022; Antonino De Francesco, *Vincenzo Cuoco. Una vita politica* (Bari, 1997).
64 'Lo spirito pubblico', *Il Giornale italiano* (6–27 October 1804), republished in Fausto Nicolini (ed.), *Scritti vari*, 2 vols. (Bari, 1924), vol. I, 115–24.
65 'Il Regno d'Italia', *Il Giornale italiano* (1–6 April 1805), republished in Nicolini (ed.), *Scritti vari*, vol. I, p. 157.
66 Capra, 'La condizione degli intellettuali'.
67 Meriggi, *Milano borghese*, p. 41.
68 Carlo Capra, 'Nobili, notabili, elites: dal "modello" francese al caso italiano', *Quaderni Storici*, 37 (1978), 13–41.
69 Marino Berengo, *Intellettuali e librai nella Milano della Restaurazione* (Turin, 1980); Marco Meriggi, *Amministrazione e classi sociali nel Lombardo-Veneto (1814–1848)* (Bologna, 1983).
70 Kent Roberts Greenfield, *Economics and Liberalism in the Risorgimento. A Study of Nationalism in Lombardy 1815–1848* (Baltimore, MD, 1934); Alessandro Galante Garrone, 'I giornali della restaurazione', in Castronovo and Tranfaglia (eds.), *Storia della stampa italiana*, vol. II; Alessandro Galante Garrone and Franco della Peruta, *La stampa italiana del Risorgimento* (Bari, 1979), 3–246; John Davis, 'Cultures of interdiction. The politics of censorship in Italy from Napoleon to the Restoration', in David Laven and Lucy Riall (eds.), *Napoleon's Legacy* (Oxford, 2000), 237–56.

10 Russia, 1790–1830

Miranda Beaven Remnek

The emergence of politicised civil society is often preceded by the growth of public opinion. This can in turn be traced to those social spaces where an increasingly responsive press interacted with other sites of debate. In this way the press, along with venues such as learned societies, salons, coffee houses, cafés, clubs, theatres, and masonic lodges, helped to foster the exchange of ideas and formation of opinion. In the West, these institutions arose in close succession,[1] but in Russia, the pace of change was slower. Often thought to have been a country where political stringencies resulted in stunted growth, Russia in the early nineteenth century was, however, in a state of flux,[2] as this chapter will demonstrate. This was true despite the autocracy's secure position and the lack of attempts to introduce public participation in government on the French model. Indeed, the first real tremor came only in 1825 with the Decembrist Revolt that accompanied the rise of Nicholas I to the throne, and the upheaval was quelled at no great cost to the autocracy.[3]

Even government officials were often unable to influence policy in significant ways. Granted, there were exceptions. In 1826, the elder statesman and legal specialist M. M. Speranskii first proposed using locally produced provincial gazettes as a vehicle for government decrees, statistical data and information of general interest or benefit to the public. In the decades to come, these organs provided a significantly broader number of provincial readers with the information they needed to begin a political dialogue. Even so, only a few appeared immediately (such as *Tiflisskie vedomosti* (*Tiflis Gazette*) in 1828–32).[4] Indeed, according to W. B. Lincoln, 'one of the most critical shortcomings of Nicholas I's system had been that it had failed to produce any politically or socially responsible group whose voice was heard in the highest spheres of Russia's government'.[5] Thus, as far as direct political participation was concerned, opportunities at most social levels were decidedly minimal throughout the late eighteenth and early nineteenth centuries.

Nevertheless, Russians belonging to the educated sphere of society were sometimes allowed more freedom than their compatriots, and the beginning of the period covered by this book was marked by the onset of Catherine II's expansive reign (1762–96), in which the educated were encouraged to express their opinions relatively freely. A prime example was the activity of the prominent educator and freemason Nikolai Novikov. Indeed, some scholars have insisted that a civil society already existed in eighteenth-century Russia: but one marked by education, not nobility. Thus, Marc Raeff designated society of the period as a 'civil society of the educated'.[6] But the liberality that offered the educated greater freedom of expression was cyclical in its extent. Developments in France so alarmed the authorities that the years 1790–1800 became a period of restraint. True, lone voices continued to present Russia's problems for scrutiny. One famous example was a manifesto of 1790 by the nobleman A. N. Radishchev, who used his private press to publish 650 copies. Entitled *Puteshestvie iz Peterburga v Moskvu* (*A Journey from St Petersburg to Moscow*), the piece was a thinly disguised 'travel account' depicting the excesses of Russian life. Suggesting that Russia's fear of politicised public space was evidence of its immaturity, the author affirmed: 'The better grounded a state is in its principles ... the less danger it incurs of being moved and swayed by the winds of shifting opinion ... An open-hearted man who does good and is firm in his principles lets anything be said about himself.'[7]

Yet voices such as these were usually stifled, thanks to the undulating but pervasive presence of censorship. There may be a tendency to overdramatise the extent of censorship in Russia: some scholars note that the history of Russian journalism differs from journalism in the West in that vigorous official censorship was absent during its first 100 years.[8] But the usual approach is to emphasise the growing power of press restrictions, based in part on sources like Radishchev's *Puteshestvie*. In a chapter on censorship his protagonist meets a would-be reformer at Torzhok (west of Moscow) who advocates tolerance and freedom of the press. Although the protagonist reminds the reformer that, by virtue of Catherine II's decree of 1783, any citizen 'is now permitted to own and operate a printing press', in framing the reformer's response, Radishchev affirms: 'Now anyone may have the tools of printing, but that which may be printed is still under watch ... The censorship of what is printed belongs properly to society ... Leave what is stupid to the judgement of public opinion; stupidity will find a thousand censors.'[9] Catherine, however, was unable to agree: Radishchev's *Puteshestvie* was seized, and the author exiled to Siberia in 1790. Other events of similar severity occurred in this decade: Novikov was imprisoned in 1792 after a long period of publishing activity, and though released in the reign of Catherine's son Paul I, which began in 1796, he was forbidden to resume his journalistic activities. Indeed, the five-year reign of Paul is known as a period of particular severity, culminating in an unenforceable ban on the importation of all foreign books.[10]

In contrast, the early reign of Alexander I, who ruled from 1801 to 1825, imitated the early years of Catherine II, and the period was rich in new cultural and educational endeavours. One of Alexander I's immediate moves in 1802, during his early liberal period, was to transfer the censorship apparatus away from the police to the newly established Ministry of Education. He also developed a new, liberal censorship code in 1804.[11] Yet certain pro-French compositions began to encounter prohibition, and by 1811, supervisory powers over censorship were restored to the police. A temporary lull occurred during and after the war of 1812, but repression returned in greater force with the reactionary tendencies of the second half of Alexander's reign. The reconstitution of the Ministry of Education in October 1817 as the Ministry of Religious Affairs and Public Instruction did not bode well. Mysticism was on the increase, and although police control over censorship had been reduced again in 1817, by 1818 there was virtually no discussion of serfdom or anti-government views in the periodical press, which was subject to special persecution.[12] In 1819, M. L. Magnitskii of the enlarged Ministry of Education executed his notorious purge of faculty at the University of Kazan. Government intrusions into intellectual activities continued to multiply, and in 1822, instructions were issued to disband masonic lodges throughout Russia.[13]

The subsequent reign of Nicholas I, which began in 1825 and ended in 1855, can be similarly divided. The first two years or so were a period of tension following the uprising of December 1825: noteworthy was the new censorship code of 1826 known as the Cast-Iron Statutes. But these were amended in 1828, and the revised code ushered in a ten-year period characterised by a subtle but noticeable maturing of Russian society and culture. True, political restraints continued and some writers suffered at the hands of censors. But only three journals were closed down in the course of the reign, and recent research affirms that 'writers came into conflict with the regime on surprisingly few occasions'.[14] Book editions and serials circulation increased dramatically, and Russian culture at the middle levels of society made progress. However, the fact that even in the late 1850s Alexander II recognised the need to create an intricate system of publicity (*glasnost'*) – whereby both conservative and progressive elites would be permitted to debate their views *within* the political framework of autocracy[15] – demonstrates that insufficient strides had been made towards the creation of an active public sphere.

No discussion of the Russian press and its effect on civil society can thus be attempted without realising the degree of its dependence on the whims of censorship. Although the early nineteenth century witnessed a continued expansion of the press – as well as in the number of gathering places such as clubs, cafés, theatres and masonic lodges – the extent of these institutions was less than in Western Europe, and as a result, even participation in less politicised spheres was limited. As late as 1839, there was, according to some, what may be called a 'culture of silence'. The disastrous storm which blew up in that year, when many were sailing from Petersburg to take part in the Peterhof festival, caused several hundred deaths. Yet the visiting Marquis de Custine noted no major outcry:

> What numberless accounts... would not such a catastrophe have given rise to in any other land except this... How many newspapers would have said... that the police never does its duty... Nothing of the kind here! A silence more frightful than the evil itself, everywhere reigns. Two lines in the *Gazette*, without details, is all the information publicly given; and at court, in the city, in the saloons of fashion, not a word is spoken....[16]

Nevertheless, this essay contends that as Russia moved into the nineteenth century, its press – though hampered – succeeded in contributing both directly and indirectly (through its interaction with other institutions) to a growing maturity in contemporary society that was based in no small measure on a larger social consciousness and greater recognition of civil obligations.

Periodicals had begun their steady expansion, as in the West, in the eighteenth century. But in Russia newspapers were not the most important type. Besides Peter the Great's *Vedomosti (News)* published from 1703 to 1727, there were only two major titles: the Academy of Sciences' *Sanktpeterburgskie vedomosti (St Petersburg News)* published twice a week beginning in 1728, and Moscow University's *Moskovskie vedomosti (Moscow News)* begun in 1756. Both were published by government-run institutions and, glossing over economic issues, limited their coverage to political news. *Moskovskie vedomosti* first appeared in an edition of only 600 copies (although Novikov, once in charge of Moscow University Press, managed to bring up the edition size to 4,000 copies). Nor did *Sanktpeterburgskie vedomosti* circulate widely in other towns (perhaps because of its price of four rubles an issue).[17]

Journals, on the other hand, showed more vitality. The early part of Catherine II's reign was a time when journalistic debate earned imperial favour, marked especially by the so-called satirical journals of the 1760s in which Catherine herself participated. The journalistic battles were particularly intense in 1769–74, when Catherine and Novikov debated in print over the question of serfdom. This liberality was followed by the decree of 1783 which permitted private individuals to set up presses in provincial cities.[18] Thus, the scene was set for a number of advancements in the period 1790–1840: both in the power of the press and its influence on the public sphere. However, these developments were not linear. Indeed, the 1790s ushered in a period of restraint. True, brand new presses continued to arise: including Tula (1790), Kozlov (1791), Kursk and Nizhnii Novgorod (1792), Kostroma (1793), Smolensk and Kharkov (1795), Vladimir and Zhitomir (1798). But events in Europe had already prompted a significant tightening by the beginning of the decade, culminating in Catherine's decree of 1796 which ended any remaining freedom of the press and instituted administrative censorship.[19] Indeed, it is no coincidence that the one form of serial publication that began to thrive in the 1790s was the almanac. The almanac was also popular in Europe, but in Russia it was to take on a special role (particularly in the 1820s): its publication on an annual rather than a more frequent basis was less likely to raise the suspicions of censors, enabling it to include extracts from texts that could not be published in their entirety.[20]

Reversing this trend, the early 1800s (marked by Alexander I's coronation in 1801) saw a marked rejuvenation of the Russian press. At least sixty-nine periodical titles began their existence, and again, most were journals rather than newspapers.[21] Many were specialised titles like Moscow University's *Istoricheskii zhurnal* (1809–30) or the Academy of Science's *Tekhnologicheskii zhurnal* (1804–15), although this latter journal was designed to popularise science. Other, more general, titles were often short-lived: a major exception was N. M. Karamzin's *Vestnik Evropy* (*Herald of Europe*), lasting from 1802 to 1830. New newspapers were often the organs of official agencies, such as *Sankt-Peterburgskie kommercheskie vedomosti* (*St Petersburg Commercial Gazette*), 1802–10. In 1809, two more official papers appeared, the Ministry of Internal Affairs' *Severnaia pochta* (*Northern Mail*) and *Senatskie vedomosti* (*Senate News*). Most titles were still limited in periodicity, and *Severnaia pochta*, for example, appeared only twice a week. But the new publications began to emphasise economic information, which was a major development and one that became even more noticeable in the following decade.[22] Further expansion of the press after 1811 was impaired by the Napoleonic Wars, which brought upheaval to the publishing sphere as to others. Russian export turnover had already decreased from 127,873,000 rubles in 1805 to 75,988,000 by 1808, signifying economic problems that were only compounded by Napoleon's devastating entry into Russia in 1812.[23] The weekly journal *Syn otechestva* (*Son of the Fatherland*) (1812–52) issued a more frequent supplement from 1813 to 1818 entitled *Listki politicheskogo soderzhaniia*

(*Sheets with Political Content*) that was clearly intended to make up for the paucity of newspapers,[24] and the face of the Russian press in the post-war years remained somewhat schizophrenic.

On the one hand, new interest in history brought a marked increase in historical works, and the public taste for history was also satisfied through journals. Besides *Vestnik Evropy* and *Syn otechestva*, other titles included *Ruskoi vestnik* (*Russian Herald*) (1808–24) and, later, *Sibirskii vestnik* (*Siberian Herald*) (1818–24). In addition, the historical fervour created by the milestone publication in 1816–18 of Karamzin's *Istoriia gosudarstva Rossiiskogo* (*History of the Russian State*) led to endless but instructive social debate that was abetted by discussion of this *oeuvre* in the press, and particularly in journals like *Vestnik Evropy*, *Syn otechestva*, and, later, *Severnyi arkhiv* (*Northern Archive*), (1822–28). In other words, an event driven partially by the press played a very real part in the expansion of the reading public.[25] New newspaper titles also appeared. The military *Russkii invalid* (*Russian Veteran*), issued two or three times a week from 1813 and then daily from 1816, survived until 1917. The period also saw the appearance of the first provincial newspaper, *Kazanskie izvestiia* (*Kazan News*), published 1811–20, followed by *Vostochnye izvestiia* (*Eastern News*) in Astrakhan in 1813, and *Rossiiskoe ezhenedel'noe izdanie* (*Russian Weekly Edition*) in Riga in 1816.[26] But the press remained backward in several respects. First, its physical appearance showed little innovation: even the influential journal *Vestnik Evropy* used type reminiscent of the reign of Catherine II. In addition, public tastes still struck some observers as limited. Alexander I's educational reforms were materialising at a languid pace, and in 1815, a commentator in *Vestnik Evropy* gave the continued lack of school attendance as the reason for the demand for 'coarse novels', to the exclusion of non-fiction materials.[27] Most importantly, the freedom of the pre-war years was gone. Alexander surrounded himself with increasingly conservative ministers and the repression of these years resulted in the great instability of new periodicals, and encouraged the vogue for the less heavily censored almanac.

Alexander I's death and the problem of the succession prompted the Revolt of 1825. It was harshly suppressed by his brother, Nicholas I, giving rise to a period of renewed censorship and police repression. But after the loosening in 1828 of the Cast-Iron Statutes, the following decade was one of progress for the Russian press. The period 1825–34 was marked by the publication of N. A. Polevoi's *Moskovskii telegraf* (*Moscow Telegraph*). Often termed the most influential journal of the period, *Moskovskii telegraf* was innovative in its deliberate focus on the general reader irrespective of social level.[28] Yet its cultural impact was less than that of two other press organs, the private newspaper *Severnaia pchela* (*Northern Bee*), which also began in 1825, and the later journal *Biblioteka dlia chteniia* (*Library for Reading*) (1835–64).[29]

In addition to such developments, an important but neglected section of the Russian press during this period involves titles published in foreign languages. As noted by V. G. Sirotkin, in the period 1702–1917, over 100 newspapers and journals were published in St Petersburg and Moscow in a variety of languages other than Russian: most often in French, German, English, Italian and Polish.[30] These included foreign-language editions of Russian papers like *Russkii invalid*. Sirotkin distinguishes four main periods in the evolution of the foreign-language press in the first quarter of the nineteenth century: 1803–5 (economic papers and literary journals in German); 1806–7 (the Russian government's anti-Napoleonic *Journal du Nord*); 1808–14 (bureaucratic patriotic journalism); and 1815–22 (discussion of constitutional and serfdom issues in the foreign-language press). It is known that the Russian nobility often read in European languages: hence, these sources constituted an important vehicle for the exchange of ideas. However, at issue in this essay is the broadening of the public sphere, and as such, greater emphasis is placed on the Russian-language publications that were the only choice of lower-class Russians, as well as elites.

Indeed, in evaluating the relationship of the press with the developing public sphere in Russia it is important to distinguish the extent of its impact on different socio-cultural groupings and public venues. Although social groups in pre-revolutionary Russia began to diversify as the nineteenth century progressed, in the previous century the four principal bastions of society amounted to no more than four estates (nobility, clergy, townspeople and peasants). In terms of social prestige (though not in size), the nobility was the primary group. But its impact on government was less clear-cut. Its allegiance was necessary to the autocracy, but it was not as yet self-conscious in any real political sense. Thus, the nobility's main sphere of interaction was social, and its primary public venue – at least in the capitals – was the salon. This ties in well with the approach taken by Jürgen Habermas, which explained the new consciousness of the individual as a construct apart from the family and the state, and discovered through reading, polite conversation and commercial interaction.[31] Indeed, although commercial activity was hardly a characteristic of upper-class Russian society in the early 1800s, the other two were hallmarks of salon-based culture, for the salons were places where the social elite would meet on a regular basis to converse and listen to literary readings.[32] To what extent did salon society deal with political issues? The answer depends to some extent on the type of salon, and on periodisation. Some of these groupings were purely social, and political engagement was not an issue. But others attracted writers and other nobles with greater intellectual curiosity. And while, prior to 1825, the Alexandrine autocracy did not permit the existence of political societies or clubs like those that characterised English society in the 1650s, literary societies were rife, if sometimes short-lived, and their political undercurrents were well known. A good example is the Arzamas society, founded in 1815 by a group of litterateurs including A. S. Pushkin and P. A.Viazemskii. The main activity of the circle was the composition of parodies of the Slavonicised language of their literary opponents, but these were thinking men who could not ignore political issues.[33] After 1825, however, open discussion of political topics was dangerous, and the literary salons were ostensibly non-politicised gatherings.

A further point concerns the degree to which the Russian press participated in the development of the public sphere that the salons signified. Here the answer depends on the type of publication in question. In 1802, the writer N. M. Karamzin, in his famous essay on the book trade in Russia, noted that 'many nobles, even in comfortable circumstances, still do not take newspapers',[34] and one encounters few references to the discussion of newpaper material in the salons themselves. This, of course, does not mean that the nobility in general did not read newspapers. Besides mainstream Russian papers like *Moskovskie vedomosti* and *Severnaia pchela*, their tastes ran from foreign-language editions like the *Journal des Débats* (published from 1815) to specialized titles like *Zemledel'cheskaia gazeta* (*Agricultural Gazette*), begun in 1834. The first of these, according to a story set in the early part of the century by Prince Odoevskii, was the only newspaper available to petty provincial landowners in 'my late uncle's village'. At the other end of the scale, the second and third of these titles were read by Nicholas I on a daily basis.[35] The fourth was read by the lady-in-waiting and society figure, Anna Osipovna Smirnova, as she tended to her conservatory on her estate in Moscow province. As Prince Viazemskii noted: 'her knowledge was varied, her reading instructional and serious, though not to the detriment of novels and newspapers'.[36]

In the salons, however, another type of serial publication – the almanac – was far more in evidence. Almanacs were composed of short pieces and extracts which made them highly suited to the convention of reading aloud associated with contemporary poetic discourse, and although – after a brief vogue in the late 1790s (ten titles) – they sank in popularity in the post-Napoleonic decade (five titles), they reached their heyday in the late 1820s (sixty-seven titles) and early 1830s (fifty-two titles) as the hallmark of salon culture.[37] Indeed, as remarked by the writer I. I. Panaev, 'writers of the thirties were not interested in any European political events. None of them ever took a look at any foreign newspapers ... For our fellows, the writers, the appearance of some *Northern Flower* (a major almanac published 1825–32) is a hundred times more interesting than all these political news'.[38]

In several ways, therefore, the salons were an integral part of the developing public sphere. They represented an important venue for social interaction and, on occasion, face-to-face political discussion, while their primary organ – the almanac – served as a transitional form that set the stage for the more comprehensive thick journals of the 1830s.[39] The almanac's success made clear that a regular public forum was needed for the sampling and analysis of literature that went beyond the restricted space of the salons. As a result of its ability to publicise extracts from controversial works – such as Alexander Pushkin's *Evgenii Onegin* and Alexander Griboedov's *Gore ot uma* (*Woe From Wit*) – in ways that were less threatening to the authorities, the almanac also fostered the activation of public space by providing a makeshift repository for politicised dialogue.[40]

Despite their importance, the significance of the salons and the almanacs they fostered was clearly not that they attracted a variety of readers from different social levels or many subscribers in total.[41] Thus, one must look for other zones of intersection between social groups and the press. Salons existed in Russia throughout the years 1790–1830, but in the 1820s and early 1830s another grouping, the circle, began to grow more prominent.[42] Circles differed in several ways from salons. They were linked with Moscow University, far from the drawing rooms of St Petersburg; they involved primarily academics and intellectuals; and although they shared a passion for romantic literature, their main interest was German idealist philosophy. An important earlier group was the Lovers of Wisdom (*Liubomudry*), formed in 1823. Perhaps the best known circle centred around the young intellectual, Nikolai Stankevich, who entered Moscow University in 1830. Circles gradually became an ever more important feature of the cultural scene.[43] According to some, the reason for their emergence centred on the poverty of Russian intellectual life. Opportunities for self-promotion in the press were hampered by both limited numbers of journals and censorship difficulties. The critic M. O. Gershenzon (born in 1869) wrote that in the 1830s, intellectual life flourished in groups and circles because its public apparatus (books, journals, lectures and communication with the West) existed in 'the most insignificant quantities', and so individuals sought support in a circle of like-minded friends.[44] Thus, even though they were small groupings that met in apartments and other venues even more private than the salons, these circles played an equally important role as a crucible for an expanding public sphere.

In particular, circles stretched the boundaries of cultural interaction by admitting members from lower social levels. Stankevich came from a noble family near Voronezh, but other associates of his circle – Vissarion Belinsky (from a poor doctor's family), Aleksei Koltsov (son of a cattle dealer) and Ianuarii Neverov (later a civil servant) – were of plebeian origin. Yet despite the influx of members to these circles from less privileged groups, in general their motives were not political. Although circle members suffered from the atmosphere of oppression, most were more interested in philosophy than political or social thought and looked on political radicals with distrust.[45] Hence, their connections with the press involved not newspapers – and certainly not almanacs – but journals. Journals, like almanacs, had joined the publishing scene well before the 1820s. As noted, many were short-lived: such as *Zhurnal iziashchnykh iskusstv* (*Journal of Fine Arts*), 1807, and *Dramaticheskii vestnik* (*Drama Herald*), 1808. Earlier, more substantial titles included Karamzin's *Vestnik Evropy*, N. I. Grech's *Syn otechestva* and F. V. Bulgarin's *Severnyi arkhiv*. In the late 1820s and 1830s more intellectual titles were prominent: Polevoi's *Moskovskii telegraf* was joined by M. P. Pogodin's *Moskovskii vestnik* (*Moscow Herald*), (1827–30) and N. I. Nadezhdin's *Teleskop* (*Telescope*), (1831–6), the latter being the main outlet for the Stankevich circle.

To differing degrees these incarnations of the Nicholaevan era began to transform themselves in important ways. First, journals now exhibited an 'encyclopaedic' subject focus: *Moskovskii telegraf* emphasised romantic fiction, but also carried information on current French fashions. Secondly, and as a result, they included longer prose essays and extracts, thus contributing not only to the spread of fiction, but also, as noted by Jon Klancher in regard to the late eighteenth century in England, to a new role as pinion of the public sphere; indeed, journals became the new public sphere by displacing the primary public gathering place (the salon) as the preferred medium of debate.[46] True, the debate was hardly politicised. While journals like *Syn otechestva* included the word 'political' in their titles, debate was clearly limited within the framework of Nicholaevan censorship. Yet journals did provide a forum for heated discussion. Often their arguments reflected their profiles. In the late 1820s, *Moskovskii telegraf* was a staunch proponent of romanticism, *Teleskop* (in the 1830s) an opponent. Often they voiced a topical concern: as in the debate on literary commercialisation led in 1835–6 by S. P. Shevyrev in *Moskovskii nabliudatel'* (*Moscow Observer*) (1835–9), N. V. Gogol in *Sovremennik* (*Contemporary*) (1836–66) and Belinsky in *Teleskop*.

In the foregrounding of the journal the circles played a nurturing role: one of the primary manifestos of the early 1830s was an essay published in *Teleskop* entitled 'Literaturnye mechtaniia' ('Literary Musings') by Belinsky (staunch member of the Stankevich circle).[47] But the journals were not merely the property of intellectuals. In fact, the great achievement of the 1830s was the broadening of reading across middle- to lower-class communities: largely due to a journal that was criticised for its intellectual poverty, Osip Senkovskii's *Biblioteka dlia chteniia* (*Library for Reading*). Begun in 1834, it quickly attracted a large following. Typical rates since the 1700s had been in the 600 to 1,200 range. In fact, it is no understatement to say that journalism prior to the appearance of *Biblioteka dlia chteniia* had existed for the few.[48] But *Biblioteka* soon reached 7,000 subscribers. Although this figure hardly matches some Western totals, it is worth noting a formula proposed by Prince Viazemskii in 1848: 'Sometimes a journal here has four or five thousand subscribers, consequently perhaps as many as 100,000 readers.'[49]

If true, where were these new readers from? Many thought the provinces. In this they followed Belinsky, who wrote graphically of *Biblioteka dlia chteniia*'s reception in those quarters. Contributors to the journal were heatedly supportive of landowner interests: indeed, it occasionally opened its pages to members of the provincial gentry for the discussion of agricultural questions. However, others give prominence to urban middle-level groups like civil servants and emerging professionals.[50] There was, however, another new audience in Russia – the merchantry – that was less aligned than the gentry, bureaucracy and professional ranks with the sometimes provocative journals noted above. In the West, the bourgeoisie played a major role in building civil society, but the Russian merchantry was less developed. Prominent Moscow merchant families such as the Alekseevs, Guchkovs, Usachevs, Kumanins, Dolgovs and Moskvins were hampered by socio-economic problems to such an extent that only the first two survived beyond mid-century. Moreover, Moscow merchants were 'distinguished above all by extremely narrow horizons... and a strong emphasis on religion'.[51] Their enterprises were primarily commercial, and they found little time for political involvement. For these reasons most observers discount the role of the merchantry in the development of civil society in Russia.

Perhaps most important in substantiating such an argument is the issue of literacy. The third merchant guild averaged 76,067 members from 1829 to 1835 (against 2,624 in the first and second guilds),[52] but it was the least educated. True, illiterate merchants were often successful. Besides the status achieved by the peasant millionaire Fedor Guchkov, P. A. Bugrov – an illiterate state peasant from Nizhnii Novgorod – acquired

7 million rubles.[53] Yet even when literate, merchants were often poorly educated. According to the Moscow School District Curator in 1819, children in gymnasia were those of poor provincial officials or merchants, and 'neither group finishes the whole course...' Thus, the prevailing image of merchants matched the following description of provincial Arkhangel'sk in 1834 by A. V. Nikitenko: 'The Russian merchants live in filth and trade like swindlers...'[54] Observers also noted the public reticence of the merchantry. The merchant memoirist G. T. Polilov-Severtsev criticised his grandfather for his guarded personality (although his reluctance to mention the Decembrist Revolt of 1825 was not uncommon).[55] This also applied to public office. Theoretically, the merchantry offered unpaid municipal service in return for freedom from military duty and corporal punishment. But as late as 1842, the Governor of Tula wrote that 'in almost all the cities the merchantry decline election to office'.[56]

Nevertheless, in the early 1800s, 'merchant life was beginning to be affected by the winds of change'.[57] Some merchants put on short German-style coats and shaved their beards. There is also evidence that merchants had begun to display interest in education and public service. The prominent agronomist A. T. Bolotov remembers a two-month stay in provincial Kozlov in 1788, where he held numerous philosophical discussions over tea with a merchant named Dmitrii Egorovich Borodin. The writer Alexander Herzen formed a good opinion of the educational level of merchants he encountered during his exile in Viatka in 1835.[58] Examples of public service may also be found. First-guild merchant I. F. Baranov from Vladimir inherited his father's manufacturing business in 1838 and agreed to serve as *gorodskaia golova* (mayor) of Aleksandrov by popular request.[59] As more and more merchants joined the public sphere, the press played an ever larger role in their lives. But in contrast to the situation with more privileged groups, the limited evidence of merchant reading more often emphasises newspapers.[60] In his article of 1802, the writer Karamzin contrasted the nobility's occasional lack of interest in newspapers with different practices among lower-class groups: 'the merchants and townspeople', he wrote, 'already love to read them'. In 1816, E. T. Polilov was setting up his own hemp business in St Petersburg, and preserved in his diary a newspaper clipping concerning awards received by Russian merchants for the application of steam to sugar refinement. Nor was this the only evidence of his interest in the press; around the time of the great Petersburg flood in November 1824, he included a clipping referring to a similar disaster on the island of Guadeloupe.[61]

Other such images abound. Merchant-class Russians, like other groups, attempted to avoid the high prices charged for printed materials prior to the 1830s by subscribing to the circulating libraries ever more frequently encountered on the Russian cultural scene.[62] E. T. Polilov, in St Petersburg, subscribed to a circulating library in 1832, as did the merchant youth I. V. Selivanov while at school in Moscow, also in the 1830s.[63] There were even some merchant-class women who began to acquire print materials, usually from a male relative. Polilov's youngest daughter, Iuliia, was an avid reader. Her tastes ranged from a story by Gogol, 'Noch' pod Ivana Kupala' – found in an earlier version (1820–30) of *Otechestvennye zapiski* – to women's fashions appearing in 1831 in the newspaper *Severnyi Merkurii* (*Northern Mercury*). Iuliia also indulged in the contemporary practice of reading aloud with her father. Their reading included materials from the press: she attempted to read to him from *Severnyi Merkurii*, but he asked instead that she read from the largely military newspaper, *Russkii invalid*, as an example of better writing.[64]

Indeed, just as journals were broadening their grasp among different social groups, so too were newspapers. Most earlier papers were official organs, but the most prominent new title, Bulgarin's *Severnaia pchela*, was a private undertaking: though since Bulgarin was a government agent it was heavily subsidised for 'services rendered'. It was also noteworthy in other respects. After six years as a thrice-weekly publication, in 1831 it became Russia's only daily paper (indicating its popularity). Its tie with the government earned it the privilege of becoming the first unofficial paper authorised to carry political news. In fact, the presence of political news was the main source, thought Pushkin, of its impressive readership.[65] *Severnaia pchela*'s readers included socio-cultural groups relatively new to the sphere of news and comment. Among the new audiences were legions of civil servants required by the bureaucracy of early nineteenth-century Russia, and who began to participate in the strengthening public sphere through the medium of newpapers. Indeed, as noted by the critic Pavel Annenkov:

> We left Petersburg [in 1840] engaged in an occupation unusual for it. Petersburg had taken up the reading of foreign newspapers... Ten years previously, in the early 1830s, our public had been very little interested even in such an event as the French Revolution of 1830 ... Now the situation was somewhat different ... What had previously constituted ... a privilege of the highest aristocratic and government spheres now became a common practice.[66]

Besides its growing influence on various social groups, there were other sites of the developing public sphere where the press played a role. Political clubs *per se* were not a feature of the Russian scene, but Petersburg and Moscow society were well equipped with social – and commercial – clubs. The oldest was the St Petersburg English Society (S. Peterburgskoe angliiskoe sobranie), founded in March 1770. It arose from the custom practised by foreign traders – largely Englishmen – of gathering in one of the local hotels, where they spent time conversing, reading newspapers and playing cards.[67] Despite the fact that foreigners were largely responsible for its founding, Russian names began to appear in the lists of members. By 1780, so many people wanted to join that the membership total was sealed at 300, and it was decided to admit no members with ranks higher than 'Brigadier': an important feature from the perspective of broadening social interaction.[68] Nevertheless, many prominent figures belonged, and it was perhaps because of fear of foreign influence that in 1798, the Society was closed for three days in the darkest period of Paul I's reign. But in 1801, the membership cap was raised, and in 1802, the Diplomatic School was given special privileges, and many foreign diplomatic personnel attended the annual dinners. In the period 1808–10 an attempt was made to russify the club by compiling its records in Russian (rather than German), but this did not take root until 1817.[69]

Besides this club, St Petersburg's Noblemen's and Merchants' clubs were also well known. Moscow had four by the early nineteenth century: the English, German, Noblemen's and Commercial clubs. Custine recorded that the Petersburg Noblemen's Club gave magnificent winter balls; indeed, some clubs reached a healthy size. Although the membership of the Petersburg English Club was relatively modest, the Noblemen's Club accommodated as many as 3,000 persons.[70] Nor were these clubs socially exclusive. True, the journalist Faddei Bulgarin, in his novel *Ivan Vyzhigin* (1829), paints the Moscow English Club as the haunt of high society: 'Old men ... [among whom] the distinction of rank is observed ...'[71] But besides the move to exclude high ranks seen in Petersburg, both Moscow's Commercial Club and the Noblemen's Club admitted *raznochintsy* (men of different ranks),[72] constituting an association of people of the middle sphere. And, despite their service as 'safe havens', the clubs were not restricted to men: ladies of 'middle rank' visited the Commercial Club's evening dances.

Coffee houses also grew in importance in Russia in the early nineteenth century, although they were not portrayed by visitors as active public fora. Even in 1839, the acerbic Custine was to note: 'The interior of a Russian coffeehouse is very curious ... The waiters ... serve you with excellent tea ... coffee and liqueurs; but this is done with a silence and solemnity very different from the noisy gaiety which reigns in the cafés of Paris.'[73] However, A. D. Galakhov's memoir of Moscow's new coffee house indicates otherwise; the café received visitors morning, noon and night.[74] They included artists and teachers, as well as some who worked with different organs of the press.

In both clubs and coffee houses, news sources were well in evidence. From the date of its foundation in 1770, the St Petersburg English Society set aside a room for the reading of foreign and local newspapers to which the Society subscribed. They were clearly used, for one of the Society's first rules was the imposition of a 5 ruble fine for newspapers removed from the premises.[75] Much later in 1836, the Marquis of Londonderry found it to contain 'all the Russian and some German and French journals', and Kohl noted that Petersburg coffee houses were provided with 'the best English, French and German newspapers'.[76] The availability of Western imprints is confirmed by Cynthia Whittaker, who notes – in reference to a slightly later date – that the young *raznochinets* Nikolai Chernyshevskii (born in 1828 to the family of a Saratov priest) 'could sit in St Petersburg tea-houses and read the *Journal des débats* and other Western publications'.[77]

The central coffee house in Moscow also provided Russian newspapers like *Severnaia pchela* and journals like *Biblioteka dlia chteniia*, *Otechestvennye zapiski*, and *Moskovskii nabliudatel'* (which served as enticements along with billiards). Furthermore, new issues helped heighten the public debate according to Galakhov, since 'the conversations and pronouncements, always more or less heated, and transforming themselves into unfinished arguments, became even more lively and noisy with the publication of a new issue of a monthly journal, or some newspaper feuilleton or other (in *Severnaia pchela* on Saturdays)'.[78] That the journals created frequent arguments stemmed from the fact that:

readers had already divided into literary parties that held different opinions on the direction, contents and other particularities of the periodical press. Some preferred *Biblioteka dlia chteniia* for its ... wit and for the choice of articles ... others, in contrast, preferred *Otechestvennye zapiski* and *Moskovskii nabliudatel'* as more serious publications with an educational bent. The only private newpaper of the time, *Severnaia pchela*, which drove away a certain circle of readers with the *feuilletons* of Bulgarin, in fact attracted another circle by the same *feuilletons*, and appealed by its accessiblity of content, ease and transparency of argument, wit, humour, and smooth and melting language.[79]

The Russian public sphere also received reinforcement from the theatre. In fact, theatres often gave rise to coffee houses: Galakhov notes that, as in Europe, cafés arose close to theatres because actors needed a space in which to prepare for and review performances.[80] But the theatre itself – unlike many other Russian institutions – had always been linked with the lower portion of society. Thus, even as theatres became more gentrified as the eighteenth century progressed, they retained their identity as a public gathering place associated with average citizens: court theatre attendance encouraged by Anna Ivanovna and Elizabeth Petrovna was deliberately also made available to well-dressed merchants, in order to swell audiences.[81] The mixing of classes was a trend that continued, especially away from St Petersburg. Moscow audiences were more democratic:

besides civil servants they included merchant youths 'avid for culture', and drawn even to Shakespeare. The enthusiasm of civil servants is confirmed by A. A. Kharytonov, who entered the War Ministry in 1835. When he became office assistant, he had time for cultural activities, but once he became section chief, his work left him no time 'for reading or for frequent visits to the theatre': a change he regretted.[82] And although the middle-level Moscow goldsmith P. M. Vishniakov was too busy to attend himself, he allowed his children to do so.[83]

Russian audiences were also able to feed their appetites for drama through the medium of the press. The 1820s saw a sharp rise of interest in West European romanticism and drama, and this was largely promoted by various journals of the time. These included *Syn otechestva*, *Moskovskii vestnik*, *Moskovskii telegraf* and *Teleskop*.[84] Authors like Shakespeare, Goethe, Schiller, Scott and Hugo were widely represented in these journals, and their appearance in print clearly prepared audiences for live performances. Besides Shakespeare (in translation) and Schiller, the 1820s saw a number of dramatic representations from Scott's novels earn widespread recognition. Indeed, the theatrical element in Scott's overwhelming popularity in Russia was vital: although he did not reach the height of his fame until the second half of the decade, the plays based on his works had been performed since 1821, and it was even the practice to attend society balls wearing costumes drawn from Scott's novels.[85]

The enthusiasm of audiences for live theatre notwithstanding, it is clear that the authorities feared the press as an equally powerful source of public interest in drama. This is seen in the closure of Polevoi's *Moskovskii telegraf* in 1834 precisely because its negative review of a patriotic play by N. V. Kukol'nik (that lauded the Emperor) would probably be read by too many people to permit the embarrassment to be overlooked. The public's enthusiasm for *Moskovskii telegraf* – often termed the best journal of the period – was probably not misread by the authorities. This journal contained a wide range of romantic material, prompting the critic A. A. Grigor'ev to ask in 1861: 'Is it any wonder that everything young and fresh was enthralled by it?'[86] Polevoi's review was merely the final straw in a long series of articles unpopular with the government, but the fact that a brief review of a play was considered sufficient grounds for closure underscores the growing power in Russia of both the theatre and the press as instruments of public engagement.

Admittedly less 'public' than the gatherings in nearby theatres (but representing a sphere of socio-cultural interaction that was equally, if not more, compelling to those who belonged) were the numerous masonic lodges that arose in Russia throughout the period under review. The lodges necessarily constituted private gathering places until 1810, but then the government summoned lodge directors to the Ministry of Police and, while placing them under government control and requiring their documents for review, gave official sanction to their existence.[87] A less well-known characteristic of the lodges is that they boasted a complex social composition. Russian freemasonry is often viewed as limited to the nobility: D. D. Lotareva described Russian masons as 'largely from nobility in the capitals and provinces', though some were 'representatives of university and literary circles, and artistic types'.[88] But as Douglas Smith has noted, 'the lodges ... remained open to all groups that formed the Russian public'.[89] And Russians from different spheres did indeed belong. Although among the more than 3,000 Russian masons in the eighteenth century around 1,100 came from the military and civil service, the next largest group comprised 300 or so merchants.[90] The Moscow Astreia lodge active in 1783 included merchants, while in 1788 St Petersburg's Urania lodge admitted two Jewish merchants, who rose quickly through the hierarchy. In fact, the urban lodges in which foreigners predominated were often composed primarily of merchants (as in the case of the Holy Catherine lodge in Arkhangel'sk).[91] With this in mind, it is interesting to ask whether there was any connection between the involvement of Russian merchants in masonic lodges and the fact that numerous Russian merchants of the early nineteenth century were more cultured and interested in serious publications than is usually thought to be the case.[92]

It is, of course, common knowledge that masons were a particularly bookish group: more than 2,000 Russian titles of a mystical and aesthetic character are known, not counting many manuscript titles. It thus seems likely that merchants who joined the lodges were encouraged to read masonic literature (and the fact that most masonic literature consisted of manuscript copies of foreign texts in Russian translation would not have put these titles beyond their grasp).[93] The converts would then have been in a position to foster intellectual practices amongst others in their immediate circle. It is also possible that merchants encountered masonry in other ways. For besides meetings at the lodges, correspondence and the fruits of printing presses (both official and secret), other methods of proselytisation were speeches at the Friendly Society (Druzheskoe obshchestvo) and public lectures.[94] It is known that in addition to their visits to theatres, merchants also began to attend university lectures in Moscow in the early nineteenth century:[95] they may therefore have attended masonic lectures at the same time. If true, this would constitute a fascinating component of the developing Russian public sphere that has hardly been imagined. Nevertheless, extensive research remains to be done.

The three institutions mentioned above (clubs, theatres and lodges) all served as a public gathering spaces for groups that included the middle ranks of Russian society, but additional institutions played a similar role. One more may be mentioned: the learned society, which grew in significance during these years. Notable dates include the creation of the Volnoe ekonomicheskoe obshchestvo (Free Economic Society) in 1765 and the Moskovskoe obshchestvo istorii i drevnostei rossiiskikh (Moscow Society of History and Russian Antiquities) founded at Moscow University in 1804. In 1805, the University of Kazan founded its own historical society, as did the University of Kharkov in 1817.[96] The intersection between these societies and the press was not always marked: the main project of the Moscow History Society (a critical edition of the chronicles) did not progress rapidly. But the wheel had been set in motion. In reference to the late 1840s, Lincoln notes that the prevailing view of *glasnost'* (as a means to permit men who supported change to participate in a broader discussion) was nowhere more evident than in the activities of certain civil servants connected with the Imperial Russian Geographical Society, whose main organ, *Geograficheskie izvestiia* (*Geographical News*), became a major repository for discussion of the peasant question.[97] In other words, this cursory survey of selected social groups and public sites – and their links with the press – has underscored the extent to which the Russian public sphere was developing in the first half of the nineteenth century.

This chapter has demonstrated that in many respects the greater Russian public – despite its lack of opportunities – was not the unthinking, uncritical, or even non-existent, mass that it is sometimes portrayed as being. True, the writer Ivan Turgenev – much like Gershenzon after him – had the following to say about Russia under Nicholas I: 'Although "lettres" existed at this time, "literature" did not . . . regardless of greatly talented individuals, literature as a profession, with standards at least partially or implicitly recognized by a large public . . . did not yet exist . . . or only in the most impoverished form.'[98] But the evidence presented here indicates that in many arenas, public engagement, interaction and debate on literary and other topics were indeed beginning to occur. Even more importantly, the Russian press was not as ineffective as is sometimes suggested. Again, the evidence presented here serves to highlight the extent of its dissemination. This is further confirmed by foreign travel accounts: the Englishman Richard Venables noted in 1837 the presence of newspapers in every home.[99] Even allowing for exaggeration, it is fair to point to a marked upswing in access to, and interest in, newspapers and other forms of periodical publication taking place towards the end of the period under review, and preparing some sectors of the public for more solid social engagement in the period of the Great Reforms beginning in 1861.

NOTES

1 Margaret C. Jacob, 'The Mental Landscape of the Public Sphere: a European Perspective', *Eighteenth-Century Studies*, 28, 1 (fall 1994), 95–113, p. 96. See also Marvin B. Becker, *The Emergence of Civil Society in the Eighteenth Century: A Privileged Moment in the History of England, Scotland and France* (Bloomington, IN, 1994).
2 Important sources for the socio-cultural and political development of the period under review include Janet Hartley, *A Social History of the Russian Empire 1650–1825* (London, 1999); Gary Marker, *Publishing, Printing and the Origins of Intellectual Life in Russia, 1700–1800* (Princeton, NJ, 1985); Nicholas Riasanovsky, *A Parting of Ways: Government and the Educated Public in Russia, 1801–1855* (Oxford, 1976); David Saunders, *Russia in the Age of Reaction and Reform, 1801–1881* (London, 1992); and Elise Kimerling Wirtschafter, *Structures of Society: Imperial Russia's People of Various Ranks* (DeKalb, IL, 1994).
3 See A. G. Mazour, *The First Russian Revolution, 1825* (Stanford, CA, 1961).
4 Marc Raeff, *Michael Speransky, Statesman of Imperial Russia, 1772–1839* (The Hague, 1969), p. 291; L. P. Burmistrova, *Provintsial'naia gazeta v epokhu russkikh prosvetitelei: gubernskie vedomosti Povolzh'ia i Urala 1840–1850 gg.* (Kazan, 1985), pp. 39, 41–2. Most provincial gazettes emerged after 1838, when governors began to follow instructions from the Ministry of the Interior to publish such titles regularly.
5 W. Bruce Lincoln, 'The Problem of *Glasnost'* in Mid-Nineteenth-Century Russian Politics', *European Studies Review*, 11 (1981), 171–88, p. 172.
6 Marc Raeff, 'Transfiguration and Modernization: the Paradoxes of Social Disciplining, Paedagogical Leadership and the Enlightenment in Eighteenth-Century Russia', in Hans Erich Bödeker and Ernst Hinrichs (eds.), *Alteuropa – Ancien Regime – Frühe Neuzeit: Probleme und Methoden der Forschung* (Stuttgart, 1991), 99–115, p. 109, quoted by Douglas Smith, *Working the Rough Stone: Freemasonry and Society in Eighteenth-Century Russia* (DeKalb, IL, 1999), p. 58.
7 A. N. Radishchev, *A Journey from St Petersburg to Moscow*, ed. R. P. Thaler (Cambridge, 1958), pp. 165–6.
8 Jay Jensen and Richard Bayley, 'Highlights of the Development of Russian Journalism, 1553–1917', *Journalism Quarterly*, 41 (summer 1964), 403–15, 436, p. 403.
9 Radishchev, *A Journey from St Petersburg to Moscow*, pp. 164–5, 171.
10 Sidney Monas, *The Third Section: Police and Society in Russia under Nicholas I* (Cambridge, 1961), pp. 135–6. Besides its impracticality, the ban exposed the authorities to ridicule because it included printed music.
11 See especially Charles A. Ruud, *Fighting Words; Imperial Censorship and the Russian Press, 1804–1906* (Toronto, 1982).
12 Monas, *The Third Section*, p. 136; V. G. Berezina, *Russkaia zhurnalistika pervoi chetverti XIX veka* (Leningrad, 1965), p. 54.
13 A primary source for this development is 'Unichtozheniia masonskikh lozh v Rossii 1822 g.', *Russkaia starina*, 18 (March 1877), 455–79; (April 1877), 641–64.
14 Saunders, *Russia in the Age of Reaction and Reform*, p. 155.
15 Lincoln, 'The Problem of *Glasnost*", p. 173.

16 Marquis de Custine, *Empire of the Czar: A Journey Through Eternal Russia* (New York, 1990), p. 269.
17 Jensen and Bayley, 'Highlights of the Development of Russian Journalism', pp. 403–5; B. I. Esin, *Russkaia dorevoliutsionnaia gazeta, 1702–1917: kratkii ocherk* (Moscow, 1971), pp. 10–14; P. N. Berkov, *Istoriia russkoi zhurnalistiki XVIII veka* (Moscow, 1952), p. 64. The high price of printed materials was an issue up until the early nineteenth century. Even then, when an annual subscription to *Sanktpeterburgskie vedomosti* cost 40 rubles, the monthly wage of an average civil servant amounted to no more than 60–80 rubles, or 840 a year; see Sergei Gessen, *Knigoizdatel' Aleksandr Pushkin* (Leningrad, 1930), p. 19.
18 Esin, *Russkaia dorevoliutsionnaia gazeta*, pp. 15–16.
19 Jensen and Bayley, 'Highlights of the Development of Russian Journalism', p. 407.
20 For more on this special role of Russian almanacs see below, and also M. Beaven Remnek, 'Russian Literary Almanacs of the 1820s and Their Legacy', *Publishing History*, 17 (1985), 65–86.
21 Esin, *Russkaia dorevoliutsionnaia gazeta*, p. 17. Sources differ as to production totals. Jensen and Bayley, 'Highlights of the Development of Russian Journalism', p. 407, cite eighty-two new periodicals between 1801 and 1811. On this period see also Berezina, *Russkaia zhurnalistika pervoi chetverti XIX veka*.
22 E. S. Likhtenstein, 'Akademicheskaia kniga', in *400 let russkogo knigopechataniia, 1564–1964*, vol. 1: *Russkoe knigopechatanie do 1917* (Moscow, 1964), 257–67, p. 264; Jensen and Bayley, 'Highlights of the Development of Russian Journalism', pp. 407–8.
23 M. N. Kufaev, *Istoriia russkoi knigi v XIX veke* (Leningrad, 1927), pp. 60–61.
24 N. M. Lisovskii, *Bibliografiia russkoi periodicheskoi pechati 1703–1900 gg.* (Petrograd, 1915), p. 51; Esin, *Russkaia dorevoliutsionnaia gazeta*, p. 17.
25 J. L. Black, *Nicholas Karamzin and Russian Society in the Nineteenth Century: a Study in Russian Political and Historical Thought* (Toronto, 1975), pp. 137, 142. It should not be assumed that the multi-volume history was disseminated merely to upper-level Russians. The German traveller J. G. Kohl remarked that in 1837 he often saw a group of merchants' servants sitting together listening to one who read aloud, and Karamzin's *Istoriia* was a title he often saw in their hands: J. G. Kohl, *Russia: St Petersburgh, Moscow, Kharkoff*... (London, 1842), p. 223.
26 Esin, *Russkaia dorevoliutsionnaia gazeta*, p. 17; Jensen and Bayley, 'Highlights of the Development of Russian Journalism', p. 408.
27 M. V. Muratov, *Knizhnoe delo v Rossii v XIX i XX vekakh; ocherk istorii knigoizdatel'stva i knigotorgovli, 1800–1917 gody* (Moscow, 1931), p. 56.
28 V. G. Berezina, 'Zhurnal N. A. Polevogo *Moskovskii telegraf* (1825–1834) i chitatel' ', *Vestnik Leningradskogo universiteta* 2 (1981), 38–44, p. 38.
29 *Biblioteka dlia chteniia* immediately drew new readers in the provinces to sport a total of 5–7,000 subscribers: far more than the 1,200 subscribers to *Moskovskii telegraf*. And it is likely that, to some extent at least, *Biblioteka dlia chteniia*'s expanding readership was not the audience associated with

Moskovskii telegraf but the broader audience already associated with *Severnaia pchela* (which drew from 4,000 to perhaps as many as 10,000 subscribers during its early years). On *Severnaia pchela*'s circulation rates see B. D. Datsiuk, *Russkaia zhurnalistika 30-kh godov* (Moscow, 1948), p. 6. Datsiuk suggests 10,000 – as does Arline Boyer ('A Description of Selected Periodicals in the First Half of the Nineteenth Century', *Russian Literature Triquarterly*, 3 (1972), 465–73, p. 469). It is possible that they derive this figure from an estimate given by Moscow University professor S. P. Shevyrev ('Slovesnost' i torgovlia', *Moskovskii nabliudatel'*, 1 (March 1835), 5–29, p. 8).

30 V. G. Sirotkin, 'Russkaia pressa pervogo chetverti XIX veka na inostrannykh iazykakh kak istoricheskii istochnik', *Istoriia SSSR*, 4 (1976), 77–97, p. 77.

31 Jacob, 'The Mental Landscape of the Public Sphere', p. [95].

32 A major resource for this topic is William Mills Todd, *Fiction and Society in the Age of Pushkin: Ideology, Institutions, and Narrative* (Cambridge, MA, 1986).

33 See especially B. Hollingsworth, 'Arzamas: Portrait of a Literary Society', *Slavonic and East European Review*, 44 (1966), 306–26.

34 N. M. Karamzin, 'O knizhnoi torgovle i liubvi ko chteniiu v Rossii', in his *Sochineniia*, 3 vols. (St Petersburg, 1848), vol. III, 545–50, p. 546.

35 V. F. Odoevskii, 'The Sylphide', in *Russian 19th-Century Gothic Tales* (Moscow, 1984), 297–320, p. 298; P. Karatygin, '*Severnaia pchela*, 1825–1859', *Russkii arkhiv*, 4 (1882), 241–303, p. 280; Custine, *Empire of the Czar*, p. 241.

36 A. O. Smirnova, *Zapiski, dnevnik, vospominaniia, pis'ma* (Moscow, 1929), p. 66; P. A. Viazemskii, 'Salon A. O. Smirnovoi-Rosset', in N. L. Brodskii (ed.), *Literaturnye salony i kruzhki: pervaia polovina XIX veka* (Moscow, 1930), 208–12, p. 210.

37 The figures are taken from T. S. Grits, V. Trenin and M. Nikitin, *Slovesnost' i kommertsiia: knizhnaia lavka A. F. Smirdina* (Moscow, 1929), pp. 190–91.

38 Quoted in Nicholas Riasanovsky, *A Parting of Ways*, pp. 164–5.

39 Russian literary monthlies of the nineteenth century were known as 'thick journals' (*tolstye zhurnaly*) because of their many pages. A key source is Deborah A. Martinsen (ed.), *Literary Journals in Imperial Russia* (Cambridge, 1997).

40 A portion of *Gore ot uma* was published in the almanac *Russkaia Talia* in 1825.

41 This is suggested by a review of four almanacs in my research database of 11,898 subscriptions to twenty-two Russian imprints, 1825–46. The titles in question are *Mnemozina* (1825), *Nevskii al'manakh* (1830), *Sirotka: literaturnyi al'manakh* (1831) and *Russkaia beseda* (1841, 1842) – for which the subscription totals are only 157, 48, 162 and 626. Furthermore, the subscriptions came largely from high-ranked subscribers; the first two titles included entries for only two and seven merchants respectively.

42 The major source remains Brodskii (ed.), *Literaturnye salony i kruzhki: pervaia polovina XIX veka*.

43 Edward J. Brown, *Stankevich and his Moscow Circle, 1830–1840* (Stanford, CA, 1966), pp. 4–17. Admittedly the concept of circles is usually applied to relatively small intellectual elites. But as I stress in my dissertation – 'The Expansion of Reading Audiences in Russia, 1828–1848', University of California, Berkeley (1999), p. 189 – one can also apply the concept to other

newer gatherings (like groups of female friends and young professionals) that grew in number in addition to the more traditional, male-dominated, family reading circles.
44 M. O. Gershenzon, *Istoriia molodoi Rossii* (Moscow, 1908), p. 212.
45 Brown, *Stankevich and his Moscow Circle*, pp. 7, 12.
46 For Klancher's discussion see his *Making of English Reading Audiences, 1790–1832* (Madison, WI, 1987), p. 23. As noted in my dissertation (p. 203), the designation of the salon as a 'public' space is a relative concept in the Nicholaevan context (the salons were far from accessible to the average Russian). But the emphasis here is on large social gatherings as opposed to intimate readings.
47 According to D. S. Mirsky, this essay may be regarded as 'the beginning of Russian intelligentsia journalism' (*A History of Russian Literature from its Beginnings to 1900* (New York, 1958), p. 172). At this time Belinsky stood for the expression of social consciousness in literature, establishing the civic trend later so powerful in Russian criticism (W. E. Harkins, *Dictionary of Russian Literature* (Westport, CT, 1971), p. 165).
48 M. A. Antifeeva, 'Zhurnal A. Smirdina *Biblioteka dlia chteniia*', in *Knizhnoe delo Peterburga-Petrograda-Leningrada: sbornik nauchnykh trudov* (Leningrad, 1981), 37–47, p. 44.
49 M. I. Gillel'son, *P. A. Viazemskii: zhizn' i tvorchestvo* (Leningrad, 1969), p. 324.
50 V. G. Belinsky, 'Nichto o nichem, ili otchet g. izdateliu *Teleskopa* za poslednee polugodie russkoi literatury', in idem, *Polnoe sobranie sochinenii*, 13 vols. (Moscow, 1953–9), vol. II, 7–50, p. 20; Datsiuk, *Russkaia zhurnalistika 30-kh godov*, pp. 8–9; V. G. Berezina, *Russkaia zhurnalistika vtoroi chetverti XIX veka (1826–1839 gg.)* (Leningrad, 1965), p. 20.
51 Jo Ann Ruckman, *The Moscow Business Elite: a Social and Cultural Portrait of Two Generations, 1840–1905* (DeKalb, IL, 1984), pp. 16, 75.
52 Calculated from Roger Portal, 'Aux origines d'une bourgeoisie industrielle en Russie', *Revue d'histoire moderne et contemporaine*, 8 (1961), 35–60, p. 38.
53 Ruckman, *The Moscow Business Elite*, p. 75; Manfred Hildermeier, 'Social Change in the Russian Merchantry During the First Half of the Nineteenth Century', in D. K. Rowney (ed.), *Imperial Power and Development: Papers on Prerevolutionary Russian History; Selected Papers From the Third World Congress for Soviet and East European Studies* (Columbus, OH, 1990), 116–33, pp. 125–6.
54 R. G. Eimontova, 'Prosveshchenie v Rossii pervoi poloviny XIX veka', *Voprosy istorii*, 6, 10 (1986), 78–93, p. 84; Aleksandr Nikitenko, *The Diary of a Russian Censor*, ed. and trans. Helen Saltz Jacobson (Amherst, MA, 1975), p. 51.
55 G. T. Polilov-Severtsev, 'Iz dedovskoi khroniki', in idem, *Nashi dedy-kuptsy: bytovye kartiny nachala XIX stoletiia* (St Petersburg, 1907), 1–80, p. 24.
56 Thomas C. Owen, *The Corporation under Russian Law, 1800–1917: a Study in Tsarist Economic Policy* (Cambridge, 1991), p. 10; Daniel Brower, 'Urbanization and Autocracy: Russian Urban Development in the First Half of the Nineteenth Century', *Russian Review*, 42 (1983), 377–402, p. 397.
57 Ruckman, *The Moscow Business Elite*, p. 75.
58 A. T. Bolotov, *Zapiski Andreia Timofeevicha Bolotova, 1738–1794*, 4 vols. (St Petersburg, 1871–3), vol. IV, pp. 413, 416, 427, 431, 459; Burmistrova, *Provintsial'naia gazeta v epokhu russkikh prosvititelei*, p. 62.

59 *Nekotorye cherty iz zhizni Aleksandrovskogo 1-i gil'dii kuptsa i pochetnogo grazhdanina Ivana Fedorovicha Baranova* (Moscow, 1849), p. 16.
60 I refer here to organs of the press, and do not imply that merchants read only newspapers. My dissertation has shown not only a surprising degree of merchant interest in reference materials, but more especially an enthusiasm for fiction that was proportionately greater than in other middle- to lower-ranked groups like lesser civil servants and professionals.
61 Karamzin, 'O knizhnoi torgovle i liubvi ko chteniiu v Rossii', vol. III, p. 546; Polilov-Severtsev, 'Iz dedovskoi khroniki', pp. 12, 21.
62 The traveller J. G. Kohl observed that he saw 'an abundance' of circulating libraries in St Petersburg in 1837 (*Russia: St. Petersburgh, Moscow, Kharkoff...*, p. 89). For more on the libraries see especially A. A. Zaitseva, '"Kabinety dlia chteniia" v Sankt-Peterburge kontsa XVIII-nachala XIX veka', in *Russkie biblioteki i chastnye sobraniia XVI-XIX vekov* (Leningrad, 1979), 29–34.
63 Polilov-Severtsev, 'Iz dedovskoi khroniki', p. 32; I. V. Selivanov, 'Vospominaniia o Moskovskom kommercheskom uchilische, 1831–1838 godov', *Russkii vestnik*, 36, 12 (1861), 719–54, p. 752.
64 G. T. Polilov-Severtsev, 'Divan: dnevnik kupecheskoi devushki', in idem, *Nashi dedy-kuptsy: bytovye kartiny nachala XIX stoletiia* (St Petersburg, 1907), 83–142, pp. 107, 123.
65 Berezina, *Russkaia zhurnalistika vtoroi chetverti XIX veka*, p. 53.
66 Pavel Annenkov, *The Extraordinary Decade: Literary Memoirs*, ed. Arthur Mendel, trans. Irwin Titunik (Ann Arbor, MI, 1968), p. 62.
67 *Stoletie S. Peterburgskogo angliiskogo sobraniia, 1770–1870* (St Petersburg, 1870), pp. 1–3. Membership fees had risen to 150 rubles a year by 1820 (p. 14).
68 This point should not be taken too far. Imperial Russian society was heavily dependent on a system of service ranks known as the Table of Ranks, founded by Peter the Great in 1722. It involved three spheres (court, military and civil), each one composed of fourteen ranks. The rank of *brigadir* did not survive into the nineteenth century, but in the eighteenth it was equivalent to the early nineteenth-century rank 5 (*statskii sovetnik*), a rank of considerable stature conferring hereditary nobility (James Hassell, 'Implementation of the Russian Table of Ranks During the Eighteenth Century', *Slavic Review*, 29 (1970), 283–95, p. 284).
69 *Stoletie S. Peterburgskogo angliiskogo sobraniia*, pp. 5–15.
70 Custine, *Empire of the Czar*, p. 439.
71 Faddei Bulgarin, *Ivan Vejeeghen, or, Life in Russia*, 2 vols. (London, 1831), vol. I, p. 218. The German Club catered to an even lower audience, 'predominantly artisans'; however, its clientele was primarily foreign and so less relevant as an integral component of the Russian public sphere.
72 The term *raznochintsy* was used to describe the increasing numbers of Russians who did not strictly belong to the one of the four traditional 'estates' in Russian society (nobles, priests, townspeople and peasants). They included groups like retired soldiers, sons of men with lifetime nobility, sons of priests, educated commoners, semi-professionals, and so forth.
73 Custine, *Empire of the Czar*, pp. 440–41.
74 A. D. Galakhov, 'Literaturnaia kofeinia v Moskve v 1830–1840 gg.', *Russkaia starina*, 50, 4 (1886), 181–98, p. 182.

75 *Stoletie S. Peterburgskogo angliiskogo sobraniia*, p. 3.
76 Charles Vane (Marquis of Londonderry), *Recollections of a Tour in the North of Europe*, 2 vols. (London, 1838), vol. 1, p. 100; Kohl, *Russia: St. Petersburgh, Moscow, Kharkoff*..., p. 210.
77 Cynthia Whittaker, *The Origins of Modern Russian Education; an Intellectual Biography of Count Sergei Uvarov, 1786–1855* (DeKalb, IL, 1984), p. 119.
78 Galakhov, 'Literaturnaia kofeinia v Moskve', pp. 182–3.
79 Ibid., pp. 184–5. It is obvious that Galakhov's remarks do not refer to the early 1830s. *Moskovskii nabliudatel'* began publication in 1835, and *Otechestvennye zapiski* did not re-emerge until 1839 – although its impact on the press scene was immediate.
80 Galakhov, 'Literaturnaia kofeinia v Moskve', p. 181.
81 Malcolm Burgess, 'Russian Public Theater Audiences of the Eighteenth and Early Nineteenth Centuries', *Slavonic and East European Review*, 37, 88 (December 1958), 160–83, pp. 160–63.
82 Mirsky, *History of Russian Literature*, p. 146; A. A. Kharytonov, 'Iz vospominanii', *Russkaia starina*, 81 (January 1894), 101–32, p. 120; (February 1894), 96–130, p. 97.
83 B. B. Kafengauz, 'Kupecheskie memuary XIX v.', in *Moskovskii krai v ego proshlom* (Moscow, 1928), 105–28, p. 114.
84 I. I. Zamotin, *Romanticheskii idealizm v russkom obshchestve i literature 20–30-kh godov XIX stoletiia* (St Petersburg, 1907), pp. 86–7.
85 Ibid., pp. 87–9, 149; Iu. D. Levin, 'Prizhiznennaia slava Val'tera Skotta v Rossii', in *Epokha romantizma: iz istorii mezhdunarodnykh sviazei russkoi literatury* (Leningrad, 1975), 5–57, p. 7.
86 Berezina, *Russkaia zhurnalistika vtoroi chetverti XIX veka*, p. 38; A. A. Grigor'ev, *My Literary and Moral Wanderings* (New York, 1962), p. 78.
87 A. N. Pypin, *Masonstvo v Rossii: XVIII i pervaia chetvert' XIX v.* (Moscow, 1997), p. 333.
88 D. D. Lotareva, 'Nekotorye istochnikovedcheskie problemy izucheniia masonskoi knizhnosti v Rossii v kontse XVIII-pervoi polovine XIX veka', in *Mirovospriiatie i samosoznanie russkogo obshchestva (XI–XX vv.): sbornik statei* (Moscow, 1994), 142–63, p. 142.
89 Smith, *Working the Rough Stone*, p. 23.
90 Ibid., p. 24.
91 Ibid., pp. 27–8.
92 In my own research database of 11,898 subscriptions to twenty-two Russian imprints published 1825–46, 9.1 per cent emanated from the merchantry.
93 Lotareva, 'Nekotorye istochnikovedcheskie problemy izucheniia masonskoi knizhnosti', p. 146.
94 Ibid., p. 143.
95 Eimontova, 'Prosveshchenie v Rossii pervoi poloviny XIX veka', p. 82.
96 Anatole G. Mazour, *Modern Russian Historiography* (Westport, CT, 1975), p. 70.
97 Lincoln, 'The Problem of *Glasnost*", p. 176.
98 Monas, *The Third Section*, p. 133.
99 Richard Venables, *Domestic Scenes in Russia* (London, 1838), p. 131.

Index

Abeille du nord, 25, 40
Abréviateur universel, 194
Absolutism, and public sphere, 17
Académie française, 176
academies, 207
Academy of Sciences, 227, 228
Accademia letteraria, 218
Act of Union, 113, 122, 123
Actes des apôtres, 194, 196–7 n. 2
Adams, John, 33, 140–1, 146, 151, 152, 170
Addison, Alexander, 140
advertisement tax, 119, 124
advertising, 3
　in cosmopolitan press, 27
　in Dutch papers, 51
　in Ireland, 115, 119, 124, 126, 129
　in Italy, 204, 206
　in Britain, 100, 108
advertising papers, 73, 159
　see also *Affiches*
Advocaat der Nationale Vrijheid, 63
Affaires de l'Angleterre et de l'Amérique, 33, 160, 175
Affiches, 183, 188
Albany Gazette, 148
Albany Plan of Union, 146
Alekseev, A. V., 235
Alexander I, 226, 228, 229
Alexander II, 226
Alien and Sedition Acts (US), 8, 140–1, 151
Allemannia, 83
Allgemeine Deutsche Bibliothek, 72–3
Allgemeine Zeitung, 38, 77–8
almanacs, 228, 231–2, 244 n. 41
Altona, 28
Ambigu, 25, 27, 40–1
America, 140–158
　foreign reporting in, during colonial period, 146
　government printing contracts in, during colonial period, 148
　libel laws in, during colonial period, 150
　newspaper content in, during colonial period, 145
　number of newspapers in, 148–9
　patriot press in, during colonial period, 150
　see also United States
American Revolution, 26, 28, 35, 161, 177
　and French press, 164, 173, 174, 175
　coercion of newspapers during, 151
　influence on German press, 69
American Revolutionary War, 49
Ami du peuple, 185, 188, 192
Ami du roi, 184
Amiens, peace of, 38
Amsterdam, 5, 9, 49, 61
Amsterdamsche Courant, 50, 51, 61
Anderson, Benedict, 52, 55
Angely, barons d', 25
Anna I, Tsarina of Russia, see Ivanovna
Annales politiques du XIXe siècle, 25
Annales politiques, civiles et littéraires du dix-huitième siècle, 26–7, 29, 160–1, 175–7, 184
Annenkov, Pavel, 236
Antidote, 130
Anti-Federalists, 142, 147
anti-slavery movement, 97
Antraigues, Louis-Alexandre-Henri de Launay, comte d', 40
Archenholz, Johann Wilhelm von, 74, 95, 106
Argus, 99
aristocrats, 207, 218
Arndt, Ernst Moritz, 74, 78
Artaud, Jean-Baptiste, 165
Articles of Confederation, 152
Arzamas Society, 231
Ascendancy, Protestant, in Ireland, 117, 118
Aspinall, Arthur, 100, 107
associations, 13
Athlone, prosecutor, 59

Index

Attucks, Crispus, 147
audience, see readership
Austria, 81–2, 83–4, 216
Avignon, 28, 165

Babeuf, Gracchus, 196
Bahrdt, Carl Friedrich, 84
Baker, Keith Michael, 10, 22 n. 58
Ballina Impartial, 126
Bamberger Zeitung, 81
Bankes, Henry, 97
Baranov, I. F., 235
Barker, Hannah, 4, 16
Bastille, fall of, 34, 36–7, 184
Batavian Republic, see Netherlands
Batavian Revolution, see Netherlands
Bath and Cheltenham Gazette, 138 n. 129
Baudus, Louis, 25, 38, 43 n. 8
Bavaria, 83–4
Bayard, François-Louis, 199 n. 34
Beaugeard, Ferréol de, 188, 194
Beccaria, Cesare, 209, 210, 215
Belfast News-Letter, 115, 119, 120
Belgium, 36
Belinsky, Vissarion, 233, 234, 245 n. 47
Bellegarde, 193
Benhamou, Paul, 27
Berlinische Monatsschrift, 74
Bernard, Francis, 150
Bernard, François, 60
Bertin d'Antilly, Louis-Auguste, 25
Bertuch, 72
Bianchi, abbé, 27
Biblioteka dlia chteniia, 230, 234, 236, 238, 243–4 n. 29
Biester, Joachim Erich, 74
Bill of Rights, US, 149, 152
Bischoff, Johann Nikolaus, 70
Black, Jeremy, 7
Blackstone, William, 101
Blessington, Countess of, 123
Bödeker, Hans, 13, 75
Bolotov, A. T., 235
Bonaparte, Louis, 64
Bonaparte, Napoleon, 7, 16, 27, 99, 213, 216
  and British press, 38
  and censorship, 186
  and control of press, 14, 38, 216–17
  and German public, 69
  émigré press incites his assassination, 41
  use of press by, 78
Böning, Holger, 73
book fairs, 71

book market, in Germany, 71–72
book production, in German language, 71
book reviews, 211
books, 71–2, 182, 226
booksellers, in Italy, 204
bookshops, 71
Borger, 54
Borodin, Dmitrii Egorovich, 235
Bosch, Bernardus, 62
Boston Gazette, 146, 150
Boston Massacre, 146–7, 151
Boston News-Letter, 5, 143
Botein, Stephen, 142
Bouillon, 28, 38
Boyer, Pascal, 29, 33, 169
Boyton, Charles, Rev., 129
branding, 4
Brazil, Prince of, 28
Brewer, John, 93, 107
bribery, 7, 32, 100
  see also subsidies
Brissot de Warville, Jacques-Pierre, 8, 29, 189, 190–1, 194
Britain, 93–112
  and émigré journals, 41
  constraints on press in, 97–9
  extra-parliamentary politics in, 95–6
  newspaper content in, 93
  number of newspapers in, 103–4
  politics, coverage in foreign press, 35–6, 164, 166–9, 174, 175
  press subsidies in, 40–1
  press, and peace of Amiens, 38
  provincial press in, 100
  radical newspapers in, 96, 99
  taxes on newspapers in, 98
  unstamped papers in, 98
broadsides, in US, 147–8
Brooke, John, 22 n. 58
Brown, Richard D., 142–3
Brumaire, coup d'état of, 186
Brunswick, Duke of, 28
Brunswick movement, 129
Bugrov, P. A., 234–5
Buijnsters, P. J., 53
Bulgarin, Faddei V., 233, 236, 237, 238
bureaucracy, 216, 236
burghers, 55
Burke, Edmund, 97, 101, 118, 122
Burrows, Simon, 14
Bute, earl of, 96, 101

cabinets de lecture, 27
cafés, see coffee houses
Cairo, readers in, 27

250   Index

Calonne, Jacques-Ladislas-Joseph, abbé de, 25
Caminer, Domenico, 202, 204
Caminer, Elisabetta, 215
Caminer, Gioseffa Cornoldi, 215
Campbell, John, 143
Canada, 152
capitalism, 11
Carey, James, 147
Carey, W. P., 120
Carleton, William, 130
Carlsbad Decrees, 84
Carra, Jean-Louis, 188
Carson, James, 116
Cast-Iron Statutes, 226, 229
Castlereagh, Robert Stewart, Viscount, 40, 100
Catherine II, Tsarina, 225, 227
Catholic Association, 128, 129
Catholic Board, 125
Catholic Emancipation, 123, 129
Catholic Question, 127
Censer, Jack, 12, 17, 22 n. 58, 183
Censeur, 25, 38
Censeur des journaux, 193
censorship, 5, 7, 11
    in Austria, 80
    in France, 37, 184
    in Germany, 78–81, 84, 84–5
    in Italy, 210–11
    in Napoleonic Europe, 37–8, 80
    in Russia, 225–7, 228
Central Coffee House, Moscow, 238
Cerisier, Antoine-Marie, 29, 60
Cérutti, Joseph-Antoine, abbé, 192–3
chambers de lecture, 27
Charlemont, Lord, 117–18
Charleville, Lady, 123
Chernyshevskii, Nikolai, 238
Christian IV, Duke of Deux Ponts, 32, 38
Christie, Ian, 100
Chronicle, 125
Church of Ireland, 129
circles, in Russia, 232–3, 234, 244–5 n. 43
Circolo costituzionale, 216
circulation, of newspapers, 5
    in Britain, 103–4, 105, 106–7, 126
    in colonial America, 148, 149
    in France, 26–7, 187, 194
    in French language, 26–8, 161, 203
    in Germany, 73, 74, 76
    in Ireland, 115, 119, 126, 132
    in Italy, 205–6, 212, 217
    in Russia, 226, 227, 234, 236, 243–4 n. 29

    produced in Netherlands, 26, 50, 58, 60–1
Cisalpine Republic, 216
citizenship, Dutch concepts of, 55
civil society, 52, 55, 58, 218, 224, 225, 226–7
clergy, 195
Cleves, as French publishing centre, 28
Clonmell, Lord, 121
clubs, 11, 12, 13, 27
    constitutional, in Italy, 215–16
    in Russia, 227, 236–7
    political, in French revolution, 191
Cobbett, William, 106, 144
Cobden, Richard, 102
coffee houses, 7, 9, 10, 11, 27, 49, 195, 206
    in Britain, 104, 107
    in Ireland, 116, 118, 120, 128
    in Russia, 227, 237, 238
    in Venice, 206–7
colonial assemblies, in America, 144
Columbian Centinel, 140
Columbian press, 6
Comet, 129
Commercial Club, in Moscow, 237
commercialisation, 70
Committee of Public Safety, 187, 192
Common Sense, 147
Compagnoni, Giuseppe, 202, 209
Condorcet, Louis-Joseph-Antoine de Caritat, marquis de, 188
Confederation of the Rhine, 69
Congress of Vienna, 83
Conservative Association, 129
conservative press, in Britain, 93
Constantinople, 27
Constitutional Congress, 144
Conway, F. W., 130
Cooper, Thomas, 102
Copeland, David, 16
coranto, 5, 18 n. 11, 49
Cordeliers club, 186
Cork Herald, 120
Cornell, Saul, 147
Correspondance politique, 25, 26
Correspondent, 124, 126
Correspondenten, 33, 38
    see also *Hamburgische Unpartheyische Correspondent*
correspondents, employed by newspapers, 7, 33–4, 49, 77
Corriere di Napoli, 217
cosmopolitan press, 2, 14, 23–47
    and complaints of governments, 30–1
    and enlightenment, 35

Index

and political values, 35
  demise of, 41, 42
  size, 42 n. 6
Cotta, Johann Friedrich, 77–8
counter-revolution, 192
Courier d'Angleterre, 25, 26, 28, 40–41
Courier de l'Escaut, 24
Courier de l'Europe, 7, 24, 25, 26, 28, 29, 30, 31, 160, 175
  and fall of Bastille, 37
  and French government subscriptions, 32
  and Parliamentary reporting, 35–6
  and Patriot Revolution, 36
  content, 35
  editorial policy, 34–5
  editors, 28
  Paris correspondent, 33
  profits, 29
  see also *Courier de Londres*
Courier de Londres, 25, 27, 38, 40–1
  see also *Courier de l'Europe*
Courier du Bas Rhin, 24, 25, 29, 159
  banned in France, 30
  editorial policy, 34–5
  and British politics, 36
  and French Revolution, 36–7
  and Patriot Revolution, 36
  and Prussian propaganda, 32–3
  circulation of, 26, 27
  Italian edition of, 203
  Paris correspondents, 33
  suppression, 38
Courier, 103
Courier d'Avignon, 24, 26, 159, 161, 165–9, 177, 184, 191
  and fall of Bastille, 37
  and Papal authorities, 165, 169–70
  coverage of American Revolution, 167–9
  coverage of foreign politics, 166–169
  coverage of France, 166, 173
  coverage of Seven Years War, 166–7
Courrier de Monaco, 165
  see also *Courrier d'Avignon*
Courrier de Strasbourg, 188, 194
Courrier de Villeneuve-lès-Avignon, 194
Crisis, The, 147
Croker, John Wilson, 128
Cuoco, Vincenzo, 217
Cushing, William, 152
Custine, Marquis de, 227, 237
Custodi, Pietro, 216

Dagverhaal [Journal] of Batavian National Assembly, 63
daily newspapers, 5–6, 77, 149, 203, 236
Damiens, 173
Darnton, Robert, 12, 21 n. 47, 22 n. 58
debating societies, 11
Decembrist revolt, 224, 229
Declaration of the Rights of Man and Citizen, 8, 185
Defenders, 118
Défenseur de la vérité, 193
Democraten, 48, 63
Denker, 53
Denmark, 31
Desmoulins, Camille, 185, 186, 191
Deutsche Chronik, 74
Deutschland in seiner tiefen Erniedrigung, 81
Deux-Ponts, duchy of, 28
Diario di Roma, 205
Diario ordinario di Roma, 203, 211
Diario veneto, 202, 203, 206
Dick's Coffee House, 116
Dickinson, John, 141–2
Didot, 196–7 n. 2
Directory, 187
Donna galante, 215
Dramaticheskii vestnik, 233
Drogheda News-Letter
Du Breuil, Jean-Pierre Tronchin, 32
Duane, William, 141
Dublin, 132
Dublin Castle, 113, 123
Dublin Evening Mail, 114, 126, 127, 129–30, 134
Dublin Evening Post, 119–20, 121, 123, 124, 125, 130, 134
Dublin Journal, 116, 120, 124, 126
Dublin library, 128, 130
Dublin press, 125, 128
Dublin Satirist, 125
Dublin Society, 116
Dublin University Magazine, 113, 130–1, 133
Dublin Weekly Journal, 116
Duckett, William, 136, n. 67
Dutch gazettes, 159, 169–70
  see also cosmopolitan press, international gazettes
Dutch Reformed Church, 55

Edenton Tea Party, 155 n. 7
editorial comment, 25
editorial content, in Italy, 209–10, 213
editorial policy, German journals, 75
editorials, Ireland, 124
editors, 6, 118 and *passim*
education, primary, 9
educational provision, 8, 9

educational reforms, in Russia, 229
Egypt, 27
Einkommende Zeitung, 5
Eisenstein, Elizabeth, 3
elite press, 27
Elizabeth I, Tsarina of Russia,
  see Petrovna
  émigré publications, 23
  émigrés, 25, 41
Encyclopédie, 117
Engelsing, Rolf, 56–7, 71
England, 4, 93–112
  and freedom of the press, 16
  literacy rates, 9
  press laws, recommended for Germany, 84
  public sphere in, 11–12
  see also Britain
enlightenment
  and cosmopolitan press, 35
  in Germany, 69
  in Ireland, 131
  in Netherlands, 52, 54, 55, 56, 58
  and content of German journals, 74
enragé journalists, 193
ephemeral literature, 57
Esprit des cours de l'Europe, 31
essay papers, 96
Estates-general (France), 184
Estratto delle notizie di Vienna, 202
Europa, 204
European public sphere, 23, 42
Evening Mail, (England), 103
Evening Mail (Ireland), 124, 129, 130
Evening Post, 124, 125
Evgenii Onegin, 232

fair-sexing, of newspapers, 15
Farnham, Lord, 129
fashion, 233
fashion journals, 72
Fatherland Society, 59
Fauche-Borel, Louis, 40
Fauchet, Claude, 188
Faulkner, Richard, 116, 131
Faulkners Dublin Journal, 114
Federalist Papers, 142, 148
Federalist party (US), 140, 142, 147, 151, 153
Fenno, John, 150
Fergusson, 130
Feuillant, Etienne, 190
Feuille de Flandres, 194
Feuille de salut public, 187
Feuille villageoise, 192–3

Filangieri, Gaetano, 208
Finerty, Peter, 122
Finn's Leinster Journal, 122
Firmian, Count, 202
First Amendment, 8, 141, 152
Flesselles, Jacques de, 38
Flood, Henry, 117, 118, 121
Florence, 201, 202, 204–5
Flying Post, 116
foreign correspondents, see correspondents
format, of newspapers, 115, 182
Formica, Marina, 205
Fouilhoux, Charles, 33
Fox, Charles James, 96, 167
Fox's Libel Act, 98
France, 2, 4, 26, 159–200
  and international papers, 26, 30–4, 165–77
  and news management, 33
  censorship in, 14, 39–40
  invades Avignon, 165
  links with Irish papers, 122
  literacy rates, 9
  number of newspapers in, 161
  postal revolution in, 26, 32
  press historiography of, 183
  press policy under Bonaparte, 38
  press subsidies by, 32, 186–7
  public sphere in, 11–12
  repression of press in, 161
  revolutionary newspapers in, 6, 16, 24, 182–200
  see also French Revolution
franchise, in US, 142
Frankfurt book fair, 71, 79
Franklin, Benjamin, 144, 147
Frederick II, King of Prussia, and press, 79–80
Frederick William II, King of Prussia, and press, 80
free associations, 207
Free Economic Society, 241
freedom of the press, 8, 16, 186, 190–1
  in Britain, 101–3
  in France, 16, 185, 186
  in Germany, 82, 84, 85–6
  in Ireland, 115, 131
  in Netherlands, 14, 15, 16, 51, 59, 63–4
  in United States, 16, 140–1, 151–2
Freeman's Journal, 117, 118, 125, 129, 120, 124, 126
French and Indian War, 143, 146, 148, 149
French émigré editors, 25, 28
French émigré newspapers, 24–25
French press, domestic reporting, 173

Index

French Revolution, 7, 24, 26
  and cosmopolitan press, 23, 36–8
  and coverage of British Parliament, 181 n. 59
  and French press, 182–200
  and German censorship, 80
  and Irish press, 121–2
  and Italy, 212–14
  and public opinion, 12
  and public sphere, 12
  debates in Britain, 97
  effect on German press, 69, 76
  historiography of, 177
  suppression of press freedom, 14
French sister-republics, 14
French-language press, 12, 23, 51
  in US, 157 n. 48
  see also Cosmopolitan Press, International newspapers
Freneau, Philip, 144
Frisi, Paolo, 210
Fructidor, coup d'état of, 186

Galakhov, A. D., 237, 238
Galdi, Matteo, 212, 216
Gallois, Léonard, 183
gambling dens, 27
Gazetiers, 27
Gazette anglo-françoise-américaine, 33
Gazette d'Altona, 24, 43 n. 8
Gazette d'Amsterdam, 24, 26, 51–2
  and American propaganda, 33
  and French Revolution, 37–8
  and Maupeou crisis, 31
  and Patriot Revolution, 36
  bribed by France, 32
  Italian edition, 203
Gazette d'Uirecht, 24, 26, 30, 31, 32
Gazette de Bayreuth, suppression, 38
Gazette de Berne, 24, 31, 36–7
Gazette de Bruxelles, 24
Gazette de Cologne, 24, 25, 32, 35, 36
Gazette de France, 7, 26, 159–60, 161–5, 174, 187
  circulation, 177
  coverage of foreign politics, 162–5
  coverage of France, 161–2, 173
  coverage of French foreign policy, 162
Gazette de Frankfort, suppression, 38
Gazette de La Haye, 24, 30, 31
Gazette de Leyde, 7, 24, 25, 27, 29, 51–2, 169–73, 174, 177, 184
  and American propaganda, 33
  and French government, 169–70
  and French Revolution, 36–7, 38
  and Habsurg realms, 30
  and Patriot Revolution, 36
  circulation, 26, 203
  content, general, 27
  diplomatic complaints against, 31
  editorial policy, 34–5,
  finances, 29
  foreign coverage, 170–1
  Italian edition, 203
  Paris correspondents, 33–4
  readership, 27, 170
Gazette de Paris, 194, 195
Gazette des Deux-Ponts, 24, 27, 32, 35, 37, 38
Gazette universelle, 184, 187
Gazettes, 7, 15, 16, 24, 209
Gazzetta civica napoletana, 203
Gazzetta di Milano, 202
Gazzetta enciclopedica di Milano, 201, 203, 211
Gazzetta toscana, 202, 211
Gazzetta universale, 202, 203, 205
Gazzetta urbana veneta, 205
gazzettes, 5
Gazzettino ebdomadario della Sardegna, 202–3
Gebildeten, 69–70, 85–6
Gedicke, Friedrich, 74
Geissel, 74
Gellner, Ernest, 52–3
General Evening Post, 119, 120
Genoa, 201
Genovesi, 208
Gentz, Friedrich von, 74
Geograficheskie izvestiia, 241
George III, 164, 166, 168, 169
Gérard, 25
German Club, 246 n. 71
German Question, in 1814–15, 83
Germany, 5, 69–86
  civil service in, 69–70 and *passim*
  emergence of political press in, 73
  imperial book commission, 79
  literacy rates in, 9
  newspaper content in, 76, 77
  newspaper periodicity, 77
  newspapers as mass medium in, 76
  number of newspapers in, 76, 81
  politicisation of public in, 69
  public opinion in, 82, 85–6 and *passim*
  public sphere in, 11–13 and *passim*
  role of state in public sphere in, 15, 86 and *passim*
  suppression of press freedom in, 14
Gershenzon, M. O., 232, 241

Giffard, John, 120, 121
Giffard, S. L., 123, 129
Giornale degli avvisi e notizie del Piemonte, 202
Giornale enciclopedico di Milano, 201–2
Giornale fiorentino istorico-politico letterario, 202, 205, 210
Giornale italiano, 217
Giornale veneto, 203
Girondin newspapers, 186
Girondins, 186, 193
Giroud family, 165
Giunta degli Studi, 210
Glaneur historique, 31
Glasgow, 27
Glorious Revolution, 16
Godechot, Jacques, 183
Godwin, William, 107
Gogel, Isaac, 63
Gogol, N. V., 233
Gordon, George, 120
Gordon Riots, 166, 170
Gore ot uma, 232
Görres, Joseph, 70
Gorsas, Antoine-Joseph, 188
Gough, Hugh, 14, 16
Grand Lodge, 117
Grand Master of the Order of Malta, 31
Grant, Charles, 125
Grattan, Henry, 117, 121, 122
Graziosi, Antonio, 202, 205
Great Reforms, 241
Grech, N. I., 233
Griboedov, Alexander, 232
Grigor'ev, A. A., 239
Groningen, 49–50
Guchkov, Fedor, 234
Gueudeville, 31
Gutenberg, Johann, 3
Gutenburg press, 6

Haarlem, 49
Habermas, Jürgen, 10–13, 16, 104, 113, 131, 142, 154, 177, 183, 196, 230
and public sphere, 20 n. 44, 22 n. 58, 84, 86
Habsburgs, 210
Hague, The, 49
Hamburg, 28, 38, 73
Hamburgische Unpartheyische Correspondent, 76, 77
see also *Correspondenten*
Hamilton, Alexander, 142
Hamilton, Andrew, 150

Hardenberg, Karl Auguste von, 82
Harp of Erin, 122
Harris, Benjamin, 143, 145
Harris, Bob, 94
Harris, Michael, 105
Hatin, Eugène, 183
Hébert, Jacques-René, 184, 186, 192, 194
Hegel, Georg, 55
Hellmuth, Eckhart, 13, 15
Heraclyt en Democryt, 63
Herzen, Alexander, 235
Hespe, Johan Christiaan, 59, 61, 64
Hibernian Journal, 121, 124, 126
Higgins, Francis, 114, 120, 121
History of Printing in America, 153
History of Rogues and Raparees, 113
Hodgson, Solomon, 99
Hoen, Pieter 't, 59, 61
Holland, newspapers in province, 49
see also Netherlands
Hollandsche Spectator, 53
Holt, John, 146
Holy Roman Empire, 31
Hone's Register, 106
Hoppen, Theodore, 128
huguenots, 23, 28, 117
Hutchinson, Thomas, 150
Hyde-Neuville, Guillaume, 40

Il Caffè, 209, 215
illiteracy, see literacy
Imperial Russian Geographical Society, 241
Indies, readers in, 27
Infelise, Mario, 204, 206
information, as a commodity, 5
information sources, 7
Inquisition, 210
intellectuals, 206, 208–9, 216, 217, 232
intelligentsia, in Germany, 69–70
Intelligenzblätter, 73
international affairs, reporting, see individual countries
international elite, 23
international gazettes, 8, 23–42, 24, 41, 207, 165–77
and French foreign policy, 173–5
and French revolution, 36–8
banned in French revolution, 38
collapse, 27
typology, 42 n. 7
international newspapers, 8, 23–42
see also cosmopolitan press, international gazettes

Index

Ireland, 4, 113–139
  foreign reporting in, 116
  government newspapers in, 120, 123, 124, 126
  government patronage in, 120, 124
  government repression of newspapers, 122
  literacy rates, 9
  nationalism in, 131
  population growth in, 132
  press prosecutions in, 123, 125
  public sphere in, 134
  radical newspapers in, 118
  sectarianism in, 113–14, 118, 127–8, 130, 133 and *passim*
Irish Magazine, 125
Irish rebellion, 118, 120, 122, 132–3
Irish-language newspapers, 135 n. 15
Isabella, Maurizio, 14
Istoricheskii zhurnal, 228
Istoriia gosudarstva Rossiiskogo, 229
Italian language versions of foreign newspapers, 202
Italian Republic, 216
Italy, 2, 201–23
  Catholic Church and press control in, 210
  currency equivalence, 219 n. 16
  foreign newspapers in, 203
  foreign reporting in, 203–4, 213
  government and press in, 210–11
  government and public opinion in, 211–12
  government newspapers in, 201, 202, 203
  impact of French revolution in, 14, 207
  intellectuals in, 206, 208–9, 216, 217
  Kingdom of, 216, 217
  nationalism, 213, 217
  newspaper content in, 203–4
  newspaper distribution in, 203
  newspaper periodicity, 203
  political geography, 201
  political groupings, 213
  press and French invasion in, 14, 212, 213
  public opinion in, 207–9 and *passim*
  public sphere in revolutionary period in, 213–16
  publishing industry in, 204–5, 211
  republican newspapers, 212–3
  Revolutionary Triennium in, 211, 212–13
  revolutionary womanhood in, 215
Ivan Vyzhigin, 237
Ivanovna, Anna, 238

Jacobin club, 187, 195
Jacobinism, in Italy, 216
Jacobins, 193
Janus Verrezen, 62
Janus, 62
Jay, John, 142
Jefferson, Thomas, 150, 153
Jesuits, 32
Johns, Adrian, 3
Johnson, Samuel, 106
Johnston, James, 151
Joseph II, Emperor, 30, 210, 211
Journal constitutionnel du département du Gers, 192
Journal de Bruxelles, 33, 160, 174, 175, 187, 190
Journal de Genève, 33, 160, 174
Journal de la montagne, 195–6
Journal de Marseille, 188, 194
Journal de Toulouse ou l'observateur antiroyaliste, 199 n. 39
Journal de Turin et des provinces, 202
Journal des dames (New York), 40
Journal des débats, 190, 231, 238
Journal des Luxus und der Moden, 72
Journal du département de l'Ain, 192
Journal du département de Loir et Cher, 199 n. 42
Journal du Lot, 191
Journal du Nord, 230
Journal du soir, 187, 190
Journal encyclopédique, 23, 31
Journal général de l'Orléanais, 194
Journal patriotique de la Bourgogne, 191–2
Journal patriotique de la Dordogne, 191
Journal révolutionnaire de Toulouse, 191
journalism, as profession,
  development of, 188–9
  in Germany, 70
  in Ireland, 124
  in Italy, 216, 218
journalist, concept, in Italy, 209
journalistic style, 184
journalists, 6, 7
  French, 29, 188
  role of, 190, 191, 210
  status, of, 189–90
  earnings, 205
journals, 72, 74–5, 233–4
Jumel, Jean Charles, 192

Kant, Immanuel, 10, 74
Karamzin, Nicholas Mikhailovich, 228, 229, 231, 233, 235, 243–4 n. 25
Kazan, University of, 226

Kazanskie izvestiia, 229
Kendal Chronicle, 101
Kharytonov, A. A., 239
King Street confrontation, 147
Klancher, Jon, 233
Klein, Ernst Ferdinand, 85
Klein, Rebecca, 108
Kluit, Adriaan, 61
Knox, Vicesimus, 102
Koenig, Christoffel Frederik, 67 n. 54
Kohl, J. G., 243 n. 25
Koltsov, Aleksei, 233
König steam press, 6
Konijnenburg, Jan, 63
Koopman, 53–4
Kukol'nik, N. V., 239
la Font, de, family, 170
La Lecq, Nassau, 57
La Motte, comte de, 27
la Varenne, Jean-Baptiste de, 31
Lackington, James, 106
Lacretelle, J.-B., 198 n. 30
Lameth, Charles de, 182
Langlois, Isidore, 193
Latin literature, 71–2
Launay, de, governor of Bastille, 36–7
Laveaux, Jean-Charles, 186, 188
Le Blanc, Joachim, 165
Le Blanc, Mme, 165
Le Fanu, 130
leading articles, 213
Leagues of friendship, 12–13
learned societies, 52, 241
Leeuwarden, 50
Leicester Chronicle, 99
Leipzig, 5
Leipzig book fair, 71
Leo XII, Pope, 127
Leopold II, Emperor of Austria, 210
letters to editors, 15, 94–5, 96
Levant, 27
Lever, 130
Lévi-Strauss, Claude, 5
Levy, Leonard, 150
Leyden, 49
Leydse Courant, 61
Libel Act (Britain), 7
libel laws, 7, 150, 185
libel trials, 14–15, 125
libraries, 107, 207, 235–6
Licencing Act, 16
licensing, of newspapers, 5, 7, 145
Limiers, Madame de, 32
Lincoln, W. B., 224, 226, 241

Linguet, Simon-Nicolas-Henri, 8, 27, 29, 160–1, 175–7, 184
literacy, 8–9
  in Britain, 9, 106
  in Central Europe, 9
  in Germany, 71
  in Iberian peninsula, 9
  in Ireland, 9, 115, 119, 124, 125–6, 132
  in Italy, 206
  in Mediterranean basin, 9
  in Russia, 9, 234–5
  in Scandinavia, 9
  in United States, 141
  measurement of, 20 n. 38
literary journals, 116, 159
literary societies, 231
Liverpool, Robert Banks Jenkinson, Lord, 100
Lloyd's Evening Post, 102, 107
local news, 7, 93, 142–3
Lojek, Jerzy, 23
Lolme, Jean de, 101–2
London, 5, 9, 25, 28–9
London Corresponding Society, 106
London Irish, 123
London newspapers, 6
Londonderry, Marquis of, 238
Longo, Alfonso, 210
Lotareva, D. D., 240
Louis XV, 161
Louis XVI, 37, 38, 161, 175, 177, 186
Louisiana purchase, 157 n. 48
Louvet, Jean-Baptiste, 193
Lover, 130
lower-class readers, 94, 235
Lucas, Charles, 116, 117
Luzac family, 170
Luzac, Elie, 61
Luzac, Etienne, 31, 170
Luzac, Jean, 29, 33, 170–1
  and American Revolution, 35, 170, 171
  and Belgian revolt, 36
  and Dutch patriots, 170
  and Polish patriots, 170
  editorial policy of, 34–5

MacDonnell, 125
Mackintosh, Sir James, 38
MacMahon, Joseph Perkins, 28
Madden, R. R., 113
Madison, James, 142, 153
Magee family, 123
Magee, John, 121
Maginn, William, 123
Magnitskii, M. L., 226

Index

Mallet Du Pan, Jacques, 25, 28, 29, 30, 190
Manchester Gazette, 94
Manchester Herald, 94, 99
Manchester Reformation Society, 106
Mangan, 130
manuscript gazettes, see *nouvelles la main*
Manzon, Jean, 29, 32–3, 35, 36
Marat, Jean-Paul, 184, 185, 188, 192
Maria Theresa, Austrian Empress, 210
Mason, George, 152
masonic literature, 240
masonic lodges, 10, 13, 117, 226, 227, 239–40
Masonic Order, 127
mass marketing, 4
Massachusetts Spy, 147
Maupeou coup, 31, 171–173, 177
Maza, Sarah, 12, 21 n. 47
McDougall, Alexander, 150
McLuhan, Marshall, 2
McNally, Leonard, 120
Meditazioni sulla economia politica, 208
Mein, John, 151
Mendelssohn, Moses, 74
Menschenvriend, 62
merchants, 4, 14, 28, 234–6, 240, 247 n. 92
Mercier, Louis-Sébastien, 182, 193
Mercure britannique, 25, 26, 28, 29, 30
Mercure de France, 25, 160, 174, 187
Mercure universel, 25, 40
Mesmont, Germain-Hyacinthe de Romance, marquis de, 25
Messenger, 125
Metternich, Clemens, Prince, 82, 84
Middelburg, 50
Middle Ages, 5
Milan, press in, 201–2
Minerva, 38, 74
Mirabeau, Honoré-Gabriel Riquetti, comte de, 184, 188
Moldavia, 27
Molesworth, Lord, 116
Momory, 186
Moniteur, 7, 38, 39, 80, 184–5, 187, 190
Monitor, 101
Monitore cisalpino, 213
Monitore di Roma, 213, 214
Monitore napoletano, 213, 214
Montgelas, Maximilian von, 83
Montlosier, François-Dominique Reynaud, comte de, 25, 38
moral weeklies, 73
Morande, see Théveneau de Morande, Charles
Morelli, Maria Augusta Timpanaro, 205

Morénas, François, 165
Morgan, Henry, 120
Morning Chronicle, 99, 100
Morning Post, 99, 100
Moscow Society for Russian History and Antiquities, 241
Moscow University, 227, 228, 232, 240, 241
Moser, Friedrich Karl von, 74
Moskovskie vedomosti, 227, 231
Moskovskii nabliudatel, 233, 238, 247 n. 79
Moskovskii telegraf, 229–30, 233, 239, 243–4 n. 29
Moskovskii vestnik, 233, 239
Mosvitianin, 236
Muller, Statius, 54
Murray, William J., 29, 188

Nadezhdin, N. I., 233
Naples, 203
nation state, 3
National Adviser, 101
National Assembly (France), 185, 189, 190
National-Chronik der Teutschen, 81
Necker, Jacques, 37
De Nederlandsche Criticus, 54
De Nederlandsche Spectator, 53
Negro, Piero del, 207
Neilson, Sam, 134
Netherlands, 2, 5, 28, 31, 48–69
  and French-language press, 12, 28
  Batavian Revolution in, 48, 56, 62, 63
  civil society in, 52
  constitution of 1798, 63
  control of press under Batavian Republic in, 64
  decline of newspaper press in, 64
  diplomatic complaints to, 30
  early newspapers in, 49–50
  freedom of the press in, 14, 15, 16, 51, 59, 63–4
  historiography, 56
  National Assembly, 63
  nation-building in, 52–3, 55
  patriot newspapers in, 58–60
  patriot refugees from, 61
  Patriot Revolution in, 7, 16, 35, 36, 49, 56, 58
  political structure, 52
  press in, and French Revolution, 62
  public sphere in, 52, 58 and *passim*
  reading revolution in, 56–7
  suppression newspapers in, 62
Neue Graue Ungeheuer, 74
Neuwieder Zeitung, 76

Neverov, Ianuarii, 233
New York Gazetteer, 151
Newcastle Chronicle, 99
news agencies, 7
news information, 14, 23, 74
news letters, 7, 143
news management, 8, 32
newsbooks, 5
newspaper, definition of, 4
newspaper finances, 29, 100–1, 119–20, 205, 187–8, 194
newspaper prices, 104, 124, 126, 170, 205, 227, 243 n. 17
newspaper shareholders, 6
newspaper staff, 6
newspapers,
  and political partisanship, 17
  and reading revolution, 57
  and state, 16
  evolution of, 2, 5–6, 18 n. 11, 75
  production methods for, 187
  renting of, 50
  see also cosmopolitan press, international newspapers, international gazettes, provincial newspapers, and entries for individual titles and countries
New-York Journal, 146
Nicholas I, 224, 226, 229, 231
Nicolai, Friedrich, 72
Nieuwe Post van den Neder-Rhijn, 62
Nikitenko, A. V., 235
noble readers, 14, 161, 195, 230, 231
Noblemen's Club, in Moscow, 237
North Briton, 101
North, Frederick, Lord, 96, 101, 167, 168, 169
Northern Star, 114, 121, 122, 134, 136 n. 67
Notizie del Mondo, 202, 204, 205, 209
Notizie del Mondo, Venetian version, 202
Notizie per l'anno, 203
Notizie politiche, 203
nouvelles la main, 160, 204
Nouvelles extraordinaires de divers endroits, see *Gazette de Leyde*
Nouvelles politiques, 198 n. 30
Novellista veneto, 203
novels, 57, 72
Novikov, Nikolai, 225, 227
Nuova gazzetta veneta, 202, 206
Nuove di diverse corti e paesi, 203, 204
Nuovo Postiglione, 202

O'Connell, Daniel, 125, 127, 128, 129–30
O'Connor, Arthur, 122

Ockerse, Willem Anthonie, 48–9, 50, 63, 64–5
Octennial Act, 117
Odoevskii, Prince, 231
official publications, 7
Oprechte Haerlemse Courant, 50
oral communication, 7, 142–3
Orange Order, 118, 125, 129
Orange press (Ireland), 130
Orangist newspapers (Netherlands), 60
Orangist party (Netherlands), 58
Ordinari Post-Zeitung, 76
Otechestvennye zapiski, 236, 238, 247 n. 79
Otis, Harrison Gray, 151
Ouderwetse Nederlandsche Patriot, 60
Oxford Gazette, 18 n. 11

Paape, Gerrit, 62
Pahl, Johann Gottfried, 81
Paine, Thomas, 147–8
Palm, Johann Philip, 38, 81
Palmer, Robert R., 56
pamphlets, 4, 12, 15
  anti-Napoleonic, 78
  in Britain, 96
  in France, 182, 184, 189
  in Germany, 78
  in Netherlands, 51, 57
  in US, 147–8
Panaev, I. I., 231–2
Panckoucke, Charles-Joseph, 33, 160, 174, 187
Paoli de Chagny, François-Etienne-Auguste, comte de, 25, 40
Papal state, 203
Parini, Giuseppe, 202
Paris pendant l'année, 25
Paris, 24, 33
Parisian press, 184, 194
Parker, James, 150, 153
Parlements, 171–2
parliamentary reform movement, Britain, 97
parliamentary reporting, 35–6, 103, 144
Parnell, Henry, 116
Patriot Revolution, see Netherlands
Patriot, 124, 126, 130
Patriote français, 184, 194
Patriotic Societies, in Italy, 215–16
Patriotisches Archiv, 74
patriots
  in Italy, 213, 214, 215, 217
  in Netherlands, 59, 60
  in Ireland, 120

patronage, 7, 150
  see also subsidies
Paul I, Tsar of Russia, 28, 225–6
peasants, 192–3
Peel, Robert, 114, 123, 125, 132, 134
Peireth, Wolfgang, 15
Peltier, Jean-Gabriel, 23, 25, 29, 38
Pennsylvania Journal, 148
Père Duchêne, 186, 192, 194, 195
Perkins MacMahon, Joseph, 29
Perthes, Friedrich, 79
Peter II, 227
Peterhof festival, 227
Pétion, 185
Petrovna, Elizabeth, 238
Philadelphus Letters, 118
Philantrope, 53
philanthropic societies, 13
Philippeaux, 193
Philosooph, 53
philosophes, 32
philosophic books, 12
Phipps, Sir Constantine, 116
Pilot, 128
Pimentel, Eleonora Fonseca, 214, 215
pirate editions, 175
Pitt, William, 96, 99, 118
Pius VI, pope, 211
poetry, 116
Pogodin, M. P., 233
Poland, 32, 33, 163
Pole, Wellesley, 124
Polevoi, N. A., 229, 233, 239
police, in Russia, 226, 239–240
Polilov, E. T., 235, 236
Polilov, Iuliia, 236
Polilov-Severtsev, G. T., 235
Political Register (*Cobbett's Register*), 106
Politieke Blixem, 64
Politieke Kruyer, 49, 59–60, 64
Politique hollandais, 60
Poniatowski, Stanislaus-Augustus, 32, 33
Popkin, Jeremy, 12, 22 n. 58, 27, 183
popular opinion, 14
Porcupine's Gazette and Daily Advertiser, 144
Portugal, 41
Posselt, Ernst Ludwig, 78
Post van den Neder-Rhijn, 49, 58–60, 62
Pour et le contre, 25
press laws, 185, 186, 210
Press, 121, 122
pressure groups, 125, 127
priests, 193
print culture, 2, 3
printers, 6, 142, 182, 204–5

printers' guilds, 204
printing, speed of output, 6
printing technology, 6, 17
print-type, 229
private presses, 227
Proclamation Fund, 124, 126, 137 n. 87
propaganda, 3
  American, 33
  Austrian, 83–4
  British, 40
  in Germany, 81, 82–3
  Napoleonic, 38, 39–40, 81, 82, 86, 217
  Prussian, 82–4
proprietors, of newspapers, 6, 114, 115, 118, 148
prospectuses, 194
Prospetto degli affari attuali d'Europa, 202
provincial newspapers, 5, 6
  in Britain, 103, 105
  in France, 184, 194
  in Russia, 229, 242, n. 4
Prudhomme, Louis-Marie, 187, 194
Prussia, 79–80, 82–4
  and *Courier du Bas-Rhin*, 32–3
  censorship regime, 79–80
  complains about *Gazette de La Haye*, 30
  intervention in Patriot Revolution, 36
  press policy, 82
  primary education, 9
  see also Germany
pseudonyms, 58, 141
public, concept of, 8, 11, 94 and *passim*
public addresses, 143, 153
public ceremonies, 143
public houses, 107
  see also taverns
public mind, 213–14, 217
public opinion, 9, 10, 11 and *passim*
  definitions of, 9–10
public opinion polling, 81
public reading, of newspapers, 206
public sphere, 12, 14, 20 n. 44 and *passim*
  and governments 15
  and Habermas, 10–13 and *passim*
Publick Occurences, 143, 144
Publick Occurrences Both Forreign and Domestick, 145
publishing privileges, 7, 50, 205, 211
Pue, Richard, 116
Pue's Occurrences, 114, 115, 116
Pushkin, A. S., 231
Puteshestvie iz Peterburga v Moskvu, 225

radicalism, in Britain, 93
Radishchev, A. N., 225

Raeff, Marc, 225
Ragguagli di vari paesi, 202
railways, 6
Rao, Anna Maria, 205
Rasori, Giovanni, 216
Raznochintsy, 246 n. 72
readers, 4
readership of newspapers
  in Britain, 13–14, 94, 104–6, 107
  in France, 14, 16, 23, 161, 192–6
  in Germany, 13, 71, 72, 73, 76
  in Ireland, 114, 124
  in Italy, 14, 205, 206, 207, 214
  in Netherlands, 13–14, 50
  in Russia, 14, 230–1, 234
  in United States, 13–14, 142
  of cosmopolitan press, 28
  of Dutch gazettes, 27
  see also circulation
reading aloud, 76, 236
reading circles, 76
reading clubs, 52
reading habits, 182
reading revolution, 56–7, 71, 206
reading societies, 13, 71, 72, 207
Real-Zeitung, 76
Rebmann, Andreas Georg Friedrich, 74
Rédacteur, 187
Reformation, 3
reformist associations, 52
Regents, 58
Regnier, Jacques, 25, 38, 40
Reichspostreuter, 76
Reilly, Richard, 116
Reinier Vryaarts openhartige brieven, 61
religion, 214
religious newspapers, 155 n. 5
Remnek, Miranda Beaven, 4, 14, 15
Renaissance, 5
Renaudot, Théophraste, 15, 159
Renunciation Act
reporters, 144
reporting practices, 6–7
Repubbreca spiegata co'lo santo Evangelio, 214
Republican party (US), 140, 151, 153
Republikein, 63
Reveil, 25
Revere, Paul, 146
Révolutions de France et de Brabant, 185
Révolutions de Paris, 184, 187, 194
Rheinische Merkur, 70
Rhineland, 28
Richelieu, cardinal, 15, 159
Riformatori dello Studio, 211

Ristori, Giovanni, 205, 209, 210, 216
Rivington, James, 151
Robespierre, Maximilien, 185
Rockingham Whigs, 101
Roland, Jean-Marie, 186
Roman Empire, news media, 5
romantic fiction, 233
Rome, 203
Roper, David, 153
Roubaud, abbé, 165
Rousseau, Jean-Jacques, 10, 29
Rousseau, Pierre, 31
Royou, abbé, 188
Russell, Benjamin, 153
Russia, 4, 224–47
  and *Courier du Bas-Rhin*, 32
  and French revolution, 225
  exports, 228
  foreign newspapers in, 40, 236, 238
  foreign-language press in, 230
  government and masons in, 239–240
  government attitudes to theatre in, 239
  government papers in, 228
  growth of newspaper press in, 227
  intellectuals in, 232
  Ministry of Education, and censorship, 226
  Ministry of Religious Affairs & Public Instruction, 226
  number of newspapers in, 230
  periodicity of newspapers, 228
  political participation in, 224
  reception of western literature in, 239
Russkii invalid, 229, 230, 236
Russkoi vestnik, 229
Ryan, Mary, 13

's Gravenhaegse Courant, 50, 61
Sabatier de Castres, abbé Antoine, 25
salons, 10, 11, 230–2
Sanktpeterburgskie kommercheskie vedomosti, 228
Sanktpeterburgskie vedomosti, 227, 243 n. 17
sans-culottes, 186, 192, 195–6
Sardinia, 202–3
satirical journals, 227
Saunders News-Letter, 115, 121, 124
Savoy, kingdom of, 202
scandal, 184
  see also sensationalism
Schiller, Friedrich, 78, 239
Schlözer, 74
Schneider, Euloge, 188
Schubart, Christian Friedrich Daniel, 70, 74

Schudson, Michael, 142, 144
Schweizer, Karl, 108
Scienza della legislazione, 208
Scotland, 9, 100
Scott, Walter, 239
scribal culture, 3
Secret Service accounts, Britain, 101
Secret Service Fund, Ireland, 120, 124
secularisation, 3
sedition, definition in French revolution, 185
sedition laws, in Britain, 7
seditious libel law, Britain, 98
seditious libel trials, in colonial America, 150
Selivanov, I. V., 236
Senatskie vedomosti, 228
Senkovskii, Osip, 234
sensationalism, 113, 184
serfdom, 227
serial publications, 3–4
Serres de La Tour, Alphonse Joseph de, 28, 29
servants, 243 n. 25
Seven Champions of Christendom, 113
Seven Years War, 26, 69, 171
Severnaia pchela, 230, 231, 236, 238, 243–4 n. 29
Severnaia pochta, 228
Severnyi arkhiv, 229, 233
Severnyi Merkurii, 236
Sgard, Jean, 12, 188
Shakespeare, William, 239
Sheehan family, 129, 134
Sheil, R. L., 128
Sheridan, Richard Brinsley, 102
Shevyrev, S. P., 233
Shields, David, 13
Sibirskii vestnik, 229
Sicily, 203
Sidmouth, Lord, 101
Simes, Douglas, 17
Sirotkin, V. G., 230
sister republics, 213
smallpox inoculation, 145
Smirnova, Anna Osipovna, 231
Smith, Douglas, 240
Smith, Martin, 94
smoking rooms, 27
Smyrna, 27
Soave, Francesco, 201
Società di incoraggiamento delle scienze e delle arti, 218
Società di pubblica istruzione, 216
sociétés d'amateurs, 27

Sons of Liberty, 150
Southey, Robert, 97, 106
Sovremennik, 233
Spain, 41
Spectateur du nord, 25, 38
Spectateur national, 198 n. 32
Spectator, 53
Spectators, 15, 53–55, 56, 57–58, 62
Spenerscher Zeitung, 80
Speranskii, M. M., 224
Spezieria di Sondrio, 210
St James Chronicle, 123
St. Petersburg English Society, 236–8
Staatsanzeigen, 74
Staatsman, 57
Staffetta del nord, 202
Staffetta di Sciaffusa, 202
Stamp Office records, Britain, 103, 104
stamp taxes, 117, 119–20, 132, 186
Standard, 123, 129
Stanhope press, 6
Stankevich, Nikolai, 232, 233
Star of Brunswick, 129
steam press, 6
steam printing, 17
Stecchi, 207
Stein, Karl vom und zum, baron, 82
Stephens, Mitchell, 3
Storia dell'anno, 202
Struensee, Johann Friedrich, 31
Sturkenboom, Dorothée, 55
Stuttgart, censorship in, 81
subscription clubs, 76
subscription reading rooms, Britain, 107
subscriptions, 26, 193–4
subsidies, to newspapers
  in Britain, 99–101
  in France, 32, 186–7
  in Ireland, 114, 120, 124, 126
suppression fees, 7
surveillance of the public, 81
Sweden, 40
Swift, Jonathan, 113
Swinton, Samuel, 33
Switzerland, 12
Syn otechestva, 228–9, 233, 239
Syndercombe Letters, 118

Table of Ranks, 246 n. 68
Talot, 193
Tanucci, Bernardo, 210
taverns, 10, 143
  see also public houses
taxes, on newspapers, 93, 104, 131
  see also stamp taxes

Tekhnologicheskii zhurnal, 228
Teleskop, 233, 234, 239
Termometro politico, 214
Terror, 184, 185-6
Teutscher Merkur, 75
theatres, 227, 238-9
Théveneau de Morande, Charles, 28, 29-30, 36, 37
thick journals, 4, 244 n. 39
Thomas, Isaiah, 146-7, 153-4
Times, 6, 7, 103
Tocqueville, Alexis de, 153
Tournal, Sabin, 165
Townshend, Lord, 116-17
trade journals, 108
Traveller, 123
travelling times, 202
Treuttel, Jean-Georges, 188
Tribun du peuple, 196
Tribuno del popolo, 213, 216
Tunis, 27
Turgenev, Ivan, 241
Turgot, Anne-Robert-Jacques, 174
Turin, 202
Tuscany, 202

Ulster, 119
Ultra Tories, 129
Union Star, 121
United Irishmen, 120
United Provinces, see Netherlands.
United States, 140-158
  and propaganda, 33, 35
  and revolutionary France, 151
  freedom of press in, 16
  national consciousness in, 13
  politicisation of press in, 149-50
  public sphere in, 13, 142
  race, and public sphere in, 141
  constitution of, 149
Università della Stampa, 204
urban culture, 10
Vaderlandsche Byzonderheden, 61
Valckenaer, Johan, 63
Valcour, Aristide, 188
van Effen, Justus, 53
van Engelen, Cornelis, 53
van Goens, Rijklof Micha, 1, 60
van Hamelsveld, Ijsbrand, 62
van Paddenburg, 59
Vasco, Gianbattista, 210
Vedomosti, 227
Venables, Richard, 241
Venice, 5, 201, 202, 203, 204, 211

Venturi, Franco, 203
Vera repubblicana, 215
Verduisant, 25
Vergennes, Charles Gravier, comte de, 160, 164, 171, 173, 174-5, 176
Verri, Alessandro, 208
Verri, Pietro, 208
Vestnik Evropy, 228, 229, 233
Veycrusse, Jean, 30
Viazemskii, Prince P. A., 231, 234
Vieux Cordelier, 186
Village Record, 153
Villers, Charles, 25
Vincent, David, 106
Virginia Gazette, 148
Vishniakov, P. M., 239
Vistengof, P., 237
Volnoe ekonomicheskoe obshchestvo, 241
Voltaire, 31
Volunteer's Journal, 119, 121, 122, 136 n. 67
Volunteers, 118, 121
Vossische Zeitung, 76, 80
Vostochnie izvestiia, 229
voting, in US, 142
Vrouwelyke Spectator, 53

wage levels, 104, 243 n. 17
Waldstreicher, David, 13
War of American Independence, see American Revolution
War of Austrian Succession, 161
War of Liberation (1813), 70, 81, 82, 83, 84
Warder, 129, 130
Waterford Herald, 122
Webster, Noah, 149
Weekly Oracle, 116
Weekly Register, 129
Weil, Hans, 85
Wellesley, Arthur, Duke of Wellington, 99
Wellesley, Lord, 99
Wellesley, Richard Colley, marquess, 125
Westmorland Gazette, 101
Wexford Herald, 129
Whalley's News Letter, 116
Whig historians, 93
Whitefield, John, 143
Whittaker, Cynthia, 238
Wieland, Christoph Martin, 70, 75
Wilkes, John, 96
Wilson, Robert, 108
Windham, William, 103
women readers, 195, 215, 236
  and literacy, in US, 141

and political news, 155 n. 7
and press, in Ireland, 131
and press, in Italy, 215
and public sphere, in US, 141
women's journals, 72, 215
Wood, Alexander, 123
working-class readers, 105–6
World, 100

Wyvill, Christopher, 99

XYZ affair, 151

Zemledel'cheskaia gazeta, 231
Zenger, John Peter, 150
Zhurnal iziashchnykh iskusstv, 233
Zöllner, Johann Friedrich, 85

For EU product safety concerns, contact us at Calle de José Abascal, 56–1°, 28003 Madrid, Spain or eugpsr@cambridge.org.

www.ingramcontent.com/pod-product-compliance
Ingram Content Group UK Ltd.
Pitfield, Milton Keynes, MK11 3LW, UK
UKHW010859060825
461487UK00012B/1246